What Readers Are Saying

A Surgeon's Odyssey is extraordinary! This brilliant, compelling narrative allows readers insight to the deep details of Asian culture and faith. Dr. Richard Moss holds nothing back. His tales are shocking, gruesome, hysterical, triumphant, and tragic.

Dr. Moss recounts his journey through Asia as he seeks to combat Third World disease and train local surgeons. Through this unbelievable expedition, Moss identifies and exposes Asia's cultures, faiths, geography, history, politics, and dangers. His stories describe the unimaginable truths of Asia from its most captivating beauties to its deepest sins. Throughout his pilgrimage, Moss poses questions about culture and faith that help shape his own beliefs. It is a powerfully thought provoking piece. Readers undergo a vicarious experience that far outweighs the Western understanding of Asian culture.

Odyssey of a Surgeon is an all-out feast of Third World reality from the mind of a brilliant writer and surgeon. I was laughing out loud, crying, angered, overjoyed, shocked, and changed by this book. *A Surgeon's Odyssey* is a priceless masterpiece and an indispensible gift to Third World literature.

Tiffany Moncrief, Freelance Christian Writer and Musician

A Surgeon's Odyssey is a fantastic journey through third world Asian medicine, culture, and spirituality. Dr. Moss's odyssey exposes the reader to people and worlds that would otherwise remain hidden. A must read for the adventurous!

Diane Larson, RN
Charge Nurse of Endoscopy Services
Memorial Hospital Outpatient Surgery Center

A Surgeon's Odyssey is captivating. Few people pursue their dreams to the extent Dr. Moss has fulfilled his. As a brand new surgeon, he set off for Asia to teach in University hospitals and help patients with complex head and neck cancers. His journey is one of growth: spiritually, professionally, and relationally. The reader gains candid insight into his triumphs and failures and gets a glimpse into the many facets of third world Asian culture. It is an adventure during which at times I was amused, appalled, bewildered, shocked, and always interested. I found myself cheering him on!

Karen Kolb CRNA
(Certified Registered Nurse Anesthetist)
Memorial Hospital and Health Care Center
Jasper, IN

Moss is a captivating storyteller who from the first page masterfully pulls the reader into the world of his life as a young, head and neck surgeon. Well aware of society's expectations yet willing to follow his heart, Moss leaves the familiarity of the West to treat patients and find adventure in the faraway lands of the East. His story is one of struggle and determination as Moss seeks to bring healing and restoration to patients facing debilitating cancers. Readers will be swept away in this incredible journey through South Asia. *A Surgeon's Odyssey* is a fantastic read!

Kimberly Wagner
Children's Book Author, and Featured Writer at
Smithsonian National Air and Space Museum

I highly recommend this book of an intriguing and heart-tugging journey through lands and cultures and unthinkable poverty. The descriptive, vivid detailed writing puts you there in the midst of it with the author as if you're experiencing it all unfold before your own eyes. It is entertaining as well as enlightening and inspiring.

Nancy Blessinger
Registered Respiratory Therapist
Christian mother

I first met Richard three decades ago standing likewise in the visa queue of a Bangladeshi consulate in Calcutta, and we've duly reported to each other on our progress ever since. Having lived and worked in most of the same places covered in A Surgeon's Odyssey —although dealing with a different cast of characters— I know something of which he speaks. The techno-clinical aspects of practicing desperation oncology on quite another planet; the vicious infighting within the medical, diplomatic, and "international development" bureaucracies; and the rising —or not— to Judaeo-Buddhist imperatives is extraordinary.

Alan Potkin, Ph. D.
Team Leader, Digital Conservation Facility
Center for Southeast Asian Studies/Burma Studies Center
Northern Illinois University, USA

Dr. Rick Moss—a tremendously gifted author and physician—shares with the reader his amazing story of dealing with the tender aspects of compassion as well as his known science as he faces an unfamiliar territory in Asia treating very serious malignancies against all odds.

The reader is rapidly drawn into the story with Moss's quick-witted, colorful and detailed style of writing. He doesn't try to disguise the grisly details of what he saw. Instead, he shares the authenticity of human suffering in the third world.

A **Surgeon's Odyssey** is a masterpiece penned by a man who came to understand that it was truly his vocation to serve God by unselfishly and literally caring for humankind.

Maureen Gutgsell
Pharmacist and Catechist of the Catholic Faith

I feel as if I were on an exciting journey with Dr. Richard Moss from the sheer imagery of his descriptions during his travels in Asia. The excitement of a young, idealistic surgeon as he battled his way through hardships and poverty, his own and that of his patients, enthralled me from beginning to end.

Lori Johnson, RN
Administrator
Memorial Outpatient Surgery Center

This story, in the long questing tradition, needs relating if for no other reason than it tells of yoking the spiritual with the material as primary to life. BETTER THAN A GOOD READ...AN ESSENTIAL ONE...you'll often see yourself in Ricky's story for he faced emotional obstacles common to us all... It belongs on the bookshelf as a modern tale next to the Iliad, the Odyssey, Ulysses, and the biblical Exodus.

John F.X. Ryan, Jr., Former Managing Director,
Sovran Limited and Pac West Distributing, Inc.
Executive Assistant, Lieutenant Governor,
State of Indiana

A Surgeon's
ODYSSEY

A Surgeon's
ODYSSEY

Richard Moss, M.D.

ARCHWAY
PUBLISHING

Archway Publishing books may be ordered through booksellers or by contacting:

Archway Publishing
1663 Liberty Drive
Bloomington, IN 47403
www.archwaypublishing.com
1 (888) 242-5904

ISBN: 978-1-4808-5952-4 (sc)
ISBN: 978-1-4808-5951-7 (hc)
ISBN: 978-1-4808-5953-1 (e)

Library of Congress Control Number: 2018903932

Print information available on the last page.

Archway Publishing rev. date: 7/23/2018

I dedicate this book to my many patients and their inspiring bravery in the face of intolerable disease and circumstance.

Acknowledgements

The following friends and family members assisted me in the preparation and publication of this book. John F.X. Ryan was involved in this manuscript from the beginning, offering insights and encouragement. He pushed me to tell the complete story. I recoiled at the additional labor but his insistence has made the manuscript infinitely better. My daughter Arielle was ruthless in her editing, insisting I make it more a story than a travelogue with character development and good dialogue, critical to the end product. Aaron Steele produced a wonderful map of the journey; he also unlocked the Chiang Mai section from a floppy disc when everyone else had failed: invaluable. Lori Johnson, Alan Potkin, Tiffany Moncrief, Kim Wagner, Diane Larson, Karen Kolb, Nancy Blessinger, and Maureen Gutgsell, generously read, advised, and endorsed the manuscript. Dan Barrett provided an exceedingly kind and moving foreword.

I thank my wife, Ying, for her forbearance, accepting my obsessions, and taking care of our four children, as I nestled in the attic writing the story. She also played a critical role in the "Odyssey." My four children, Arielle, Noah, Adina, and Isaiah mean everything to me and in their own ways provided encouragement. I will always acknowledge the role of my beloved mother, of blessed memory, in everything I do including the writing of this book. She will evermore be an inspiration to me. My four brothers, Cliff, Lon, Jeff, and Larry, helped shape me as a young boy in the Bronx and appear in some of the flashbacks in the story. We are brothers forever. I thank the cast of exotic and compelling characters I met during the journey with special reference to my good friend Uttamo, of blessed memory, and Jaroon. I thank my colleagues, the faculty, residents, and students at the various medical centers in each of the nations I was privileged to work in. Then there were the countless patients afflicted with terrible disease who honored me by allowing me to treat them. They ultimately were the purpose of this surgeon's odyssey, this pilgrimage of healing.

Foreword

In a place, far from the comforts of America, an unknown adventure was about to begin involving a young man from the city of New York. This individual had grown up in a neighborhood in the Bronx in a not-so-nice area, rife with crime and drug addiction. His family was near the poverty line. Overcoming his environment and supported by an encouraging and loving mother, this man, through the sheer power of his character and dedication to making a difference in a world full of human suffering, had recently completed his residency in Otolaryngology – Head and Neck Surgery (ENT or Ear Nose and Throat). Most physicians upon concluding years of schooling, the expense of college and medical school, a five-year residency and one-year fellowship, would be thinking about starting a practice and cashing in. Not so Dr. Richard Moss.

In the future, he would become known in several lands and countries as a healer, a teacher, a savior of people afflicted with horrible disease and pain, an emissary of kindness and charity. On this cold winter day, with snow flurries and bitter wind swirling in lower Manhattan, in a Chinese Restaurant of all places, a decision was made that would cast a long shadow, affecting many lives in the future. This young surgeon, a single man, married to his profession, would pursue his long-standing dream of service to humanity in some of the poorest nations on earth.

Dr. Moss then takes you into a world that most of us know nothing about. You follow him through South Asia as he educates and informs, makes hard decisions, seemingly performs miracles, and yes, commits painful mistakes. He experiences exhilaration and joy, but also despair and self-doubt.

A Surgeon's Odyssey is written in exquisite, mind-boggling detail. Through it, one experiences the same fulfillment, triumph, and tragedy that Dr. Moss experiences. You will laugh and you will cry. You will encounter the fears and hopes of his many anguished patients. You will stand in awe as you follow this young surgeon in his effort to save lives and help patients in advanced stages of horrible disease. He gives them hope. He gives them a second chance at life. When necessary, he gives those with incurable disease the dignity and courage to face the inevitable. Dr. Moss performed his surgical wonders for little or no compensation. And not infrequently, he had to operate under challenging and backwards conditions. Yet, Dr. Moss proves to the reader that the brotherhood of man truly transcends the sovereignty of nations and religions of the world. His deep personal beliefs raise him to a higher calling and demonstrate that faith in God elevates us and provides meaning and purpose to human life.

You will hear from little known luminaries and visionary characters that cross the path of the good doctor as he leads us on his quixotic journey through mysterious lands including Thailand, Malaysia, Singapore, Indonesia, Nepal, India and Bangladesh. He explores Buddhism especially but other faiths too such as Islam, Hinduism, Christianity, and his own Judaism. He encounters Buddhist sages and becomes a monk in a forest temple. You will meet his beautiful and dedicated wife, Ying, and learn of his unusual Asian marriage and how she saved his life. You will follow him in his wide-ranging jaunts on his trusty motorcycle through stunning and sometimes dangerous terrains. You will participate in and learn with him vital lessons about poverty and suffering, exhilaration and despair, disease and healing, life and death.

This saga has it all. Dr. Moss gives the reader a glimpse of his three-year expedition into an exotic world, a true-life quest that is inspiring, uplifting, and tragic. It is Dr. Moss's second outstanding gift to the world, the first being his stirring first book, *Matilda's Triumph*. Dr. Moss overcame so many challenges in life to become one of America's extraordinary exemplars. He is a great surgeon, a good-will ambassador for his country, a humanitarian, an inspiration, a God-sent healer. He has given us an incredible account, a story for the ages.

Danny J. Barrett
Director, International Agreements
Commander, US Naval Forces, Japan
Yokoska, Japan

The Odyssey

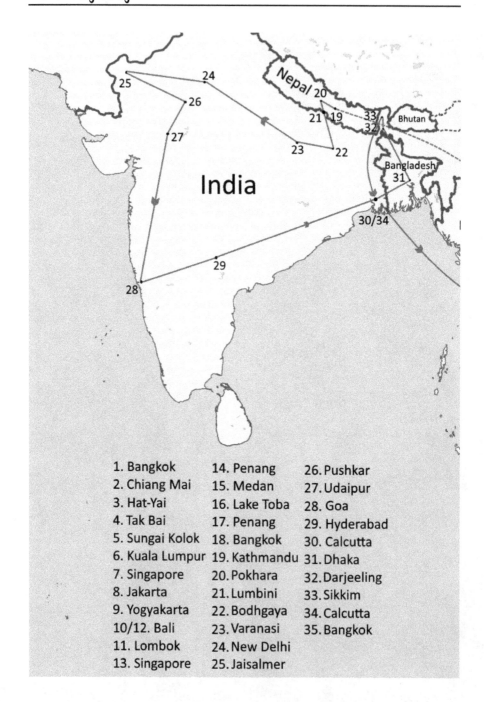

Nepal
Bhutan
India
Bangladesh

1. Bangkok
2. Chiang Mai
3. Hat-Yai
4. Tak Bai
5. Sungai Kolok
6. Kuala Lumpur
7. Singapore
8. Jakarta
9. Yogyakarta
10/12. Bali
11. Lombok
13. Singapore
14. Penang
15. Medan
16. Lake Toba
17. Penang
18. Bangkok
19. Kathmandu
20. Pokhara
21. Lumbini
22. Bodhgaya
23. Varanasi
24. New Delhi
25. Jaisalmer
26. Pushkar
27. Udaipur
28. Goa
29. Hyderabad
30. Calcutta
31. Dhaka
32. Darjeeling
33. Sikkim
34. Calcutta
35. Bangkok

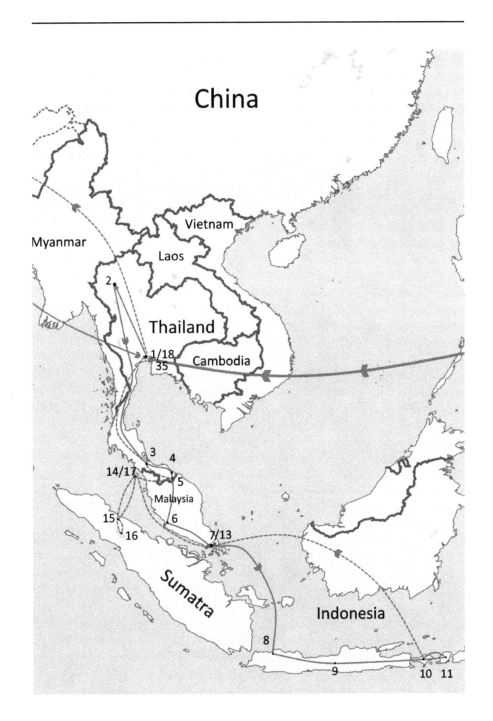

I. Prologue

Chapter 1

I was delivered from grinding indecision in the most unlikely of places - a Chinese restaurant in New York City's Chinatown. A second floor walk-up called "Number 1" on Canal Street, a real dive. The portions were big, and the price was right. There were dozens of other joints like it in the neighborhood, but I always came here.

There were windows overlooking the bustling street below. Incandescent light bulbs dangled from the ceilings, casting a stark glow on the wooden tables, the plastic tablecloths, the creaky metal chairs, and linoleum. Holding court at the register was a wizened matriarch who barely spoke English.

"Hello again," she nodded, remembering me.

I circled my order on the menu. "The usual."

"Very good. Please have seat."

I sat down at a table next to the window. I found relief in gazing at the traffic, the crowds hurrying by, the madness and frenzy of downtown Manhattan. The place was empty. And quiet. Perfect for my purposes. I had to decide what to do with my life.

I had completed my residency training in Otolaryngology, also referred to as Ear Nose and Throat, or, even more simply, ENT. I had worked at the New York Eye and Ear Infirmary on 14th street in Manhattan, a revered old institution near famous Tompkin's Square Park, a classic New York haunt and affectionately referred to as "Needle Park." I had traveled across the continent to the dream city of San Francisco where I completed a fellowship in facial plastic surgery. Now, fully fourteen years after making the decision to become a doctor, I found myself at age thirty-three having actually completed the deal. Now I was ready to start a practice, and, yes, earn money, an essential staple that had always eluded me.

Coming from humble origins, I found the allure of money enticing. Born and raised in a tough neighborhood in the Bronx, the fourth son in a family of five boys, my brothers and I had been exposed to most of the common pathologies of the inner city. Indeed, my family had more than its fair share. It began early in my childhood when my mother and father divorced after years of squabbling. My mother, who had only a high school education, had to raise the five of us alone. How many days I remembered walking alongside her, listening to her weeping, overwhelmed by the burden of supporting us with almost no resources. She did her best, working full time in Manhattan, taking the train back and forth everyday, and coming home to shop and cook. It was not easy. Growing up in the Bronx in general had become a problem. The neighborhood was not safe. And there were other concerns. Some of the brothers got involved in drugs including heroin and cocaine. It was all there, the whole turbulent scene - growing up in a broken home in the Bronx - the drugs, the violence, the bad influences drawing you one way or another.

The waiter arrived with the food, a plate of simmering boneless chicken with cashew nuts and broccoli slathered in a brown glaze of oyster sauce and ginger.

"It's very hot," he warned.

The piquant aromas drifted from the plate and into my eager nostrils, arousing my appetite. It was bliss. Secular but near-messianic bliss. I dove in, taking deep and abiding pleasure in demolishing the tender pieces of chicken dripping with oyster sauce and spicy slivers of ginger, enjoying the debauchery of crunching cashews and broccoli between my upper and lower molars. It was more than just gustatory gratification. It was tactile and auditory. Visual and olfactory. It was a comprehensive assault on the senses. I knew I had made the right decision to return here.

Through those difficult days as a kid in the Bronx, I managed to do well in school. Books were my refuge and through study I escaped some of the devastation occurring around me. I entered college, not a small feat for our ragtag crew. When I was accepted to medical school my family was ecstatic. I had beaten the odds. I could have wound up dead on the streets with a needle in my arm like friends and others from the neighborhood. Now, after 14 years of study and training, I was done with the whole protracted ordeal and poised for a career in medicine and hopefully success, both professional and financial. So, considering everything why was I now toying with the idea of leaving the country to work for virtually nothing in developing nations instead of staying right here and earning money for the first time in my life?

There were other elements that weighed in as well, not the least of which was the desire, if for only a short time, to get out of the highly regimented and Spartan existence I had been living in medical school and residency. I had watched, after all, more than a decade of my life go up in smoke, consumed in the fires of unending study, testing, and nights and weekends on call. After living most of my adult life by roughly four or five year Mao-esque plans – that is, four years of college, four years of medical school, and five years of residency training - wasn't it time for a change? On top of that, I harbored an enduring wanderlust, a desire to live abroad and see the world, a dream I had been nursing for years but had to delay until I completed my training. I also fostered a desire to hurl myself into the turmoil and tumult of the third world, treating disease at its unmitigated worst. I wanted to work as a cancer surgeon in places where patients had little or no access to proper health care and presented at appalling stages of their disease. This seemed worthy to me. Why not devote a life to such endeavors? Not to mention the call of adventure! The Indiana Jones of Otolaryngology. A kind of Saint George of ENT, seeking cancer dragons to slay with a surgeon's knife as lance, my "Ascalon." The allure was powerful and tempting. But for a pauper like me, the glow of anticipated revenue also seduced.

Don't do it, it's a trap! A passionate voice shouted within my head. *Once you're in practice, you'll never leave. Obligations and responsibilities will follow just as surely as the seasons. It's now or never!*

Then another voice, equally demanding, argued on behalf of stability and income. *Ah, go ahead, start a practice. You can go abroad later, after you've lined your pockets a bit. You need to fatten your bank account first.*

No, the voice lusting for adventure countered. *Go now, or you'll never have the chance!*

After devouring the last fragment of cashew, I settled in with a small dish of pineapple chunks and the traditional fortune cookie. I stared at the little cookie suspiciously as it lay innocently atop the dish of pineapple. Poking at it, I wondered if I could glimpse its message. I picked it up, examining its contour and color. After a moment's pause, I took a bite, brutally ripping the cookie apart with my teeth. A crumbled strip of white paper fell from my mouth. I picked it up and unfurled it.

"Do not forsake your dreams for material security."

A lightning bolt struck direct from the Middle Kingdom. It had sliced through the layers of confusion. I was not superstitious but more than ready to accept this otherworldly mandate. Perhaps it was what I wanted all along. My dilemma was real. I was torn. But now I saw unambiguously the path before me. It was not everyday that the sacred inscription of a Chinese fortune cookie decided one's destiny. But then why not? I had been lurching hesitantly towards the idea of playing dice with my life for years. I had rolled a seven.

I surrendered myself to the delicious wisdom of the fortune cookie, the ultimate New York oracle - and I would follow its sublime decree. It was a welcome reprieve. It suited me. I had faced down the inner voice that leaned inevitably towards security and material wealth, when deliverance from that was what I sought.

I also happened to be carrying with me another dispatch from the East, flirting uneasily with what now seemed an irresistible offer. It was a crinkled blue envelope with delicate but indecipherable calligraphy printed on its upper right corner. On the left side a series of small postage stamps with the handsome countenance of the King of Siam. The stamps were postmarked "Chiang Mai, Thailand." Also below the script, in bold English, were the words, "Department of Otolaryngology, Chiang Mai University."

I had earlier sent out a series of letters with my resume to various universities and hospitals in different countries in Asia. I was drawn to Asia. I knew that was where I wanted to go. I delicately peeled open the envelope being ever so careful not to damage the Thai characters or the stamps.

July 13, 1987
Dear Dr. Moss,

Thank you for your kind letter of June 9, 1987. I would like to tell you something about our hospital and department. Chiang Mai University Hospital is a regional medical center for the north of Thailand. There are more than 1500 beds. Our department of Otolaryngology is very busy with many cases of head and neck cancer. We have most of the equipment you need to do surgery and take care of patients. We like to invite you to stay with us for one year and send you a contract starting October 1, 1987. Your pay is 11,975 baht per month (about 475$) and we provide accommodations for you in our guesthouse. I know this is very little by your standards, but in Thailand you can live a modest lifestyle with this. You don't have to worry about speaking Thai. Chiang Mai is popular with the westerners. We have tourists and many Thai people here can speak English too. We need a lot of help with the head and neck cancer patients. I hope you can come here to work. Everyone here will be very excited.

Sincerely,
Acharee Sorasuchart
Head
Department of Otolaryngology

Thailand suddenly loomed large in my imagination, spurred by the letter and some travel books I had skimmed recently about the country. Visions of swaying palm trees, glittering rice fields, and magnificent Buddhist temples with elaborate statuary passed through my mind. I heard soft voices singing lilting melodies to a background of traditional Thai music. Teams of oxen pulled little boys perched on rickety wooden wagons with tall, spoked wheels along winding dirt paths. Barefoot women in wide brimmed sun hats and sarongs harvested rice from boundless rice paddies in the midday sun. I seemed to have acquired wings and was magically transported to the verdant, emerald pastures of Thailand. I could almost feel the soft mud beneath my feet as I planted a kernel of rice.

There was also a spiritual element to this journey that I could not ignore. I was seeking something. I wanted to help the neglected and diseased. But I wanted something else. I wanted to understand healing, its essence, and embrace it as something sacred. I was searching to live it in its fullness and become a healer. I would leave the palace of America, the comforts of this great and comfortable nation, to experience the suffering of other lands. I was hungry for the East, an American on a journey to the Orient. I would not be blind or oblivious to the reality of what I was assuming, of the contests and inevitable failures that awaited me, the thresholds I would have to cross in my pursuit of healing and worthy purpose. Nor did I know where I would go beyond Thailand or if it would all end there in a blaze of glory or disaster. But I had settled on this path. This was my Grail-quest, my crusade, my noble venture, my *Kiddush* or sanctification, and I would embrace it.

I thanked the Chinese grandma at the cash register at the "Number 1" restaurant on Canal Street in lower Manhattan. She and her unpretentious eatery had helped me. I would begin my journey to a strange and alluring land in Southeast Asia on the basis of a friendly and inviting letter from Thailand - and a Chinese fortune cookie.

II. Chiang Mai, Thailand

Chapter 2

Midnight, December 3, 1987. An auspicious time, only two days before the King of Thailand's sixtieth birthday. My plane had just landed in Bangkok's Don Muang airport. I collected my luggage and found my way to a taxi. The driver, a short thin man, introduced himself in broken English.

"Hello sir, welcome to Bangkok," he said.

"Take me to the 'Royal Hotel,'" I said. The name elicited encouraging nods of approval.

"Oh, very good hotel, sir." The doors slammed, and we were off.

Curiously though, despite his initial enthusiasm for my hotel, the driver seemed intent on giving me every chance to size up an array of other hotel options. He ushered me to one hotel after another, none, I noted, with the name "Royal Hotel." I was received at each point by a smiling proprietor who did his best to convince me of the virtues of his particular guesthouse. Explaining that I had reservations elsewhere, I politely refused. The driver and I would then march back to the car to repeat this exotic charade somewhere else.

I didn't mind the slow progress as it gave me a chance to gauge the measure of this sprawling Gotham at a time of night where you could actually drive unimpeded. The fare had already been agreed on so the additional mileage and time were on him. Despite going without sleep for 24 hours, the impact of actually being in Thailand had raised my adrenalin levels enough to keep me alert. This initial immersion into Asian life in the back of a Bangkok taxi was actually enjoyable, although I realized my driver was trying to maneuver me into a pre-arranged lodge to procure a commission.

Finally, we arrived at the Royal Hotel. I checked in, dragged myself to my room and immediately went to sleep.

I took my time getting up. After a long, hot shower and an American style breakfast replete with eggs, toast, and home fries, I found myself standing in the hotel foyer, looking through the glass doors that separated me from the streets of Bangkok. This was not the Bangkok I recalled from last night when the boulevards were silent and still. This was Bangkok in its daytime fury with vast armies of vendors and pedestrians lining the sidewalks, and waves of some of the most lethal traffic in the world converged upon the streets with unrestrained vengeance. Where the haze, dust, and noxious gases clouded the senses and the incessant noise hounded you without relief. A city seemingly designed to maximize chaos. A place that had almost overnight transformed itself from a charming river village laced with canals, temples, and meandering dirt roads to a concrete and asphalt nightmare of over six million.

I hesitated for a moment before walking into the path of the electronic eye that would signal the glass doors to open. The maze of streets jammed with cars and faces hurtling past just beyond the protective membrane of the glass doors seemed surreal. A kinder reality existed here in my nice hotel up in my air-conditioned room, tethering me to my first-world luxuries.

Within moments of my first fledgling steps outside my sanctuary I was besieged by a phalanx of smiling rickshaw, "tuk-tuk," and taxi drivers, all intent on taking me to wherever my heart desired. Some even whisked me over to the side asking with mischievous grins, "What is your pleasure?"

Not having the slightest idea of what I'd like to do in this vast city, I extricated myself from the friendly coterie of drivers and hoofed down a broad avenue known as Rajadamnern, which led past the Democracy Monument located in the center of a busy intersection. I crossed the street to get a closer look. About halfway there, a wave of terror overcame me. In one hair-raising second, I heard the sound of rubber and tar screeching against each other. My heart leapt into my esophagus as some 20 motorcycles and a bevy of honking cars behind them came to an ear splitting halt mere inches from my quivering body. The small legion of motorcyclists now stood with engines idling, gazing dispassionately at the spectacle of a hapless Westerner clearly out of his element. Curiously, they were not angry like they would be in New York City. Staring from my own precipice across the gulf of cultures, I sensed something different in this country already, a quality of patience and restraint that I admired. Perhaps, it was the Buddha's influence at work, some 2500 years later, insinuating himself into the fabric of life here in Thailand. I bid a hasty retreat back to my sidewalk oasis, out of harm's way, impressed by their self-control. There was not a single off-color epithet or fist shaking angrily in the steamy air by anyone. They had waited politely while I returned to safety. The chaos of the roads then quickly resumed.

I found my way to the "Amulet Market" in Wat Rachanada where sacred talismans of every description were sold for a multitude of purposes, primarily protective in nature. Most were images of the Buddha, but there were others of various gods and goddesses. Some deities offered protection for the wearer from such things as disease or bullets or automobile crashes. Others helped you to find success in business or to attract a member of the opposite sex.

Reclining Buddha, Bangkok, Thailand

I was browsing around wearing my white Rebock sneakers and jeans, snapping pictures furiously with my camera. While looking around and behaving as any tourist would, a pudgy, Thai in his late thirties, who spoke broken but decipherable English, approached me. He smiled a lot, had gold caps on his two front teeth, and wore spiffy blue trousers and a red Lacoste shirt. I seemed to be the only English-speaking tourist in the whole of Bangkok. He appeared overwhelmed by the possibility of practicing English with me.

"Hello. My name Somchai. You speak English, sir?"

"Yes."

"Where you come from, sir?" he continued.

"America."

"Oh, America! Very big country, and strong. Everyone rich there." I am quickly alerted to the word "rich."

"Not everyone."

"Sir, I like practice English with you. I am student. Please, let me go with you, practice English.

We crossed the street to the Golden Mount. This was a glittering, gilded "chedi" atop a man-made hill containing relics of the Buddha originally given to Rama V, the fifth King of the current "Chakri" dynasty by then British Viceroy of India, Lord Curzon, at the turn of the century. We began our ascent up the 318 steps of the long circular staircase.

By step 160, the salt from my sweat had crystallized above my eyebrows. It was hot in Bangkok, and with the added burden of 318 spiraling steps I wondered how auspicious my visit to the Golden Mount really was. As if reading my thoughts, Somchai offered another suggestion.

"Richard, I like suggest you better idea. Too hot, no?" I happily awaited deliverance. "We ride Thai boat in klongs (canals). You enjoy, I guarantee." I considered the offer. Clean air, dashing along in a motorboat with a refreshing breeze, enjoying the sights as they whisked by. Why not?

Somchai contracted a long, sleek boat with an obese and surly looking man wearing a dirty bandana tied around his head and a stained T-shirt. The business arrangements were meted out with surprising dispatch, and within seconds the three of us were seated in the boat darting south on the Chao Phraya River. Somchai wore something of a satisfied, even smug expression on his face. When I inquired as to the cost of this little journey, he assured me that it would be inexpensive. He muttered something about 50 baht (2$) per kilometer, promising it would be "very reasonable."

We turned right into a smaller tributary of the Chao Phraya River and headed into the intricate network of klongs that formed the primary method of travel and trade for many in this part of Bangkok known as Thonburi. We passed ornate and colorful temples, countless river dwellings and houseboats where people cooked, washed, traded and gossiped. The whole gamut of life sprawled before us along the river's edge. We visited briefly a few of the temples and markets and spent perhaps an hour before finally returning to the dock.

Feeling refreshed after this little splash of traditional Thai life, I was ready for the bill. I remembered the approximate price of 50 baht per kilometer, and estimated we may have traveled 8-10 kilometers. I wondered if I was being undercharged for such an enjoyable journey. Somchai gestured to the heavyset boatman who scrawled out some figures on a crumbled piece of white paper. He handed the bill over to me with Somchai gleefully watching. I read the figures and was rendered speechless. Written in blue ink were the figures 122 kilometers, which when multiplied by 50 equated to the tidy sum of 6100 baht or about 244 dollars. Now there was no way we had traveled 122 kilometers. I looked at Somchai whose smile had suddenly changed to an expression of befuddlement. He raised his shoulders and gestured moronically towards the boatman as if to say, "Don't look at me, it's him."

I looked at the boatman who remained a study of sweating stone. He was safe behind the impenetrable wall of not knowing a word of English. I looked back at Somchai whom I now suspected.

"There's no way I'm giving you 6100 baht," I said. I opened my wallet, and peeled out two crisp purple notes each worth 500 baht (20$). Somchai, switching sides suddenly insisted rather aggressively that it was not enough. "You owe *me* 4400 baht!"

"Owe *you* 4400 baht," I said angrily. "You set this whole damn thing up, didn't you?"

Somchai made a sudden move for my open wallet. I grabbed him by his shirt and pushed him away. "You must pay money!" he screamed in my face. He had gone from a bumbling fool passing himself off as a student to a belligerent con man trying to steal my money in broad daylight.

"Back off now! You've got your damn money's worth out of me!" I stared hard at two dark eyeballs and then stormed off the boat and onto the dock.

Even at 1000 baht I'd been duped, but I accepted this as part of my initiation into Asia. I left my two co-conspirators dividing the spoils while I returned to the refuge of my hotel.

After completing my second day in Bangkok, I had recognized defeat. I could not stand this place. All my life I had been under the impression that having been raised in New York City, I had dealt with the ultimate in urban nightmares. Two days in Bangkok had proven me wrong. By the end of my second day, I was buying a ticket for a second-class sleeper to Chiang Mai.

Chapter 3

I scanned the platform for the train to Chiang Mai. I boarded, arranged my luggage, and found a seat. With a little bump, the train lurched forward and slowly picked up speed. The buildings and crowded streets raced by. We passed the outskirts of town and were soon plunged into the inescapable essence of Thai life and culture - the rice fields - stretching out in all directions, the lush pastures saturating the land with their soothing hues of emerald-green and lemon. Facing the open window with this sweeping vision of the East rushing by, and dusk slowly settling in, I could not have imagined a better place to be than on a train to Chiang Mai.

The sound of the wheels racing over the tracks were hypnotic. It was odd for me to be here in this land, so removed and distant from all that I had known growing up in the Bronx. Although a board certified Head and Neck Surgeon with a fellowship in Facial Plastic Surgery, I remained connected to my past and my family. I still saw myself on a continuum with that same boisterous, pugnacious boy from the Bronx with all the rough edges and rowdy tendencies intact. I thought of my mother and four brothers. We had our troubles growing up without a father. I was an oddity. I had shot up through the competitive world of medicine. I had mastered the dense treatises of anatomy and disease. My brothers thought me strange. I did not want to disappoint them and especially my mother. But such an adventure was peculiar to them. I suspected they resented it. Why would I travel so far from home, from New York where we grew up and the family still lived, on so outlandish a mission as this, earning nothing? It made no sense to them. I came from nothing and should understand the importance of financial security. How pompous and immodest.

"You're a schmuck, Ricky," I imagined them saying. "A real schmuck."

And I smiled at my immodesty, at my eccentric mission to the Far East, at my beloved brothers and mother, at the Bronx, at my childhood. The sky darkened, the train catapulted forward, the wheels sounded their magnificent metallic cadence, and the moon reflected in the unending estuaries and fields and paddies.

I wondered about the interplay of culture and healing, of disease and death in Siam, a Buddhist Empire. How would a religion founded on the notion of suffering, impermanence and non-self influence its adherents when it came to health and sickness? In my days as a medical student and later as a resident and fellow, I knew well the American attitude. Americans expected prompt diagnosis, treatment, and cure. They feared sickness and death. They sought eradication of the disease process. They wanted to live. Perhaps attitudes differed in Asia? I imagined so.

I sensed the Thai would be more accepting of their fate and unwilling to undergo aggressive measures to extend life a month or two or more. Which attitude was preferable? Life at any cost or acceptance of the inevitable? As a hard-charging young surgeon, I knew what I wanted. But perhaps the Thai would teach me something on this matter.

I thought of this in my glazed stupor, rolling in and out of slumber, mesmerized by the careening locomotive, its soothing rhythms, its subtle intonations and tempo, a wondrous sound. It mattered not that I slept soundly or not. I was floating on a dream, wandering in a stream of disconnected sensations, memories and fleeting reflections that intersected in a curtain of wonder and fantasy.

When I was five, I went sleigh riding down a steep hill in our neighborhood in the Bronx known as "Dead Man's Hill." The hill ran down Crotona Park East towards Boston Road and the "El" on 174th Street. It had a metal barred fence at the bottom. My mother forbade me to go down. But I went anyway and rammed head first into the metal bars. I was bleeding from a scalp wound. I lay there in the snow, blood pooling around me, staining the whiteness.

An ambulance appeared and whisked my mother and I off to Fordham Hospital. In the Emergency Room, the physician sutured my scalp wound, took an X-Ray, and determined there had been no skull fracture. "You're okay, Ricky," Mom cried, "There's no fracture. You're going to be okay."

Ten days later, we visited Dr. Pinski, our family doctor whose office was on Hoe Avenue right next to my grandparent's apartment and Aunt Sophie's and Aunt Rae's. Dr. Pinski removed the stitches, examined the wound, and pronounced me fully recovered. Other than a three-inch ridge in my scalp, covered by hair but detectable to this day, I felt fine. As my mother and I walked home together, holding hands, I remember inquiring about medicine.

"How do you get to be a doctor, Mom," I asked.

"It takes a lot of work and study, son."

"Do you think I could become a doctor?" I asked.

"Yes, you can."

We held hands and crossed 174th Street under the "El." We walked past the metal barred fence that I had smashed into only ten days ago that had brought near calamity, not even stopping to look or comment, the horror and panic of the moment now only a fleeting memory. We strolled up Crotona Park East, the eastern border of Dead Man's Hill, to our building at 867 Crotona Park North.

"I would like to become a doctor, Ma," I announced to my mother as we walked up the stairs to our apartment, 2C, on the third floor.

"Okay, Ricky," Mom said, smiling.

And I thought not about this again until years later. Yet I wondered as the train wound its way north, slicing the turgid, invisible air, alive with promise and mystery, if that earliest interaction with the medical profession had begun the process that had brought me to this moment, galloping within this metal stallion to Chiang Mai. I gazed outside my window at the enveloping darkness. I noticed not the rocking and lurching, the pitch and heave, the sharp velocity of the charging projectile carrying me forward. I was at peace in my little sleeper, gazing out through the broad window at the blackness flecked by the star-lit canopy and the incandescent golden moon fixed in the heavens. We passed over bridges, ravines, and streams, the fields and paddies spreading outward from the parallel tracks into infinity, the din of the train a glorious symphony.

My mother had given me a sense of destiny. It was not intentional. It was just that she favored me, and so I grew up with the sense of being the Chosen One. I expected grand causes and efforts. This enterprise was only the manifestation of that inchoate sense of purpose. It might have taken other forms. But this one suited me. My background propelled me. I was connected to my past, a humble past, an American past. I had no status, wealth, or family connections to explain such a boon to myself. It was my mother and family and a generous nation and system that rewarded initiative that allowed this to occur.

The next great portal and testing ground awaited me. The ensuing awakening beckoned. I wanted to engage in grim but noble struggle with overwhelming disease under the worst of conditions. This drew me irrevocably to my destiny in the third world, in Asia, in Thailand, in Chiang Mai, the seat of *Lanna*, the Kingdom of a Million Rice Fields.

In my first semester of my first year at Lehman College, I had taken liberal arts courses including English, Ancient Classics, Contemporary Literature, and American History. Twelve credits. Not too taxing. And Straight A's at the end of it. But not a science or pre-med course to be found. I was not thinking about medicine. Not driven in that direction. I was a humanities guy. I liked writing, politics, and history. I thought about journalism. Words and language were my thing. But not science, math, engineering, or medicine. In my second semester, I took more of the same, and again had a relaxed time of it.

I found school easy. It came naturally. And I had done well not just in the humanities but math and science when I had studied them in high school. I began to ponder a career in medicine. The prospect excited me. I spoke with my mother and brother Lonnie.

"It would be a dream, Ricky," Mom said. "You can do it. You're a great student. The family would be so proud. All your cousins, aunts and uncles and Nono and Nona. The first one in the family. It would be wonderful. I would be so proud, Ricky. You can do it."

Lonnie was more cautionary. "It's a lot of work," was all he would say.

I met my faculty advisor, Mr. Jeffries, a white-haired individual and member of the English department.

"Forget it," he said. "The candidate to acceptance ratio is 50:1. You are competing against the best. Medical school is expensive. Don't waste your time. It is too difficult and costs too much."

"I got straight A's, barely trying. Both hands tied behind my back. I can do the same in pre-med. I did well in science in High School. No problems."

"So why are you taking humanities?"

"I wasn't thinking pre-med, but I am now. I am more inclined towards the humanities, but I can go do science as well."

"Don't waste your time. It is demanding. You will be frustrated. I can't tell you how many have come and gone through the years with the same sudden epiphany. They all wanted to become doctors. They loved the romance of it. The challenge. The dream. The sense of purpose. The status. The money. Whatever the motivation, I can't tell you how many were profoundly disappointed in the end. All of them began with high commitment and inspiration and went down in flames. It will not be easy and most likely you will fail. I advise you to forget it and save yourself the frustration. Pursue humanities, which seems to interest you. Writing, Journalism, History. Forget medicine."

And so I gave up my little dream of becoming a doctor.

The rapid passage and melodic sound of the train lulled me. We continued northward on our journey, train and I, accompanied by my companions in the darkness - the night sky, the stars, and the moon casting diamonds everywhere.

Chapter 4

The next morning I was up before dawn. My friend and spiritual guide, the train, awakened me as it had all night with its melodious chant: the splendid ensemble of the massive locomotive hurtling through the charged, sultry air on wheels of steel atop iron rails. The pure weight and force of tons of metal, engine, cargo and people surging forward in space and time, beneath a lucent, velvet horizon, roaring past the countryside of the heartland of Siam were transporting in many ways, not all anticipated.

I glimpsed the earliest waves of scarlet sunlight streaking across the glittering rice fields, revealing the undulating, hilly terrain of northern Thailand. When the train pulled into Chiang Mai, it was early, and the air was cool. While waiting for Dr. Sorasuchart to pick me up, an elderly Thai man walked up to me. He was tall for a Thai, had greying hair, and a military bearing.

"Sawadee khrap" I said.

"Sawadee khrap!" he retorted sharply by way of both correcting my pronunciation and returning the greeting. "Do you speak Thai?" he asked.

"Uh, no."

"Well that it is okay," he said, "I can speak your language."

He mentioned that he was a landowner with, indeed, a military background. Describing for me his large country estate, he invited me to join him sometime for dinner. He then posed a curious question that by western standards, at least, would have seemed out of place, but here in Thailand, I gathered, it was not. "Are you married?" he asked.

"Uh, no."

He looked at me and said, in his brisk way, "I can find you a Thai wife." I did a double take. Find me a wife? Just like that? "Really?" I laughed.

"Yes," he responded.

"You mean a beautiful one, with long, black hair?"

"No problem! I can find you one. Let me know when you are ready." My eyebrows raised, and I cleared my throat. "Uh, how do you go about doing this?

"Never mind, I will take care of it."

Just as I was about to inquire further into the logistics of such an arrangement, I noticed a petite, well-dressed woman, hurrying towards me with a middle-aged man following closely behind.

"Dr. Moss," the frail looking woman asked. "Yes. Dr. Sorasuchart?" We shook hands warmly. Acharee Sorasuchart, head of the department of Otolaryngology at Chiang Mai University, the one who had written me such a lovely letter six months ago, had rescued me from the matchmaker. She introduced me to her husband Sonwut who smiled broadly and shook my hand in the American style. I bid farewell to my accommodating friend, telling him I might take him up on his offer, and the three of us walked over to their car.

I opened the back door to get in. Dr. Sorasuchart opened the front door and insisted that I sit in the front. Still very much the westerner, I politely deferred, insisting that she have the seat of honor. "Dr. Moss," she smiled, "please take the front seat, you are our guest." I accepted. With Sonwut driving, we headed into town.

"I am a General Surgeon, Dr. Moss," Sonwut said, "a member of the Department of General Surgery at Chiang Mai University. I am sure we will also have the pleasure of working together," he smiled. He was a kindly man with a good sense of humor.

"I will look forward to that," I said.

"My English is not bad but still a work in progress. I have worked with western doctors before and so have had some practice," he said.

"That will come in handy, I'm sure," I said grinning. "Thank you," I nodded. He had a handsome face and was of medium stature.

Although I would be working with Acharee, it was Sonwut who did most of the talking as we drove. Acharee was rather shy. "We are delighted," she said gently, "that you have come so far to be with us." She had black hair, a pretty face, and appeared in her late forties. She smiled a great deal and had an almost maternal demeanor.

"I am delighted to be here," I said. "I really mean that. The honor is mine."

We continued down Tha Phae Road, the main street into Chiang Mai referred to by Sonwut as the "aorta" of Chiang Mai. We then turned onto a highway, got off on a smaller road, and entered a development about two miles from the center of town, nestled in the foothills north of the city. A guard opened a large gate that allowed us into the complex, and we drove to the Sorusuchart's home. Removing our shoes, a Thai custom, we entered the house.

We were greeted by their eighteen year old daughter, who immediately stood, pressed her flattened hands together in front of her face and bowed, while bending her knees. I responded in kind. The "wai" was the quintessential Thai greeting. It underscored the great importance of showing respect in Thai culture. There was much subtlety and meaning communicated in the "wai" depending on how low one bowed and where the hands touched the head or face.

Acharee escorted me to her dining room table where an appealing array of

Thai sweets and desserts awaited us. Slippers were brought for me. I sat down with Sonwut while Acharee served hot tea. Their home had two floors, a large lawn and patio, and a terrace on the second floor. It was built of grey stone with classical wood columns for the main entrance. Inside there was thick carpeting and fine wood trimming along the ceiling and walls. Dominating the center of the living room were pictures of the King and Queen of Thailand. To the side of these were other photos including one of their daughter at graduation receiving her diploma from the King himself, a prized possession.

Acharee soon joined us at the table. She encouraged me to indulge myself on the many enticing treats she had prepared while Sonwut explained some of the subtleties of the Thai language. He mentioned that the grammar was straightforward, but pronunciation could be difficult. Thai was a tonal language, so the meaning of a word could be completely altered with only a slight shift in tone. For the novice attempting to master the language this could present challenges.

"Take the Thai word 'su-ay,'" he began. "Depending on the tone, it could mean either 'beautiful' or 'bad luck.'"

"Uh-huh," I nodded, "I could see that might be tricky."

"Yes, you see Thai people are quite generous in describing women as 'su-ay' or 'beautiful,' but if you're tone described a woman as 'bad luck' it would not be well received."

He chuckled at this example. "Okay, now I challenge you to pronounce the word correctly."

I tried, but somehow my lips and tongue could not coordinate themselves to give even a close rendering. Sonwut was beside himself. "You see," he said, choking on his laughter, "it is difficult."

Acharee remained bashful. She seemed to lack confidence in her English and made only the most cautious of forays into our conversation. She did manage to explain the Thai custom of using the first name rather than the last. I was referred to as Dr. Moss in deference to the western custom, but she, for example, was called Dr. Acharee, instead of Dr. Sorasuchart, which was her last name.

We left their home and went to, as Sonwut called it, my palace, the Chiang Mai University guesthouse where I would spend the next year. It was inside the campus and a two-minute walk to the hospital. Located on a road along with other faculty homes, it consisted of two floors with separate rooms and baths for each guest. My room had a light, fan, closets, and luckily, I was told, an air conditioner. The hot season, between February and April, before the monsoons came, could be brutal.

It was not palatial by any means, but acceptable, perhaps a cut above an American student dorm. Across the road were tennis and basketball courts, recent imports from the West I assumed, and now fully occupied with students playing. Opposite the guesthouse was a guard post where a security officer monitored incoming traffic.

Tonight I would be meeting with Dr. Yupa who ran the head and neck cancer section for the ENT Department, and three residents for dinner. Tomorrow, Dr. Rak, the chief resident, would meet me at the guesthouse to bring me to the hospital.

Two things about Thai people impressed me after only three days in Thailand. The first was the manner in which they walked. They all seemed to saunter or stroll. Their feet slid leisurely along the ground in broad, smooth strokes, while their backs angled gently backward a bit. Never hurrying, they moved their heads left and right, surveying peacefully their surroundings. These graceful people had elevated the mundane act of walking to an art form. It was easy for me to admire this because all through my childhood, and even into adulthood, I had always been criticized for walking too slowly, as if it were a crime. "Why are you so slow?" was the usual recrimination. "You think we've got all day?" "I'm moving as fast as I can," I would respond meekly.

After growing up in New York, with all the hustle and brusqueness, this was a pleasant change, one of the things I knew I would love about Thailand. It occurred to me, particularly in later years, that leisurely, even *contemplative* walking could be thought of as a portable sanctuary, a form of meditation to help ward off the assault of modern life. Ironic now, I thought, to be living in a country where everyone else seemed to have the same idea.

The second observation, not unrelated to the first, was that everyone here seemed to smile. Not those wide, toothy grins commonly encountered back home, but simple, easy smiles. The type not laden with any message or motive. The Tourism Authority of Thailand had made a big deal about this, with their ubiquitous posters and brochures describing Thailand as the "Land of Smiles," but I had not taken it very seriously. In fact, it seemed to be true.

An old BMW soon pulled up, interrupting my reverie. The door opened and a tiny, frail looking woman in her forties exited the vehicle. She had black hair with streaks of grey, puffy eyes, and a wrinkled, tired face. Dr. Yupa walked slowly up to the patio where I was sitting and introduced herself. "Hello, Dr. Moss. I am Yupa. We are very pleased to have you. Welcome to Chiang Mai," she said. She bowed in a wai, which I returned. "Thank you," I said, smiling. Unlike everyone else, walking for her required some effort, and she seemed uncomfortable. Following behind her were three attractive young women. "Dr. Moss, these are three residents in our ENT department. They are Supranee, Jaruan, and Sirada," Yupa said. The three residents all bowed with a wai and smiled, which I again returned. The four women were dressed similarly. They had skirts that came several inches below their knees, elegant white cotton shirts, and all were proper and impeccably polite.

We drove to an open-air restaurant alongside a stream and a small water-fall just outside the main part of town. A waiter led us to our table. I noticed that the three residents always stayed close together and held each other's hands while walking. In Bangkok, I had observed women holding hands, as well as men. Some men would even place their arms around each other. I gathered that in Thailand, members of the same sex were permitted to enjoy a certain measure of physical intimacy with one another in public. It seemed taboo, however, for members of the opposite sex to hold hands or outwardly express physical affection.

We arranged ourselves around a hard wood table, sitting on wood benches. Yupa, reading from a menu written in Thai, ordered the food. I then looked up at the three women sitting opposite me, who, as if on cue, immediately began to giggle. I liked the sound of their laughter. They all simultaneously brought their folded right hands up to about the level of their noses and covered their mouths, as if to express embarrassment for laughing. Even their laughter was done in a stylized, charming manner.

Sirada, a little more confident than the others, spoke first. She cleared her throat and asked with perfect politeness, "Dr. Moss, how are you enjoying Thailand?" She was slender with brown, slightly curly hair, a round face, and friendly eyes. Her question immediately gathered everyone's attention. "I like Thailand very much," I answered, "I'm glad to be here." Everyone seemed quite pleased with this simple response.

Labored but pleasant conversation in fragmented English and Thai ensued. The residents struggled with their English but always spoke softly and with much deference. Yupa, having trained in Europe, spoke English well. She had a slow, deliberate manner, and frequently served as translator for the residents. "We have a tremendous amount of Head and Neck Cancer in Thailand, Dr. Moss," Yupa mentioned. "We are hoping to learn a great deal from you."

"I fully expect to learn just as much from you, if not more," I answered. And everyone smiled.

Looking across at these three delicate ladies and the diminutive Yupa, I had to wonder if these women actually enjoyed head and neck cancer surgery, a fairly demanding surgical specialty, often requiring lengthy procedures. Although there were no barriers to women back home, for one reason or another the specialty had generally remained the province of male surgeons.

"Do you like head and neck surgery?" I asked Yupa.

"Not really," she answered. Her honesty surprised me. Most people would not want to admit that they actually did not like what they did. Especially, when it was a medical career that would span three or four decades. I admired how candid and matter of fact she was. "I have a bad back and cannot stand so long at the operating table. I prefer allergy."

"Allergy?"

"Yes," she smiled, almost embarrassed.

In the field of ENT, there are no two areas more diametrically opposed than head and neck surgery and allergy. One is an exacting surgical specialty while the other is completely non-surgical.

"Why do you do it?" I asked somewhat incredulously.

"Dr. Acharee asked me." This was an interesting response.

"And you must listen?"

"Yes, I must, it is my duty." Simple enough, yet remarkable. It would be hard to imagine someone back home with a stated preference for allergy work and a bad back ever agreeing to run a head and neck department, no matter who asked. "Would you like to get out of head and neck?" I asked.

"Yes, but I cannot. There is too much work here, and we have too many patients. It is not possible." I was impressed. If there was anyone who seemed unsuited for an area of medicine, particularly head and neck surgery, it was Yupa, and yet, there it was. She seemed determined despite her physical limitations and personal interests.

After dinner we walked around the town. I spoke mainly with Yupa, whom I realized was also serving as chaperone for the ladies. The three residents walked closely together, safe in their own cocoon, hands clasped, chatting and giggling like young children. Casual strolling and conversation with any of them individually, I sensed, would have been strictly out of bounds. There was, no doubt, a formal process, carefully structured and supervised by which the sexes got to know one another in this very ritualized and traditional culture, as I would no doubt discover.

Chapter 5

Rak was a cherubic, young Thai doctor who very cheerfully introduced himself at my guesthouse the next morning. He was unusually tall for a Thai, with thick dark hair, round cheeks, and large eyes. He was a chief resident, and, I gathered from Acharee's description, a promising head and neck surgeon. His English, although far from perfect, was understandable. Acharee had mentioned that Rak would be looking after me while in Chiang Mai. Already, there were any number of mundane but important questions, which I was completely unable to answer, the first of which was how to get my laundry done and where to find hangers for my clothes. Rak would assist me in navigating that strange world out there.

"Hello, Doctor *Richahd*, nice to meet you," he greeted me with a curious northern Thai twang, stretching the vowels.

"Thanks, Rak, for picking me up."

"How was your sleep, Richahd," he asked.

"Fine," I lied, because, in fact, it was terrible. The Thais had apparently fallen in love with the motorcycle and drove it at all hours of the night, making deep sleep an unattainable goal. A pair of earplugs would be added to my shopping list.

"I am so happy," Rak smiled, his congeniality infectious.

We walked together through the campus, passing through corridors and adjoining buildings enroute to Suandok Hospital, the main teaching hospital for Chiang Mai University. It was a large and imposing white building, 15 floors high with over 1500 in-patient beds, and a massive outpatient facility on the ground floor. Numerous Thai flags and other decorations were draped over much of the outside of the building in commemoration of the King's sixtieth birthday.

We entered the elevator in a crush of Thai humanity, which in itself was something of an experience. In just this tiny microcosm you could glimpse the full spectrum of Thai society. Half the occupants in the elevator appeared as if they had just ridden in on their bullocks from an outlying village. They were scruffy and small, with hair asunder, possibly chewing something like beetle nut, in sandals and cotton shirts, rolled up trousers or, for the women, sarongs. Some of the workers wore official grey uniforms or jeans. Then the usual assortment of nurses, doctors and residents, some wearing white coats, but most with shirt sleeves and an open neck.

The elevator arrived at the tenth floor, the ENT floor. We passed through a sunlit hall where numerous patients and their families were lounging about together and entered the wards. Once there, Acharee and Yupa greeted us, both dressed gracefully in colorful blouses.

"Hello *Ajarn* Moss, how are you?" Sirada had mentioned that "Ajarn" was the respectful title given to teachers and professors in Thailand.

"Good morning Ajarn Acharee, Ajarn Yupa."

"Ajarn Moss, we will begin grand rounds with you now. Everyone is waiting. We will go first to the treatment room," Acharee said.

Inside the treatment room, a large group of doctors, residents, medical students and nurses were buzzing about. When we entered everyone immediately became quiet. I noticed about ten or twelve young faces standing in the front, some in the typical, short white coats of resident doctors. This I took to be the team of residents I would be working with.

Behind the residents, looking very timid in the presence of the American doctor, were some fifteen medical students. They shuffled about nervously. Several nurses, clad in white gowns and bonnets were also present.

Sprinkled amongst the residents were the faculty members, including Acharee and Yupa, the grand ladies of the department. These two were the main powers, although their bearing was more that of protective hens overlooking their young brood of students and residents. On the opposite side of the throng, standing isolated and distant, a shadowy looking character leaned against the wall with arms folded in a cocky sort of way. He was slight, paper thin, and had a narrow, prudish face, thin slits for lips, glasses, and just a hint of a scowl. Dressed rather fashionably, he had on, amazingly, a tie. His complexion was pale green, and he did not seem particularly thrilled to see me. Perhaps he was the young Turk, the alpha male of the department, who viewed me as an interloper and a threat. Of everyone there, his was the only chilly reception I had received.

Acharee stepped to the front and introduced me. She then began speaking in Thai, perhaps explaining a little about my background. Looking at me frequently, she smiled, as if to apologize for speaking in her language. Turning towards one of the residents, she then signaled for the first patient.

A young man, no more than 20, entered the room.

"This patient came to us because of pain with swallowing. He has something in the back of the tongue. Two biopsies have come back as negative. The report indicates only chronic inflammation," Yupa said by way of introduction.

"Chronic inflammation" was a benign, non-specific diagnosis. I suspected there was still concern about possible malignancy, hence his presence in this room for me to examine.

I sat down before the patient with my head mirror in place. Somewhere in a dark corner of my mind, I wondered if I was being set up to fail, recalling my experience with the "hang yao" in Bangkok. I asked for a face cover and a pair of gloves. A reusable cloth mask was given to me. I had heard that tuberculosis was endemic in Thailand, so I planned to wear a mask and gloves for every patient I examined.

I noticed that the mask had been brought out of a stainless steel bin with sterile forceps by a resident wearing gloves. The bin had a latch that had to be opened and rested on a cart with other steel bins and containers holding additional sterile instruments. The outside of the bins were warm having just been taken out of the autoclave. In addition to the bins and containers, there were glass bottles containing all sorts of colorful liquids, each one labeled in Thai and English, including ethanol, betadine, mercurochrome, peroxide, and saline. There were bins for forceps, clamps, scissors, needle holders, retractors, gloves, bandages, masks and hats. Underneath the top level of the cart was a second level for disposing of contaminated instruments and dirty dressings. I admired the handiness and frugality of their little set up. In the US, virtually everything was disposable, usually coming individually wrapped in plastic or paper to be used once and discarded. The waste was staggering. In Thailand, they obviously could not afford such extravagance. They managed to function effectively, maintaining sterility, but within the bounds of affordability.

I put on my mask and opened the folded cloth that contained the sterile rubber gloves. While putting on one of the gloves I noticed that it was quite stiff. I pulled a little harder, and the whole glove ripped apart.

"Ajarn Moss," said Acharee, "our gloves are a little stiff because we use them over again after sterilizing. I am sorry."

Another pair was brought. I then faced the seated patient and shined my headlight directly into his open mouth. Holding the patient's tongue with a piece of gauze, I passed a small round mirror into his mouth to visualize the back of his throat. The residents huddled closely behind, peering in over my shoulder.

After looking for a single moment it dawned on me, with all the clarity of a bolt of lightning, exactly where I was and what I was doing. This was the third world, so to speak, a poor, developing country with very sick patients suffering with advanced, neglected disease, and all my training and background in the States would not be adequate for dealing with what I now had to face.

The kid's tongue was completely gone. Nothing you could really call a tongue. Although he seemed rather cheerful, this young man had a large cancer that had completely consumed the back of his tongue. It had even extended up onto his tonsils. All that was left was a series of irregular pink humps and ridges covered with a bad smelling glaze of infected slime. It appeared almost volcanic, a ghastly eruption that had converted his mouth into a geologic ruin of cliffs, fissures, and gullies.

I then asked the young man to say "eeee." This maneuver allows visualization of the vocal cords. Not surprisingly, he could barely speak. Along with the muffled sound came an even stronger dose of the same putrid smell of rotting flesh I had already noticed, made worse by the added force of his exhalation.

I nodded to myself, released the young man's tongue and withdrew the mirror. I then felt his neck and detected golf ball sized lymph nodes running down both sides.

In this first case, I had encountered something worse than I had ever seen in the US, and in someone only 20 years of age! I felt as if I had been ambushed. If this were only the first case, what would I see in the course of an entire year? Worse than that, what diseases would I be expected to have answers for from my loyal following here? I found myself hurtling through the vacant chambers of my cerebral cortex wondering what I was going to recommend to my audience of more than thirty health professionals gathered eagerly around me. I wondered, too, about my lofty goals of "healing."

We had had advanced cases in my residency at the New York Eye and Ear Infirmary and then during my fellowship at the University of California in San Francisco. I recalled one diminutive Hispanic patient I had seen at the Infirmary by the name of Pablo, a Puerto Rican who spoke no English, recently emigrated, with a large cancer he had neglected in his hypopharynx or lower throat. He required a complete resection of this throat and reconstruction with a skin-muscle flap from his chest. He had numerous complications post-operatively including the dreaded *fistula* or breakdown of the repair resulting in leakage of saliva into his neck. He required aggressive wound care and a prolonged recovery before being able to return home. On the other hand, he was a smoker and a drinker, in his fifties, a non-English speaker from the third world with poor access and limited resources, and so met the usual risk and lifestyle factors associated with advanced throat cancer. Furthermore, within the Head and Neck Cancer pool of patients in the US were many other cases of far more limited nature and stage and hence eminently curable. Most such patients did not require extensive, mutilating surgery. Perhaps radiation alone would suffice. This was because Americans sought medical care much sooner when they sensed something amiss, at earlier stages in the course of the disease. They had greater access and resources and enjoyed much higher cure rates as a result with less invasive interventions. Yet here, in my first patient, was a 20-year-old non-smoker, absent any of the typical risk factors, with a deforming tumor that had fully consumed his tongue in hideous, revolting fashion, rendering it a foul-smelling gorge of festering debris that surely must have caused symptoms in this poor, young man well before this late hour when early diagnosis and treatment were possible. It was unnerving.

I masked my confusion with a professorial clearing of my throat. Adjusting the collar of my white doctor's coat, I shifted in my seat, placing my sweaty palms upon my knees. Sixty-some eyeballs were glued to me with an additional sixty eardrums waiting patiently for my recommendations.

"Uhhhh," the first official utterance of the great American doctor.

I procrastinated a little longer. I needed time to consider further the implications of this case. What should I advise? I knew it was cancer, whatever the biopsy report said. A large cancer and in a 20 year old boy! How did he get this? More importantly, how did it change the treatment for a youth as compared with someone in his fifties or sixties, the more typical age in the States for something like this? Should I recommend a total glossectomy in a 20 year old? Cut out the entire tongue and voice box? What kind of life was it for a kid with no tongue or voice? Or should I just go with radiation and chemo, recognizing that this would never cure him?

I had no idea, and I prayed no one would ask. Somehow the prospect of cutting out the tongue of a 20 year old disturbed me. If he was older, maybe, but a 20 year old? I didn't know what to say. If I went with surgery, the resulting disability was horrific. If I went only with radiation the tumor would be back in months.

I started to feel a very uncomfortable sensation in my chest, like a tight band encircling me. I felt hot too. This white coat and suit were bothering me. Why did I have to put this damn white coat on? Everyone here was comfortable in their shirtsleeves and open collars, but I had to play the professor and wear the big white coat with a suit and tie.

The pleasant bouquet of faces peered at me anxiously, still smiling. They didn't seem to suspect my indecision. Good! I felt like I was going to make a fool of myself on my first patient. I remembered the biopsy report. That's right. "Chronic Inflammation." Non-definitive, non-specific. Vague, unclear, confused, exactly the way I felt. But at least I had a definitive non-definitive biopsy report to hold on to. Salvation!

"I believe," I intoned gravely, "that we need to perform another biopsy." Splendid. Even profound. No one suspected. I continued slowly. "In as much as the prior biopsies were non-specific, I believe we need to know exactly what we're dealing with. I strongly recommend a third biopsy."

The audience lit up. Of course, that was it. Another biopsy! After all, we were still not sure. I then expounded, in stately tones, about the outer layers of chronic inflammation that surround cancers in the throat. "Because of the adjacent infection we must be sure to get a very deep bite," I uttered with growing confidence. They seemed to love the sound of this word, "bite," and repeated it aloud to themselves. "This to ensure that we obtain an actual piece of tumor tissue."

"Excuse me Ajarn Moss." My head jerked nervously in the direction of a timid female voice emanating from the crowd. It was a tiny figure, a young female resident wearing of all things, a Mickey Mouse sweater. Her name was Siripon. She had fluffed up hair, a pleasant face and looked as if this question had pressed her to the outer limits of her courage and fortitude. I began to feel that tight band forming around my chest again. Was this young girl about to pin me to the wall with the dreaded question? What treatment I would recommend if it came back as cancer, which it obviously was?

"Ajarn Moss, how do you make sure we get a good biopsy?" she stammered bravely in adorable English. *Thank you, God.* I would not have to reveal my uncertainty. The band around my chest loosened. This question I could answer handily, even with a little pedagogical aplomb.

"First of all," I began throatily, "I would recommend doing it under general anesthesia." This meant putting the patient asleep as opposed to just numbing it with an injection of lidocaine or local anesthesia. I was told that biopsies here, because of the sheer volume of cases, were frequently done under local anesthesia: a practice that would guarantee you the loss of all your patients in the US. It seemed a little barbaric, but then attitudes towards pain and comfort may be different here. Still, with two biopsy attempts, and nothing to show for it, maybe the third one should be done under general anesthesia to ensure accuracy.

"Also, after taking the first biopsy, you should return to the same location, for a second bite." That onomatopoetic syllable again seemed to titillate the crowd. "We can do a very thorough exam of the patient while he's asleep and better assess the full extent of the tumor." I was coming into my own now. "Remember that when examining patients with cancer of the tongue, palpation is probably more important than visualization. With your fingers palpating you can tell how deeply the tumor has invaded." Rapt. My audience seemed to be imbibing these pearls in silent reverie.

I had been saved. We were miles from the dreaded question now. No one had forced me to answer what I actually intended to do for the patient. I could gather my wits before recommending we cut out a 20 year old's tongue and voice box. Meanwhile, I could consult the textbooks or the medical literature, maybe even an emergency phone call to one of my professors back home.

"Ajarn Moss, let us examine the next patient, please," Acharee said.

"Fine."

"We already know the diagnosis, but we are not sure what to do."

"Okay."

"We will bring the patient now."

"Good, let's take a look." I was getting a little nervous again. She seemed to be preparing me. Did she notice anything? Maybe that last one was just a warm up.

An old scrawny man was escorted in by one of the residents. The left eye and side of his face were covered over with a large gauze pad. He sat down in the examining chair and looked out at the crowd with his one uncovered eye.

"Ajarn Moss, this patient came to us two weeks ago with a tumor on the left side of his face, coming from the maxillary sinus. The biopsy is positive for cancer," Yupa said.

"So it's coming from the sinus?"

"Yes."

"Was a CT scan done?"

"No. The patient could not afford one."

"Where did you take the biopsy from?"

"The face," she said. The face! Now that was worrisome. Usually a biopsy of a sinus cancer is taken from inside the sinus where the tumor originates. In advanced cases it may grow into the nasal cavity. But the face! How big was this thing anyway?

"Let's take a look." I tried to sound confident.

I peeled off the gauze pad taped to the man's face. I immediately became pale. The midportion of his left face was gone. Just like the young man's tongue. In place of the normal skin and facial contour was an appalling mass of surly red beef. His left eye was clouded over and pushed up against the roof of the orbit, and his left nostril bulged with thick, brawny tumor.

This case was worse than the last one, and we already had the biopsy report showing cancer. I could not hide behind "chronic inflammation" again.

"Very advanced," I said, trying to conceal my discombobulation.

"Yes," replied Yupa sympathetically.

"It's not possible to get a CT scan?" I wondered meekly.

"We cannot. We use the CT scan very rarely here. It is just not possible."

The patient impressed me. He looked at me with his one good eye and smiled. He muttered something in Thai, patted my arm and laughed. He didn't seem bothered by the condition of his face. In fact, he seemed more relaxed than I was, which was odd.

"Ajarn Moss, what do you think? We will follow your recommendations," Yupa said.

I was in a quandary. I could not delay treatment since there were really no further tests needed. The biopsy report was positive for cancer. A CT scan could not be done. Did I want to operate or not?

"It's very advanced," I repeated again.

"Yes."

"Do you get many cases like this?"

"This one is unusually advanced," Yupa commiserated.

"Quite large," I burped, noticing a little acid reflux.

"A very aggressive tumor," Yupa replied.

Yupa was making me feel better. It was advanced even by her standards. For me it was exponentially worse than anything I had ever seen. Did it invade the skull? How would I reconstruct the face after I removed the tumor? If I was treading frantically with the first case, by now I was sinking fast.

"Do you have a fiberoptic scope," I asked.

"Yes."

Saved again.

"I think it would be a good idea to carefully evaluate the nasopharynx. A tumor of this size may have spread there, which would make it inoperable."

"We have a fiberoptic scope in the clinic. You can examine the patient there."

"Splendid."

We continued.

"...24 years old with a large lump in his neck," said Yupa about the third patient now sitting before me.

"How long has he had it?" I asked.

"Several years."

"Getting larger or the same size?"

"The same size."

"Has it been infected?"

"No."

"Nothing else on physical exam?"

"Everything else is normal."

Good. Now this was reasonable. I would have some fairly straightforward suggestions for this. An unknown primary? A congenital cyst? A lymphoma? Tuberculosis? My mind was spinning with ideas and differential diagnoses. I was coming into my own now. Getting warmed up. At last, something that didn't blow me out of the room.

I sat down, performed my routine exam, and found nothing but a soft, mobile six centimeter mass on the right side of the patient's neck.

"Has anyone needled it?" I asked.

"Needle?" Yupa asked.

"Yes, you know, a fine needle biopsy."

Puzzlement quickly spread among the ranks. A fine needle biopsy? Apparently something new around here. Good. I was finally the expert!

At this point, a middle aged, balding Thai man in a grey safari suit whirled into the room, bristling with command and authority. He had a large, round unsmiling face, was short and plump. It was the first time since coming to Thailand that I had encountered anyone that could be thought of as plump and bald! A statistical rarity, I imagined, in this country. Acharee introduced us. This was the esteemed Dr. Kobkiat, the former chairman of the ENT department, recently promoted to associate dean. He greeted me with a warm, American style handshake.

Kobkiat looked to be in his fifties and had done his residency training in Chicago, at a time when it was relatively easy for foreign graduates to come to the US. In the 1980s, this had changed. The US had closed the doors, leaving positions available only for Americans. Kobkiat, though, of an earlier era, had gotten in just under the wire. This gave him, I suspected, formidable clout as the US seal of approval carried tremendous weight.

"Fine needle biopsy?" Kobkiat asked. "Please demonstrate." I sensed a slight edge in his voice. Perhaps he wanted to establish the pecking order in his kingdom.

Residents scrambled for a syringe and a 21-gauge needle. A shiny, glass syringe was delivered and placed on the table by the patient. I put on my sterile, reusable rubber gloves, without tearing them, and worked the syringe. The plunger moved up and down the glass shaft much more smoothly than the plastic throwaways we used in the US.

Other residents were applying the betadine antiseptic to the patient's neck. No explanation was offered the patient beyond a word or two muttered quickly in Thai.

In a moment, everything was ready. With everyone huddled around, I grasped the syringe in my right-gloved hand, positioned it just below the mass and plunged the needle deep into his neck. I withdrew the plunger, and the syringe immediately filled with bright yellow straw-colored fluid. I removed the syringe and applied pressure to the neck.

"Send this for routine culture and sensitivity, AFB stain, and cytology," I said. Residents rushed forward with the necessary vials and labels. "I needle all neck masses," I said, turning to Kobkiat. He had, in manner at least, thrown down the gauntlet. With this biopsy, I had picked it up.

"What do you think it is, Ajarn Moss?" A timid voice from one of the residents.

"I would guess it's a branchial cleft cyst."

The crowd seemed pleased with this little display, and I was beginning to feel better.

"Ajarn Moss, we will go to the wards now to make rounds," Acharee said.

The momentum had suddenly shifted.

Acharee escorted me from the treatment room and onto the wards. The rest of the throng, including Yupa and Kobkiat, followed closely behind. The halls were sunlit and clean. There were several men dressed in blue denim shirts and a couple of women in sarongs and sandals who were quietly sweeping and dusting.

"We have over 80 beds, and they are always filled," said Acharee. "Sometimes we must place them in the halls."

"You're kidding. Eighty beds?"

"Yes, or more." That easily made this the largest department I had ever worked in. I noticed the cots in the halls where many of the patients were staying.

We passed the nurses station and entered the first large communal room with about 16 beds neatly lined up side by side, garrison-style, on each side. Large windows flooded the quarters with light. Dressed in their white hospital pajamas, the patients waited for the doctors.

The first patient was a young man who sat cross-legged at the foot of his bed. As with all Thais, he seemed quite relaxed despite the fact that he had a series of walnut sized lumps peppering both sides of his neck. Other than that he looked fine. He dutifully wai'd Acharee and Yupa.

"This is a 19 year old man with cancer of the nasopharynx," said Yupa. In five years of ENT in the US, I had seen perhaps 2 or 3 cases, but remembered that this often affected people of Chinese ancestry. I figured this too was another routine cancer found here, given the high percentage of Thai that were of Chinese descent. "He was found to have elevated liver enzymes, and a liver spleen scan showed multiple mets (metastatic disease) to the liver."

Why is this man smiling so much? Does he realize that at the age of 19 he has a terminal disease?

There was also something odd also about his eyes. Yes, of course! His right eye turned inward. *My god! The tumor has spread to the brain.*

"He also has a lateral rectus palsy because of intracranial spread," Yupa added as if reading my mind. "He was treated with radiation about six months ago, but unfortunately the disease has come back."

Hopeless, absolutely hopeless.

"Any suggestions?" Yupa asked.

"Do you have chemotherapy protocols here?"

"We do have a protocol, but it is very expensive, and can only be used on selected patients."

"Based on their ability to pay?" I asked.

"No, based on whether the patient has any chance for long-term cure," Yupa answered.

And, clearly, this unfortunate individual with metastatic disease to the brain and liver had none. "In America, we would tend to give it to anyone who might need it, even those with incurable disease," I said.

"We cannot do that here," Yupa said pleasantly. "We must be very cautious with our resources and give it only to those who can be cured. It is not for palliation."

We continued on our way from bed to bed. There was no shortage of patients with advanced disease.

We came upon a man I guessed to be in his forties. "This patient had radical radiation for a cancer in his throat," said Yupa, "but the tumor has come back. What will you do?"

Like the other Thai patients, he was smiling, something I found remarkable considering their abysmal prospects. He sat upright and was attentive, yet calm, as if he had not a care in the world. I noted the skin of his neck, which looked like dried leather from the radiation. "Was it a very advanced tumor?"

"Yes, I'm afraid so."

Again I felt myself backed into a corner. The man needed surgery, but after having had radical radiation therapy the risks were high.

"You know the complication rate goes up considerably after radiation, especially with the skin he's got," I said.

"Yes, I know," said Yupa.

"His options are not good," I said.

"I agree," Yupa nodded.

I felt his skin. It was brawny and dry. Little peeled flakes of skin littered his collar. "He needs to have surgery."

I was not crazy about his odds.

We passed through the wards, moving from patient to patient, each case as difficult and formidable as the last. Many of the patients were right out of ENT textbooks, rarely seen, if ever, back in the States - especially the infectious diseases, which had been, for the most part, eradicated. There were brain abscesses, acute mastoiditis, cavernous sinus thrombosis, leprosy, tuberculosis, maggots, parasitic disease, and others. Of course, there was the continuous parade of hopelessly advanced cancer cases. I had managed to see in a single day the equivalent of a career's worth of unusual pathology back home.

It was daunting but affecting because of the incredible challenge it represented. And despite it all, I was finding my footing. I recalled the many steps and questions that preceded the decision to come. I recalled the fortune cookie, the appealing letter Acharee had sent me, and the train-ride up from Bangkok. I recalled the many doubts and concerns. And, yet, none of that now mattered. The reality of that decision, of Acharee's letter, of Head and Neck Cancer in the Third World and specifically in Thailand, the intense suffering and need that existed, and the team and structure that was in place here to battle this scourge, this dedicated cadre of residents and doctors and the hospital, which I had now joined, transcended that. Such concerns loomed small and meaningless in the face of the overwhelming hardship that I had witnessed in only my first day. I relished this. I could not have asked for a more fulfilling chance than this. I was thankful I had not weakened or second-guessed myself, thankful I had not changed my mind. I would have to think quickly and make decisions on the basis of limited experience and incomplete information, but I was here - and elated. I could make a difference.

Grand Rounds soon finished. It was 9:30 AM. Everyone dispersed, and I was left with Acharee, Yupa, and another young female ajarn named Niramon. She was an attractive woman, with glasses and short-cropped hair. Having studied in Canada for a year, she spoke English fairly well. We walked into the faculty office where a large bowl of exotic fruit and a plate of Thai sweets had been prepared. The secretary in the office brought me a cup of hot tea. I sat down with my three colleagues.

"I spoke too much, didn't I?" I asked.

"Not at all, it is what we want," Niramon said.

"Are you sure?" I liked the reassurance.

"Yes, we have so much to learn."

"So it went alright?"

"Very much so."

Chapter 6

I recalled a pivotal moment in my move towards medicine and hence my work in Asia. I was living in the Swami Rudrananda Yoga Ashram in Big Indian, New York, in the Catskill Mountains with my older brother Lonnie and some sixty other souls seeking spiritual enlightenment. Lonnie had moved there first and I followed a couple of years later. A friend from the Bronx, Mark Schlosberg, from Sedgwick Avenue right behind our building on University Avenue, moved up after visiting Lonnie and ran the Antique Store, one of the ashram businesses. Mark was Lonnie's age, very devoted to his spiritual practice, and like an older brother to me. He was also from the old neighborhood. I trusted him.

"I got straight A's," I told Mark as I entered the store. I had just completed my second year at Ulster County Community College, in Stone Ridge, near the ashram, after my freshman year at Lehman College, this time with a year of Biology and Inorganic Chemistry. "I'm thinking of applying for Chiropractic school," I said.

The year before I had enrolled in a tech college in Delhi, about an hour's drive from Big Indian. I was going to take a course in carpentry, to be a builder. We had a construction company at the ashram, which I worked for and liked. I wanted to pursue construction. A week or so before the class began, I received a letter from the college indicating it had been cancelled because of a lack of enrollment. This chance occurrence at so early an age as I was deciding my career path was not insignificant. I switched to Chiropractic and began taking the necessary prerequisites. I went from wood, nails, and bricks to bones, joints, and ligaments.

"Are you crazy, Ricky," Mark said, staring at me as if I were the biggest fool in the world. "You're an A student. Why would you go into Chiropractic? Go for medicine."

"Medicine takes a lot of time. Chiropractic is only four years. Less expensive too," I said.

"Listen to me. You've got the grades. You're smart. You're going into medicine. That's it. Now do it."

I was taken aback. But I knew Mark was looking out for me. I had thought of medicine but was not sure I could do it. Perhaps this was the push I needed to make such a commitment. A week later I applied to Indiana University in Bloomington, Indiana. I would pursue a career in medicine.

While my life in Chiang Mai revolved around my work at the hospital, nights and weekends gave me the opportunity to peak beneath the surface of this growing town and see the underside of life in the north of Thailand. Chiang Mai was not an ordinary town by anyone's measure. It possessed an amazing mix of culture and tradition and a rich history dating back almost a thousand years. But it was an ancient city caught in the tempest of changing times and circumstances, unwittingly serving as the backdrop for a multitude of sins and tragedies.

The old part of town contained magnificent Buddhist temples, some four or five hundred years old, where the monks, barefoot, cloaked in orange robes, chanted and meditated. Every morning, as the sun rose, the monks went out with their alms bowls to meet the faithful, who would bow and make offerings of food, this beautiful ritual enacted across the city and the nation. The people too, in the way they interacted with one another, seemed engaged in an ancient, stylized dance, with every gesture and word nuanced carefully to demonstrate honor and deference. Their musical tonal language, which had the texture and rhythm more of a song or melody, provided a delightful sound to their conversations. In these regards, Chiang Mai was timeless, delicate, and lovely.

But right alongside these hallowed and revered aspects of life in Chiang Mai, stood other more temporal realities, a seething, subterranean pool of lecheries and cravings, the most entrenched of which was the sex trade. Flesh peddling was a part of life here in Thailand, from Bangkok to tiny hilltop villages, and each night the town geared up for the unbridled pursuit of carnal pleasure. Come nightfall, the women descended upon Chiang Mai, the great Sodom of the north, from the mountains and hamlets, filling the clubs, bars and brothels with the flower of Thailand's womanhood. All of them were looking for the same thing, a chance to make money using their bodies as their livelihoods as it has been for time immemorial. Most of the girls went to the many brothels of Chiang Mai and sat behind large glass windows with numbers on their lapels, waiting to be picked by leering male customers who sat on the other side of the great glass divide. The brothels were more like sex factories, the more attractive girls partaking in as many as ten sexual liaisons in the course of an evening's work. In the more posh clubs, the girls were higher priced and a single encounter or two would suffice. But it went on night after night, and Chiang Mai was the setting where these lustful dramas unfolded each night, a sexual beehive packed solid with raging hormones, where men and women pursued each other hotly for their own purposes and desires.

Everyone came to Chiang Mai looking for different things, and Chiang Mai seemed able to satisfy them all. There was good food, splendid temples, a fascinating culture and way of life, and, yes, there were many beautiful women. It was an amazing blend of the sacred and the profane, a place where the world of the senses intermingled almost seamlessly with the austere realm of the spiritual and transcendent.

There was a street that formed the eastern border of the old city known as Moon Muang road where many of the westerners hung out. There were a couple of restaurants that offered western food and in general catered to western sensibilities. Of all the joints, none was more popular than the "Bierstube," a German run place that was the great meeting hall for expatriates. It was here where I learned about the seedier side of life in Chiang Mai and met a lot of compelling, bizarre, and intriguing people.

George, an Aussie, was a very well known Westerner, or *farang*, living in Chiang Mai, who ran a bookstore and breakfast counter just down from the Bierstube. Living in Chiang Mai for years, he had married a local Thai girl and had a beautiful boy that everyone knew and loved. Unfortunately the boy was born with a myelomeningocele of the lower spine, which made him incontinent and unable to walk without a brace. Still, it hardly seemed to affect the lad's disposition. He got around well enough and was a local favorite in his own right at the Bierstube.

"He's a good bloke," George said to me one morning at his bookstore, admiring his son who was scampering about, leg braces and all. "You'd never know there was a problem the way he carries on."

George was also the world's leading authority on motorcycling in the north of Thailand and had maps detailed to the tenth of a kilometer of every dirt road, small village or hill tribe camp in the northern provinces. He could wind his way through the jungles and forests bordering Burma or Laos better than any local, and, weather permitting, made weekly forays himself. Something of a speed freak, George generally raced along the back roads of Thailand at 125 kilometers an hour or more and knew no fear.

In his bookstore, George had photo albums filled with the innumerable out of the way places he had visited, so before any trip to the northern hills and jungles, you could stop in at George's, pick up some of his maps, run through his photos and plan your journey. It was a great service for travelers unfamiliar with the terrain. I stopped in one morning to get advice about a motorcycle trip up north.

"I want to see the Golden Triangle. Maybe do a river trip or visit the Hill Tribes," I said.

George pulled one of his albums out and we pored over them together.

"I'd recommend a trip to Fang and then Tha Ton. You get on the Kok River and ride the ferry down to Chiang Rai. Spend the night there and come back the next day," George said. "Or you can spend the night in Tha Ton and leave early the next morning. It takes about four hours on the ferry to Chiang Rai. There's a giant Buddha in Tha Ton overlooking the Kok River. Make sure you see it."

"Any Hill Tribes?" I asked.

"Along the way on the Kok River, you can stop off at *Mae Salak* and take a bus or ride your motorcycle to the Lahu Village. From there you can trek to other Hill Tribe villages. There are many. Shan, Lisu, Yao, Thai. There are even some Chinese refugee villages."

"I would need a few days for that," I said.

"Yes, at least two or three."

He showed me pictures of the towns, the Kok River, and the ferry.

"What about Chiang Rai?"

"Visit Wat Phra Keo, the original temple that housed the Emerald Buddha that now sits in the temple of the same name in Bangkok," George said. "There's a replica of the Emerald Buddha there now."

"You can get your motorcycle on the ferry?" I asked.

"Yes, no problem. The Thai do it all the time."

"What about the 'Golden Triangle?'" I asked.

"That refers to the area in the north where Thailand, Burma, and Laos meet."

"That's where they grow all the opium?"

"Yes, still do," he said, rubbing his face. "The Hill Tribes in particular. That's their big cash crop. They came over from Burma and China after World War II and settled in northern Thailand. Poppy grows well on hillsides. Perfect for them. There are still opium warlords there, but not like the old days during the Vietnam War. Then you had everyone jumping in. The CIA, Burmese, and Chinese military guys. We had the old KMT there, the Kuomintang, the anti-communists from China that fought for Chiang Kai Shek and his nationalist army."

"You're kidding? The old Chinese army under Chiang Kai Shek? I had no idea they were up there."

"Yes, they used the money from the opium trade to fund their military operations against the Chinese Communists along the Burma-China border. Still at it but nothing like before. True believers. I don't blame them. Better than the commie bastards running China now."

"I didn't realize how big this was."

"Oh, it's major. The heroin used to come out of the Middle East until the Golden Triangle took over. With all the GIs during the Vietnam era, it really took off. Now the US and the Thai government are trying to wipe it out. Poor Hill Tribe blokes have no way of surviving. Thai Army Rangers burn up the poppy fields and destroy the heroin refineries. No way for the Hill Tribes to make their way," George said.

"So what do they do?"

"Not much. They get to watch their livelihood being hacked or burned to the ground."

"I know we don't want heroin to be produced. But it's a quandary since the Hill Tribes know nothing else. Have they tried to get them to learn other trades or cultivate different products?"

"The Thai government and royal family tried a crop substitution program. Tea, coffee, corn, herbs. A total failure. They're also trying to get the Hill Tribes to assimilate into mainstream Thai culture, learn the language, get a Thai education, earn a living like Thai do, farming the usual things like rice or learning more traditional trades."

"Any success?"

"Not really. Hard to get the buggers to change their ways."

"Maybe tourism?" I suggested.

"Oh, yeah, some of the more clever types are taking advantage of that already. But that has problems too. There are abuses. And they lose their traditions. No easy answers, I'm afraid," George said.

"Are they still cultivating poppy?"

"Oh, yeah. Plenty of pockets still left. Can't eliminate all of it. But a lot of the trade has moved to Laos."

"But they still grow it up there in Thailand?"

"Yes, still do. But much less. It is illegal in Thailand to cultivate poppy for profit, but they let the Hill Tribes grow it for personal use. Funny, really. They love their opium."

"I'll have to visit the Hill Tribes."

"Oh, yeah, don't want to miss that while you're here. Just let me know."

George, not necessarily through personal experience, was also an expert on "places of entertainment" as he delicately called them, and could describe number and street corner of almost any brothel in any town, no matter how remote or small. This expertise was less well publicized, but for those who were interested, George could supply the information, right down to number of the girl behind the glass screen and price tag. "If you're ever interested in the brothels, let me know. I can fix you up with that too," he winked. "Truth be told, any town you're in, just ask the locals for the 'ladies.' They'll know exactly what you're talking about."

A fixture in town, George was easily recognized whenever he flashed by on his famous gold colored Honda motorcycle, the one with the seat and handles covered in fur - a regular Asian cowboy.

Chapter 7

As the weeks passed, I adjusted to my new routines and responsibilities at the hospital. I worked closely with the residents and other Ajarns in the operating room, on the wards, and in the clinics, and found it all very satisfying. Of all the various activities I was involved in, perhaps the most important was the head and neck clinic.

Every Monday, at one o'clock, the faithful converged just outside the doors leading to the ENT outpatient department. They began assembling at noon and slowly filled the rows of long wooden benches. By one o'clock, they were standing in the aisles.

They were here for the head and neck clinic. It turned out to be by far the busiest of all specialty clinics because in Thailand head and neck cancer was rampant.

The patients were, for the most part, simple villagers or farmers wearing wide brimmed straw hats. They appeared to have just come in from the fields. Some carried large woven baskets filled with rice to take to the market afterwards. Their skin was wrinkled and dark from the many years working in the sun.

Many clearly bore the marks and wounds of their disease, usually large lumps on their necks, some the size of grapefruits. In some cases, the tumor may have eaten through the overlying skin of the neck or face, forming a horrid, fleshy welt of exposed cancer. Some of the tumors oozed or actively bled and came wrapped in thick pads of gauze.

There were patients with tracheostomy tubes in their necks, placed because a tumor had choked off their airway. Other patients had discolored, leathery, dry skin from prior radiation. Postoperative patients who have had their voice boxes removed came in with a breathing hole or stoma at the base of their necks; others may have had part of their tongue and jaw removed, bearing the stigmata and deformities of those procedures.

The head and neck clinic officially opened when Yupa and I came to the clinic. Boonrit was the third member of the triumvirate, but he tended to come late, if at all. He was the pale green, sickly looking doctor I had noticed on my first day, and since my arrival his appearance at the head and neck clinic had become erratic. I knew he was not pleased with my being here.

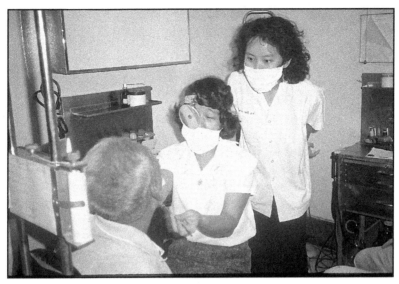

Dr. Yupa in clinic

Yupa and I were met with the usual team of residents, students and nurses. The head nurse of the clinic, Sunata, greeted me warmly.

"Hello Ajarn Moss," she said with a bow.

"Sawadee khrap," I said, returning her bow. In her mid thirties, Sunata was very friendly and always did her best to make me feel comfortable.

I took my place in the center of the crowd of residents on a stool situated next to the patient's seat. Yupa sat next to me.

The first patient, a middle aged man, entered the room and sat beside me. I immediately noticed three things about him. First, he had a metal trache tube in his neck to breathe from, suggesting there was a large cancer blocking his voice box. Second, he had a large lump on the right side of his neck. Third, he was smiling. There was something comical about that smile. Comical in that I could not possibly fathom what he was smiling about and the incongruity of it seemed humorous.

"He came to clinic two weeks ago. He have trouble breathing. We must do emergency trache, sir." Sumet, a first year resident with a curiously shaped head was presenting the patient. His head was narrow at the mouth, gradually expanded outward, culminating at his forehead, which was massive, giving the impression of an inverted trapezoid. He looked funny, and his personality matched his appearance. Endlessly stumbling over himself, he was one of these blissfully, happy people who didn't seem to mind making a fool of himself.

"We perform biopsy when we do trache, sir. It come back today. The result say," he unfolded a dirty blue piece of paper he had been carrying around in his shirt pocket, "squamous cell carcinoma. Thank you sir."

"Anything else, Sumet?"

"Oh, uhh, no, sir. He have cancer." I paused waiting for any further morsels of information.

"Well, did you see anything during the biopsy?"

"Oh, yes," he began fumbling through the patient's chart finally locating the operative report. "He have large cancer of the - uhh - throat, sir. Tumor invade voice box and is very big."

"Is it circumferential?" A pause, and then a puzzled look. Yupa quickly intervened in the mother tongue. Sumet nodded and laughed.

"Oh, yes - circum - circumferential. Yes sir, it is, uhh, so big, I believe so. Yes, I think so. It may, uhh, be circumferential."

"So it wraps around the whole throat?"

"I - I think so sir."

I put him out of his misery. "It's a massive tumor involving the throat and voice box, which has spread to the neck, and he's going to need a major operation. Right, Sumet?"

"Uhh, yes sir, sank you sir, I sink so." He quickly sat down.

"Okay, let's take a look. Fiberoptic please."

This was a gift from the Japanese, a brand new Olympus fiberoptic scope, a long black snake-like device or "scope" for looking at the voice box. I was overjoyed to find they had one because it made head and neck exams so much easier. It came in a cushioned case, and the nurses treated it like precious jewelry. They opened it and handed it to me with great solicitude. The light source was attached and switched on.

"*Yu ning ning* (don't move)," I said, inserting the scope through the patient's right nostril. I guided it through the hills and valleys of the patients nasal cavity, past the soft palate, and down into the throat. The patient coughed a bit but soon stopped.

Amidst bubbling pools and rising vapors of rotting tumor, I could make out a large cancer that had invaded deeply into the larynx (voice box) and that had advanced along the back of the pharynx, well on its way to encircling the entire throat in a wall of solid tumor. It was a wonder the patient did not suffocate prior to the trache.

I tried to advance the scope past the tumor. The patient began coughing violently. I quickly removed the scope. The patient reached for the spittoon and wretched up a great green gob of cheesy mucus with small chunks of tumor debris. The sounds emerging from his throat were seismic.

I examined the patient's neck. On the right side was a large fixed mass the size of a tennis ball. The skin overlying the neck mass was swollen, red, and fixed to the underlying tumor. It appeared to be on the verge of rupturing.

On the opposite side of the neck, two smaller lumps were identified. It was another example of very advanced disease, but a fairly common presentation for head and neck cancer in Thailand.

"What do you want to do with this, Sumet?"

"I-I don't know, sir." He shrugged. I looked around and opened up the floor for answers. "Do you want to radiate it?" I ask rhetorically. Everyone knew that radiation alone was not going to touch this tumor. Radical disease required radical treatment, and that meant surgery, although radiation would be needed post operatively.

"What do you want to do? Pitchit?" Pitchit was a promising and well-read second year resident.

"I-I-I believe this is circumferential tumor of hypopharynx with bilateral metastatic disease to the neck. He will need a total laryngopharyngectomy and bilateral neck dissection.

"Do you want to radiate post op?"

"Yes sir."

"How should we reconstruct the throat? Sirada?" Elegant and lovely as always, Sirada responded, "With a pec major flap."

"Any other possibilities?"

"A gastric pull up," Rak said.

"Do you have a general surgeon here that can do that?"

"I think so, Richahd."

I looked over to Yupa to get her input. She nodded her agreement. This patient would need his entire throat and larynx removed along with the lymph nodes on both sides of his neck and some reconstructive procedure to reconnect his mouth and stomach.

The next patient came in to be examined. "This patient is 26 years old, and, uhh, have l-lymph nodes on both sides of the neck. We b-believe there is something in nasopharynx." Siripon, the pretty first year resident I had met the first day, was presenting.

"And what would you like to do now?" I asked Siripon.

"We should take a biopsy."

"Good. You can put him on the schedule." This innocent suggestion triggered an unexpected tangle of puzzled looks. "Something wrong?"

"Uhh, Ajarn Moss, we do not need to place the patient on the schedule," Siripon said. Curious.

"Well, when do you want to do the biopsy?"

"Now."

"Now? You mean right now in the clinic?"

"Yes, Ajarn."

"The patient will agree to it?"

"We always biopsy the nasopharynx in the clinic, Ajarn."

"Really?"

"Yes."

I was amazed. A biopsy of the nasopharynx (directly behind the nose) was not a big deal, but back in the States we had always done it in the operating room, usually under general anesthesia. If it wasn't a big deal, we at least made it one back home. We ordered blood tests, an EKG, and chest x-ray. Consent forms were signed. Discussions regarding the procedure were held. Histories and physicals were completed. The patient was admitted the morning of the procedure. Once wheeled into the operating room, a gaggle of nurses, aides, and residents tended diligently to the patient and attached him to an array of complex gadgets, monitors, probes, and lines. The anesthesiologist then delivered a number of medications intravenously to induce sleep and muscle relaxation and finally complete paralysis, after which, the patient was intubated (a tube placed into the airway to breath through) and whisked off to sleep. At this point, and not a second sooner, the biopsy of the nasopharynx was taken. Here in Chiang Mai, they managed to accomplish the same thing right here in the clinic and without anesthesia.

"The patient can tolerate it?"

"Yes, Ajarn," said Siripon.

"You've done this before?"

"Yes, Ajarn."

"Isn't it uncomfortable for the patient?"

"They tolerate it, Ajarn."

I watched the first year resident discuss for less than five seconds the planned procedure with the patient. It amounted to, I guess, telling him that he needed a biopsy. Nothing more. Siripon then sprayed topical Novocain into the nose. Grasping a long biopsy forceps in her right hand, she gently guided it along the floor of the patient's nose until it reached the back wall. The patient moved a little, but controlled himself. She opened the forceps and plunged it into the tumor. After closing the forceps she pulled back. An audible "wahk" could be heard. The patient winced. She quickly removed the forceps from his nose and deposited the biopsy specimen into a vial held by one of the nurses. The patient muttered something in Thai. It was clearly not something he relished, but then it was over. There was a tiny trickle of blood in his throat, which soon stopped. Otherwise he was fine.

It occurred to me that the whole convoluted process that American patients routinely go through in performing the very same procedure all boiled down to that one instant of discomfort, when that abrupt "wahk" could be heard. I wondered if our emphasis on patient comfort, admitting them, placing them under general anesthesia, was worth the time and expense?

The patient left the area.

I was impressed. I didn't know if I could get away with it in the US, but it certainly worked in Thailand.

Chapter 8

Robert was another Chiang Mai ex-pat I met at the Bierstube. An American from southern California, who lived and worked in Japan for six months out of the year and in Thailand for the remainder, to spend all the money he had made in Japan. He taught and edited English in Japan, got paid handsomely for it, and lived like a king the rest of the year in Chiang Mai. He had a brand new white Honda motorcycle and regularly took 1000-kilometer jaunts all over Thailand, tearing up the roads, dodging ten wheel trucks, risking life and limb for the adrenalin rush of high speed biking in Asia.

"The Japanese pay well, Rick. Enough to keep me very comfortable in Thailand for half the year," he said one morning at the Bierstube.

"Do you need any training or a degree?" I asked.

"Nope. I'm just a native English speaker," he said. "The Japanese never challenge you. They're so damn polite. What are they going to do? Question my English? Not going to happen. You or anyone can do what I'm doing. It's very pleasant. I couldn't ask for a better job."

He spent most of his time in Chiang Mai, nursing his great weakness, the women of Chiang Mai on a nightly basis.

"It's a perfect life. Japan and Thailand. I love Thai women. They're beautiful. And they don't hassle you like American women. I can have a different one every night. It's heaven, Rick."

By day, Robert was always alone, eating at the Bierstube, lounging for hours over a plate of home fries, toast and eggs, chased by a fresh squeezed orange juice or a yogurt shake. At night though, you could never find him, but if you did it was usually with two women, one on each arm. The next time I saw him, he was walking on crutches down Moon Muang road, en-route to the Bierstube, left leg in a cast. "What happened, Robert?" I asked.

"I broke my leg last time out on the motorcycle. Crazy Thai truck drivers. The worst in the world. No respect for motorcycles. He was honking his horn like a maniac, forced me off the side of the road, and I took a spill. Broke my damn leg. Some locals got me to a hospital. I didn't need surgery. Just a cast. It's a pain, but it'll come off in six weeks," he said.

But in other ways, I could see he hadn't slowed down at all. Hanging on each arm were two lovely Thai ladies, watching him with all the worry and concern of nervous mothers. "You look like you're doing fine," I said.

"Couldn't be better, Rick," he said, with a wink and a nod.

If you had to break a leg somewhere, there was no better place than Chiang Mai.

Chapter 9

I had moved to Bloomington, Indiana to attend Indiana University in my junior year. I was a pre-med student like hundreds of others smitten with the romantic vision of becoming a physician. I was taking Organic Chemistry, first semester, the great "weed-out course" as it was known that brutally winnowed the class, purging the majority of students who would not go on to the promised land of medical school. It was a horrendous course, teeming with compulsive and sometimes desperate premed students most of whom were not going to make it.

The emotions and stress levels ran high, especially before a test. The Teaching Assistants and professors all knew how much was riding on this. Some were compassionate. Others were less so, relishing, it seemed, their status as arbiters of the fate of the hundreds that filled the vast auditorium in the hallowed Chemistry Building off Third Street.

I approached it and all tests in similar fashion, which was to say as a samurai. I had read the novel, "Shogun," by James Clavell, about feudal Japan, and had been influenced by its depiction of samurai culture. I had also studied "Bushido," the code of the samurai that emphasized duty, discipline and honor, and absorbed it into my personal philosophy and way of life. Death was not to be feared. Rather, we sought death, especially a good and honorable death.

I prepared myself before every test with meditation and concentration techniques. I recited invocations and dressed in accordance with the occasion. This meant an orange T-shirt for purity and fire. Over that, I wore my red corduroy shirt symbolizing blood and death. Upon my desk, I placed my Swiss army knife, a symbol of the coming spiritual battle and my willingness to die if necessary in the contest.

The professor paced up and down the aisle, trying, it seemed, to calm the troops. He looked at me. "What's all this?" he asked, noticing my colorful garments and the Swiss army knife on the desk.

"Oh, nothing, just my pre-test sanctification and mental preparation ceremony," I said.

"I see," he said nodding. "You think it helps?"

"Yes, sir, I do, along with untold hours of studying and mastery of the material."

"Good answer," he said, nodding with a hint of approval. "Curious. Never saw it before, but who knows? Good luck, son."

"Thank you, sir." I saw it as a blessing of sorts.

Chapter 10

William, the fat bearded Brit, taught English in Chiang Mai University. Something of a Puritan in this sinful city, Will was a cantankerous, testy soul who waxed philosophic and looked with disdain at the unrefined gutter habits of his fellow *farang*.

"I am a frustrated intellectual," William announced to me one evening at the Bierstube. "I haven't come near fulfilling my academic ambitions. I walk around the darkened corridors of the English Department at Chiang Mai University pontificating like a madman, attempting to preserve some vestige of my withering claims to academic distinction," he said dejectedly.

"In front of students or empty halls?" I asked, smiling.

"Either. I'm not picky."

I could easily imagine my plump British friend generating windstorms of unbridled brilliance before the barely comprehending throngs of Thai students. Perhaps in some recess of Will's mind, under the influence of his own bluster, he fancied himself to be teaching before the best and brightest of jolly old England, in the hallowed halls of Cambridge or Oxford.

"Is there much difference?" I asked.

"Not much, I'm afraid," he said.

"Don't take it so hard, William," I said. "Maybe your career in Thailand could be a jumping off point, a resume enhancer, for a triumphant return to the great institutions of higher learning back in Britain."

"If only it were so," he said. "But let's face it. I am a middle aged academic with no career, no future, no hope. They have no interest in me. I don't know what to do with myself, why I am even here. And especially Chiang Mai. What am I doing in so primitive a place, surrounded by lurid gluttony of all sorts?"

Will stuck out at the Bierstube, an intellectual eccentric in this assembly line of food, booze, and flesh. Always alone, pondering great thoughts. Odd as it seemed, he showed up for a pork chop or sauerbraten almost every night. He seemed to like it here despite his protestations. And there was room for him. Somehow he fit in, a strange twist in the overall weave, but it seemed to work.

"What do you make of your compatriots and fellow farang?" I asked one evening.

"I despise them," he answered without hesitation. "They are contemptible, even beneath contempt, with their obnoxious lusts and obsessions, their little sex dolls, their drinking and uncouth behavior. No appreciation of the finer things of life. They wouldn't know refinement if it smacked them between the eyes. Miserable louts."

William was also an expert on Thai antiquity and culture and could hold you spellbound as he expounded on the significance of some turning point in Thai history or the finer points of Thai culture. I spoke to him often on just such matters, particularly in regards to the impact of Thai culture on medical care.

"I have been impressed with the serenity of Thai patients in the face of utterly devastating medical news," I said. "They remain unperturbed. They act as if I were discussing sports or the latest gossip when I am, in fact, delivering a death sentence. They amaze me. Their composure is extraordinary."

"It is true," he said. "It is the reverse of our hyper-dramatic Western culture and self-absorption. It is the impact of Buddhism and traditional culture, but it is more than that. When a Thai shows emotion it is among the worst things he can do. He loses face. He can never do that."

"I have noticed," I said, nodding.

"There are two Thai expressions that explain the Thai temperament. The first is *mai pen rai*, which is roughly translated as 'never mind.' The Thai use this expression all the time when encountering inconvenience or disappointment. It reflects an attitude of acceptance and detachment from the inevitable frustrations of life, both minor and tragic. They may sit in traffic for hours and not raise a peep, develop, as you mentioned, a life threatening disease and not bat an eye, narrowly miss a head on collision with a ten-wheel truck, and not give it a second thought. If I had to pick a single expression that came closest to characterizing the Thai philosophy of life it would be "mai pen rai."

"As a cancer surgeon, "I said," I have observed this quality often in my patients. Their equanimity when confronted with a diagnosis of fatal disease and no chance for cure or terrible post-operative complications. They have also been remarkably friendly and helpful in assisting in the care of family members requiring protracted wound care, therapy, and hospitalization. They accept it in a way that I think many Americans would find difficult. I have seen '*mai pen rai*' at work."

"Indeed," Will said. "There is another Thai expression that captures this. '*Chai-yen*,' which translates literally as 'cool heart.' There was no greater compliment a Thai could give someone than to refer to him as '*chai-yen*.' As a corollary, to describe someone as '*chai-raun*' or 'hot heart' was the worst insult. That is Thai culture."

Another time I found him defending what he referred to as the "Western Canon," the great works, thoughts, writings, and deeds of Western Civilization against the attacks of a certain greying, unkempt, longhaired individual whom I had never met before. "The great thinkers of the West, from the Stoics, Aristotle, and Cicero, to Augustine to Aquinas, to Galileo, Bacon, Descartes, and Newton, to Locke, Smith, Burke, the American Founders and beyond have changed the world immeasurably for the better," Will said.

"Yeah, but what about Western Imperialism?" the longhaired one retorted.

"You, my cretinous friend, are a caricature of an aging campus radical, an old fossil uttering tired clichés devoid of substance. You have no appreciation of the debt you and the world owe to the West, and the great men of the West, yes, the 'dead white males' you referred to earlier. We all, together, stand on a vast mountain created by those men. A mountain of freedom, rights, the rule of law, and incredible artistic, musical, and scientific advances that have improved the lot of millions. Miscreants like you that grew out of the sixties embrace a toxic cocktail of post-modern cultural relativism. You discard objective truth. You set a whole new standard for moral and intellectual sloth."

Will was getting into his delivery, his face pink and robust, his eyes glazed over, his stomach twitching with excitement, flecks of food caught on his beard and mustache. I had never seen him so animated.

"Yeah, man," said the aging hippy, "but the West created so many problems. It's Western imperialism man. Western colonialism. Capitalism. The West is responsible, ripping off the poor and developing countries."

"Oh, I see, and there has never before been colonialism, or empires, or imperialism until the West," Will said. "The world began in 1500. No Ming empires. No Muslim Empires including the disastrous Ottomans. No Persian or Mongolian empires. No Aztec, Mayan, or Incan empires in Central and South America. No Mali or Songhai Empires in sub-Saharan Africa. Only Western empires and Western imperialism."

"Yeah, the West is to blame," the man repeated.

"Of course. The West is always to blame for a certain kind of malcontent. But empire, conquest, slavery, and colonialism are the way of the world and have been for all time. Evil is a universal. But it was the West that fought those tendencies and gave us human rights, abolished slavery, and created democracies, unique in world history. You are an anti-Western dunce with no appreciation for how much the West has given you and the world. All quite predictable, brain-dead college campus leftism. But one would have expected someone of your age to outgrow this simplistic rot. Now begone from my sight and return to the sewer from whence you came."

The man blinked, shrugged, and shuffled out the saloon doors of the Bierstube. Will showed just a glimmer of a smile, a rarity for him. I applauded him for his fine elocution and defense of the West - and the facile thrashing of his hapless opponent.

"Well done, Will," I said.

As wild and exotic as life was outside of the hospital, so it could be within. And as much as I enjoyed the larger world of Chiang Mai and Thailand that surrounded our temple of disease and healing, it was for this world, the world of medicine and surgery, and delivering the long suffering, that I committed myself. It was to our small army of students, nurses, residents, and faculty similarly resolved to this contest that I dedicated myself. As always, it was hectic with pathology. Cases that demanded our highest attention and keenest efforts. But there was also the insertion of Thai culture into our medical practice that surprised and gave insight to the strange world of Thai superstition and myth.

I did surgery on a man with a large tumor of his tongue. It was a difficult case that required the removal of most of his jaw. The procedure took over eight hours, but after the operation the patient did well. On the tenth day, he was eating, and after two weeks he was ready to go home. At that time, he complained of difficulty urinating. A urologist was called in to examine the patient who informed us that he had an enlarged prostate. While he was here, the urologist suggested that a procedure be done to alleviate the patient's symptoms. A fairly routine operation, it was performed under general anesthesia and took less than an hour. The patient and family agreed, and so we gave our blessings to the urologist to operate.

After the procedure something unexpected happened. The patient never woke up. Explanations included stroke, hypoxia, the anesthetic, and others, but no one ever really knew why. The operation had been uneventful until the end when he failed to regain consciousness. He was sent to the Intensive Care Unit and seen by neurologists and internists, but nothing could be found. He was comatose and remained blissfully asleep with little or no chance for recovery. After a week or so, he was returned to our wards with no change in mental status.

One morning while making rounds with the residents, a pleasant Thai woman approached me. She appeared educated and introduced herself in broken English as the daughter of the unfortunate man who had lapsed into a coma. I was amazed at how delightful and at ease she appeared, considering what had occurred. She had a simple request.

"Ajarn, may I take father home before die?"

Take him home like this? I was impressed. Apparently she wanted his last days to be spent at home. *But wouldn't it be difficult, I wondered, to care for him at home, even if he only lives a few more days?*

"Are you sure you can do this?"

"Yes, Ajarn. It is better."

"Really?"

"Yes."

"Okay. I'll speak with the residents."

"Thank you, Ajarn."

I found her demeanor surprising and curious. She seemed calm. There was no anger or bitterness about the horrible outcome. I didn't know that many Americans would have been as forgiving.

The next day I watched residents and students place the old man on a stretcher and wheeled to the elevator, attended by the daughter and other family members. After they had gone, I remarked to Rak how enlightened it seemed to bring family members home to die, rather than keeping them in the hospital.

"That is part of it, Richahd, but there are other reasons."

"Oh, like what?"

"Uhh, how do you say in English, uhh - oh, yes! I think you call them ghosts."

"Ghosts?"

"Yes, ghosts."

"You mean like 'spirits?'"

"Yes, Richahd. You call them ghosts, no?"

"Uh, yeah."

"Thai people believe in ghosts. Did you know that?"

Rak explained that when a person died it was thought that his or her spirit lingered, stirring up trouble prior to being reborn in the next life. Apparently, apart from wanting father to die at home surrounded by loved ones, there was yet another motive behind her desire to move Dad from the hospital before dying.

"All Thai people are afraid of ghosts and dead bodies," Rak said. "No driver will agree to take the father home after he died. The daughter wanted to take her father home before he died. Otherwise, she would never be able to find anyone to agree to transport him home after he died unless she paid a high fee, which she could not afford. A Thai driver would not deliver a dead body because he would be afraid that the spirit or 'ghost' of the dead person would cause hardship in his life and bring him bad luck."

I nodded.

"You see, Richahd," Rak continued, "an angry ghost could cause the driver to lose his wife, get violently sick, or die in a car accident. Ghosts of recently deceased were ones to be avoided by anyone not a close family member. If a brave driver still transported a dead body, and none of these disasters occurred, then something else equally bad would."

"What's that?"

"The driver would lose all his business because nobody would ever ride in his car again."

"Why?" I asked.

"Because the ghost would attack them too."

"Really?"

Yes. That is Thai belief. The driver would have to change careers or get rid of the car, which no Thai taxi driver could afford."

"Amazing."

"But if the immediate family owned their own vehicle, then it was permissible to transport a dead body, since the spirit would not disturb his own family."

"But if you could not afford your own car, you had a problem," I said.

"Yes, the only solution was to bring him home before he died."

Once alerted to this belief I watched it in practice many times. Thai people will never let a loved one die in the hospital unless it could not be avoided. For all the usual good reasons for bringing a family member home to die, there was one more I hadn't considered - angry ghosts.

Chapter 11

Another one of the routines I quickly became involved with was the combined cancer clinic where Yupa and I joined our colleagues, the radiation oncologists, every Tuesday morning. Like everything else here, it always provided interesting cases and complicated situations. This Tuesday, as usual, Yupa and I met first upstairs in the ENT office and went together to the radiation department.

The first patient was an old man, very thin and emaciated, who was treated six months before with radiation for cancer of the tonsil. He was in for routine follow up.

The old man opened his mouth with some difficulty. Yupa peered in with her light and tongue blade and noticed something right away. She motioned for me to have a look. Bad news. The tumor had come back. The two radiation oncologists also take a look. They spotted it quickly as well. The old man had cancer again.

I wondered what to do for the old man. He was old and weak and had already received radiation. The tumor could be resected, but it would take a major operation, and the chance for complications were high. He was far from the ideal candidate for such an ordeal, but what else could we do? It was his only chance.

He would need a CT scan if we could obtain one for him, and possibly an angiogram. Then a biopsy. Perhaps a liver-spleen and bone scan to make sure there was no distant spread. I methodically listed everything he would need in my head: chest x-ray, EKG, and routine blood tests; also nutritional supplementation with a nasogastric tube to prepare him for the operation. He would be in the hospital for at least a month, possibly longer. After all this, there was no guarantee of a cure. Still, it was better than nothing, and we couldn't just leave it.

Yupa was speaking in Thai to the old man. The radiotherapists were listening, and nodding in agreement. Perhaps she was explaining the surgery. She suddenly stood up. The patient was helped from the examining chair and escorted to the door. He left by himself. Strange. I wondered where he was going.

"I sent him home," said Yupa, smiling.

"You mean just go home? With the cancer still there?"

"Yes."

"But, doesn't he want you to do anything?"

"No, he said he prefers to go home."

"And do nothing?"

"Yes, sometimes it is better to do nothing."

I never considered it. It seemed odd to me, yet there was a simplicity and elegance about it that seemed so perfectly natural. Up till now it would have been the furthest thought from my mind. I remembered wondering about this very thing on the train ride up from Bangkok. I anticipated that in a Buddhist nation, a Third World nation, where the people lived according to their traditions, close to nature and its cycles, understood death intuitively as an integral part of life, that such a people would be more accepting of death. I suspected that many of them would reject heroic measures to salvage a life at all costs. Still I was not ready to accept it.

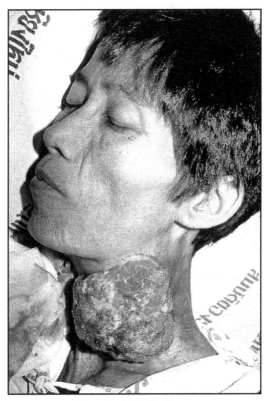

Advanced Neck Cancer

"Did you explain to him," I asked Yupa, "that we could do surgery, remove the tumor, and possibly cure him?"

"We did. But we also discussed the risk of complications particularly after radiation. We were concerned about his age and medical status and whether he would survive the surgery."

"True," I said.

"We also explained that even if the surgery went well, the tumor could still return or may have already spread to distant structures rendering the entire procedure a wasted effort and very costly and traumatic."

"I agree. But did you give him the option?"

"We did. He made the final decision. He wanted to go home."

The old man could now return to his village to spend the remaining months of his life with the people he loved. He had given radiation a chance, and it had failed. He would not agree to further treatment, especially surgery, with the chances for cure so low. That he was going to die didn't seem to matter. Perhaps, he felt it was time.

There was an old expression about the cure being worse than the disease. In Thailand the doctors had no difficulty in recognizing that situation. Their culture (and legal system) allowed both doctor and patient the freedom to accept nature's course, and the inevitability of death. Dying with dignity in the right place with familiar faces can be more important than struggling against all odds for a life that probably could not be saved. The Buddha taught of the reality of impermanence. It would be difficult for most Americans to accept, but sometimes death was the final healing. I recognized that I was not ready to accede to this. I would have pushed him more aggressively to have the surgery. In America, there would have been no question. Something would have been done. It may have involved chemotherapy and most likely major surgery. In some institutions, perhaps, radioactive seed implants or brachytherapy. The patient and family would have insisted, as would have the Cancer team. The entire system and mentality in the States would have driven us to action. But not here. It was the opposite. Which was correct? Perhaps, the Thai had it right.

Chapter 12

I was enjoying my life in Chiang Mai. Enjoying my role as visiting American surgeon, helping and teaching in the third world. I was photographed and had a bio placed in the hospital bulletin. I visited with the Dean and assistant Dean of the medical school and the director of the hospital. I was wined and dined at the homes of many of the faculty. Any engagements or gala affairs with other visiting lecturers or diplomats from, say, the American consulate always included an invitation for me. Everywhere I went I had a contingent of residents and students following closely behind, and I was busy with lectures, patients and surgery. Treated very well, I was quite content and fulfilled in my new world. Up until the day, that is, that I met a patient named Chatchai.

I was first introduced to Chatchai in the head and neck clinic. He was a healthy looking man of 33 years with flowing black hair, and a big smile. He had, unfortunately, a cancer of his throat that had been treated already with radiation, but unsuccessfully, because the cancer never fully went away. Chatchai's skin was discolored, flaking, dry and leathery from the radiation. Its appearance concerned me, but I had no choice. His only chance at this point was surgery. The planned operation called for removal of his voice box, part of the tongue, and the lymph nodes on both sides of his neck. It was a decision I would long regret.

The first few days after surgery, Chatchai did well enough. By day five though, the warning signals began to go off. He developed fever, and the wound edges became red and inflamed. By day seven, the entire incision line had broken down, and pus and saliva were pouring out of his neck. By the tenth postoperative day, the skin overlying his entire neck had dried, blackened and sloughed off, eaten up by infection and poor circulation. His neck lay open, like a fileted fish, with all the underlying structures moist and exposed. Worst of all were the two carotid arteries. These two great vessels, lying on each side of the neck, carried blood to the brain. They had been previously irradiated and were now bathed in a continuous soup of saliva and pus. Pumping ominously amidst the infected debris and slough, the weakened walls of this vessel dried and thinned a little more each day. It was only a matter of time before that last thin layer of the vessel would give out, and the carotid would open up in an angry gusher of blood. A carotid blowout is the single greatest fear of a head and neck surgeon. It can kill a patient in minutes from exsanguination or leave him comatose or paralyzed on one side of the body. The conditions for such an outcome were optimal.

Multiple debridements were carried out, but nothing seemed to help. Layer after layer of dead tissue was removed, but the infection and slough continued. In all my life, I had never seen such a hopeless case.

I was in the head and neck clinic one afternoon reviewing some charts with Yupa, when the phone rang. Yupa answered, listened, and quickly hung up. She looked at me anxiously. "There is a problem upstairs. Chatchai is bleeding. You are needed immediately."

I rushed up to the tenth floor and into the large communal room where Chatchai stayed. When I arrived, I found the room frantic with nurses, students and residents, all gathered around Chatchai's bed. I waded in through the layers of people and encountered my own worst fears. Chatchai was swimming in his own blood. His clothing and bed were stained with it, and pools of blood had formed on the floor below him. Pale and clammy, Chatchai was nearly in shock.

The room was a frenzy, everyone desperately trying to keep Chatchai from bleeding to death. Nok, the first year resident, was applying pressure to the right side of his neck, slowing the bleeding. Tateb, another resident, was slicing through his right forearm with a scalpel, looking for veins to start a line with. Another resident was shoving a subclavian line in just below the left collarbone, and a medical student was performing a cut down on the left leg. Blood that had poured out of Chatchai's neck was being sucked up into syringes and sent for type and cross. Nurses were scrambling for bags of intravenous fluid, sutures, clamps and vials of dopamine. Another nurse attempted futilely to measure his almost non-existent blood pressure. A stretcher was wheeled in to bring him down to the operating room.

On the verge of a grisly death, Chatchai remained remarkably composed. Fully conscious, he lay peacefully on his bed, and impassively allowed this insult and invasion of his body to take place.

"Is the operating room ready?"

"Yes, Ajarn."

"Start transfusing him as soon as you get the blood. I'll meet you downstairs."

"Yes, Ajarn."

I stepped aside as the stretcher carrying Chatchai was pushed to the elevator, followed by a small band of residents, all engaged frantically in some life saving activity. The most important task was that undertaken by Nok. She raced alongside the stretcher with her right index finger pressed firmly on Chatchai's carotid, preventing yet further bloodletting from the moribund patient.

In the wake of Chatchai's rapid departure, the aftermath of a carotid blowout lay in full evidence about the room. It looked as if a small war had taken place. The stains and puddles of blood lay everywhere, along with the gauze pads, clamps, scissors, and other essential armaments. The aides and nurses studiously cleaned and rearranged everything, as if nothing had happened.

Downstairs in the operating room, Nok's little finger pressed on Chatchai's neck, represented the sole obstacle between life and death for him. Dutifully holding her finger in place, she offered this as a sacrament to the sanctity of one man's life. If this single finger were to tire or cramp, it would end quickly. There was not even a moment for switching fingers with someone else.

Chatchai was put to sleep. Instruments were assembled, and the surgeons lined up on either side of the operating table. All the while, Nok stood beside him in street clothes, with her finger in place. I took my position at the head of the table and asked for a retractor. For the first time in my surgical career, I knew true fear. Could I find the carotid quickly enough? Could I control it? And what about the other side? That carotid, too, was fully exposed. Would that blow in the next day or two?

I asked Nok to remove her finger. In an instant, a red gush of blood came pouring out from the patient's neck.

"Put your finger back!"

"Suction!"

"Stop it! Stop it!"

Nok jammed her finger back into Chatchai's neck. My heart was pounding. Could I control this without my patient bleeding to death? I was afraid. My head was throbbing. I could feel the adrenalin pouring into my body. My heart raced, my stomach tightened, and my hands shook. I was terrified I was going to lose the patient. With Nok's precious finger secure on the carotid, I stalked this wild beast before it struck again. I gained control of the vessel low down in the neck, and clamped it, a minor victory of sorts, but still incomplete. I needed superior control before it was safe. I followed the artery up along its length until I came to the hole. A tiny 3 or 4 millimeter opening, like a window into oblivion, where the wall of the great carotid artery had blown. It seemed so harmless now, and yet this small rent had brought my patient to the threshold of death.

I tied off the carotid and removed the weakened segment. The immediate threat of death was over - for now. But I was not relieved. Just over on the other side, lay the other carotid, equally as vulnerable to rupture as this one. And there was not a thing I could do. If it went, Chatchai was dead. I watched it, swimming in a broth of infected secretions, pulsing away with each beat of his heart. My other concern was whether Chatchai could withstand tying off this carotid. With the blood loss, and loss of half of the circulation to the brain, there was a good chance he would have a stroke or lapse into a coma.

59

We applied a dressing to the neck, and the residents transferred him to the recovery room.

That night I visited Chatchai in the intensive care unit. He was awake and alert, and seemed to recognize me. I was relieved. He apparently had not suffered a stroke. I still agonized about the other carotid, fully expecting to be called that night for a second, fatal rupture. I did not sleep well.

The next morning, I visited Chatchai and asked him to move his left arm. He could not. I asked him to move his left leg. Again, he could not. It had come to pass after all: a massive delayed stroke. His left arm and leg were limp, useless appendages. I was devastated.

My world came crashing in. I thought of the young man I had met just a month ago, and what horror I had visited upon him by my decision to operate. He had become a bedridden invalid, with an infected neck, unable to eat or speak. He had been subjected to numerous procedures, the trauma of a carotid blowout, and now this - a massive stroke resulting in paralysis of half of his body. I berated myself. Why had I agreed to operate? Couldn't I see his skin had been burned beyond hope, that he would suffer serious complications? I felt as if I had been trapped. Snared by my hubris and the arrogant belief that I could cure anything. Beyond this, I was a visiting American surgeon, invited here to teach. How laughable that seemed now.

I would live through this agony of self-doubt for some time. Chatchai though, the one who had suffered all this, was kind. In the morning when I visited him, he would lift his right functioning hand to his head in a kind of half wai, and give me a thumbs-up sign. Amazingly, he appeared happy to see me. His wife and mother were also there, smiling and assisting. These two stayed with Chatchai day and night, fanning him, exercising his paralyzed limbs, helping him in and out of bed. And they also remained friendly. It was as if they sensed that I too had suffered a kind of mortal wound, and rather than bitterness offered compassion instead.

About five months after his initial surgery, Chatchai was ready to leave the hospital. After several additional procedures, I had gotten the neck to close. He required a wheelchair because of the paralysis, but he was ready. I accompanied him, his wife and mother to the elevator and watched them go. I escorted them personally, bidding them farewell and thanked them for what they had done for me. When I watched the elevator doors close, I felt some relief but not much.

Chapter 13

My experience with Chatchai had become the stuff of rumor and gossip. It was my personal disaster, an albatross tied securely around my neck. It had also become a valuable weapon for one of my colleagues.

Sometime after Chatchai had blown his carotid, Yupa invited me to her office for a talk. She seemed embarrassed by what she had to say and struggled to find the right way to put it. After an uncomfortable moment, she finally informed me that a letter had been written and sent throughout the hospital to all the various heads of departments, the director, associate deans, and the dean himself, about the complication Chatchai had suffered. The letter was condemning in nature and described in some detail the long and difficult road Chatchai had traveled since I first operated on him. In addition to the hospital faculty, the author had taken the trouble to send the letter to the editors of various influential newspapers, not only in Chiang Mai, but in Bangkok as well. Not stopping there, the letter had even been forwarded to the chairman of the Thai Medical Council, the man responsible for overseeing all of medicine in Thailand. In addition to this, the letter had even found its way to the desk of then Prime Minister of the country, Prem Tinsulanon. The final twist in this well thought out scheme was that the letter had also been sent to the wife and mother of the patient, and to the patient himself.

I was angry and embarrassed. To insult and discredit me, not just in the eyes of the medical faculty, but before the local and national press, the Ministry of Health, and the Prime Minister himself was vicious and slanderous. But the final dagger was to deliver this black epistle to the patient and his family. The effort to destroy me was complete. My adversary was thorough.

"Who do you think did it?" I asked.

Yupa smiled apprehensively. She seemed to know, but didn't want to say the name.

"Was it Boonrit?" I asked.

"I think so," she whispered uncomfortably.

"You're sure?"

"Yes... it was him."

"How did you find out?"

"We were told by one of the faculty."

"What should I do?"

"Nothing. Just continue your work. He hurts himself by this, not you."

"Maybe I should leave. Look at the trouble I have caused."

"You cannot leave," she answered firmly. "We need you. We have too many patients. Who will take care of them?" Her response was quick and forceful. I nodded. "I want to talk with Boonrit," I said.

"I understand," Yupa nodded.

I found Boonrit on the wards making rounds with the residents. "I want to speak with you," I said. He tightened a little. Dismissing the residents, he turned to me.

"What's the matter with you?" I asked coldly.

"What are you talking about?"

"The letter. Why'd you write the letter?"

"What letter? What are you talking about?"

"Don't play games."

He paused. "How do you know I wrote it?"

"Who else would? Who else knows the case?"

"I did it... for the patient."

"For the patient?" I asked incredulously.

"Yes. Look at how he has suffered."

"It was a terrible thing that happened, but how does the patient benefit from your letter?"

He said nothing.

"And why did you send the letter to the newspapers? To the Prime Minister? To the patient's own family?"

He did not respond, nor did he appear contrite. In fact he seemed to be gloating. "You publicized this tragedy to embarrass me, and you have," I said. "But you have also hurt the patient. Complications happen Boonrit, they happen to the best of us. Anyone who picks up a knife long enough will have complications. You should watch yourself. Things have a way of evening out. Watch your own cases and don't worry about mine."

I turned and left the floor, leaving Boonrit sitting smugly in his chair.

Relations did not improve between Boonrit and me. But two months later, I ran into him while making rounds, standing with Acharee by the nurses' station. I could tell something was amiss. He was pale and nervous; he looked at me anxiously, avoiding my eyes. Acharee seemed to be comforting him in her maternal way. Turning to me, she explained what had happened.

"Boonrit's patient died last night," she said softly. "He bled to death. He was only fifteen, and the mother was there when it happened. He was her only child." Boonrit continued to stare limply, like a pale ghost, at the floor. "It happened so quickly, there was no way to save him. Boonrit tried, but it was too late."

"Who was it?"

"The boy with tracheomalacia."

Boonrit had operated on a young boy with tracheomalacia, a disease that softens the windpipe and interferes with breathing. He had worn a trache tube, and Boonrit wanted to remove it so he could breathe normally without a trache tube. It was a legitimate case, but a tough one. Boonrit still could not remove the trache tube from the patient without the airway collapsing.

"He had operated several times," Acharee continued. "After the last procedure, the trache tube had eroded into the boy's innominate artery." This was one of the great vessels coming off the aorta in the chest. "It ruptured suddenly last night, causing the young boy to exsanguinate."

It was a bloody, fearful, horrible death. Boonrit was there and had tried to stop it but could not. The boy drowned in his own blood as it gushed uncontrollably through the small rent in his windpipe and down into his lungs. The horror and panic of those last terrible minutes had also been witnessed by the poor mother who stood there helplessly, watching her only child struggle and choke to death like a butchered animal.

I knew very well the pain and guilt Boonrit was experiencing. I also perceived the irony of the situation. My conversation with Boonrit earlier had become prophecy, for now he stood naked and alone in the aftermath of his own disaster.

In that one moment after listening to the story, I thought about the unexpected tragedies of life. I thought also about the great privilege it was to wield a surgeon's knife. The art of surgery, both brutal and sublime, conferred great honor upon the surgeon. But it was an awesome burden as well. Surgeons straddled two worlds. One of healing. The other of horrific mistakes and complications that shook us to our core. One was a realm of accomplishment and fulfillment, even gallantry and honor, a great good that sustained us and propelled us forward in our efforts to cure. The other was one of profound setback, remorse, and self-doubt. Yet, complications were inevitable. The more challenging the cases and the sicker the patients, the greater the risk of tragic consequences. One had to learn from one's mistakes and not repeat them, and improve the trajectory with time. But the searing pain from horrible outcomes should in some way edify and educate, and engrave deeply the lessons of caution and prudence. Wielding the surgeon's knife remained the ultimate responsibility, and death and disability always lurked.

I told Boonrit I was sorry and shook his hand. He looked at me through a glaze of despondency and shame but with a measure of gratitude that I had not gloated or taken advantage of his misfortune. I saw how wounded he was. I then left for the operating room.

I never had trouble with Boonrit again. No more letters, bad mouthing, or backstabbing.

Chapter 14

Songkran, the traditional Thai New Year, was just around the corner. It began April 13, lasted three days, and was reputed to be uproarious. And nowhere, throughout the kingdom, did the celebrations reach fever pitch quite like they did in Chiang Mai.

Any new year, regardless of culture or nation, is about renewal. The Thai people combined this spiritual view of the New Year with the cathartic medium of water, in a somewhat secular expression of purification. My first introduction to the more watery aspects of Songkran occurred the weekend before the New Year actually began. I was riding on a motorcycle through several small villages to the north of Chiang Mai, in Mae-Sa valley, when I noticed a gathering of some ten to fifteen Thai youngsters on the side of the road armed with pails, buckets and barrels of water. I didn't think much of it as the holiday did not begin for several days. They began gesturing for me to slow down as I approached them.

"Slow done, sir, if you please," I heard one of them say innocently.

Thinking they may have wanted to speak with me for some reason, I slowed down and drove over to them. As I got close, I was abruptly slammed with ten or so pails of ice water.

"What the hell?" I blurted out, nearly choking. I fortunately kept my balance and sped off, realizing that at least here in Mae-Sa valley, Songkran had arrived.

I received many more splashings that day, but all of it was mere preliminary to the grand event in Chiang Mai on April 13, where drenching took on a whole new dimension. Prior to the festivities, though, as Rak explained after clinic, there were other obligations that came first.

"On the evening before Songkran," Rak said, "housewives give their homes a good cleaning. They will throw out old clothing and household items. Thai people believe that anything old and useless must be discarded or it will bring misfortune to the owner."

"As in bad luck?"

"Yes. Some believe that it is the same as throwing out bad attitudes or thoughts."

"A spiritual 'housecleaning'?"

"Yes."

I saw similarities here with the *kashering* or making "kosher" one's home and kitchen by observant Jews before Passover, a rigorous "spring cleaning," which too had an internal or spiritual dimension.

"On Songkran morning," Rak said, "young people bring gifts and pour scented water on the hands of elders and parents to show respect. We do the same for our teachers. Tomorrow, the nurses, students, and residents will go to the ENT clinic to pay respect to Doctor Acharee and other faculty. You are welcome to come, Richahd."

As a *farang*, I was not obligated to participate, but I wanted to show my respect.

"I would like to go," I said.

"I will take you."

When we arrived the next morning, there was a line of students, nurses, and residents who had come to the clinic. They turned to wai me. "Sawadee khrap," some of them said. They seemed pleased that I had come and smiled warmly. I took my shoes off and stood in line. When I came to Acharee, she seemed embarrassed.

"Ajarn Moss," Acharee said, "you don't have to do this. It is only for Thai." She smiled at me like a loving mother.

"*Mai pen rai,*" I said. "I owe you so much." I poured the ritual water on her hands, wai'd, and bowed.

Rak was standing behind me. When he completed the ritual, he joined me. "Ajarn Moss, I am very happy you came today," he said. "Ajarn Acharee appreciated it very much."

As we walked out of the hospital, he said, "There are other customs we have, Richahd, that you may find exciting."

"Like what?"

"Today we will visit the temple and offer food and gifts to the monks. We pour water on their hands, as here. Then they bless us by splashing us with water. We release live birds and fish at the temple. For good karma or *tham boon*, to make merit. We bring caged birds to the temple and free them. Or we carry fish in small bowls and pour them into canals or ponds at the temple."

"I have seen that."

"What do you think of our customs?

"I like them. Very spiritual."

"Richahd, I must leave you. I will go to my ancestors who have died. My family and I will pour scented water on their ashes and graves."

"It is a beautiful tradition."

"Be careful of all the water today," Rak said, as he walked away. "You will get very wet."

I rode my motorcycle over to Tha Phae road, in the center of town. There were already large crowds of Thais and westerners on the streets, gathered for the purpose of soaking one another. The high-spirited Thai took the ritual of pouring water on the hands of respected elders, and expanded it exponentially into a Dionysian free for all, bringing into play plastic bags, buckets, barrels, and steel drums of often ice cold water. Pick-up trucks careened up and down the avenues packed with young Thai who showered passersby and other vehicles. Fountains were set up on corners for refills. People walked around with bags and buckets of water, drenching one another.

I walked into a temple just off the main road. There I encountered a pretty young Thai woman named Wan. I had met her once before at the Chiang Mai cultural center where she worked evenings. I had tried to get to know her then, but she rebuffed me. Now she greeted me with scented water poured gently down my shoulder from a ceremonial silver cup.

"*Sawadee ka*, Ajarn," she said, wai'ing me.

"*Sawadee khrap*," I said, returning her wai. I poured water down her shoulder although not scented.

She smiled. "I will take you to light incense and pour water on the Buddha," she said.

She escorted me to a Buddha statue. Other Thai were there lighting incense, holding them between their outstretched hands positioned in front of their foreheads and bowing to the Buddha. They placed incense before the statue along with hundreds of other burning incense sticks already there. It created a large plume with a soothing, pungent fragrance. They stood and grasped the silver cups, filled them with scented water, and poured it down the shoulder of the Buddha. Then they wai'd the statue again.

"Please try it, Ajarn," Wan said.

She handed me several sticks of incense and arranged herself next to me. We kneeled and wai'd the Buddha.

"Now we pour water. This is *tham boon,* making merit," she said. "It will bring you good luck."

We stood together, poured scented water down the shoulder of the Buddha and then wai'd the statue. Wan smiled and wai'd me. She was elegant, I thought. Her movements feminine and graceful. No wonder Thai women intrigued Western men. We walked to Tha Phae road.

The word *Songkran* came from a Sanskrit word, *samkranti*, that meant transformation or change. In this festival I noted the fusion of culture and religion, of Thai custom and Buddhism. I liked the integration of the different spheres. I was comfortable with Thai sensibilities. I felt an internal shifting or "change" when I paid respect to Acharee and again at the temple before the Buddha with Wan. I was becoming Thai, as if fulfilling Songkran's call for transformation. I now merged with their world, with the realm of Buddhism and Thai tradition, with a people and culture, with my patients and work as a cancer surgeon, joined as one.

Wan found a good location for us on the crowded street. "There will be a procession now of many large Buddha statues. We must ready ourselves. It is time for *tham boon*. Making merit," she said.

I smiled at her intensity. "You take your Buddhism seriously," I said. She seemed intent on gaining as much spiritual merit from the day as possible. Our interests converged. I sought the same thing.

"Here they come," she said.

It was the oddest procession I had ever seen but appropriate to this country, culture, and occasion. Carried on flat bed trucks, the large Buddha statues proceeded down Tha Phae road enroute to Wat Pra Singh, a famous temple in the old part of town.

"See how they are decorated," Wan said excitedly.

Indeed, each statue was draped with garlands and decorative flower arrangements and accompanied by beautiful Thai maidens in traditional dress. Elaborately covered in flowers as well, the trucks passed slowly down the street, stopping periodically to allow the ritual pouring of scented water on the Buddha images by the people.

Wan grasped my arm and urged me to splash the statues. From the street to the top of a truck required splashing. We were out of range for "pouring." But it seemed acceptable albeit less dignified than the gentler pouring of water down the shoulder of the statue. "It is okay, Ajarn. You may splash. It is good for merit," she said.

We participated in this for several hours. The array of statues, their beauty, size, and variety, was extraordinary. The effort required to arrange such a procession, I thought, must have been daunting.

Hundreds of statues passed, each of them splashed ceremonially by the throngs below. There was a celebratory, Dionysian, even bacchanalian quality to the day. It occupied a fine line between spiritual devotion, renewal, and making merit on the one hand, and pure, explosive release on the other. The Thai seemed eminently capable of navigating that line and traversing the two disparate realms. As devoted to Buddhism as the Thai were, they were not puritans. They knew how to revel and carouse. The event occupied the same space for me. It was spiritual and transformative, yet festive and ecstatic. And so it seemed for Wan and everyone else.

"There is music, Ajarn," Wan said, directing my attention to the procession once more.

Bands of local musicians playing traditional Thai instruments and music now came down the avenue on the same large flat bed trucks. "You may splash them too," Wan said laughing. "It may not make merit for you, but it is part of the fun."

I watched the musicians playing while graciously if not stoically submitting to the drenching from their fellow citizens below.

"They sound good considering," I said.

I was happy to have Wan accompany me for Songkran. I did not know where it would go but for now it was my good fortune to have her.

"Ajarn, there is another legend of Songkran," Wan said.

"What is that?" I asked.

"It will rain," she said. I had heard of this but was skeptical. The rainy season was months away. There had not been one day of rain, not even a single drop of rain or a cloudy day since I arrived five months ago.

"There is not a cloud anywhere," I said, looking up.

The sky, indeed, was a luscious blue canopy unpunctuated by a single cottony cloud, nothing even remotely suggesting a storm front.

"It will rain, Ajarn," she said seriously. "It always does."

"I have heard of this. But I don't think it will happen today."

I was cynical because it was the middle of the hot season, and the rainy season was more than two months off. *Songkran* day had thus far been as hot and sunny as any other. But at 5 PM, as the musicians began pounding their traditional drums, as if calling out to the heavens, dense clouds gathered and the temperature dropped. Thunder and lightning appeared in the distance. Wan pointed all this out to me although she scarcely needed to.

"You see, Ajarn," she said, giggling mischievously.

The sky darkened and the wind blew. I noticed a drop of rain, followed by another and another. Within minutes the clouds had opened, blanketing the streets with sheets of rain.

"It is incredible," I said in amazement.

It was the perfect fulfillment of the day, a cosmic union, it seemed, between humankind and nature, one invoking the other in celebration of the New Year. The collective wishes, prayers and watery antics of the people of Chiang Mai had reached up and touched the clouds, releasing their full force and fury in an eruption of unrelenting rain. There was pandemonium on Tha Phae road. The Thais, already exhilarated, exploded with the arrival of the rain, almost as if this otherworldly blast from above was proof of the power and influence they still wielded over the gods.

"I told you, Ajarn. It never fails," Wan said. We walked the streets together, drenched by the rain and the splashing, which went on superfluously, perhaps, despite the downpour.

And so, on this thirteenth day of April, in the ancient village of Chiang Mai, the capitol of Lanna, in the kingdom of Siam, the Thai welcomed the new year, soaked each other, and the heavens answered. It was a day of spirituality combined with revelry and celebration. A blending of the two realms. Of the Buddha and Dionysus. Of the Exalted and the Worldly.

After Songkran, I didn't see another drop of rain for more than two months.

Chapter 15

Wan and I continued to communicate. Each evening, just after returning home from work, I was treated to the sound of her soft voice over the phone, asking me where we could meet. I noticed though that our meetings were always in some neutral corner. I was not allowed to pick her up or drop her off at her home nor would she ever meet me at mine. When sitting on the back of my motorcycle, I also noticed that she was careful never to make contact with my body. One time, when entering the "Riverside Cafe," a popular music club on the Ping River, she abruptly stopped, turned and walked out. She looked back into the cafe nervously to see if there was anyone there who may have recognized her, and said, "I am sorry Richard, I cannot go in there." There was no further explanation, and we quickly left.

I always wondered about these strange quirks but soon realized what was going on. From her perspective she was taking an awful chance by going out with me. As a respectable Thai woman, this would be looked upon very critically, and she had to avoid anyone who knew her, especially members of her family. Eyebrows would be raised and questions asked. Had her family met the man or counseled her about this? Was she having sex with him? Everyone knew about western attitudes towards sex. Had she compromised herself already?

One Friday evening, Wan invited me to *tham boon* at the temple. She was a devout Buddhist and visited the temple regularly. With ceremonial flowers and sticks of incense, we paid homage to the Buddha together. She seemed delighted that I was interested and respectful of her religion.

The next day, Wan and I met at the Chiang Mai Zoo. While watching the reptiles and snakes, Wan turned and looked at me with an anxious expression on her face. She told me she had an unusual dream last night and was troubled. I asked her what the dream was about. She hesitated before speaking, but finally told me. "Last night, I dreamt I had been bitten by a snake." I had no idea what the significance of this was, but after some gentle prodding, she finally let on that according to legend, when a woman dreams that a snake has bitten her it means that she will soon marry. I jokingly wondered to myself if I should offer congratulations, but by the look on her face I realized that I was probably the leading candidate for that honor. "That's an interesting dream," I said moronically. I otherwise kept quiet, and we continued our walk.

I didn't hear from Wan for over a week. As she had no phone, and she never allowed me near her home, I had no way of contacting her. One day, I ran into her accidentally at the hospital. I asked her why I hadn't heard from her. She told me politely that she was *"mai wang"* (not free). "Mai wang?" From wanting to get married to "mai wang." Although I wasn't in the market for marriage, I figured we could continue seeing each other. But that was not to be.

I thought about this sudden turn of events and eventually put it together. During the day, Wan was a secretary at the department of Anatomy at the University. As this was part of the medical campus, gossip from the hospital undoubtedly flowed freely. It was probably common knowledge that I was friendly - if only on a platonic basis - with a couple of the nurses from the wards. In her traditional culture, being seen with me in light of this would have compromised her, particularly since I had no plans to marry her. Whatever her feelings may have been, she could not risk this. She quickly became *"mai wang,"* and I never saw her again.

It wasn't too long after Wan and I parted ways that I ran into a Thai beauty named Daeng. She was a sensual woman, athletic, and unusually tall for a Thai. I met her at a popular bar, owned by an expatriate from southern California, where she was serving drinks. I invited her to join me. I had my usual orange juice while she had a glass of Mekong whiskey, which she downed in one or two gulps. She finished her drink with a flourish, slamming her glass down on the table and gave me a suggestive wink. She then stood up, grabbed me by the arm and nearly carried me out the door. Jumping on the back of my motorcycle, she whooped like a cowboy while I started up the bike. We headed directly over to her place.

Daeng used to work the bars in Pattaya, the famous resort outside of Bangkok that catered to westerners. Women from all over Thailand went to Pattaya to earn money in the usual way, which was to sleep around with western men. Daeng had some painful memories, it seemed, from those days, and possessed a bitterness and toughness about her, which was very unusual for a Thai, particularly when it came to westerners.

One night, while we were walking into a cafe called the Chiang Mai Pavilion, she recognized a westerner, possibly a former lover, who had per-haps offended her in some way, although I had no idea. I noticed her mood immediately change. She tensed up, gritted her teeth, and released my hand. She then walked right up to the guy, and said, without a moment's hesitation, "You never talk to me like that again, you motherfucker." The poor guy was dumbstruck, but he seemed to know what she was talking about because he didn't say a word. She left him looking stupid and embarrassed, and walked back to me. I didn't say a word.

Underneath that toughness though, Daeng was very vulnerable, always wary, it seemed, of the next disappointment. We got together frequently over the next few weeks, riding my motorcycle around town, stopping in at different clubs, listening to music. But no matter how I reassured her, there was always a fear in her that I would let her down and do to her what, I imagined, many others had already done. Whenever I would leave her she would grab my arm, raise her finger, and warn me, almost imploringly, "Don't *jao-shu* me, Richard, okay? Don't play around."

I understood Daeng and was sympathetic. I knew that in Thailand women were disadvantaged in their relationships with men. Traditional Thai women wanted to marry and build a family. They were dedicated to that. But other women were readily available for sexual liaisons, which could occur on a nightly basis. Thai men, including married men, could find pleasure and comfort outside of marriage at any time. Bars and brothels were ubiquitous.

Considering the culture and accepted practices, Thai men enjoyed significant advantages in the relationship between the sexes. It was this tendency that Daeng recoiled against and rejected, understandably so. She had been on the wrong side of it on multiple occasions. She hoped, perhaps, that I would be different. In truth, however, I was not seeking marriage.

One night I visited her at her home, and knew something was wrong. She looked at me and said, "You *jao-shu*. I saw your motorcycle at the bar. You butterfly me, right?" She had recognized my motorcycle parked outside a bar, but in fact I was innocent.

"I was only listening to music."

"You *jao-shu* me, Richard."

"No, I didn't do anything. Nothing happened."

"I know you, Richard, like all men. You are all the same."

That night she could not sleep. She had a shot of whiskey, but it did not help. She muttered to herself over and over as if struggling with some question. Finally, she turned to me, and asked, "Richard, do you love me?"

"Well, uhh, I certainly care a great deal for you," I said stupidly.

"I understand Richard. That is my problem. You like me but don't love me, just like everyone."

I knew this was coming. She wanted marriage and stability. She wanted to belong to someone and to have a family, like most women, particularly in traditional cultures like that of Thailand. But I would not be the one. I was on my own journey, and it didn't include her or anyone else. I flew solo. I was married to my work and only my work. I would not compromise this pilgrimage of healing. Most people would not undertake such a journey in the first place, preferring income, practice, home, family, and stability instead. But I was on a mission. I would not be a householder. Unfortunately for Daeng, I would be another name on a long list of male disappointments.

The next night when I visited her, she was distant. "I cannot see you anymore," she said. "I am marrying a Dutchman that I met six months ago in Pattaya. He is sending me money every month. And a ticket to fly to Amsterdam next week."

I was caught off guard but not really surprised. "I understand," I said. "I don't blame you at all."

Daeng had thrown the whole thing open with her question last night.

"I don't love him, Richard," she said, "but he loves me. And he sends me money. With this money I built a home for my mother and two sisters in Lamphun."

One could question her fidelity and character, going out with me while all this was going on. But that was life, I supposed. The injuries and derelictions went both ways. I would imagine the Dutchman might have changed his mind had he known. I also recognized that if I had answered differently last night, Daeng might have forgotten her plans with him. But without my promise she would not risk the money and security for just another pleasant evening and a motorcycle ride. I never saw her again.

Chapter 16

As a fourth year medical student at the Indiana University Medical Center in Indianapolis, I nursed a strong case of wanderlust. The senior year in medical school afforded an opportunity to satisfy that appetite. We could schedule up to three months of elective time in an approved course almost anywhere in the world. With my interest in Japan and samurai culture there was no question where that would be. I contacted several teaching centers in the larger cities in Japan by mail and received the most delightful letter from Dr. Shozo Tateishi, a thoracic surgeon at Kyoto University, in Kyoto, the ancient capitol of Japan. In the letter, Dr. Tateishi had written that he would "try to help me realize my goal." Within a few months I was flying into Osaka airport where Tateishi received me and drove me to his home. I took off my shoes, as was the custom, donned slippers, and entered his traditional home with tatami floor mats and shoji panels. I met his lovely wife Kyoko, a pediatrician, and their five daughters, or, his five "kittens," as he referred to them.

"Rick-san," he then said, "please have a bath." The offer surprised me at first, but I remembered this was part of traditional Japanese culture, which I found fascinating. Afterward, I was given a bathrobe and slippers. I could not have been more relaxed in a home of strangers I had only met today. We had dinner and enjoyed an alluring assortment of Japanese delicacies. Below the low-lying table the floor was sunken to make it easier to sit, with small heaters underneath to warm our feet. Tateishi insisted that I try "saki" or Japanese rice wine, in small porcelain cups.

The next day I accompanied Tateishi and assisted in surgery, made rounds, met the residents and faculty. He arranged for me to observe other medical and surgical specialties. I also enjoyed the mystical and artistic enchantments of Kyoto, replete with innumerable grand, yet intimate Buddhist temples, Shinto shrines, and feudal castles, as magical and wondrous a city as could be imagined.

Japan was the first foreign country I had ever visited. It will always hold a special place for me. I have remained in touch with Sensei Tateishi. In his last letter since learning of my travels to Asia, he called me his "prodigal son." Indeed. He was a father and mentor to me. In a sense, I began my Asian journey in the most splendid of ways seven years ago with him.

It was not uncommon in my work at the hospital to encounter clinical situations that made me very uncomfortable. In fact, it was routine. But over time, feeling uncomfortable became something I learned to live with. My comfort level also changed with time. I learned to handle things that only months before made me very nervous. Still, there were many tight moments when I really didn't know what to do.

I saw a patient with a cancer that was already pushing out the side of his neck from a large lymph node where the tumor had spread. Despite its advanced stage, I felt it could be removed and scheduled him for surgery. For some unknown reason, the patient disappeared. The next time I saw him was in the operating room two months later. The only problem was that by now the tumor had eaten out a huge swath of skin and had grown to the size of a grapefruit. I looked at Rak. "What happened? We booked this case two months ago."

"He had to wait, Richahd. We have so many other cases, there is no time to do them all."

"But look at the size of this thing. It's almost fixed. How do I know I can get it out. Did you get an angiogram to see if the carotid was involved? Or a CT scan? This thing is tremendous."

Rak shrugged his shoulders. "I know Richahd, but the patient is asleep."

"I see."

"What will you do?"

I rolled my eyes. "He's asleep already, there's nothing we can do. Let's operate."

Rak and I struggled with this large cancer, but like so many times before, we got it out. We sewed him up and sent him to the wards. He recovered uneventfully.

I had gotten used to this sort of thing. Operating on big cases without the benefit of a work up or studies. Just cut and get the damn thing out. After a while, you start to surprise yourself. By the end of the year in Chiang Mai, I had not ordered a single angiogram on a patient and almost never a CT scan. Most of the time the patients couldn't afford them anyway.

With this case and so many others, I observed my gradual transformation. I realized from the first day how ill prepared I was for this journey and all I would be asked to do. I had committed grievous errors of which Chatchai was the most dramatic. There had been others. There were crises of confidence and bouts of self-doubt. I was always in the process of catching up. Preparing for difficult cases with little or no guidance. Questioning myself. Researching. Making calls to a mentor-friend in the States, Steven Sobol MD, Otolaryngologist par excellence, for advice and consolation. Often, I did not know what to do but acted anyway despite limited knowledge.

I was in a war. I paid ransoms and liberated prisoners. There were casualties and botched rescues. I had been wounded in the clashes. The land was uncharted. But I had to move and make decisions - to save myself as much as my patients. I accepted this trial. Yet each step was filled with peril. Every decision a disaster waiting to unfold. My inexperience and mistakes haunted me. The nature of the pathology was overwhelming. My footing remained insecure. My unease persisted. In the depth of my uncertainty, I clung to one reality, my wish to heal. With the passage of time, I had ascended if but slightly. My view of the territory was better. The cases remained as daunting and hopeless as ever. I knew I was a target. My every move scrutinized. I could not afford another misstep. The department and the University would not tolerate it. Another Chatchai-esque calamity would have crushed me and ended my career. I treaded cautiously. I was alone and could share my thoughts with no one. I lived in solitude like a monk. But I would continue my work.

Another patient had cancer in the mouth and already had two operations. Each time the cancer came back. Now it had spread everywhere. It was in the muscles, and the jaw, and had extended up toward the base of the skull. The parotid gland and facial nerve were involved. It was big, and I didn't know if I could get it out.

Pitchit, an excellent resident whom I trusted, shared my anxieties. He thought it had spread too far and voiced this opinion during rounds. But what could I do? The patient was in terrible discomfort and could barely open her mouth. The tumor produced a foul smell in the middle of her face, and she could not eat or sleep. Should I leave her to this miserable death or try to save her? Most of the doctors thought it was too far gone and recommended she be left alone. Was I being too brave? I had placed my personal reputation on the line by doing this case.

"I wonder if I should be operating."

"It w-will be difficult."

"Do you think I should cancel it?"

"You cannot. She is asleep."

I remembered vividly the CT scan showing the massive tumor enveloping the entire jawbone and side of her face, sweeping up like a dark wave to the skull. I was convinced the tumor was too damn big to resect, only it was the wrong time to come to that decision.

Like two warriors going into battle, we slowly placed our gowns and gloves on, and stood on either side of the table. There was none of the usual banter or joking before a case. Only the silence that was broken when I asked for the knife. Pitchit, like most residents, was usually interested in operating, but this time he wanted nothing to do with it. He handed me the knife.

I took it and began the surgery. Four hours later we were done. Somehow, despite its size, we were able to get the tumor out. We reconstructed her mouth and the side of her face and the patient was eating ten days later and ready to go home.

There were many such moments in Chiang Mai, when I felt very alone; many chances I took when surgery could have been lethal but also represented the only chance to cure. You were compelled to action by the suffering of your patients. But the memory of Chatchai was never far. You were always one case away from disaster, including death and disability, and the trashing of your reputation. A surgeon could not afford terrible outcomes and had to pick his cases carefully. Yet there were times when one simply had to act and assume the risks. The patients demanded it. Their illness called for it. Their agony and suffering required it. It was life or death with grim options and one's back pressed against the wall. It was a protracted war of attrition. I accepted this. It was jungle medicine. One learned to act within the limits of knowledge and outrageous pathology. It was a frightening conflict. Yet, I was married to this fate. I would grow hesitantly and painfully into this life and journey.

Chapter 17

The patient on the table was covered from his neck down to his ankles, front and back, in some of the most colorful, brilliant tattoos I had ever seen in my life. He was a walking work of art. He also had a large cancer in his throat that had spread to his neck, bulging out ominously like a large lumpy potato.

"Goodness, they're beautiful," I said to Rak, admiring the tattoos of the patient now asleep on the operating table. "Why'd he get so many?"

"For protection. Many of our people have them."

"Protection from what?"

"From everything. Evil spirits, enemies, even disease."

"Disease, huh."

"Yes, Richahd, many of them believe this."

I felt the patient's neck with my gloved hand as Rak and I lined up on each side of the table. The ornate turquoise and crimson tattoos almost seemed to dance in the brilliant glow of the overhead lights, stretched out boldly by the mass of tumor lying just below its decorative surface. The combination of the two was strange: an unlikely synthesis of art and deformity, of fanciful life and a disease that killed.

It was a strange sensation bringing the knife down onto such painted flesh, cutting through it and staining it with the patient's own blood. Would it be any different than slashing a beautiful painting? Was there not some other way, I wondered, less defiling, to cure this man, than to ravage his neck, which had been transformed into art?

There was no other way, of course. His neck had already been defiled and not by us. The brutal work of salvaging him, of separating him from the disease that lay just beneath his skin, was the task at hand. Nothing would keep us from that, not even the delicately rendered patterns arrayed before us.

Rak and I finished the operation, successfully removing the cancer from the patient. We sewed his neck up and recreated the beautiful artwork with all the methodical precision of art-restorers. We lined up the edges, matched the colors, and maintained the continuity of the designs. The line of incision would of course form a scar that would be an eternal reminder of our transgression, an unfortunate but necessary intrusion. I hoped the scar would not diminish the protective power of the images.

Chapter 18

Ladda was a nurse I had become good friends with over the months although strictly on a platonic basis. Having spent a year studying in Australia, she spoke excellent English. She had a younger brother, age 23, who was intending to marry the following year. Prior to marriage, as so many young Thai males do, he planned to become a monk for the three month Buddhist Lent period, which began in July, coinciding with the rainy season.

"The ordination ceremony will be tomorrow at the temple in my village. You will find it very interesting."

"When does it start?"

"The actual ceremony is tomorrow morning, but before that we must prepare him. Tonight at the temple we will have the ceremony known as *Sukhwan Nak*. It is a very sensitive time, and we must protect him."

"From what?"

"Evil spirits."

"I see."

"We can go together this evening."

We drove to her village, Santeewan, after work on my motorcycle, about fifteen kilometers east of Chiang Mai. Santeewan was a small community of perhaps three hundred families who lived together amidst the rice fields and forests, each home or gathering of homes connected to others by small dirt paths. Ladda and I went directly to the temple and parked the bike outside. Inside, there was a large crowd of villagers surrounding a young man whom Ladda pointed out as her brother. He was dressed in the usual village attire, but his head and eyebrows had already been shaved in preparation for his ordination tomorrow.

"Once he shaves his head, he is no longer part of our world," Ladda said. "But until he becomes a monk tomorrow he is not part of their world either. He is between the two worlds, and therefore very vulnerable. We must stay with him through the night to protect him."

"From evil spirits?"

"Yes. He is a *Nak* now, which means dragon. By becoming a dragon during this transitional time, it is hoped that evil spirits will avoid him."

"And all the people?"

"They must also stay with him through the night to protect him. The more of us, the better."

Buddhist Temple, "Old" Chiang Mai

We sat down with the other villagers. Her brother, the *Nak*, sat in the center of this large defensive circle. I noticed the friends and family passing around protective white threads, which they tied around their wrists, and three sets of candles, which were passed around counterclockwise. A garland of flowers with money attached from villagers was hung around the neck of her brother and then deposited in a ceremonial silver bowl. There were burning sticks of incense filling the room with their pungent odor. In addition, six or seven intoxicated men with traditional drums were pounding them and singing uproariously, warding off evil spirits lurking about.

Ladda handed me a drink. "Try this," she said.

I drank some. "What's this?" I said, wincing.

"N*arm kao* or homemade rice whisky."

"It is strong," I said, drinking some more.

"The villagers make large jugs of it for the ceremony. It gives strength to the musicians, so they can play all night."

The music, singing and drinking went on and on while the young *Nak* sat peacefully within the protective perimeter of the villagers. Some of the musicians tired and handed their drum off to others who immediately assumed their duties, maintaining the wall of sound that assured the *Nak's* safety.

"This is *chien mahk*, or betel nut," Ladda said, handing me a gooey black substance wrapped in a leaf.

"What is it?"

"It is betel nut, limestone paste, and betel leaf. It is common in Thailand. They are all chewing it now," she said, pointing to the others in the room.

"To give them strength?"

"Yes."

"And you want me to use it also?"

"Yes. Place it in your mouth next to your cheek and let it absorb. Now you will be able to stay up through the night," Ladda said.

I put some in my mouth against the inside of my cheek. I felt my heart race and my ears buzz. "It is stronger than pure nicotine," I said.

"Much stronger. And stronger than caffeine. It is a stimulant."

Between this and the rice whiskey, I was galloping at full throttle like everyone else.

Another drunken villager handed me a drum. I banged it with the others, contributing to the protective cordon of noise around the Nak who sat safely in the middle of our circle within the confines of a Buddhist temple, as safe as we could make him. A steady supply of *narm kao* and betel nut powered us. We continued for hours. At around 4 AM, I called it a night. "Are you staying up?" I asked Ladda.

"Yes. I have to remain with my brother. He lives between the two worlds. We must protect him until he is a monk tomorrow. Then he will be safe in their world. Now we must stay here and guard him."

"Until morning?"

"Yes," Ladda said.

I handed off my drum, walked out of the temple, found a large red passenger truck with a flat roof and climbed on top. Dizzy, drunk, and exhausted, I lied down, feeling content in this strange Thai world of spirits and demons. The drums and laughter and singing in the temple continued in the distance, surrounding me with their soft resonances and including me, it seemed, in their protective vigil. I gazed at the broad black canvas of sky dotted by stars. Within seconds, I was asleep.

At about 8 AM, Ladda climbed up the truck to wake me. "Hurry, you must come quickly or you will miss the ordination."

I hurried down from the truck, and Ladda and I motorcycled two kilometers up a dirt road to the other side of the village where an elaborate procession was about to begin.

"There he is," Ladda said.

"Wow."

Dressed in an elaborate pink and gold costume adorned with jewels and ornate embroidery, the *Nak* wore an equally ornate and bejeweled ceremonial hat. He had intricate patterns of make-up painted on his face, including numerous radiating stars.

"He looks quite otherworldly in those pink sunglasses," I said.

An equally colorfully garbed pony carried him. Some 150 villagers of all ages began the procession, wearing yellow flowers in their hair, dancing the traditional Thai dance, splashing water, laughing and singing. Just behind the villagers, the *Nak* rode atop his decorated steed. One of the villagers held a tall ceremonial umbrella over him.

"It is quite an ensemble," I said.

We moved forward to join the group.

"He seems quite removed, very detached and poised," I said, "considering all the excitement around him."

"Yes," Ladda responded. "He is entering the world of the Buddha."

The young man, whom I had met on other occasions, and who seemed ordinary enough, appeared changed by the process. "This is not just a ceremony for him. He takes it seriously," I said.

The mood in the large gathering was festive. Musicians played traditional instruments, energizing everyone with their driving music, touching not only those already in the procession, but other villagers who poured out from their small wooden homes and stood along the dirt road, drawn to the spectacle of the *Sukhwan Nak*. Some of the villagers smiled or waved, while others, unable to resist the spell, joined in the ceremony, taking up the traditional Thai dance, and merging into the larger group.

The procession stopped at various locations along the path where a Buddha image was present. Here, the *Nak* was carried from the horse to pay respect to the Buddha. "The *Nak* never walks himself," Ladda said. "His physical body is of no consequence. Only his mind, his practice, and *dhamma*. He must devote himself only to *dhamma*."

I was drawn to this and to Buddhism in general. I recognized the importance of separating from the "real" world, the world of the senses and the subsequent absorption into the realm of consciousness and spiritual refinement required in monastic life. But I was still drawn to my work in the "real" world as a surgeon. My purpose was to attack disease not to attain enlightenment. I did not want to distract myself. But Buddhism intrigued me. Perhaps, at some point the two paths would merge in my life.

The *Nak* wai'd the Buddha statue and cleansed his hands in a ritual silver basin. The villagers carried him back to his horse, and the procession continued as before. The musicians played their enchanting melodies, the villagers rapturously dancing, smiling, pouring water, and sharing yellow flowers with one another.

When we arrived at the temple, the procession circled the *Bot* (ordination hall) three times, while the Nak threw coins into the air.

"This symbolizes rejection of the material world," Ladda mentioned.

They hoisted the *Nak* over the threshold of the *Bot* and into the central hall. Once inside, the Nak changed from his ritual dress and hat and into the white robes handed to him by his father, who then guided him to the abbot of the temple.

"This is a very proud moment for my father," Ladda said. "A fulfillment of his duty to pass on the tradition to the next generation. It is a highpoint for him and our family."

The *Nak* bowed three times before the abbot and asked permission to be ordained. Holding his hand, the abbot recited from Buddhist scripture about the transient nature of earthly existence and explained to him about the life he would soon lead. He placed a yellow sash on his body.

"This symbolizes his acceptance for ordination. Now, he is no longer a *Nak*, but an aspirant on the threshold of entering the monastic life. He is joining their world now and will soon be safe from the spirits," Ladda said.

Her brother, now an "aspirant," went to a raised platform, surrounded by other monks from the temple. The abbot spoke to him for some 45 minutes, while he sat on his knees, hands pressed in the wai position.

Two monks then took the aspirant out of view where he assumed the saffron robes of the monk. Upon returning to the hall, he recited, in Pali, the vows he must uphold.

"The most important," Ladda explained, "were the vows of celibacy, the restrictions against the taking of life, engaging in magic, using intoxicants, and eating anything after twelve noon."

The father then offered the alms bowl to the abbot of the temple, who, in turn, placed the sling of the bowl over the head of the aspirant and around his neck and shoulder. The aspirant stood to face the large Buddha image in the center of the hall, while the two monks requested the larger community of monks to accept him.

"He has his alms bowl and his orange robes. He has been accepted into the monastic life as a member of the Buddhist clergy. He is now in their world. He is a monk. We can relax. He is safe," Ladda said.

The ceremony concluded with the monks chanting and the new monk pouring water from a silver chalice into a bowl. "With this ritual, he passes all merit acquired by becoming a monk to his parents."

The father then performed the same ritual.

"This assures that my father's parents will receive some of the merit as well."

As we rode home, Ladda said, "It is a very important ceremony in Thai culture, Ajarn. Did you enjoy watching?"

"I will never forget it."

Chapter 19

"It's time I visited the Hill Tribes," I said to George, the Aussie motorcycling guru.

"Oh, yeah, you're due a visit, I would say. Certainly before your year here is up. I know you're almost done."

"Right."

"Thousands of westerners flock to them every year."

"So tell me about them."

"The 'Hill Tribes' are a mix of distinct ethnic minorities. They live in the mountains of northern and western Thailand. Most are semi-nomadic. They migrated to Thailand from China, Tibet, and Burma over the last three hundred years. People are bloody fascinated by them."

"How many are there?"

"About five hundred thousand."

"Have they assimilated at all?"

"Some have, but most have kept the old ways."

"What are the names of the tribes?"

"Lahu, Karen, Akha and Jingpaw are some of them. There are others."

"What do they do?"

"Grow opium. Some try traditional farming but not too successfully."

I decided to visit one of the "Hill Tribes." There was a great allure to visiting them, untouched by modernity, before they were lost forever through absorption into the dominant Thai culture. Inadvertently, though, the travel agents and tourists were speeding up the process and eroding the traditions of these ancient peoples, who suddenly found that posing for pictures or begging was an easier way of making money than farming. I had resisted going, thinking that I did not want to add to the steady erosion of their traditional way of life, but I finally gave in to my curiosity. I limited it to a hill tribe that was rarely visited by other westerners and only for a single night.

"It's 120 kilometers north of Chiang Mai," George said as he pored over one of his maps of northern Thailand. "Then you turn left off the main road and follow a dirt trail about six kilometers."

"What's the name of the village?"

"Huey Tong. It's a Lahu Hill Tribe."

"What's the dirt road like getting there?"

"Normally, it's not too bad, but with the rainy season, forget it. It'll be terrible. It's very steep up to the village, and it'll be nothing but mud. But if you want to get to a hill tribe village where none of the tourists go, that's the one."

"Do they speak Thai?" I had picked up a working knowledge of the language.

"No, only Lahu. But there's a school there, part of the Royal Project. There'll be someone there who can speak Thai."

"Are they friendly?"

"Don't worry, they won't eat you. They're really quite civil in most ways."

"You think I'll have trouble getting there by motorcycle?"

"You'll make it, but you'll be one dirty bloke by the time you get there."

I gulped down my orange juice. "Thanks, George."

"No problem. Don't forget to fill up with gas."

I put on my helmet, motorcycling gloves, sunscreen, thick socks, and sneakers, and long heavy shirt in preparation for the journey. Heading north out of Chiang Mai, I drove the 120 kilometers to the turn off for Huey Tong. After the first couple of kilometers, the dirt trail narrowed and steepened, and I began going up and down the many hills and valleys in the area. The trail was pure mud from the monsoons, and by the time I was half way there my legs and sneakers were caked in it. After an hour or so more of sliding around in the mud, I finally reached the outskirts of the village. Just before reaching the main part of the village, I heard two young voices calling out to me from the side of the trail. I turned, and saw two Lahu children, a boy and a girl, perhaps five years old, motioning for me to stop and join them. They were dressed in traditional Lahu garb, albeit tattered and dirty, which consisted of a black shirt and tunic and black and white leggings. They were barefoot. I stopped my motorcycle, got off, and walked over to them. As I neared them, they made a gesture, bringing index finger and thumb together in a circle, much like we use in the states to indicate that something is "A-Okay." A sly sort of grin and a wink accompanied this. Then they began rapidly stroking their tongues with their index fingers, which I took to mean they were looking for food. Finally, and without a great deal of subtlety, the two little angels began rapping all four of my muddy pockets with their knuckles, carefully listening for the sound of coins. Apparently, there had been other westerners here before, so they had already learned some tricks. I sighed, recognizing that I was now joining the ranks of the millions of tourists each year contributing to the despoliation of another traditional culture.

I noticed an aging Lahu woman, wrinkled and stooped, appear out of a thatched roof bamboo hut up on the hill. She walked out without a shirt on, her wrinkled breasts sagging to her navel, and beckoned for me to join her. With the two children, I followed her into her hut, where she and another bare chested old lady were sitting on the bamboo floor. There was a tiny alcohol lamp with two packages of black greasy stuff and a makeshift pipe resting on the floor between them. The black stuff I took to be opium, something hill tribe people were famous for, and the old gals were getting stoned.

The first lady motioned for me to sit down next to her, which I did. She then held the pipe up to my face and offered me a puff. I declined. She then elbowed me gently in my ribs, as if to express her annoyance, and took a big drag on the pipe, inhaling deeply, and then slowly released the hot, pungent smoke out through her nostrils. She smiled, and offered me a puff. Again I politely declined. She then pulled up to me, on her knees, grabbed one of her sagging breasts, and, amazingly, shoved it in my face. Almost gagging, I politely declined this as well. Looking me right in the eye, she took another heavy drag, blew the smoke in my face and held the pipe against my lips. Having refused her peace pipe once already, not to mention one of her withered breasts, I figured it was time to make at least some gesture of conciliation. I mouthed the pipe and drew in ever so slightly, keeping the hot smoke in my mouth, and then blew it out without really inhaling. I repeated this clever maneuver once more, which seemed to pacify my enchantress. I didn't really know what she was up to, but my greatest fear was that she would try to get me stoned and then rape me. The two little kids were watching all this and gave me the thumbs up sign after my second drag. When I started to stand up, she too rapped my pockets for change. Now, I realized what she was after. I pulled out my wallet and unloaded ten baht (40 cents) for my two drags. She smiled, and I returned to my bike. Welcome to the Lahus.

Another kilometer up a very steep hill, the last half of which I had to walk because the mud was so thick, I found myself in the very primitive looking village of Huey Tong. There were about forty Lahu families here, a total of about two hundred people. The homes were all very simple, consisting of bamboo floors, raised off the ground on tree stumps, bamboo walls, and thatched roofs. Dried plant stems and fibers held everything together. The village climbed the side of a mountain, and a large stream ran through the valley below separating this side from the opposite mountainside, where most of the farming took place. The surroundings were lush and tropical, and with the orchestration of clouds and blue sky against the mountain profile and the patchwork colors of cultivated land in the distance, the scenery was spectacular. I could hear the sound of villagers singing, children playing, and the low roar of the stream echoing below.

Hill Tribe Children

I noticed any number of dogs, cattle, goats, chickens, pigs, and even a horse. The people were all dressed in traditional garb, including the black tunic, shirt, and black leggings. Many of the children ran around naked and, as with the old ladies, some of the women were topless. The men and women often brandished machetes used, I presumed, for cutting and harvesting crops. Many of them, including some of the children, smoked a large home-made cigar stuffed with tobacco and rolled into a banana leaf. The women usually carried large baskets on their backs to the fields for gathering crops. Young mothers too continued to work, holding their small children on their backs like tiny packages wrapped neatly with cloth shawls.

I ventured into the village, where all the huts were connected by small dirt paths, and soon came upon a one-room schoolhouse where I met the teacher of the village, a young Thai man by the name of Chan, who lived here along with his wife, Lampoi. Speaking in Thai, he introduced himself and joined me in a little tour of the village. We walked together to the opposite mountainside where the Lahu were working on the cornfields.

"*Ajarn*," Chan said, "just three years ago, these fields were used solely for the cultivation of opium. We have taught them to grow corn instead, but many of them continue to grow opium. We are very close to the 'golden triangle' where most of the opium going to your country is made."

It was amazing to think of the strange web that connected these simple people in their tattered rags with the streets of New York where the opium they grew wound up as processed heroin.

"The hill tribes are very interesting for westerners, but for us they are a problem. It is necessary to teach them our ways."

We returned to the village. Chan invited me to spend the night in his hut. I was given one corner of the floor and a light blanket.

Later on in the afternoon, while walking around on the muddy paths connecting the various homes, I heard the sound of a pig squealing. Walking over, I saw four or five Lahu men surrounding a piglet and its mother, attempting to capture the little piglet. The large mother pig kept fighting off the men, trying to come between them and her kid. The piglet stayed close to its mother until the large pig was finally beaten off with sticks and the little one caught. After corralling the piglet, I realized I was to be treated to a sight I was not prepared for. I watched the young men hold the squealing piglet down and slice its neck open with a machete. The mother continued trying to return to her piglet and save it, but the men kept beating her back with their sticks. A large bucket was placed just below the open neck, catching the blood as the piglet squealed and squirmed. Dogs, smelling the blood, dashed forward, licking the small drops that splashed to the ground. As the blood continued to drain out of its neck, the piglet's squeals softened to a whisper. The animal gradually weakened and died. The mother pig walked off to the side as if recognizing there was nothing it could do. Although I knew this happened all the time, I was not accustomed to it. I saw great sadness and despair on the part of these two creatures fighting for life. I was devastated.

The dead animal was carried off for butchering. The Lahu men saved everything. The internal organs, skin, hooves, knuckles, ears, and even the snout of the poor beast were considered edible. The blood was also used for food. It was allowed to congeal and placed in a large pot of soup, which was cooked over an open flame underneath one of the huts.

Dusk was approaching. The farmers were returning from the fields carrying primitive digging and cutting tools and baskets filled with corn. The temperature cooled as the sun set, and mist was settling over the mountaintops, ablaze in orange light. I noticed many of the villagers heading to the stream for what appeared to be the big social event of the day, the nightly bath. Everyone gathered together and bathed in the icy stream water; some removing their clothes, others more modest, only their tops. There was much laughter and discussion and the mood was very festive.

I waited for everyone to finish and then took my own bath. The water was frigid. While drying myself off, I noticed a young Lahu man waiting for me. I finished dressing when he came up to me and said something I was not expecting to hear in this remote village. Smiling broadly, and showing all of his front teeth, I heard him say the two magic syllables, "Lay-dee?"

'Lady,' I thought to myself. I couldn't believe it. Even here? He looked at me quizzically and awaited my response. Sex with a hill tribe girl? Somehow it didn't seem like a good idea. "Uhh, no thanks," I answered in Thai.

"Very good, only fifty baht (2$)," he insisted.

"No thanks," I repeated again. "It's time to eat. Let's go home." We walked together back to the village.

Returning from my bath, night had fallen, and Lampoi, Chan's wife, was preparing some food. She was utilizing a large bowl made of masonry over a wood fire and cooked right on the floor in her hut. She had already made rice and invited me to join her for some. Sitting next to her, I watched her prepare what I took to be the main course. She picked up a small metal container with about ten large beetles crawling about. "They are fresh," she mentioned, perhaps thinking this would whet my appetite. "I just caught them today." One by one, she reached down into the container, grabbed the beetles, tore off their legs and threw them into a pan, live, to be sautéed in hot oil over her makeshift stove. I watched the poor creatures struggling in vain to escape the sizzling oil, the stumps of their legs moving frantically, but to no avail. The oil popped and cracked. Ten roasted beetles on a plate of rice.

Speaking in Thai, Lampoi asked me if I would like to have some with my rice. "No thanks," I answered politely. She laughed. "It is very delicious, especially with pepper." I consoled myself with my bowl of rice. I knew the Thai ate all manner of insects regularly, from crickets to millipedes. They were sold in markets everywhere. This was one traditional culinary delight I would avoid.

After dinner the three of us sat in the middle of the hut on the floor around a small alcohol lamp in the center of the room. As Chan was a central figure in the village, we had a large number of Lahu visitors. Many came to see the strange western visitor as well. Afterwards, I ventured out alone into the darkness and enjoyed the spectacle of the night sky, moonless, but punctuated by innumerable twinkling stars, an occasional comet or shooting star, and the ever present roar of the stream in the distance.

I slept on the floor in my clothes with a thin blanket above me and the hard bamboo floor below. It was cold, but I managed to catch a few hours of sleep. The next morning, after waiting for a heavy monsoon to pass, I bid my friends, Chan and Lampoi farewell and walked half a kilometer down to my motorcycle. It was right where I had left it, buried six inches in mud. I turned it around and began the journey back to Chiang Mai.

Chapter 20

Jaruan was an unassuming and gentle Thai woman, thirty years of age, who, more than any resident I ever worked with, lacked the necessary confidence that was needed to be an effective surgeon. She had to be pushed, prodded, and, on occasion, yelled at to do more. Whereas most residents needed to be restrained or checked from some misguided surgical adventure based more on overzealous enthusiasm or the desire to learn, Jaruan stood on the opposite end of the spectrum, consoling herself with performing the simplest procedures and refusing to learn anything new.

There was nothing so terrible about her particular attitude towards surgery. Not everyone was meant to do major cancer operations. The problem here was one of timing and place. Timing, because I was in Chiang Mai to work with the residents, and she was one of two chief residents that fate or karma had blessed me with, which meant that she and I would have to work closely together and often. Place, because this was northern Thailand, where head and neck cancer was widespread, which assured us of a steady stream of patients requiring major surgery. All of this placed Jaruan and I on something of a collision course.

I was in the fourth hour of a long cancer case. Struggling with two large metal retractors, I tried to provide good surgical exposure for my resident assistant Jaruan. Although I referred to her as my assistant, she was actually doing the case, and I was performing one of the ultimate acts of self-sacrifice for a surgeon by guiding her through the operation. For the most part I told her step-by-step, which cut to make, which vessel to tie, which structures to preserve and which to remove. Her hands became my hands, performing the same maneuvers I would be doing myself. To a layperson, it would seem that this was an easy road. All the senior surgeon had to do was give instructions while the resident did all the work. In actuality, nothing could be further from the truth. Taking an inexperienced resident through a case could be a tedious, even excruciating labor of love that could pinch your coronaries and burn holes in your stomach. It was perhaps the single greatest test of patience and inner composure in the entire field of medicine: a true offering of oneself on the sacrificial altar of teaching and imparting one's knowledge to the next generation.

Of course I had been the recipient of just such generosity in my days as a young resident. I recalled my first ear case done under the supervision of the chairman of the department of Otolaryngology at the New York Eye and Ear Infirmary, Glen Agostino, along with the chief resident, Ezra Habil, who was assisting me. Ear surgery was different than Head and Neck surgery, or perhaps any other specialty, and required much practice and attention to detail. It was a tiny world with very dense, critical anatomy in a compact area that included the base of the skull, the sigmoid sinus, a major blood vessel that drained the brain and fed into the Internal Jugular Vein, the facial nerve, which moved the face, and the inner ear. All of this contained in an area less than a square inch and encased in bone. It had to be revealed carefully and meticulously, like sculpture, not with a chisel but a drill. In elevating flaps and exposing the anatomy, I had made a botch of it beginning with raising the flap to enter the middle ear. Dr. Agostino's face grew red. His neck vessels swelled. He was beside himself with my ineptitude. Although I learned to love Otology and grew confident in it, that first case was most unpleasant.

Jaruan and I were working in a high-risk area of the head and neck. The tumor in this case had grown towards the base of the skull and was pushing against the carotid artery. This great vessel entered the skull here enroute to supplying the brain with its essential bathing of oxygen rich blood. Every effort had to be made to remove the tumor while preserving the integrity of this critical artery upon which the brain depended. The operation slowed to a standstill as even the slightest miscalculation could lead to disaster.

Jaruan continued when a small but careless jerk with her scissor unleashed a massive welling of blood, a frightening outpouring covering the valleys and hills of the patient's open neck. The horrendous torrent immediately raised an essential question as we hovered breathlessly over the bleeding patient - did she cut the carotid?

The adrenalin surge was felt immediately in the pit of everyone's stomach, as the wild frenzy to control the bleeding and keep the patient alive began. The anesthetists started up a unit of blood, ran the intravenous fluid, and prepared for the insertion of another central line. Dopamine drips were prepared. The nurses scampered to supply rooms bringing additional instruments and supplies: another unit of blood, vascular clamps, sterile sponges, umbilical tape, additional suction devices. Jaruan and I were in the thick of it. Blood stained sponges were everywhere as we attempted to control the bleeding. After several tense minutes, the bleeding vessel was found. By luck or grace it was not the internal carotid artery, but another large artery albeit less critical. The vessel was clamped and tied and the operation continued uneventfully.

Jaruan and I performed another case together that involved removing the lymph nodes from one side of a patient's neck. This required working right next to the great vessels of the neck, the carotid artery and the jugular vein, and often without the benefit of wide surgical exposure. The initial incisions were made and the skin flaps elevated. The muscle and underlying soft tissue were exposed and retracted. At this point, I noticed something odd. Jaruan peered down into that snake pit where the great vessels ran, concealed beneath the fat and lymphatic tissue of the neck, and came to a sudden, quivering halt. She then asked me a simple question.

"Ajarn?" she said innocently.

"Yes?"

"Are the carotid and jugular down there?"

"Why, yes, Jaruan, of course they're there."

In the next instant and without a moment's hesitation, Jaruan handed me the knife. I looked at her quizzically, not taking it. She rebutted with her typical enigmatic smile. She then assured me ever so sweetly that she was quite unprepared for the task of separating the lymph nodes from the patient's neck without damaging in some way one or both of those large throbbing aqueducts of blood. "Ajarn, I think it is better if you take over now." Not having the slightest desire of disturbing the great vessels as they rested peacefully in a yellow thicket of lymph node and fat, she again handed me the knife, which I now accepted. I could not deny that a part of me was almost gleeful with the knowledge that I would not have to guide her through the case as I could perform it much more expeditiously myself. I was also a little amused, even charmed by her humility and lack of pretension. In a profession where big egos are the norm, this honest admission of one's limitations was gratifying in a way.

I was the opposite of Jaruan in my days as a resident. I was relentless and wanted to do everything, including cases from every subspecialty within Otolaryngology: Facial Plastics, Otology, General, Head and Neck. I deliberately sought out surgical procedures. I saw my 4-year ENT residency as my opportunity to ensure that I had the necessary skills to take care of my patients after my formal training. We were judged in many ways as physicians. Our bedside manner, our clinical acumen and diagnostic skills, our ability to treat, communicate, and teach. But in the end, a surgeon was judged by surgical outcomes and I was committed to amassing as much experience in the operating room as possible for the sake of my future patients. This was not an uncommon attitude among residents. In me, it was perhaps more extreme. Jaruan had a completely different attitude, one that was not salutary for her development as a surgeon. While I was sympathetic to her, I felt that her approach would not get her the skills and confidence necessary to be effective.

Almost imperceptibly though, Jaruan's attitude and performance began to improve. One afternoon, after making rounds with the residents, Jaruan approached me with the operating schedule for the following day.

"We have two major cases tomorrow, Ajarn. I hope you will be able to help me with them," she said.

"Of course."

"One is a laryngectomy and bilateral necks."

"Yes, I remember."

"Will you need anything special, Ajarn?"

"Make sure frozen section is available."

"Yes, Ajarn. We will be ready for you tomorrow at 8 AM."

I noticed her confident, brisk manner. She was now eager to operate, including the bigger cases that heretofore had thoroughly intimidated her. "Good. I'll see you in the morning."

"Ajarn, excuse me, if I may say." She paused and took a breath. "We will miss you. All of the residents and faculty will miss you."

I smiled. She was referring to my departure from Chiang Mai in a couple of weeks, the end of my one-year contract with the University. "Thank you so much Jaruan."

One of the last cases I did in Chiang Mai was with Jaruan, on a patient with a large tongue cancer that required resecting part of the jaw.

"Ready, Jaruan?

"Yes, Ajarn."

I handed her the knife. The case proceeded. But instead of the usual spectacle of ham-fisted bungling, we were now treated to the cool, efficient, even slick expertise of a talented young surgeon.

"Could you retract the muscle, Ajarn?" she asked, as she exposed the great vessels of the neck, structures that before had prompted much fear and trepidation.

"3-0 silk," Jaruan asked the scrub nurse, as she prepared to ligate the vein.

"Yes, Ajarn," the scrub nurse said to Jaruan, now using the respectful title to address her.

"Clamp. Scissor."

Where Jaruan had been halting, cumbrous and confused, she now was engaged and confident. Every flip of the knife no longer heralded a fresh gush of blood and unseemly efforts to control it. The hesitant indecision had been replaced by measured, careful technique.

"Are you ready to take the jaw?" I asked.

"Yes, Ajarn." She looked to the scrub nurse. "Oscillating saw."

She split the jaw above and below the tumor, allowing the mass to fall into her hands.

"Good."

Under the sure hand of Jaruan, the anatomy and disease had revealed itself, like a figure liberated from its prison of marble by the skilled hands of a sculptor. She elevated the skin, cut the vessels in controlled fashion, and performed the surgical dissection swiftly and nimbly. Now there was pertinent anatomy to be displayed, appropriate technique to be demonstrated and, as the tumor was approached, decisive and meticulous dissection leading to its final triumphant removal.

"That was excellent," I said to Jaruan as she began suturing the skin at the end of the case.

"Thank you, Ajarn."

"I'll let you finish closing," I said, taking off my gown and gloves. "I want you to know that I'm proud of you."

She bowed her head. "Thank you, Ajarn."

I felt a sense of urgency with Jaruan. I was leaving soon. There were other places and nations to visit, and my year here was coming to an end. I felt some need to elevate her before my departure. I recalled when the hesitation and insecurity began to break. I remembered the first time she asked if she could perform a particular operation, requesting the knife before starting the procedure. She repeated this as her reluctance and indecision faded, and her confidence and skill grew. Through the residents and younger surgeons like Jaruan and others who stayed on to teach others, I could amplify my efforts. This, too, was part of the healing enterprise.

"You'll check the patient tonight?" I asked as I was leaving the operating room.

"Yes, Ajarn. I will make sure the drains are working."

"Thank you."

Chapter 21

The very last patient I saw in Chiang Mai looked oddly familiar to me, although I could not quite place him. He sat before me in the treatment room on the ENT ward with the usual crowd of doctors and students gathered around. As I examined his neck and looked at his young face, it suddenly dawned on me.

"Is this the same patient I saw almost a year ago?" I asked Yupa who was standing next to him.

"Yes."

"How ironic. He was my very first patient on my first day here. Now he is my last."

I had been fooled because the young man's head and eyebrows were shaven. He was barefoot and wearing the saffron robes of a Buddhist monk. Yet I still saw the same boy. I knew that much had happened to him since our initial visit.

He had the same innocent eyes and round face, but his neck skin was darkened and brawny from the radiation he had received. Much worse was that the tongue cancer had returned and spread everywhere. He could barely open his mouth because the tumor had infiltrated the muscles of his jaw, and his neck was thick and firm not just from the radiation but from tumor invasion. It was hopeless and tragic for so young a man.

He looked at me sorrowfully. I knew he wanted me to operate and save him. But the tumor was too advanced, and the previous radiation made it all but impossible.

I looked over at Yupa. "I wish we could offer him something."

Yupa nodded.

I hated to say no to this young man who wanted so much to live. But I had to, even though he was just a twenty-year-old boy, who never smoked or drank, and did not deserve such a fate.

"What will he do?"

"He will return to the monastery."

Tears welled up and spilled over onto his young face. He knew the reality that awaited him. He could see the decision had been made. Yupa nodded to two older monks who had accompanied him. Everyone wai'd them as they came to his side and helped him stand and leave the room, tears falling to the floor.

"Even after a year here, I am still devastated by these cases," I said to Yupa

"None of us gets used to it," Yupa said.

"We are trained to heal."

"But we have our limitations," Yupa said.

"He will have pain medicine?"

"Yes."

"Does he have family?"

"Yes."

I contemplated the message of the Buddha, who taught of the impermanence of all things. I recalled the story of the Buddha's own life, when, as a young prince, Gautama, the young Buddha, ventured forth from his palace and encountered old age, sickness, and death, which moved him to solve the riddle of suffering, ultimately leading to his own enlightenment. He shared his message of personal salvation with the world, the liberating knowledge of impermanence, and the ability of every individual to end suffering through insight. And then I thought of my poor young patient with terminal cancer, who had donned the robes of the Buddhist monk.

"I hope that the teachings of the Buddha will help him in his time of need."

With this we ended my final clinic in Chiang Mai.

It had been a year since I first arrived in Chiang Mai. Whatever I had to offer by way of teaching had been given. Whatever I could show through operating, making rounds, or attending the clinics had been offered. I had given it my full measure.

I remembered my many grievous mistakes, particularly early on. These errors had extracted a heavy price from me. They had nearly ended my journey in its tracks. Yet I now looked back on them and realized their role in my apprenticeship. I would thereafter be much more circumspect. I would tread carefully. I had suffered my defeats. But I had crossed the threshold. I bore my scars. But I could now act in a way I could not before. My path was before me.

And with everything, my companions and I had accomplished something.

I had reservations about leaving Chiang Mai and did not want to part. I had grown very fond of it here. Not only of the professional relationships and work at the hospital, but of friends outside of medicine and ultimately with the city itself. It was a magical place, Chiang Mai, nestled amidst the mountains of the northern range, with the cool nights and beautiful sunsets, with the temple, Wat Doi Suthep, peering down from its perch atop the mountain, offering protective vigil for its patrons below - those in the fray, in the heat and the agony, this city with its passions, hopes, and tragedies.

The ENT department hosted a farewell party. A large crowd of aides, nurses, doctors, administrators, and even the Dean, showed up to wish me well. There were gifts, and photographers on hand to record the event, and speeches made on my behalf. Acharee spoke of our first meeting.

"I will always remember that young man at the train station," Acharee said. "We had to rescue him from a General who was already arranging a marriage for him," she said, chuckling. "He has taught us so much. We are grateful for the time he has given us."

Kobkiat, the vice dean, who had initially viewed me, perhaps, as an interloper, also spoke. "On behalf of Chiang Mai University, I want to thank you for all you have done," he said.

I too spoke of the wonderful experiences I had and of my gratitude to everyone. "I could not ask for a better team than this. You have helped me so much. Your devotion to learning and caring for your patients is inspiring. My thanks to everyone."

A lavish Thai feast followed.

A few days later, after sending my luggage on, I stopped at Acharee's home in the early morning, the place where my visit to Chiang Mai began, and bid farewell to my two good friends, Acharee and Sonwut. It was sad to say goodbye to them, those whom I looked upon almost as parents.

"I will always remember your kindness," I said.

"Please be careful on your expedition to the south," Sonwut said. "It is a long way and the roads are treacherous. They will need your help too. You will be very busy. Good luck on your journey."

They prepared a light breakfast for me, and I was off.

"Thank you my friends and farewell."

I kick started my trusty Honda JX-110 motorcycle, which I had bought a few months ago, and was headed for the other side of the country, the southern province of Songkla near the border with Malaysia, more than 2,000 kilometers away. My life was open ended now and in a way, a year into my journey, I was only just beginning.

III. Songkla

Chapter 22

That first day, I motorcycled down to Mae Sot, a small town 300 kilometers south of Chiang Mai, located right on the Moie river, a narrow river that formed the border between Thailand and Burma. I was beginning the first leg of a motorcycle journey that would lead me almost 2000 kilometers to Hat Yai in the south of Thailand, where I would start my next assignment at the Prince of Songkla University. A year ago, I had traveled from Bangkok to Chiang Mai by train. Now, I was traversing the country by motorcycle. Just like a Thai. It was far more dangerous than rail. Thai people were aggressive on the road, the opposite of their behavior in person. And motorcycles were lowest on the highway hierarchy. But the motorcycle gave me the freedom I sought. It was a metaphor for my voyage. I embraced it as I embraced my journey.

I had made arrangements to visit and work there with Dr. Sumet, a head and neck surgeon, well known through out the country. As with Chiang Mai, I had no idea what to expect, but I was nonetheless looking forward to it. I knew that as long as I was dealing with Thai people, I would be treated well. I felt blessed to have the training that made it possible to live this way. It contained the essential elements I was looking for – adventure, altruism, and in a part of the world I had always admired - Asia.

It was a long hot drive to Mae Sot, but the last 90 kilometers were beautiful. The road weaved between mountains and stark limestone monoliths. The air cooled as I descended into the lush green valleys. There were sparkling brooks and waterfalls along the way and many small villages where the people lived in thatched huts built on stilts. Some were lounging on their open, wooden patios, smoking rolled banana leaf cigars amidst tall palm trees and meandering dirt paths.

I arrived in Mae Sot and checked into a hotel in the center of town.

The town of Mae Sot was a typical border town whose people had a reputation for settling disputes violently. There was much illegal trade going on in teak, gems, narcotics, and guns, which accounted for the unpredictability of the place. There was also an interesting ethnic mix of Thai, Chinese, Burmese, and Karen, the local hill tribe people who were engaged in violent rebellion against the central Burmese government.

There was a border crossing at the river where a boat ferried people and goods back and forth between Thailand and Burma. I knew that with the civil war going on the Burmese soldiers on the other side would not take kindly to my non-Asian face. But with so much traffic, I figured I could sneak in and get a glimpse of Burma through the back door. I parked my motorcycle off to the side and watched the local people hurrying about, carrying woven baskets and bags filled with dried fish, shrimp, rice, bamboo shoots, and mung beans. I gazed across the narrow, muddy waters of the Moei River where I could just make out the small Burmese village of Myawaddy on the other side.

Burma had a well-cultivated air of mystery about it, based in part on the closed-door policy of its military government. Tourists had a tough enough time getting in, and, if allowed, they were permitted only a one-week stay. But I had also heard that it was a beautiful country, worth every bit of the trouble. It was similar to Thailand in culture and religion, but much more traditional and less developed. I had always been curious about Burma, and with only the breadth of a narrow river separating me from it, the temptation to get in, if only to sniff around that one small village across the way, was too great to resist.

I paid my fee, walked out onto the creaking footbridge and carefully stepped down into the small boat already crowded with Thai and Burmese passengers carrying large bags of rice and spices, along with a few ducks and squawking chickens. Some of the passengers held traditional umbrellas or wore straw hats to shield themselves from the sun. I mussed my hair, slunk my head down between my shoulders, took off my glasses, and otherwise tried to look as much like the natives as possible. I thought I might be able to pass as a mix breed Indo-Burmese because I was swarthy and had dark hair. The ride to the opposite bank took about two minutes. The boat docked, and I stood up, staying as close to the other passengers as possible. No sooner did I take my first step onto Burmese soil, than two Burmese soldiers armed with machine guns materialized from behind a small wooden post. They had probably sighted me from the very first moment I boarded the boat on the other side. I noticed all the other passengers immediately scatter from the boat. I wondered if I had made a little mistake trying to visit Burma.

The soldiers ran up to me, the pads of their index fingers firmly planted on the triggers of their guns. They pointed their guns in the general direction of my chest and made it clear that the single step I had just made into their country would be my last if I didn't turn around and get back into the boat.

Under the circumstances, I should have shut up, but I thought there was a chance I could get them to ease off. I gingerly implored them in Thai to let me into their wonderful country.

"Excuse me sir," I said. "Forgive me. I work in Thailand. I am a doctor. I would like to see your beautiful country. Just a short visit to the village and back."

This turned out to be a mistake.

Without blinking an eye, one of the soldiers, very casually aimed his gun at my feet and fired off a short burst of machine gun fire into the dirt, missing me by inches.

"JESUS CHRIST!" I shrieked, hopping off the ground with my heart in my throat. I realized this was not a game. There was a civil war going on and people from both sides were probably lined up and shot everyday. One more farang in the crowd would hardly make a difference. In less than a second, acting strictly on the basis of instinct and fear, I turned, grabbed the side of the boat and jumped back in, hoping to get out of there before this maniac could fire off another burst. Once in the boat, I raced towards the back, only to find the driver cowering under his seat.

"Crap!" I grabbed him by the arm, trying to pull him up, pleading with him to start the motor. He wouldn't budge. I picked him up by the waist, sat him on the wooden plank, and told him to pull the damn cord. "Hurry up, God dammit!" I shouted. He finally stopped shaking enough to get the motor started. He backed the boat up, turned it around, and we were headed back to Thailand.

I spent a night in Mae Sot, relaxing in my room, recovering from the long ride and the day's excitement.

I left early next morning while it was still dark. As always, the industrious Thai people were up hours before me. The markets were busy, people raced by on their bicycles and motor scooters, animals were led about, and offerings were being prepared for the monks. It was a typical early morning in Thailand.

I continued south, staying overnight in whatever city I happened to be approaching as darkness fell. I passed through Nakhom Sawan, Suphanburi, and down into Nakhom Pathom, covering about three to four hundred kilometers a day. The traffic as we neared Bangkok was horrendous. Nakhom Pathom was about 50 kilometers west of Bangkok, and the half way mark of my trip. It was reputed to be Thailand's oldest city, part of a loose network of cities that emerged in the 6th-11th centuries AD in the Chao Phraya River valley. Its centerpiece was the *Phra Pathom Chedi*, the tallest Buddhist monument in the world. I circumambulated this vast edifice, admiring the many intimate Buddha images, chambers, and sanctuaries, even as I was staggered by its magnitude and scale. I rediscovered in an instant my connection to

Buddhism. The structure deserved its reputation. It was one of the grand-est things I had ever seen. It restored me after the long ride down with all the crazy Thai drivers. I rested up two nights here, enjoying the sights and sounds, before beginning the next leg of my journey down into the southern peninsula of Thailand.

I had gotten up very early the next morning to begin my run down to Surat Thani, about 600 kilometers south of Nakhom Pathom. I arrived in Surat Thani very late that night, and stayed in a hotel in the center of town before heading to Don Sak, a small, isolated fishing village, the next morning. I had toyed with the idea of riding straight south through the highlands, to a small town by the name of Thung Song, nestled in a valley surrounded by mountains on all sides. It was reputed to be quite beautiful and was a more direct route to Hat-Yai where I was ultimately headed. While I generally loved the mountains, the scenery and the picturesque villages one encountered along the way, I decided instead to take the coastal route to Don Sak.

When I left Surat Thani that morning, the sun was shining, and the sky was clear. There was nothing in the air that offered even the slightest hint of what was going to take place. About half way to Don Sak, I was hit by the worst monsoon I had ever encountered. This took me completely off guard because in Chiang Mai, in the northern part of Thailand, the monsoon season was over. None of my friends back in Chiang Mai had bothered to mention that in the south the pattern of the monsoon season was the exact opposite of the north where the monsoons had finished up more than a month ago in October. Here in the south, November marked its beginning. More impor-tantly though, this year would be the region's worst monsoon in thirty years. The last forty kilometers to Don Sak I drove through sheets of rain so thick I could barely see an inch in front of my face. The roads were completely flooded. I continued on for hours, and still the rains did not let up. I finally made it to Don Sak, a dirty little fishing village and stayed in a flophouse near the ocean.

The downpour continued. The waves came crashing in right up to my porch. The roads flooded and the power was down. This went on for days. Reports began to filter in about what was going on in other parts of southern Thailand, not far from Don Sak. Inland, near the mountains, whole villages had been swallowed up in seas of mud. Death tolls were mounting, fortunes in property and goods destroyed in a single night. Roads, bridges and rail-road lines were washed up and people were stranded, barely hanging on to their lives without food or water. I stayed huddled up in my damp hotel room for a week before the full picture emerged. I heard over a radio that at least 1,000 people were known dead, and the count was expected to climb. Large towns had disappeared overnight, consumed in horrendous avalanches of mud. This had been the worst natural catastrophe in Thailand's history.

One thing was certain - I wasn't moving. I may have to stay in Don Sak for weeks, but at least here I was relatively safe. I realized how close I had come to personal disaster. At Surat Thani, I had chosen to go to Don Sak instead of south to Thung Song in the mountains. I later found that the floods and mud had obliterated Thung Song on the same day that I would have arrived. I would have been one of the more than one thousand killed in the floods. At the last moment, for purely whimsical reasons, I changed my mind, and unknowingly saved my life. Don Sak, on the shoreline and away from the southern mountain range, although battered by the rains, was relatively safe. To this day, I don't know why I opted to go this way, especially since I generally prefer the mountains to the ocean. But in the midst of this terrible tragedy affecting millions of people, I was grateful to have been spared.

I shuddered to think about my mother and family back home. I probably would have never been recovered or identified. They never would have known what became of me, lost as I would have been in a wave of mud. My family already thought I was crazy to be working for pennies in the third world. To disappear without a trace or word would have been bizarre and unbearable. I was grateful that my brothers and especially my mother did not have to suffer that burden.

Chapter 23

During the next two weeks I was forced to stay in Don Sak. I came to know a most unlikely fellow traveler by the name of Francisco. It was strange enough meeting another westerner here. Don Sak was off the tourist circuit, having virtually nothing of interest to offer. What was even more unusual was that Francisco was a Portuguese Jew. It was quite remarkable to meet a Jew actually born and raised in Portugal. As a Sephardic Jew myself, I had always assumed that with the expulsion of virtually every Jew from both Spanish and Portuguese soil some 500 years ago during the Inquisition, there were no Jews left in either of those two countries, both of which had once hosted large Jewish populations during their own Golden Ages of Jewish culture and influence. Francisco's ancestors had managed to avoid the Inquisition and remain in Portugal through the centuries to this day by living in remote mountains in the interior of the country. Throughout his childhood he had heard many beautiful but sad tales about his exiled people with whom he had little or no contact. And somehow, over the centuries, his family had maintained the traditions and faith.

Francisco was a writer and a poet in his late twenties who had decided on this sleepy, dirty village where he had been for the last two months. He did not speak a word of Thai, and the locals here, not accustomed to dealing with westerners, knew nothing of the English language, let alone Portuguese.

"For almost ten years, Ricardo," Francisco said to me in accented English, "I have been traveling and living in strange places like this. I work for half the year to save money, and then I spend it traveling the other half. I have stayed in tiny unnamed islands off the coast of Brazil, and in the Caribbean, gazing at stars from sandy beaches at night and living off coconuts that fall from the trees. I sought refuge in the Negev desert in Israel, living there for months, wandering in the darkness, looking for God. I have settled in isolated villages in sub Saharan Africa, writing love poetry about the beautiful black goddesses I have known. I have traveled widely, but in places scarcely known to even the most intrepid travelers."

"You have been on a unique journey," I said.

"I live in my little world, Ricardo, lost and happy in my dreams, my poems and novels, with exotic people whose languages I cannot speak."

"And now you have settled in an unknown village off the Gulf of Siam."

"Yes."

"Do you get tired of traveling?"

"No. I rest. I feel the mystery of the place. I know when it is time to leave."

He had an apocalyptic side to him, I discovered, after asking him if I could read one of the novels he had written.

"I have none," he said. "I burn them as soon as I am done."

"Why would you do that?"

"I am like the Tibetans, Ricardo. They make elaborate sand paintings of mandalas, beautiful works of art that they toil over for days and weeks, only to brush them away into nothingness as soon as they complete them."

"That may be true, but it doesn't follow that you must burn your novels."

"It must seem strange to you, Ricardo."

"How many have you written?"

"Three."

"And you haven't saved any?"

"Not a page."

"Why would you work so hard only to destroy them?

"It does not concern me, Ricardo. Truly. I do not say it to be provocative. I live only for the company of my dreams. I dance and laugh with them. I am happy as a child. I want only to bring that beautiful world of my dreams to the cold realm of grey, penciled words."

"But why abort the books without giving them a chance to see the light of day?"

"Because the final product always disappoints. My efforts are doomed to imperfection. I can never translate into words the world of my imagination."

"But you can revise and refine your work until it approaches the ideal."

"No matter what, I am dissatisfied. As hard as I try, I will never be happy with them, and so I do not hesitate to burn or abandon them like the orphans they are."

"It is extreme, Francisco. But very Buddhist."

"I seek only to experience the world of the senses and the mind, and then recreate that world with words. But in the end, it is all the same. They do not matter. The world has no need of my words."

Probably no one had ever read so much as a single word he had written, although he later shared several poems and letters with me – and they were radiant and evocative, including this haunting piece from his native Portugal that escaped the fires of his bizarre passions and idiosyncrasies.

I am a happy man, growing old,
resting my soul in fields of corn and wheat,
in winters of long nights,
the seasons passing like the timeless flight of life.

It is snowing here now,
the meadows of dirt, quiet and peaceful beneath their white blanket.
The winter casts its spell.
Spring will soon be here,
the leaves on the trees dressing my poems in green.
I am a prophet of my own tribe,
following the God of the rainbows,
and the full moon over the shores of the Pacific Ocean.
I sing in Spanish, the old slave songs
from the Northern Mangrove Islands of Ecuador.
My days are my life.
That's all we have.
The children I have always had within me are born.
Now I must meet the old men that are waiting for me in
that mountain, so calmly sitting in their rocking chairs.
The streets are deserted, and I must sleep now.
I must rest my bones,
and greet the Winter and death.

Francisco sought out places like Don Sak where he could be alone with his mind, undisturbed by others, unable to speak the local language and not distracted by items of interest or beauty. Places that were simple and uncomplicated, even unappealing. As if the weird, seemingly prosaic texture of a given place served as a catalyst to his own internal impressions and flights. We became good friends during my forced detention in Don Sak, and through Francisco I learned a great deal about what went on in this seemingly insipid little town, and more specifically about what went on in our little hotel by the ocean.

One night, I was awoken suddenly in my hotel room by a loud noise. I didn't know what it was and quickly returned to sleep. The next morning, after awakening, I heard a crowd of people outside my door. I hurried out to see what all the commotion was about. I immediately noticed two police officers checking out the room just opposite mine with a small crowd of onlookers hanging around. Francisco, who was standing nearby, came over to me.

"Someone was shot last night, Ricardo," Francisco said. "Murdered."

"What?" I asked incredulously.

"In the middle of the night. There was a loud noise, Ricardo, didn't you hear it?"

I vaguely remembered awakening last night. "You mean right here?"

"Yes, Ricardo."

"You mean right next to my room?"

"Yes."

"Man, it's dangerous here."

"Yes, it is."

"What happened?"

Francisco explained that someone had been sleeping with the wrong woman, a prostitute, but someone's lover just the same. In the midst of sexual intercourse, a jealous rival burst into the room, catching both of them in the act. He angrily cursed them in Thai and pumped two bullets into the man's back. He died moaning in his lover's arms. The woman was about to receive the same fate. The man cursed her again and spat angrily in her face, smacking her repeatedly with his open hand. He then raised his gun, and aimed it at her naked chest.

"In the next instant, Ricardo, as the officer told me in his broken English, the doomed woman grabbed her necklace containing an image of the Buddha and tore it from her neck. She waved it in the man's face, screaming ancient Buddhist prayers. The man pulled back from the trigger and dropped the gun. He fell to his knees and bowed three times before the image of the Buddha, touching his head to the floor each time. He fled without a word, leaving his gun in the room."

"Even in the midst of betrayal and killing, they remain devoted to Buddha."

"They fear the Buddha and the bad karma that may come."

We watched as the police carried the dead body out of the room.

"Be careful around here, Ricardo. It can be very dangerous," Francisco warned.

After three weeks in Don Sak, word filtered down that the roads and bridges had been restored enough for safe travel. The phones were still down, so I couldn't notify anyone in Songkla, but I would show up soon enough, provided no other acts of man or God intervened.

It was strange packing my belongings in my damp, dark room. I was still living by candlelight, but I had gotten used to the strange lifestyle here. I had made friends with the locals and looked forward to our meals together, which consisted almost exclusively of fried rice and stringy vegetables. It was difficult to get supplies brought in. I enjoyed my daily excursions into town, sloshing through the mud and the unending rains for various odds and ends ranging from matches to batteries for my flashlight. It was also good to have my Portuguese friend, Francisco, around, to listen to his poems and outlandish tales of his own adventures in faraway places. He was staying on for at least another month, finishing up a novel he was working on. As soon as he finished it, he planned to set it aflame. He was a strange one, but I admired the purity of his vision. We promised to stay in touch.

I left Don Sak early in the morning as dawn began to break.

I took the coastal route, the only possible way to go even now, three weeks later, to the town of Nakhon Si Thammarat, about 150 kilometers south of Don Sak. Along the way down I saw first hand the horrible devastation the floods had wrought. Hordes of dead animals, cattle, goats, sheep, and chickens lay stiff, bloated and grey along the sides of the road. There was a terrible stench in the air from the slow decomposition of the carcasses. Homes and villages had been destroyed, bridges were down, and everywhere was the color of mud grey. The Thai people were working furiously, still digging themselves out from the catastrophe. The roads were bad, and it took hours before I arrived at my next destination.

Nakhon Si Thammarat was settled more than a thousand years ago when Sri Lankan-ordained monks established a monastery here and named it Nagara Sri Dhammaraja, which is Sanskrit for "City of the Sacred Dharma-King." The town is famous for a magnificent temple named Wat Mahathat, reputed to have been built more than a thousand years ago. Also, there were three Hindu temples, including one that housed a famous Shivalingam, or phallic shrine, which was worshipped frequently by women wanting to have children, and, finally, its gangsters. There is a burgeoning Thai mafia in Nakhon, replete with gangland slayings, "protection rackets," and other forms of extortion. As elsewhere, I had been warned to be extremely careful here.

I rolled into town after dark and checked into a hotel on one of the main streets. You could hardly tell there had been the terrible floods and mudslides by looking at Nakhon. The place was lit up, traffic was busy, and street vendors, movie theaters, stores and restaurants were open with brisk traffic.

I dumped my bags in my hotel room and immediately went outside. It felt great to be able to move around freely again. I was also starved. I hadn't had a decent meal in weeks. I hit the main street and walked into a busy noodle joint lit up with fluorescent lights and packed with customers. Sitting at an empty table, I ordered some food.

Halfway through my meal, I noticed a young Thai woman with tousled black hair, sensuous eyes, and thin pink lips sitting at a table opposite me. She was nursing a cool glass of Mekong whiskey on the rocks and seemed to be staring at me. She slowly rubbed her index finger over the rim of her glass, then into her drink, bringing her wet finger up to her lips. Looking over at me, she smiled, as she touched her finger to her tongue. I had done nothing to attract her attention.

She happened to be sitting at a table with a large party of men, all reasonably soused and rather tough looking. There was a lot of raucous laughter, macho posturing, and noisy pounding of the table with their glasses as the men ordered more Mekong. I avoided her come-on, well aware of the town's reputation and kept my eyes planted on my plate of noodles.

As if following the script of a movie, she stood up from her table, Mekong in hand, and walked over to me. The conversation at her table instantly stopped. I tried to ignore her and kept eating my food, but she sat down right next to me. I couldn't believe my luck. Under normal circumstances, like most men, I would have greeted an advance like this as a wholly fortuitous opportunity. However, under existing circumstances, a foreigner in a tough town with a table full of wild-eyed drunks just opposite me, I preferred anonymity.

The men at her table sat silently, like sphinxes, gaping at me. I could feel the weight of their collective stares. Sitting right next to me, she slowly lifted her glass of Mekong to my lips, smiling, her dark eyes looking into my own.

"Sawadee ka," she said softly.

She leaned over and touched my hair, while parting her lips slightly as if preparing for a wet kiss. She was beautiful, but I knew this was one opportunity I should let pass. She moved my head gently towards her open mouth. I resisted. She then brought her glass up to my lips. I took a sip. That was it.

As soon as I put my lips to her glass, I knew I had made a mistake. At that moment, one of the surlier looking men got up, slamming his fist on the table. He came over, leaned over the table and brought his dark face down right next to mine. I could smell the liquor on his breath. I met his hard stare, but I did not want a fight. He then reached behind to his back pocket, where I noticed the polished metal handle of a knife. This was it. My life brought to a bloody finish over a woman, like that poor guy in Don Sak. I supposed it lent a romantic quality to my misguided adventure, but I wasn't ready to end it just yet.

"I am Richard Moss," I said, speaking in Thai, "a surgeon visiting from the United States. I am an *ajarn* at the Prince of Songkla University in Hat-Yai where I will be working for the next year. I am late for my assignment because of the floods and need to get down there as soon as possible to help my patients."

The expression on his face abruptly changed. "You are an *ajarn*?" he asked in Thai.

"Yes."

He brought his hand back off the knife, his taut facial muscles loosening up, and broke into a broad, toothy grin. I breathed easier and smiled back. He shook my hand and then wai'd me. "Excuse me, *ajarn*," he said respectfully. I saw again the enormous reverence Thai people have for the medical profession. In this case, it saved me.

He then leaned over the table and whispered into my ear that this lovely flower sitting next to me was wonderful. "Take her for the night," he said, as he winked and returned to his table. And I returned to my femme fatale who offered me another sip of whiskey. She then took my hand, and we drifted off together into the Mekong night.

Chapter 24

I finally made it down to Hat Yai the next evening as the sun was setting, after a full day's drive. I found my way to the University where Dr. Kowit, the young ajarn from the Ear Nose and Throat department, was waiting for me. I had met Kowit up in Chiang Mai once before, so we were already acquainted. Kowit was to help me in arranging practical sorts of things, not unlike Rak, back in Chiang Mai. We enjoyed a meal together in town where I regaled him with some of my more recent adventures on the road. He mentioned that the floods had also struck Hat Yai, with waters almost six feet deep in the downtown area. There had been millions of dollars of property damage, but fortunately few casualties. Afterwards, he showed me to my apartment. I went to bed early that night and slept deeply. It had been a long and eventful journey down from Chiang Mai, and I was glad to stay in one place for a while.

I awoke in my apartment early next morning and looked over the accommodations. I had two bedrooms, a walk-in kitchen, bathroom, living room, and a large balcony from which I enjoyed the morning air. I also had a personal telephone, which was convenient. It was more than enough.

I sat out on the balcony watching the hospital community slowly wake up. I could see young doctors, nurses and students in their white uniforms walking over to the hospital. Motorcycles and cars drove past. Delivery trucks carrying food, medical supplies or fresh linens were making their morning run. Just below me was a large lawn where children were playing under the watchful eyes of their mothers. I noticed several tennis and basketball courts and, of course, a healthy number of joggers. There had also been a large number of joggers in Chiang Mai, yet another subtle manifestation of the fascination in Thailand with all things American including the fitness fad. In the distance, just beyond the hospital campus was a large lake, with grass-covered knolls surrounding it. Altogether, it looked like a wonderful place to live.

Kowit, who had thoughtfully brought a standing fan, and a tape recorder for me to use while here, picked me up later. We drove together in his car to the hospital to meet the ENT staff and make rounds.

The Prince of Songkla University Hospital was a white, open-air structure, situated in the center of the university campus. It was modern, spacious, and impeccably clean, with sprawling well-manicured lawns surrounding it.

It had an interesting design as well, with offices, clinics and wards occupying the outer rectangular perimeter of the building, while the center remained open to the sky, and delightfully sunlit. The central area on the first floor contained benches, trees and a fountain for a pleasant respite during the day for patients, visitors and workers. It had the feeling of a spa more than a teaching center. The hospital had been designed based on models derived primarily from the United States and reflected in every way the recent strides Thailand had made in its climb to modernity. Thailand, the former backwater, had built itself up. Prince of Songkla University Hospital was the South's shining example of progress. It was the regional center for the entire southern peninsula of the country, and, on first glance, appeared a cut or two above Suandok Hospital in Chiang Mai.

The ENT wards, which were located on the fifth floor, were bright and clean and had the look of any major, high-powered teaching hospital in the US. There were the usual Thai-style communal rooms with beds lined up consecutively, but each bed could be cordoned off from the next by curtains, and there were individual lights, suction devices and oxygen. Of immediate note was the absence of cots in the middle of the halls, patients sitting on the floor, or huge entourages of family members surrounding each patient, feeding them, fanning them, or sleeping on the floor around them, all of which I had remembered in Chiang Mai. The nurses hurried about quietly in sparkling white uniforms, the patients seemed to more or less stay in their respective beds instead of congregating out in the corridors. There was a section of private rooms for wealthier patients with all the usual trappings. The halls and floors were spotless. There was an efficient, "American" ambience here rather than the more traditional "Thai" character that I recalled in Chiang Mai, where the atmosphere often resembled more that of a small Thai village, a quality that I always enjoyed, and felt was, perhaps, more therapeutic.

The ENT staff had just begun to make rounds when Kowit and I appeared. I was introduced to the various ajarns, who, except for one, were all men. The chairman of the department was a short, unusually plump individual, with a round, almost child-like face, by the name of Sumet, who was known throughout the country for his work in head and neck cancer. He had authored books, written numerous articles in the medical literature, and had even perfected new technologies that had proved innovative and useful. He also organized and presented papers at conferences and international symposiums and was on a first name basis with professors from around the world. On first meeting him he appeared quite jovial, almost innocent in a way, but I could also sense in him a highly motivated, dynamic quality.

"Yes, yes, Dr. Moss, very good to see you," he began in heavily accented English. "We are very happy to have you. We worry about you all this time because of the floods. Dr. Kowit called me last night to tell me that you arrive safely. We are making grand rounds now, American style. Everything we try to do same as American system. Please join us," he said politely.

ENT Faculty, Prince of Songkla University

He quickly gathered the doctors who responded to him with rapt deference. I could see this was no maternal Dr. Acharee gently tending her flock.

We continued rounding with a large crowd on hand, including six or seven faculty members, a number of residents and medical students, and several nurses. One of the first patients was a particularly tough case that Dr. Sumet wanted my opinion on. He was a middle-aged man, a former teacher in fact, who had received radiation two years ago for a throat cancer. The tumor unfortunately persisted, despite the radiation, and the patient had to undergo salvage surgery for removal of his throat and voice box. After surgery, he developed an infection, which led to a breakdown of his wound. His throat opened to the skin of his neck, and saliva had been pouring out like a leaky faucet ever since. He had the usual breathing hole at the base of the neck, as was required for anyone having his larynx removed, and he could not speak. In addition though, because his throat communicated openly with his neck, he was unable to eat. As soon as he tried, the food or liquid immediately came splashing out all over his neck and clothing. He therefore required a feeding tube, which ran from his nose to his stomach. He had been this way now for more than a year, unable to speak or eat and desperately wanting a fix.

"What you like to do, Dr. Moss?" Dr. Sumet asked with an almost angelic smile.

I walked up to the patient to have a closer look. He quickly sat upright in his bed, and very eagerly showed me his wound. I saw the scars from his previous surgery, the breathing hole at the base of his neck, and the brawny, thickened skin that followed radiation treatment. There was a gaping crack in the middle of his neck where the skin and throat communicated. There were several large mounds of flesh heaped up on either side of this large opening, and saliva was barely kept at bay by the numerous white gauze pads surrounding it. Beyond the condition of his neck I perceived an unusual quality in the man himself. He was no simple field laborer from the rice paddies unconcerned about a debilitating condition like so many patients I had encountered in Chiang Mai. He appeared instead to be an educated man, who understood fully what was at stake. He seemed anxious to have something done. He also possessed a cheerful sort of optimism, which I found extraordinary, particularly considering his poor condition. An American with such a disease would not have so sunny a disposition.

"Excuse me, Dr. Moss," Dr. Vitoon, one of the faculty members, began, "I examined this patient recently. He has recurrent tumor in the throat." Dr. Vitoon delivered this rather critical piece of information in a casual, off-hand way, but it completely changed the picture. The open, draining wound was a difficult enough problem, but now we were dealing with recurrent tumor, a condition that generally meant a slow, painful death, as the tumor grew increasingly deeper into the spine and neck. We had moved from a purely reconstructive problem to one of life threatening disease.

"Did you get a good look at it?" I asked.

"Yes."

"Was it extensive?"

"It is large, but I think it is resectable," Vitoon said. Everything is resectable, I thought to myself, remembering the words of my former boss, Dr. Lucente, back in New York. But is it *curable* was always the follow-up question. One could always, in other words, *resect* something, or surgically remove a tumor, but if it killed the patient, it didn't do much good. Vitoon continued. "I think we can remove it safely. We plan for a big case tomorrow, but what do *you* recommend?"

I didn't want to overcommit myself, especially on the first case. "Let's scope him tomorrow," I said. "I want to see how large the recurrence is. If it looks like we can get around it, we can operate."

"Very good."

Just as we were about to move on to the next bed, the patient stood up and grabbed my hands, mouthing words, it seemed, of gratitude, as if he still had a voice. He held my hands for a few moments, looking at me like an innocent child. For that one instant, I sensed in him a deep yearning to be cured. He slowly released my hands, wai'd, and bowed. I returned the wai. I could not help but be very much struck by this unusual man and hoped that I could help him. We continued over to the next bed.

"Kowit, please arrange scoping for Dr. Moss tomorrow," Sumet said.

"Yes, ajarn."

The next patient was a 20-year-old girl who had never smoked a cigarette in her life, but for unknown reasons had developed a cancer that had eaten into the lower part of her throat. It had gotten so big that she was having difficulty swallowing her own saliva and had lost considerable weight.

"We have a lot of throat cancer here. We don't know why, maybe something in our soil, or too much spicy food." Sumet laughed loudly. Just looking at Sumet, his large round belly, so unusual for Thais. This was a man who appeared to enjoy his food.

Sumet opened up the forum for ideas on this poor young girl. "What you going to do?" he asked the audience.

Prasad, another faculty member, began, "It is too advanced, ajarn, and what is our chance at cure? She is too young for such surgery. I think it is better to leave her alone and only radiate her." Prasad was being affected by the young age of the patient - a mistake, I felt. Leaving this tumor alone was a death sentence, and a slow, horrible one at that. "We should not deny this girl the best chance for cure," I said, "because we think she is too young for major surgery, even though it is mutilating. We must treat her the same way we would treat a man in his fifties. Her only chance for cure is with surgery and radiation together. Without the surgery, she has no chance at all."

Vitoon quickly agreed. "Ajarn Moss is right. We should not change our treatment plan because of her age." Other opinions followed. In fact, there was considerable dissent for a group of Thai, who were ordinarily quite accommodating.

In general, this kind of tumor arose in males, who were much older. The fact that the patient was a young girl was confusing the picture, altering the usual treatment recommendations, which consisted typically of both surgery and radiation. The surgery, of course, was "mutilating" in that it was necessary to remove the throat and larynx, and the surgeons were getting cold feet at the thought of recommending such treatment for a young female. The problem was that she had "radical" disease, which was already killing her and therefore required it. It was wrong to confuse the picture and not offer her what she had to have in order to survive.

Sumet, the chairman, standing above the fray, finally cleared his throat. Instant silence. "We will operate." The issue was settled.

We saw more patients, most with some form of cancer and most requiring major surgery. As in Chiang Mai, the cases were abundant and quite advanced.

I was excited to be here and saw similar opportunities to treat serious pathology as I had in Chiang Mai. There were cases, a team of faculty, residents, and students on hand to assist, a sophisticated medical infrastructure, and an abiding interest in learning. It could not be better. It was a continuation of the same dream began a year ago. To come to developing nations and slay dragons, the healing quest enacted and lived. The commitment and passion I felt in Chiang Mai would continue in Songkla, only with the advantage of a year on the frontlines under my belt. Yet, I saw differences too. This ENT department was more self-confident. They could do the tough cases already. Dr. Sumet was a leading researcher and developer of ENT technology. The other faculty too were well read and abreast of the ENT literature. The facilities here were modern and state-of-the-art, obviously a cut above Chiang Mai. Here, I was less needed to handle the caseload or do surgery. Rather, it was an academic role I was to serve, to share ideas, research controversies, perhaps write a paper or two, and engage in the give and take of scholarly medical discourse. I saw this as valuable but also from my perspective, diminished. It would not be the same as Chiang Mai. They were well on their way here to an American standard. I preferred the more crushing circumstances and need. I wanted to be in the trenches, in hand-to-hand combat.

After seeing the last patient, Sumet quickly took me by the arm and invited me to join him for lunch. We excused ourselves and within minutes were in his car headed for a favorite haunt specializing in northeastern Thai food.

The restaurant was an open air facility with lots of tables and busy with the lunchtime crowd. Waiters ran back and forth balancing plates on their arms and taking orders. It was very hot outside, but that didn't stop Sumet. Soon after ordering, an amazing assortment of dishes arrived. There was sticky rice, eaten by hand, with dried meats, pickled vegetables, noodles, sauces, curries and spicy dips. Sumet, who seemed happiest while eating, was in ecstasy. He was not just exploding with hot curries, though, but with ideas and his own innate exuberance. As I listened to Sumet hold forth, I quickly recognized that this was a man consumed with a passion to expand and improve his department. He seemed to live and breathe his specialty. Confirming my initial impressions, he explained that he was striving to import or at least adapt the latest technology and concepts from the United States in order to keep his department up to date. He scanned the American ENT literature daily, looking for new ideas. He anxiously wanted Americans to visit his department because he wanted to learn from them. In addition, he also wanted them to learn about him. It seemed of vital importance to

Sumet that his department not only become first rate but in addition that it be recognized abroad. Especially by the United States. America was the place, the great *Mecca* of medicine from which all good things flowed. It was clear in speaking with Sumet and others before that the ultimate standard of quality and innovation when it came to medicine was the United States; and it was there where he most avidly desired some form of recognition, for himself and his institution. He mentioned repeatedly throughout our conversation that everything in his department must be "Just like America."

After lunch, Sumet gave me a tour of Hat-Yai, the South's most important city and Thailand's third largest, just behind Chiang Mai. Hat-Yai was only 40 kilometers from Malaysia, a predominantly Muslim nation and reflected this proximity in its tone and ambience. There were numerous restaurants specializing in "Muslim" dishes as well as a large mosque in the center of town. Women dressed in long black gowns (burqas) and white veils covering much of their faces were commonly seen. There were also many Chinese temples and restaurants as Malaysia and Thailand both had large Chinese populations. Singapore, which is mostly Chinese, was not too far away either. I gathered from listening to Sumet that there was a great deal of animosity between Thai Moslems and the Thai and Chinese Buddhists. The two religions and ways of life reflected utterly different traditions, and I imagined that it might be difficult for them to coexist. There had been terrorist bombings in the region, apparently by Muslim groups wanting either complete autonomy or to be annexed by their Muslim neighbor to the south, Malaysia. It was a source of anxiety for Thailand, which was determined to hold on to its four southern, predominately Muslim, provinces at any cost.

Sumet dropped me off by my motorcycle. "I must return to hospital. But you can explore Hat-Yai. Many special places you will like. Have a look. We see you tomorrow."

I cruised through the downtown section, with its large department stores, restaurants, and hotels. After wandering down a deserted street on the outskirts of town, I parked my motorcycle by a seedy looking store with Chinese letters written over the entrance. Below that was a handwritten sign in English that intrigued me. It said "Traditional Chinese Pharmacy."

I entered the store and immediately detected a curious odor. I looked around and noticed large glass cages everywhere, all containing snakes. I walked over to the proprietor, a thin, frail Chinese man, with glasses. He began speaking to me in Chinese. Realizing I understood not a word, he called over another man who spoke some English.

"My name is Anurat. I can explain to you. This is special Chinese pharmacy. We have traditional Chinese medicine here. You can try."

The proprietor nodded his head looking over at me, a big smile on his face. After a moment, he rang a bell, and two short burly Chinese men waddled in, wearing heavy gloves, which seemed a little odd to me. One of the fellows then walked over to a cage containing a thick, slithering black snake, and opened up the hatch at the top of the cage. Without a moment's hesitation, he quickly reached in and grabbed the snake by its head, pinning it to the floor of the cage. Securing his grip, he pulled the snake out of the cage and brought it to the glass counter where Anurat and the proprietor were standing comfortably. The snake hissed and flicked its tongue in anger. It coiled its long body around the arm of the man, writhing and contracting its muscles. But as long as the man held the snake's head, there was nothing it could do.

The other man then came over with a strange looking instrument that consisted of a stick with a piece of rope at the end of it, tied to form a noose. He quickly placed the noose around the head of the snake and pulled it tightly, almost choking the snake to death. The first man then grabbed the tail and held the snake vertically, with the tail up. He then systematically squeezed the body of the snake with his hand, starting from the tail and working down its entire length. He continued this peculiar maneuver for several minutes, swelling up the lower half of the snake's body. The individual holding the head of the snake grabbed a pitcher and placed it just under the snake's head. Without any warning, he pulled out a long knife and abruptly sliced the snake's head off, allowing the snake's brown blood to gush out into the waiting pitcher. The other man continued squeezing the snake's body even more feverishly, trying to get every last drop of blood. I had no idea what the heck they were doing.

After milking the snake dry, one of the men brought the pitcher of snake's blood over to the proprietor. He took the pitcher and placed it on another table and mixed ancient Chinese herbs and tonics in with the blood. After completing the concoction, he poured some of it into a large glass and brought it to the counter top.

"Mister, please, enjoy this Chinese medicine. This is the special drink that make you very strong in bed," Anurat said.

"What?"

"Don't worry. This is ancient Chinese medicine. It give you great power."

There was no way I was drinking that.

"Please. Many Chinese men come here from Singapore. Spend a lot of money. This is special snake, the best in Hat-Yai. Very strong. You try it."

"Uhhh..." He wasn't kidding.

"Okay. Don't worry. I try first. Then you try. This will make you very strong. You see." Anurat grabbed the glass and without blinking an eye downed half of it. He swallowed hard and loud. "...Ahhh. Good. Now you try."

he held the glass out for me. He was serious. "Please try, you will like it." He really wanted me to drink it. "Take drink please."

I took the glass and peered down at this dark, frothy elixir. I held it up to my mouth, smelled it, brought it to my lips and chugged it down. All of it. It was awful. I wiped my lips with the back of my hand and handed the glass back to Anurat. I felt like I had gone through a rite of passage.

"Good. Now you will see. This medicine give you great power." He seemed proud of me.

Anurat and the proprietor wai'd me. I walked out with Anurat to my motorcycle. "We have many customers," he said. "I drink Chinese medicine every week. It is the best in Hat-Yai."

The operating room was a busy place that next morning when I met Kowit. We were scoping the old teacher I had seen yesterday to assess the size of the tumor. The general surgeons were also on hand in the event we decided surgery could be done. We planned to remove what was left of the man's throat and reconstruct it by using his stomach, a procedure known, logically enough, as a stomach or "gastric" pull-up. This involved opening the patient's abdomen, isolating the stomach, and then passing it up through the patient's chest and into the neck, where we would hook it up directly ("anastomose") to the remaining part of the patient's upper throat. It was a high-risk procedure that required entering three separate body cavities, and passing the stomach up behind the heart, as it pounded away. If successful, the patient could be eating in five days. If something went wrong it could be a disaster.

The patient was wheeled into the room and placed on the operating room table. I watched as he submitted to the unpleasant poking and prodding that accompanied any major surgery: the insertion of the various catheters, tubes, IVs, gauges, central and arterial lines, so essential for monitoring the patient during the operation. He seemed strangely at ease for someone about to undergo such an ordeal. He clasped a Buddha image in his hands and smiled peacefully, as the anesthesiologist placed the mask over his face and whisked him off to sleep.

With the patient now safely under general anesthesia, I stepped to the head of the operating table. The residents were scrubbed and in sterile gowns, holding the iodine solution that would be used to wash the patient's face and body after my brief exam. Before the surgery, I wanted to take a quick look, a precursory exam only, to assess the extent of the tumor. The anesthesiologist pressed her black ventilating bag, breathing for the patient. The residents positioned the instrument table with the laryngoscopes next to me, as I sat down near the patient's head. The ENT and General Surgery teams were chatting quietly off to the side.

There was for one brief instant, a perfect serenity and magnificence to this spectacle. Silence prevailed except for the soothing and rhythmic sound of the patient's breathing, as the anesthesiologist squeezed her black bag, ushering into his lungs yet another puff of anesthetic gas. The scrub nurse switched on the light to the laryngoscope. I grasped the instrument and began the examination.

I pushed the scope down past the patient's tongue. It was tight and stiff. A bad sign. The tumor was larger than I anticipated. I removed the scope and palpated the tumor. I placed my hand down the patient's throat and felt around. "The tumor is rock hard and doesn't budge. It's fixed," I said mostly to myself. It seemed like it had already eaten into the cervical spine. I got up and looked at the CT scan on the view box. The images didn't show it. Volume averaging, I wondered. I returned to the patient to re-examine him - maybe I was mistaken. I felt again with my hand. No way. Too damn big. And fixed. I repositioned the patient's head, thinking that by relaxing the neck more, the tumor may budge. It did not. I imagined that the prior surgery and radiation may have caused the rigidity. But that would not explain this. I hated to be the one to call it off, but there was simply no way I could get that tumor out short of cutting off his head. I kept thinking about how much the poor guy wanted something done.

"Forget it. It can't be cured. It's inoperable."

The other surgeons immediately stopped their conversations and came over to look. The anesthesiologists leaned their heads in hoping to catch some of the discussion. The residents and medical students gathered around, and the nurses whispered quietly to one another. Dr. Vitoon and Kowit both examined the patient and agreed. It was too far gone. We explained our findings to the general surgeons and anesthesiologists. We cancelled the surgery and aroused the patient from the bliss of sleep.

The next morning I met Kowit by the nurse's desk, preparing to make rounds. As I turned to join him, I discovered the patient I had scoped yesterday standing before me, garbed in his hospital pajamas and the usual array of gauze pads draped around his neck. I was not at all prepared for what I now had to face. This man, who had been so buoyed with hope, flush with the expectation of a cure, had now stepped forward into the abyss. The tears that fell from his moist eyes marked his awareness of his fate most eloquently. He stood before me, arms at his side, with no gestures or movement or words from the man without a voice, but only the tears welling up and spilling over onto his face.

He had heard. He knew. He understood fully. He was not angry. He only wanted to see me, the one who had passed judgment. To gaze from the borders of his own mortality at the messenger, the one whose words had transformed him from the exalted prince on the verge of rebirth to a man of clay peering into the void. No greater portrayal of the existential angst of man alone in the world and confronted with the reality of his own impending demise could have been more poignant than the image of my voiceless patient weeping silently before me. He peered gently into my eyes, as if to impart the message of his pain, while simultaneously absorbing some fragment of empathy. I have never felt a more sweeping emptiness than that moment, looking into the tearful eyes of my patient who now knew that his disease was incurable. He then clasped his outstretched hands together to wai me, bringing his hands to his face. He bowed. I returned the wai. He then shuffled off alone to his bed, where he slowly packed his clothing and prepared to leave. I watched him walk out the door with a small suitcase in hand. He would return to his family to live out his remaining months.

It was not possible to help every patient. In the developing world in particular, where resources are limited and disease so rampant, it was often the rule rather than the exception. I recalled the many patients I had seen in Chiang Mai where, as here, nothing could be done. In particular, I recalled my last patient there, the young Buddhist monk with the advanced tongue cancer whom we had to abandon to his fate at so youthful an age. There were many others. A cancer surgeon must know when to stop, to lay one's knife on the table and offer something else instead. Some gesture of compassion, a moment of communion, perhaps. After all else, this was still the province of the surgeon. Sometimes, it could be the most valuable offering of all.

Chapter 25

During the day Hat-Yai was a fairly drab, noisy city. At night it seemed to magically transform itself into an exciting, if not downright disreputable little place. Lee Hong's was a popular Thai-Chinese restaurant in the center of Hat-Yai where I frequently ate, a perfect perch for glimpsing the multitude of sins and dramas as they unfolded in this seedy citadel in southern Thailand. I dropped in nightly for a bowl of sukiyaki, one of Lee Hong's specialties. Nok, the waitress, was a cream-skinned Thai girl with perfect black hair, pulled back in ponytail chic, who served me every night with a smile. She was also one of the best looking girls in Hat-Yai, but I could tell she had a little help from her plastic surgeon. When she moved into the light I could barely make out a double ridge running along the bridge of her nose, the telltale stigmata of a nose job. Nok's doc was good though. It was not too obvious. And her secret was safe with me. No need for everyone to know that like so many women before her, Nok too had fallen before the magic knife of the plastic surgeon. In fact, the plastic surgery business in Hat-Yai was thriving. The main business in Hat-Yai, after all, was young, pretty women wanting to look even better.

At a table just over from me sat a dark skinned Malaysian man with gold caps lining his two upper incisors, oily black hair combed straight back, a round chubby face and perspiration stains beneath both armpits. He wore two large gold rings on his plump fingers and a thick gold-linked bracelet around his wrist. He laughed loudly while puffing on his cigarette. Seated next to him was a petite Thai girl in her late teens wearing a tight black leather skirt, nylons, high heels and a red shirt. She looked like a Chiang Mai import and spoke not a word of English. This did not inhibit our silver-tongued Malay from gilding this northern lily with his rich voice. His melting eloquence was interrupted only by frequent loud clearings of phlegm from his throat. She stared directly in front of herself, occasionally tilting her head in his direction and offering only the softest of polite laughter. Her uneasiness suggested she was a newcomer to the world's oldest profession. This was not a match made in heaven, but then for one night it didn't have to be. They got up from the table. It was a dark Gulliver clasping hands with a munchkin and strolling into the neon night.

Outside the restaurant, the traffic was insane with the usual chorus of beeping horns, turning motors and cars screeching to a halt. Small bands of crazed Thai kamikaze youths shrieked by on motorcycles with eyes glazed over, faces knotted in permanent, wind-fixed sneers, shirts billowing violently like sails in a storm, kicking up the gas and craving the 98-octane, gale-force high of instant death on the streets of Hat-Yai.

Out of the corner of my eye, I made out a small invasion force of crisp, well-heeled Singaporeans walking briskly with a flotilla of sparkling Thai maidens following behind. The gals strutted their stuff, all painted up in bright lipsticks, rouge, and mascara. Their extra-long high heels clacking along the irregular pavements caused their awkward gaits, a common feature of Hat-Yai's ladies of the night. These pointy heels were an occupational hazard given the innumerable rifts, cracks and open sewers that were found in Hat-Yai. It was a concession made readily though for the advantage the few extra centimeters of height gave to being picked to play queen for a night. They were moving in the direction of the Post Laser Disc, the only video hideaway showing English-speaking cinema in the entire town. The selection at this cultural mecca consisted of such classics as Clint Eastwood's *Dead Pool* or Tom Cruise in *Cocktail*. The men assembled before the glass-covered menu, sized up the cinematic delicacies for the evening, while the waiting kittens preened and purred. After a brief discussion, they decided to sample more exciting venues elsewhere, and crossed the street, zooming in on the Zodiac disco a couple blocks away.

The Post Laser Disc was something of a haven for westerners passing through Hat-Yai, given its singular status as sole repository of English-speaking films. On any given night there, a sprinkling of westerners wetted their whistles with Singha beer, dragged on their cigarettes, enjoying some of the local color streaming by and maybe even watching the movie. Most nights, sitting off in the corner, usually alone, was Manee, another one of the many sad stories in Hat-Yai. She was a bronze-skinned buxom Thai lovely, who, for personal reasons, had limited her romantic rendezvous' exclusively to men of the western persuasion. Secretly, she was hoping for that oft sought-after dream of so many of Thailand's part-time prostitutes. She wanted to find that interested and well-off westerner who would fall in love and whisk her off into the bountiful and secure confines of matrimonial bliss, not to mention, provide a brand new home back in the village for mom, dad, and little sister.

Hat-Yai boasted other things besides flesh peddling, discos, massage parlors, and burlesques. It had some of the best shopping in Thailand, with such classic department stores as "Diana's" and "Odeans," not to mention other smaller, but well stocked shops that filled the streets with buyers and browsers. By nightfall Hat-Yai was transformed into a shimmering orchestra of neon splash with each store vying for your baht. There were also excellent open-air restaurants serving Thai, Chinese, and other cuisines, which were always jammed, and street vendors selling all sorts of interesting local delicacies as well. But if you had to say what Hat-Yai's greatest attraction was, it was the women. They were what really kept the immigration officials simmering down at the border crossing in Pedang Besar - that steady stream of lechers pouring in from Thailand's southern neighbors, Malaysia and Singapore.

Most of the women came down from Chiang Mai and Chiang Rai to reap the benefits of being so close to the Malaysian border. As a Muslim country, and a fairly strict one by Asian standards, Malaysia was an old prude compared to its seductive neighbor to the north. It was inevitable then that their Malaysian and Singaporean patrons would choose to spend their weekends and their money in Hat-Yai, only 43 kilometers north of the Malaysian border. The beautiful northern Thai women, famous for their delicate skin, were simply too enticing to resist.

I got to know Hat-Yai through a Thai man I had become good friends with by the name of Komon, who had worked for the American embassy in Bangkok for more than ten years. I was introduced to him by one of the doctors at the hospital, who thought it would be good for me to know him as he spoke English well and was an unusual character.

"I am a native of Hat-Yai, and I know it inside out. I am on very good terms with many of the more influential and wealthy citizens of the town. I enjoy, perhaps, a certain notoriety based on 'friendships' I have with the American embassy, and hence the uppermost echelons of the Thai government in Bangkok." He had an almost British sophistication in manner and language, unusual for a Thai.

Thailand, like so many developing countries, was a nation where contacts were absolutely essential to getting things done, and any advantage that could be obtained on the basis of a simple phone call or a tap on the shoulder was worth paying for. Komon seemed to be a highly sought after individual who enjoyed certain privileges based on his discrete but formidable connections. No matter where we went or which club or restaurant we ate at, everyone seemed to know him, including the proprietors, who often came out personally to greet him.

"Richard, I will take you to the 'Hawaiian Club,' my favorite place for a drink," he said one evening. We drove over. It was a vast, dimly lit hall, with a large stage in the center surrounded by individual tables. The place was seething with Thai, Chinese, and Malaysians nursing cocktails, dangling cigarettes from their lips, clouds of smoke forming overhead.

"They are here for the main event of the night, when the 'Nightingale from the North,' as she is known, Linda Supranee, takes the stage," he said as we took our place at one of the main tables escorted, as was typical, by the owner of the establishment. "She will come on at 10 PM."

As predicted, the hall darkened, the stage lit up, and the soft sound of footsteps was heard. A beautiful Thai woman with long black hair appeared. She wai'd the audience, greeting them in her soft, breathy northern voice, her face strikingly radiant. She positioned herself before the microphone and with no further words or introductions began singing love ballads from Chiang Mai. There was something about her, the way she sang, the stillness of her body, her smooth, expressionless face that held the audience rapt. Her wonderful voice seemed to emanate from some deep well of longing and filled the room with a rich, mournful sound.

"She is quite lovely," I said. Komon nodded, smiling as he observed me.

She sang for about an hour, the audience utterly mesmerized, as was I. After the applause, she politely thanked everyone and left the stage. The lights went on after several minutes, rather long I thought. "They wait until she has left the hall. No one can get close to the Nightingale," Komon said.

"I am quite taken by her, Komon," I said.

"I can see," Komon said. "She is the product of a union of a Thai prostitute from Chiang Mai and a US soldier from the Vietnam era. She never met her father and struggled, along with her mother, to make ends meet. She became a singer in Chiang Mai and moved to Hat-Yai a year ago, where she became an instant success, enjoying almost a kind of cult status. It was rumored that she had been offered a lucrative contract from a recording company in Bangkok where the offspring of mixed unions are quite popular."

"She is stunning. I wonder if I could meet her," I said. "But she is a budding young starlet on the verge of a big career. Perhaps she is inaccessible."

One night, at another performance at the Hawaiian club, after Linda had already left the stage, Komon leaned over and said he had a surprise for me. "What is it?" I asked. He didn't answer. The lights slowly came on, and Komon abruptly rose, motioning for me to follow. We both walked out of the large hall, and I followed Komon up several flights of stairs to a landing with a long hall and a single door at the end. "Ajarn," Komon said with a half smile on his face, "I've arranged something for you."

"Oh? What's that?"

"You will find out shortly."

"Great. Where do we go?"

"You have to enter that room."

"You mean that door there?" I said, pointing down the hall.

"Yes."

"Great, let's go."

"I cannot go with you."

"What are you talking about?"

"You must go alone."

"Alone?"

"Yes."

"Really?" I asked.

"Yes. This is something very special just for you. Trust me."

I looked at him, wondering what was going on. He nodded towards the door. "Go."

"Just like that," I said nervously.

Komon only smiled. "Yes. Don't worry. Just go." Nothing more. So secretive. He smiled one more time and started back down the stairs. I watched him as he descended, wondering what this wily little Thai guy was up to. He always had a cryptic quality, and although I trusted him, I never really knew what to expect. Anyway, I would find out soon enough. I walked down the corridor as he had instructed, opened the door and entered a darkened room with a single lit candle. I could barely make out a female figure sitting on a sofa.

"Please come in."

That voice! Breathy and full. It was the Nightingale. I walked in another few steps, still unsure. I knew things like this happened in Thailand, but how in heaven's name, I wondered, did Komon pull this off?

"Please come closer." I approached the sofa cautiously, without saying a word. "Sit down." I listened to her like an obedient child. She leaned over to me. "I noticed you," she said. She put her beautiful face against mine. "I wanted to meet you." I smelled her perfume. She touched my face and neck, drawing my lips to hers. We kissed. She pulled me down over her body, unbuttoning my shirt. Her lips and mouth merged with mine. I felt warm, intoxicated with this lovely body in my arms. I didn't know how it had come about or what the consequences would be, but I was no longer concerned. I surrendered myself to the darkness of the night and the subtle power of my enchantress.

I awoke at 1 AM and reached for Linda. She was gone. I switched on the light, and looked around. No one there. "Linda." I called. No answer. I checked my wallet and other valuables. Nothing was missing. I put my clothes on and walked out of the room and ran down several flights of stairs to the Hawaiian Club. It was dark and empty. An old Thai janitor was sweeping up. The night had been strange all along, but now it was getting just a little bit peculiar.

I ran across the street to another club I remembered seeing her sing at once, called the "Planet." As soon as I entered the door, a young voluptuous Thai waitress bumped into me asking, "What would you like to drink, sir?" I moved past her and into the main hall. The place was a zoo, packed with drunken Singaporeans. There was loud disco music, red and yellow strobe lights, and the smell of beer, whiskey, and sweaty males pressed tightly together. On the large center stage, a crowd of young Thai women with long blue satin robes strutted about, smiling seductively, giving everyone a good look at their pretty faces. On the last pass around the front of the stage, the women all simultaneously opened up their robes, exposing their naked, white breasts. A parade of exquisite pairs of breasts now bounced wildly around on stage to the utter delight of the crowd. The ladies swaggered around, licking their lips, teasing and cooing like cats in heat, shaking and grasping their breasts, pumping their thighs, oozing with hot sensuality. The crowd was delirious, yelling, pounding their drinks on the tables, throwing money at the ladies, drenching themselves with pitchers of beer, begging for mercy. Another woman, the Madame, waiting for just the right moment when the place seemed like it was going to burst, stepped out onto the stage, confronting the screaming audience. I could barely hear her over the howls. She held a microphone in one hand and her arm around one of the half naked beauties. She tried to quiet the mob down, speaking louder. I couldn't tell what she was saying at first, but then I heard her ask, "How much for this lovely girl?" The crowd went nuts.

"One thousand baht," someone screamed.

"Twelve hundred baht." Another man countered.

"Two thousand baht." The bidding was getting expensive. The Thai kitten on the auction block was attractive, and the boys were excited.

"Twenty two hundred baht," another voice rang out, "that's as high as I'll go." It was a fat Chinese man who slammed his bottle on the table. "No one will beat my offer." He stood, half drunk and looked around defiantly. The entire hall, almost magically, became silent. Even the hot numbers up on stage stopped gyrating long enough to have a look at the short fat man.

"I want this woman, and I will take her," he yelled.

No one budged. A friend of his, sitting at the same table, suddenly stood up behind him and poured a large pitcher of beer over his bald head. The crowd roared.

"That's too much," another man said, laughing, almost choking to death.

"Take her, she's yours."

The overweight man wiped the beer from his face, adjusted his pants, and walked up to the stage, smiling and rubbing his hands together, like a glutton before a feast. He took the girl's hand, and they walked off the stage together, a chorus of screams and catcalls following them. The bidding continued for the remaining ladies.

I looked for Linda, but she was nowhere to be found. I returned home. The next evening I got together with Komon and asked him about Linda. Not a word. He acted as if nothing happened. I pressed him further about the weird events of the past night. He gave me his enigmatic half smile and told me he didn't know what I was talking about. I returned to the Hawaiian Club. Linda, I was told, had returned to Chiang Mai and was no longer employed there. I began wondering if it had all been a dream. Did I ever really meet her? The days and weeks passed. My work at the University absorbed me.

In time, she, and that whole night, became part of the sometimes freakish, even illusory weave of my experience in Thailand. I thought about her, but it finally stopped mattering. It was part of life in the Kingdom of Siam.

One morning, I came to the hospital, and found Dr. Sumet, the faculty, residents and a large contingency of medical students standing around the bed of a patient. The patient was sitting up, cross-legged, in the middle of this large audience, an oddly expectant look on his face. The medical students had formed a line in preparation for examining him, and one by one stepped up, with tongue blade and penlight in hand, to look inside his mouth. After the dozen or so medical students completed their inspections, the residents, the next layer in the medical hierarchy, approached. They too wielded the essential sacraments of light and blade and carried out their brief exams. The faculty then followed them. All told, some 25 doctors and students had paid homage to this patient's mouth.

It was another Tuesday morning, and we were engaged in the timeless academic tradition performed in all teaching institutions around the world, known as Grand Rounds. Once a week the medical faculty, along with the residents, students and nurses, assembled and moved from patient to patient to discuss their management and progress. The chairman of the department generally led the entourage while the residents "presented" each patient, describing the pertinent historical and physical features of the patient's disease. Everyone then examined the patient. Afterwards, the chairman probed with incisive questions, encouraging the doctors to render up like small jewels, their suggestions for the care of the patient.

Mr. Boonserm, the first patient, sat up in bed, smiling at the numerous faces circling him. He was 62 years old, but appeared younger. In fact, he seemed quite robust. His reason for being here was discovered when he opened his mouth. By shifting his tongue over to the side, a cancer could be seen sitting resting on the floor of his mouth. In comparison with other cancers seen here, it was not particularly large, measuring about three centimeters. In fact it appeared readily curable, a pleasing change from the usual cases. On further examination, a small solitary lymph node was felt on the side of his neck, indicating that the cancer may have spread. Despite this, Mr. Boonserm stood a reasonable, even good chance for cure. The discussion that ensues is not one of whether to operate or not, for this case is highly operable and surgery should be done. The discussion focused more on the finer points of the operation, such as how much of the jawbone needed to be removed and how best to carry out the reconstruction.

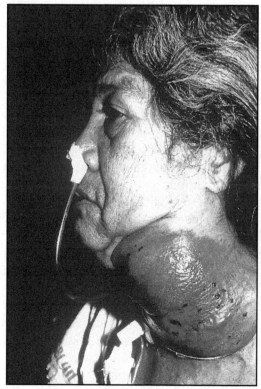

Large Neck Cancer

"It is superficial, I think we can spare the bone," Dr. Prasad said.

"But it is best not to take a chance," Dr. Vitoon countered. "We should remove the superior part of the jaw to be certain all the tumor is excised."

"It has spread into the neck already, the entire bone must be removed. We can reconstruct it," Dr. Sumet puffed.

Ideas regarding reconstruction were parried about. The patient sat on his bed, offering only a Delphic smile in the face of this multitude of suggestions regarding the fate of his jaw. We would operate on Mr. Boonserm tomorrow, and specific decisions regarding reconstruction would be decided during surgery. A resident stayed behind to discuss with the patient our plans while the rest of the team migrated over to the next bed.

The following morning, I passed Dr. Vitoon and inquired about the time of Mr. Boonserm's surgery. Vitoon, even in a land known for smiling, was notable for an unusually jolly manner. He had a characteristic high-pitched laugh that seemed to greet almost every encounter or situation no matter how grim. Not to be disappointed, Vitoon responded to my inquiry with his usual smile and high-pitched laugh. He then casually informed me that the patient had cancelled the surgery. He would have nothing to do with it. I was amazed. "What did he say?" I asked, wondering why on earth the patient wouldn't want his cancer treated.

"He didn't want to," Vitoon replied simply.

"Does he know that he has an excellent chance for cure?" I inquired.

"I explained that to him."

"He knows that by delaying his chances for survival go down."

"Yes, he understands that."

"Well, why did he refuse surgery?"

As Vitoon explained, our erstwhile patient had a different view of the natural order of things, recognizing that his own life, or death, did not figure prominently in the overall scheme of things. Rather, he grasped intuitively that regardless of whose universe you believed in, Einstein's or Buddha's, the immutable reality of this existence remained the same: our precious lives amounted to no more than cosmic dust in the slowly shifting and indifferent eye of the universe. There was no expectation of grandstand efforts to delay the final curtain; certainly nothing so splashy as a major operation that involved, for one thing, removing part of his jaw. As Vitoon explained his conversation with him, Mr. Boonserm would not be swayed.

"But the tumor will continue to grow and spread. Right now it is small. If we operate now we have a chance," Vitoon said.

"I understand," replied Mr. Boonserm.

"Then you'll have the surgery?"

"No."

"In a few months the tumor will be too big to operate on. You will not be able to eat, you won't be able to swallow your own saliva."

"I understand."

"When you return to see us we will not be able to help you. We will have no chance to cure you."

"I understand."

"It will be uncomfortable for you," Vitoon implored.

"I understand."

"Do you understand that you will die?" Vitoon finally exclaimed with some measure of exasperation. Mr. Boonserm smiled back knowingly, "I will die anyway. Whether you operate or not. So will you. So will everyone."

The inescapable logic of the patient cut short Vitoon's argument with surgical precision. The discussion was over before it started. Not that you had to explain very much to this simple farmer. He already knew that it was the local spirit powers that controlled his day-to-day existence, while the Lord Buddha and the karmic wheel of law judged the specifics of his transmigration from this life to the next. Each morning, like so many Thai throughout the country, Mr. Boonserm would bring incense, water, and other offerings to his "spirit house" to pay homage to the spirit overlord of his modest bamboo hut. He also paid respect to the spirit overseer of his rice field by making similar offerings. This of course did not inhibit his activity in the local temple, where he made frequent pilgrimages to worship the Buddha. The noble truths of the Buddha were sufficient for Mr. Boonserm.

The next morning, Vitoon and I were checking some of the patients on the wards. We passed Mr. Boonserm's empty bed. Vitoon smiled and shrugged his shoulders. It was tough for one Buddhist to find fault in the intensely Buddhist logic of our former patient. Vitoon, as surgeon, could certainly dispute it and made every effort to do so, but once the patient had locked in on his decision there was little to say or do beyond appreciating his keenly Thai attitude.

Anyone familiar with the natural course of head and neck cancer and the agony it can inflict would pale at the thought of leaving a highly curable cancer untended. Still, this was Thailand and although the majority of patients were willing to accept treatment, there were many who refused intervention on grounds not unlike our patient's. As much as I was disturbed at this patient's future course, I still respected his decision. I did not advocate or recommend it mind you, only that I appreciated the otherworldly wisdom it reflected.

It was also a reminder to surgeons that despite our elevated, "priestly" status in society, we still lived on this side of the rainbow. No matter the advanced equipment or sophisticated surgical technique we employed, there would always be those individuals who were less than impressed, patients who still opted to supervise the fate of their own bodies. Cutting on human flesh could be something of an intoxicant, with powerful mind altering, ego-enhancing effects. Among the quick acting antidotes were patients who refused what you, the surgeon-priest, had to offer. Whether the patient's decision was the correct one medically was not the issue. The verdict on that question was clear. Rather, it was that he did what was consistent with his own beliefs and worldview. He was not confused or delirious at the time of his decision. He was as composed as an azalea in spring.

Chapter 26

Several months into my stay in Hat-Yai, as I was leaving the hospital one afternoon, I passed a small group of nurses, who were heading with me towards the exit. I nodded and said hello, and they all politely returned my greeting. As I walked past the parking lot, one of them, very petite and pretty, came up from behind, riding on a little yellow motor scooter. She motioned with her hand towards the back seat of her scooter and smiled, offering me a ride back to my apartment. We pulled up shortly to my flat, where I got off. She introduced herself as Ying, seemed to speak English fairly well, and was quite lovely in a typical Thai sort of way. She mentioned that she would be happy to show me around Hat-Yai or be of assistance during my stay here. We agreed to have dinner together the next day. I waved to her and watched her ride off and then turned to walk up to my apartment. It would be a pleasant change to have some company for dinner, I thought, and she was attractive. I entered my flat, and, other than those fairly generic sentiments, did not attribute any particular significance to this chance encounter.

The next evening Ying appeared downstairs on her scooter. Thai women were the only women I knew who managed to look feminine even while riding motorbikes. She wore blue slacks, a white cotton shirt, and her hair, which had been bundled up and tucked under her nursing bonnet when we first met, could be seen now in all its oriental splendor. It was long, straight and jet-black and rolled gently over her shoulders down to her lower back. She was beautiful. We rode on my motorcycle to a favorite restaurant she recommended called "The Can," an upscale American style place right next to the main mosque in town. The loudspeakers could be heard from the minaret calling the faithful to evening prayer as we pulled up. Inside the restaurant, Ying seemed to know everyone, smiling and chatting with friends and doctors who sat at different tables. We ordered some American style food and engaged in pleasant conversation. She was an intelligent young woman and, although still very much "Thai," possessed a good deal more confidence and curiosity about the world than most Thai women I had met. When the bill came, Ying immediately grabbed it from my hand and paid it, despite my protests. She was an unusual woman, I thought.

Three months later, I found myself kneeling with Ying on a dirt floor inside the enclave of a temple before an aging, almost skeletal Buddhist monk, as he splashed water from a ceremonial bowl upon us in blessing, delivering a sermon urging us to stay together forever. I watched the old monk in his brilliant orange robes as he spoke to us, eyes closed, absorbed in his own meditation. He seemed attuned, even as he spoke, to the subtle modulations of his own psyche and body. We kneeled for nearly an hour, mesmerized by his voice, the soft monotone of his Pali chant. As I listened to him, I reflected on the string of events that had brought me to this moment. When he finished speaking, he sprayed water upon us once more in blessing. I was now a married man and considered this nothing short of a miracle.

Blessed at a Buddhist Temple

When I first met Ying, marriage was the furthest thought from my mind. I had never wanted to get married. This voyage of mine was a solo journey. I sought only to devote myself to my work. But Ying had other plans. She was dogged. She met me every day after work. We talked and had dinner. One thing led to another. We became intimate. This was dangerous. You did not do this with a "good" Thai girl, unless you were going to marry. For that reason, I did not pursue it. She did. I wanted to avoid it. Perhaps it was part of her plan to ensnare me. Or simply the passion of the moment. But now there was trouble.

"You know that I cannot get married," I told her one evening over dinner. "I am a loner. I am already married - to my work."

The words hurt her. She appeared ready to cry. Instead she said, "You will marry me. There is nothing you can do. It is no longer up to you."

"I can get on my motorcycle and disappear," I said. "Travel as I always have, alone. The same as I arrived here."

"Do not be so sure. You do not know the power of Thai culture and family honor and karma. You will not leave. You are trapped and have no choice. You will marry me, and we will continue your journey together as husband and wife."

I looked at her, not sure if I should take her seriously. I smiled at her intensity. "I appreciate your culture, but I will do what I want."

The next day Ying asked me to accompany her to visit her family in Songkla, a 45-minute drive from Hat-Yai. I had met some of her immediate family before in Songkla, including her oldest sister *Sunee* and her mother, *'Khun Mae,'* as all Thai referred to mothers, *"Khun"* being an honorific, *"Mae"* meaning mother. She had two other sisters and a brother whom I had not met. Their father had passed away recently but was a big shot in his day. He had power and influence. Their house was a four-story building. They were prosperous. That was part of Ying's purpose in bringing me to Songkla. To display the family wealth, high standing, and background. The mother and Sunee fed me and were very gracious.

Ying's family, the *Mattanyukuls*, had a big fishing business. They owned four large seaworthy vessels that plied the oceans and brought back immense, lucrative hauls. More than fifty Thai worked for them, mainly on the boats. The only son of the family, *Surat*, oversaw the vessels and went out to sea with them, but it was Ying's mother, *Khun Mae*, a diminutive lady with an iron will, that managed everything. There were aunts, uncles, cousins, nieces, nephews, and in-laws who were involved in the family enterprise and lived nearby.

The drive over to Songkla was insane. Ying drove at dangerous speeds and recklessly passed other vehicles in the curving, 2-lane road. She seemed intent on getting us killed, a form of suicide I thought given her distraught state of mind. "What are you doing," I said, looking at her.

"Are you afraid of dying?" she asked almost demonically.

She passed a vehicle with a big truck fast approaching. "Holy Crap," I shouted. "Are you nuts!" I ducked under the console to avoid what I thought was a certain head-on collision. Ying swerved at the last moment, averting catastrophe. She looked at me contemptuously. "You are afraid to die," she said.

We arrived and entered the home of one of her cousins. There were dozens of family members. It was not a friendly reception. Ying was crying. Everyone was somber. There were no formalities.

"Will you marry Ying?" an older cousin demanded with a gravely voice.

"What?

"Will you marry my cousin?"

"No, I will not. I will not be forced to marry anyone."

"You must marry Ying. It is Thai culture, not American style."

"I am a visiting surgeon from America. I respect Thai culture but I am not bound by it."

"You must honor Ying and our family and culture. You must marry her."

"You see, he is not one of us," Ying said, crying. "He does not understand our ways."

Ying's family was not happy. However reasonable my comments may have seemed to Western ears, they were not well received here.

Her brother Surat entered the room. A surly looking character accompanied him.

"You will not marry my sister?" he asked.

"No."

The family grew agitated, but Surat remained calm. He shrugged his shoulders as if to say no problem. He looked at his compatriot who nodded. "I'll take you home."

"I am sorry," I said to everyone as we left.

Ying and I sat in the back of Surat's car. He and his 'associate' sat in the front. There was a third man driving. Three people to take me home. I also noticed we were not traveling in the direction of Hat-Yai.

"I want to ask you again," Surat said courteously, "will you marry my sister?"

"No."

He shrugged his shoulder again. He murmured something to the driver in Thai. I thought I heard something along the line of "I'll do it myself." Not auspicious. Ying was crying, sitting apart from me by the window. Oddly, she wore her nurse's garb. They drove off to a side road. Surat was talking to himself, nodding, even smiling. He felt for something in his pocket. I looked at the driver who was whistling, staring straight ahead. We passed from the paved road to a gravel road and then a dirt road with dense foliage on each side. The car came to a stop.

"Ajarn, you understand that Thai culture and family are different than in America. It is very serious for us," Surat said.

"I respect your culture," I said.

"That is good. Then you understand that you must marry my sister."

I looked around. We were surrounded by jungle. Three ornery looking gentlemen were sitting in the front of the car, all of whom I suspected were armed. One was Ying's older brother who had probably protected her since childhood and still saw her as his baby sister who was being mistreated by a *farang*. She was sitting on the side, bawling hysterically. There was no one around us. No traffic at all. The *Mattanyukul* family was a proud and powerful 'Chinese' family in the area with many connections. They could not lose face. I noticed Surat again feeling for something in his pocket. In a somewhat lawless land and with a big operation like theirs, they had probably committed their share of crime including when necessary murder, all hush-hush and with the acceptance of local officials and police whom they paid off.

"What is your decision, ajarn?"

I thought about my life, my mother and brothers back in the Bronx, the neighborhood, the drugs, the violence, and craziness, medical school, my residency and fellowship, passing my boards, and then coming out to Asia. There were pitfalls and hurdles in life, unexpected developments and disasters that arose without rhyme or reason all the time. I did not realize what I was getting into when I agreed to have Ying drive me on her little motor scooter a couple of months ago, or to have dinner with her later, and allow the relationship to develop. But at this point, none of that mattered. I realized that Ying was right last night at dinner. She knew all along. I had no choice.

"I would be delighted to marry your beautiful sister," I answered smiling.

"Thank you, ajarn," Surat said. He bowed and wai'd me. The other two wai'd me as well. Ying continued crying, oblivious to the deal just struck, feeling shame, no doubt, that she had brought dishonor to the family.

These were not optimal conditions for such a decision, I realized, to say the least. I had rebelled against it. It clashed with fundamental beliefs I held regarding freedom and autonomy. I worried it would compromise my mission and journey and whether she was the right companion for me. I did not understand the hidden forces that brought me to this point. Perhaps, it was only the steely determination of a small but tenacious Thai woman to get her man and the power of 'Thai culture' and 'family honor' that she and her family had repeatedly invoked. Or the laws of karma. Or the will of God.

I had avoided marriage for almost 35 years. If Ying had not forced my hand, I may never have. I remembered the women in my past that had wanted to marry with the same ardor as Ying, but only Ying had summoned the will and external pressures needed to make it happen. She knew what she wanted and got it. She was ruthless. At the outset of our courtship, I would have considered it impossible so intent was I in remaining a bachelor. But ultimately I was forced to surrender. I reflected on her resolve and determination. They would be assets in a chaotic life like mine. I knew that problems were likely to arise between us. I would also not forget that whatever philosophical slant I gave to it, in the end she trapped me. But my road show would continue, which I considered paramount. I was devoted foremost to this, my voyage of healing.

Married

Ying and I would travel now to countries where work conditions would be very different from what I had known in Thailand. I would come to depend on her, both in and out of the operating room. Between visits to different hospitals, while traveling from place to place, country-to-country, she showed herself to be shrewd, tough, and an excellent judge of people's motives and character. On several occasions, she saved my life.

IV. On The Road

Chapter 27

June 3, 1989

Ying and I motorcycled down the coastal route that first day, heading for the border of Malaysia. We were going to travel for a while before my next surgical assignment. I wanted to see the southern edge of Thailand, ride into Malaysia, Singapore, and then over to Indonesia. We had two bags between us, small travel bags that I strapped to the rear of the motorcycle. We left Songkla, in a cloud of mystery. My colleagues in Hat-Yai were baffled by the sudden turn of events. My marriage to Ying was known by just a few. But the rumors had spread. The circumstances surrounding it were chaotic. Our relationship was not good. I also had to maintain my focus on my work. This was still my purpose and mission. I remained committed to practicing medicine in the Third World with its inevitable challenges and hurdles. I intended to pursue medical opportunities while on the road to see where I could be of service on this part of the journey.

We motored down through Yala. Ying was worried. She feared the south of Thailand beyond Songkla.

"It is not safe," she warned. "You are a *farang* and have no understanding of our problems. The western press does not cover it. The world ignores us," she said with anguish.

The four southern provinces of Thailand, which included Pattani, Yala, Narathiwat, and Sungai Kolok, were Muslim majority. There had been a decades long history of poor relations between the Thai Muslims and Buddhists that you rarely heard of in the West focused as it was on Israel and the Middle East. There had been assassinations, bombings and other terrorist attacks by Muslim separatists seeking independence from the Buddhist kingdom. They sought to either join with Malaysia to the south, a Muslim nation, or to form an autonomous Muslim principality. Where Songkla and Hat-Yai were roughly 80% Buddhist and 20% Muslim, in the southern provinces, south of Songkla, the ratios were reversed. There had also been a steady stream of Buddhists emigrating from the region as well, often selling long-held properties at liquidation prices to escape the intimidation and risk – a tactic used by local Muslims to acquire valuable real estate while emptying the area of non-Muslims.

"My cousin," Ying said, "sold her home and business. She was frightened of the threats and fled, like so many others."

The scheme was not unique to the region.

On the way, we stopped at a police post to ask for directions. Ying knew I was intent on continuing. She hoped that a word from the police might sway me. After getting directions, I heard her ask in Thai if it was safe to travel through the south. I watched the policeman's eyes open wide. He shook his head rapidly back and forth while pursing his lips, a Thai gesture that meant not to even consider it. He looked at me as if I were a lunatic.

"It is not safe," he warned in Thai.

"Thank you," I said, and we continued on our way.

Ying was terrified.

"We'll be alright," I reassured her. "I have done this."

I had motorcycled through the south when I renewed my visa for Thailand in Malaysia. I had ventured through the heart of Muslim Thailand and survived. The 140-kilometer stretch between Yala and Betong on the Malaysian border was the most remote area I had ever seen in Thailand, with curving, winding roads and numerous blind turns that would have been perfect set-ups for a takedown and kidnapping, or worse, for a lone traveler like myself. It wasn't only Muslim fanatics, who had done their share of kidnapping, bombing, and other bits of nastiness to innocents but Malaysian Communists. The Communist Party of Malaysia, a Maoist clique, was said to have their secret headquarters here and I could understand why as isolated as it was.

Despite the vast sense of isolation, the scenery through Yala was spectacular. There were rivers, lakes, streams, with verdant meadows and tall grasses, and all to myself. It was heaven. It may have been that no one was there because they were afraid and perhaps they were right to be, but I had survived it and relished the memory as one of my most beautiful excursions.

On that previous journey, I had crossed the border into Malaysia and reached the island of Penang, situated off the northwest coast of the country. I rode to the teeming metropolis of Georgetown where I arranged my one-year visa. I returned to southern Thailand, taking the same route through the border town of Betong, then up through Yala where I met no one again, enjoying the same amazing views and scenery as I had coming down, finally making it back unscathed to Hat Yai. It seemed okay, so I did not hesitate.

Perhaps it was foolhardy. But Ying had grown up with terrorism in her backyard. She had lived through it.

"When I was a kid," she had told me, "they bombed the schools, movie theaters, and markets. They killed many innocent people and frightened the rest of us. They created much fear and terror, and many Thai moved away, including my cousin. Then they took the properties and homes for almost nothing."

Many in the West never heard of this. The press ignored it, because it didn't involve Israel or the US. I didn't question her. I just went anyway and trusted that it would be all right. But this time I took a different route in deference to Ying's concerns.

"I'm not going through the mountains and the more remote areas," I said. "This will be in more populated regions along the coast."

I knew she was still worried.

From Hat-Yai we rode down route 42 and then 49 to Yala City but we would not continue down to Betong with those curvy, windy roads in the isolated hinterlands, which definitely would have freaked her out. Instead, we rode towards the coastal route to Narathiwat. It was another view, albeit less secluded, but ultimately easier on Ying.

Yala was the first of the Muslim or "Malaysian" towns we would pass through. It was the most prosperous of the four southern provinces based in part on rubber production. It was a clean city with wide boulevards, parks, and less frenzied traffic. There was an imposing mosque, the tallest building in Yala and the largest mosque in Thailand that towered over the city. We stopped by the *Lak Muang*, the shrine of the patron spirit of the town, worship of which could be traced to Brahmin influence. Most of the inhabitants within the capitol were Chinese. The Muslims tended to live in the rural areas of the province, but there was a Muslim quarter by the railroad station near the mosque. We could tell by the sheep and goats wandering through the streets, both animals staples of the *hallal* (Muslim) diet. Just outside of town, we visited the Wat Khuhaphimuk or Cave Temple with a long reclining Buddha, some 1200 years old, one of the most revered Buddha images in the south.

"I am glad the Buddha has survived here," Ying said. "This is very famous. I always wanted to see it."

"Why didn't you come before?"

"We don't go to the south."

"Because of the Muslim threat?"

"Yes."

There were other stalactite caves in the limestone outcroppings that dotted the landscape with dozens of Buddha images that we visited. A little further up the road, we stopped at the *Tham Silpa*, a cave with murals from the Srivijaya era, probably the oldest of their kind in Thailand. "Srivijaya" was an influential city-state based in Sumatra, Indonesia that was important in the spread of Buddhism from the eighth to twelfth centuries.

We ate at a local restaurant. "How are you?" I asked Ying.

"Okay."

"I know you are still nervous."

"Yes."

"We'll be alright."

We drove through Pattani, the provincial capitol, with its busy port and sailing vessels and fishermen. The smaller boats were wooden and beautifully decorated with elaborate and colorful paintings of Singha Lions, the Payanak Sea Serpent, and the Garuda (a mythical bird and vehicle of the Hindu God Vishnu and the symbol of the Thai kingdom). I didn't expect to see such images on the boats of predominately Muslim fishermen, but this was a cross-cultural region, where Thai Buddhism encountered Malay Islam.

"Who would have imagined this?" I said. The two religions coexisting peacefully, at least in the realm of boat art. I'm impressed."

"It means nothing."

"But it is forbidden for Muslims to have images. Like the Jews. Yet, here the images are out in the open."

"It is for gullible tourists. Don't be fooled."

The southern Thai, mostly Muslim, seemed darker skinned, especially the fishermen, baking in the sun all day as they did. They were rail thin, lean, and sinewy, and did not greet us with a smile but something that resembled more a glare. It was a busy port, mostly fishing boats with men hauling, lifting, and guiding boats in and out of dock, a scene of vigorous activity. A salty sea smell wafted in from the Gulf of Thailand.

"I grew up with this," Ying said, reminding me that her family was in the fishing business and owned four large fishing vessels based in the port at Songkla. "My mother ran the business," she said. "She never rested. She had to get up early in the morning to get the boats ready and then wait up late at night for the boats to come in. She divided up the fish, put them in ice and sold them. We did well but she worked so hard."

"Still going well?" I asked.

"No, we have had a disaster. We lost the four boats to the Malaysian Navy. They claimed we were in their waters and sunk them. We asked the Thai government to help us, but they are useless."

"They blew them up?"

"Yes," she said. "It was not our fault. We were in international waters. We have been fishing those same waters for years."

"My God! That's terrible."

"The family is still recovering from these losses. We still communicate with the Thai government. I did not tell you. I didn't want to burden you with my family's problems."

"Can you get your money back?"

"No. The Thai government will not fight with Malaysia over our small business."

I knew nothing of this. I could understand that she would want to hide it from me. I could also understand, given the loss and stress, how her brother Surat and his henchmen were ready to take me out that day in Songkla.

We continued exploring.

Pattani had been the center of an independent principality that included Yala and Narathiwat, hence the urge by some in the south to regain their former autonomy. We found the main mosque in town, Thailand's second largest, an open-air facility of olive tint. We listened to the call to prayer by the muezzin through the loudspeakers of the minarets, something I found jarring in this Buddhist land. But then we were in the south.

We continued on to Narathiwat about 100 kilometers from Pattani on the coastal road. It was a pleasant and soothing ride with sand-strewn beaches and clear emerald waters. The air was fresh and bracing as we wound our way down the lightly trafficked seaside road. I looked back at Ying. She appeared at ease. I saw her smile at me in my rearview mirror. She leaned her head against mine, our two motorcycle helmets clunking romantically. She said over the roar of the motorcycle, "It is beautiful, Rick, thank you." And I winked at her through the mirror.

We arrived in Narathiwat, a lovely, peaceful city by the sea. On the way in, we stopped at a Thai Muslim fishing village with the ornately painted fishing boats seen in Songkla and Pattani. We rode down to a long sandy beach just south of town to eat. We found a seafood restaurant with a table, umbrella, and wooden lounge chairs on the beach. Windsurfers at sea were taking advantage of the gusts. We stayed in an old Chinese hotel, the *Cathay*, on the waterfront, peaceful, breezy, and cheap, about four bucks for the night.

The next morning we continued south and stopped at Khao Kong to see the giant bronze Buddha, called Phra Phuttha Taksin Mingmongkon. At 25 meters, it was the tallest seated Buddha image in Thailand and visible for miles.

"I've been wanting to see this," I said. "I have heard about it since coming to Songkla almost a year ago."

"You see what you have been missing going through the mountains?" Ying said, smiling, changing her tune. "This route is safer – and very beautiful."

I photographed Ying standing next to the monument. It dwarfed her. I watched her wai it, get on her knees and bring her forehead to the floor, the highest expression of respect. Stark, golden, and majestic, the towering Buddha gazed serenely over the hills and fields surrounding it.

"It reminds me of the great Buddha at Todai-ji in Nara, Japan, the largest bronze Buddha in the world. I visited it as a medical student while studying in Kyoto," I said.

"I would like to see that someday."

"I still wonder how this massive statue sits with local Muslims."

We rode south to Tak Bai.

I had been with Ying for several months including our "courtship" before marriage. We had gone on weekend road trips and had become something of an item before things began to deteriorate. But this was different. This *was* the journey, my journey begun almost 2 years ago. Except now she was with me. I didn't mind having her, but I recognized that it would not be the same. I would of necessity close myself off to certain experiences, mainly having to do with the opposite sex. But in other ways as well. The mind and attitude of an unshackled brigand like myself changed biochemically when accompanied by another. An invisible shield formed that deflected outside influences and interactions. I was not sure I liked it. I had also been unsuccessful in arranging work or an appointment at a hospital or university on this southern sojourn, which disturbed me. What was I doing? What was my purpose now as a husband - and as a surgeon? Vacation? Traveling like any other tourist? Who was I healing on this little slog? The whole dynamic of my journey had changed. I was troubled by it.

"I hope we can arrange surgery somewhere," I said.

"We can check in Malaysia or Singapore."

"Yeah. Maybe Kuala Lumpur. I have a contact."

We never discussed the events surrounding our marriage. She and her family worried. Her brother and cronies could do nothing to me once out of the country. I was not about to ditch her. At worst, I could give her money to return without me. But I suspected she would kill herself rather than return home alone. Family honor and shame dictated that. Our journey together was based on trust. Would I do the right thing? I could easily leave her and go on my way, traveling alone as I always had. Ying had already broken the rules by getting involved with me in the first place. And now this journey too, even though we were married, was bizarre by Thai standards. For a daughter of an established and conservative family like the Mattanyukuls to marry a *farang*, hop on a motorcycle, and disappear for months was radical. Yes, Ying had broken many taboos. Her sister Sunee called me before we left.

"Please take care of my sister, Rick," she said crying, almost hysterical. "Our family worries so much."

"I will," I said.

"She is so foolish, Rick. She doesn't understand the ways of the *farang*."

"That is true."

"She should stick to our ways. They are safe. Thai women are very sensitive. They cannot give their bodies without marriage. They will kill themselves if they are rejected. We have a method for the man and woman to join together. It is slow and deliberate, so there are no mistakes. The emotions and feelings are too strong. We chaperone for two years before the man and woman can be alone. And even then they can do nothing until marriage. We are very cautious."

"It makes sense."

"They must get the blessings of both families."

"I know."

"The man must ask permission from the father to take his daughter."

"It is a beautiful custom."

"We must know that they are right for each other, so there are no mistakes. And we must know they are committed to marriage, of taking care of each other, and having children."

"Yes."

"Our way is measured and careful, but good. It is much better for everyone in the long run. For the man, woman, and children. Many Thai still have arranged marriages."

"I know."

"It is a good way. We have no divorce in Thailand. Not like America. But Western ideas have spread to Thailand and have brought problems. Now look how much suffering she has caused for herself, her family, and you. We worry so much about both of you. We don't blame you, but she is still our sister, our flesh and blood. We don't know what to expect. What you will do. She is at your mercy. I ask you to take care of her and not blame her. My mother and I worry about you and Ying. We pray to the Buddha to protect you, to keep you together, and to make you both happy."

"I want you to know Sunee that I did not push her into anything. I know that Thai culture is very conservative. I respect it. I know she comes from a good Thai family. I did not force her to do anything."

"I understand, Rick. I believe you. I only pray that you do not leave her or hurt her. She depends on you. She will never survive if you leave her. Or if you send her home. She will take her life. I pray that you will take care of her," she said, sobbing.

Chapter 28

We rode into Tak Bai, a dry, dusty village, 33 kilometers south of Narathiwat that pressed against the northeastern border of Malaysia and the South China Sea.

"There's nothing here."

We drove past a barbershop, a few *rang aharns* (small Thai restaurants), and a morning market.

"Watch that dog," Ying said. I braked and allowed the scruffy mutt to pass. There were all manner of cats, dogs, chickens, and goats roving about, looking for scraps, or resting on the grubby streets, flies buzzing around their heads. The heat was like a bludgeon. We skipped through the main part of town in less than a minute.

"What do people do here?" I asked.

"It is on the route to Sungai Kolok and from there into Malaysia."

"We can look around a little and continue on to Sungai Kolok."

We rode down a dirt road lined by trees on one side and the Tak Bai River on the other. It meandered on for about a kilometer before opening into a spacious temple enclave, stretching from its ample riverside border out into the surrounding fields and forests. A large *sala* (open air pavilion) rested on the river's edge. We came upon a brilliant pearl-white temple. It had the typical arched, tiered crimson roof pointing upwards like the wings of a falcon, with broad doors opening to its interior.

"I wasn't expecting this."

We parked the motorcycle, took our shoes off, and entered. Incense burned while candles flickered with breezes wafting in from the sea. A lone monk sat before the golden Buddha like a flame, adorned in orange robes. The shuttered-windows were agape allowing in the soothing sounds of birdsong. Ying went to her knees and bowed to the Buddha, touching her head to the floor three times.

We ventured out. In front of the main temple stood an ebony statue of an elderly monk in robes, standing, stooped of shoulder, with walking stick in hand. It was perched atop a white marble pedestal facing the ocean, receiving the salty sea mist drifting in. Ying read the inscription, which was written in Thai. "It is the founding monk of the *Wat*, Pra Cruopatphutta Kum."

I noticed the monk's quarters and then a large kitchen where the food was prepared and the monks ate. A short distance from the kitchen laid a grand open-air domicile built of wood and painted in splashes of white and sky blue. The saturated sky formed its background and white sand surrounded its base.

"It's like a painting," Ying said.

"We almost rode past it. How does something like this exist with so little attention?"

I admired the setting of this monastery, the magnificent southern style Thai architecture, the glistening Tak Bai River, and the princely palm trees plunging lazily to and fro. The waves bayed imperceptibly heralding the silent breezes borne of the ocean. The leaves and palms shifted subtly. The expanse of sand gradually evolved into terracotta earth, yielding to dense forest in the western horizon. There was the restful home of the abbot, the languorous, lucid sky, the immense hush of perfect quietude. Each component conferred with the other to form the hypnotic sanctuary known as Wat Chontharasinghe.

"I'm glad I followed my instinct to wander," I said.

We continued strolling through the temple when an elderly monk gestured to me from the door of the abbot's home.

"Come, come, welcome," he said.

He was portly, with a round face and deep, prominent eyes. His manner was a pleasant, fatherly mixture of dignity and authority. "I am the abbot of the monastery," he said calmly in English. Ying and I wai'd him.

We passed through the carved wooden door and ascended the stairs followed by the monk. He motioned for us to sit on the bare, wooden floor while he tucked his flowing, orange robes beneath him and sat cross-legged on the hard floor in front of us.

"Where are you from?"

"I am from America. This is my wife Ying from Songkla."

He nodded and smiled. "You are very curious about Buddhism and our temple," he said. He pointed towards the ceiling. "Look around. See the panels and delicate renderings. These are scenes from the Buddha's ministry painted within each divided ceiling square."

"Beautiful."

"Enjoy all you see. I think you appreciate it. It is a special place."

The wall interior was white and blue as outside, with a tree-bark brown floor and a golden Buddha image against the rear wall surrounded by lit candles and burning incense. A huge grandfather clock stood against a pillar marking ever so quietly the passage of time. Pictures of the King and Queen and the former abbots of the temple adorned the upper half of the side and rear walls. In the corner, a simple wooden platform with a thin foam cushion served as the abbot's bed.

"I am Pra Punjantaked-kat-na-rak. I am the ninth abbot to reside in this temple. We do not have many *farang* here, very few tourists. Even Thai people mostly pass by."

"Yes, I see. There are no other visitors, which surprises me."

"What are you doing in Thailand?"

"I am a surgeon from the US. I have been teaching here for two years."

"He is an ajarn?" he asked Ying.

"Yes," Ying said.

He nodded and smiled. "Very good."

"This place is a precious, undiscovered gem. How did it come to be in so remote an area, in the heart of Muslim Thailand?"

"It is most unlikely. In truth we should be part of Malaysia."

"Really?"

"Yes. You see, at the turn of the century the British who had already colonized Malaysia wanted to expand their empire. They looked to the four northern Malay states under Thai control, rich with rubber trees and mineral reserves. They wanted Tak Bai, then part of Kelantan, which today is the northeastern most state in Malaysia. Then, it was part of Thailand."

"I didn't realize."

"In 1909, the British acquired the four provinces of Terengganu, Kelantan, Kedah and Perlis. The British wanted to include in that the districts of Tak Bai, Sungai Kolok and Weng, which would have included this beautiful temple."

"That would have been a tragedy."

"Yes, but King Rama V negotiated with the British. He told them about this famous temple and how it would fall into disrepair and be inaccessible to the many Thai north of the territory just ceded to the British. Our King argued that it would be an irreplaceable cultural and religious loss for Thailand."

"And he was successful?"

"Yes. King Rama persuaded the British to compromise. In the end, they agreed to leave the districts of Tak Bai, Sungai Kolok, and Weng under Thai sovereignty, protecting this temple and setting the southeastern border of Thailand where it stands today."

"Incredible. I had no idea."

I was busily taking notes. The abbot looked at me.

"I want to write this up for one of the Bangkok papers, something I do from time to time. Either the Bangkok Post or the Nation. Both are English dailies. I am certain they would be interested in this story."

"Excellent. A surgeon and a writer. This may help you." He handed me some literature. He smiled and laughed congenially. "It is good to have curious visitors like you."

He looked outside. "The night has already fallen. Please stay. We will arrange your quarters. It will be comfortable for you here. And it is too late to travel."

The next morning, I arose early and saw that Ying had already gotten up. I went outside and found her walking with the monk amidst the temple grounds. I noticed that she was weeping. We sat on the *sala* overlooking the Tak Bai River, glowing in the crimson light of the burgeoning dawn, a peaceful setting for this conversation.

"I do not know how he feels about me, if he loves me," she had said to the monk. "I wonder if he will reject me later and abandon me."

I remembered my conversation with Sunee. I sensed that Ying would speak to the monk, a fatherly figure, rather than to me directly. That was part of Thai culture.

The abbot remained still, listening to her. I could see that he was sympathetic. He looked at me. "You must stay with her," he said. "You must help her and her family. Do not reject her. You understand Thai culture and the importance of marriage and family. I know you will take care of her and do what is right. It is your karma," he said.

I did not protest, wanting to keep the peace in my world and hers. "She has misgivings, which I understand. There are differences between Western and Thai culture. But I am married to her," I said.

I knew she was not assuaged. The wounds were too fresh. But there was a moment of peace at least for now. We sat silently overlooking the sea, a magnificent vision.

Later, I met the other monks of the temple visiting the abbot. They showed great deference and wai'd him respectfully. He received their wai's but looked away, as befitted his high status. After the monks had eaten, we had breakfast, as was Thai custom.

We spoke further with the monk.

"How is this island of Buddhism surviving with Islam?"

"Not well."

"No?"

"I do not know if Buddhism will survive in Tak Bai. Muslims surround us and they show no respect. They smoke by the temple and throw their cigarette butts around. Some defecate just outside the enclave to show their hatred."

"Disgusting."

"I have been spat upon and shouted at, even chased away. It is dangerous sometimes to go out for morning alms rounds with our begging bowls. There have been killings and beheadings of monks."

"It is a terrible atrocity," I said.

"Yes." He nodded. "It is difficult to be a monk here. It is not a good environment for Buddhist practice and culture, which is peaceful by nature."

Abbot, Tak Bai Temple

"Has there been violence within the temple enclave?"

"No. There would be a brisk response. But one never knows. If not for the Thai military and police presence we could not continue. I worry about preserving Thai culture and Buddhism in the south. I do not know if we will be able to maintain this magnificent house of Buddhism."

Tears formed. He gazed at the ground visibly shaken. I nodded sadly, as did Ying, who too was disquieted. "But I will never leave here," he said, his voice tremulous. "I will defend Buddhism in Tak Bai with my life if necessary."

I was surprised to see him cry since it seemed at odds with Buddhist practice, but I did not question or judge him. I understood the conflict he spoke of and how it could affect him emotionally, Buddhist monk or not. As a Jew I knew about it through Israel and the Middle East. I wasn't expecting it when I came to Thailand. Yet here it was.

When we motorcycled into Tak Bai I did not anticipate this temple by the sea, awash in white sand and ocean breezes. As we prepared to leave, the abbot saw us off. "There is a *farang* monk you must meet in Sungai Kolok, an American. He lives in the forest, not in a monastery. He speaks English and Thai. He can help you and your wife. Go see him."

We sped off on our motorcycle.

Just a kilometer beyond the river I could make out the forests and hills of Malaysia. "I am glad," I said, "your King saved this land for your country."

Chapter 29

We rode 40 kilometers from Tak Bai to Sungai Kolok. We needed to come here to cross the border into Malaysia. But I also wanted to meet the American monk. I was anxious to discuss Buddhism and Thai culture with him and, also, matters concerning my wife. I suspected Ying did as well. An American Buddhist monk in Thailand, fluent in both Thai and English, and knowledgeable of both cultures, would be an invaluable resource. Perhaps, as the abbot suggested, he could help us.

A river formed the border here between Thailand and Malaysia. The Malaysian influence was apparent. On the south side of the riverbank was the Malaysian town of Rantau Panjang. Sungai Kolok was nothing special. It boasted an excellent market, however. There was a post office and, of course, the brothels. Every town in Thailand, big and small, had brothels. But it did seem that the closer you got to the border with Malaysia the more active they were.

We were on a hunt for the *farang* monk, which is all we knew of him. We went around the town by motorcycle asking for him. Ying spoke to the locals in Thai.

"Do you know of the *farang* monk?" she asked a middle-aged man on a street corner. I wondered of the likelihood of random people just happening to know who he was.

"Oh, yes," was the immediate response, "he is a very wise man. He lives alone in the forest outside of town. But I am not sure where."

"Do you know of the farang monk?" Ying asked another person, a lady.

"Yes, Pra Uttamo is very famous, a great monk," she said.

"Do you know how to find him?"

"No, so sorry, he lives in the forest, but I don't know where."

"At least we know his name," I said to Ying.

"Uttamo is Pali for 'highest' in dhamma,'" Ying said, as we rode away.

We asked others. Nearly all knew of him and responded approvingly upon mentioning his name. But none knew where he lived or how to get there beyond stating that he lived in the forest on the outskirts of town.

"Ask a tuk-tuk driver," someone said.

We found one. "Do you know where Pra Uttamo is?" Ying asked.

"Yes, ma'am, I will take you there."

We followed behind him on our motorcycle, past the monastery, through rice fields, a small village, onto a circuitous muddy trail through dense forest and finally, just beyond an arcade of trees, to an isolated dwelling adjacent to a swamp. There, an older man greeted us. He was not bald as a typical Thai monk would be but had closely cropped hair and wore orange robes.

Ying wai'd him, bowing deeply. I bowed but not as deeply, sensing that a *farang* monk may not be as given to the formalities of Thai culture. Uttamo received our greeting without bowing. He said hello and nodded. I recognized an East Coast accent. We strolled down a wooden walkway over murky, dark waters, an everglade surrounded by lush undergrowth, tall grasses, and dense forest. There were insects everywhere on the surface of the marshy waters, grasshoppers, flies, mosquitoes flitting about, toads, lizards, and ubiquitous croaking bullfrogs. We passed a series of single room bungalows.

"These are our 'chalets,'" Uttamo said smiling, as they appeared quite basic. They were covered by vegetation. "Each house has a large ceramic vessel to catch rainwater underneath the gutter. It is the freshest water you will drink. There are cups in the ceramic pots for bathing purposes. My guests find it refreshing."

We walked atop the planks just above the dark waters below. There were small armies of termites marching diligently in line, foraging on the planks and elsewhere in this sweaty bayou. It was hot, steamy, and humid with a multitude of insects, amphibious creatures, and reptiles buzzing and darting about this archetypal jungle. Along the way, we encountered a long, thick black snake, about six feet long, that quickly slithered into the murky waters at the first sight of us.

"Don't worry," said Uttamo, "he's my friend. We've lived together here a long time." I found it a bit creepy but continued. There was an open-air pavilion or *sala* situated in the middle of this teeming swamp. We sat down on the hard wood floor overlooking luxuriant rice fields baking in the tropical sun.

Ying was distraught. She spoke in Thai. Uttamo listened.

"After being with Rick I have learned that Jewish people are selfish," she said.

Uttamo nodded and spoke also in Thai. *"Pra pen khon Jew,"* he said, which meant, "I am a Jew." And with this auspicious introduction thus began our visit with Pra Uttamo, who, I now realized, was not just a fellow American but a fellow Jew. I should have figured.

Ying did not so much as blink with this initial *faux pas*. It mattered naught. She did say *"kaw tode"* or "pardon me." But then continued. I understood she was troubled and did not take offense.

"He does not understand our culture. Thai women are not the same as *farang*. We are different," she said.

"What is upsetting you?"

"I am afraid of him."

"Has he done anything?"

"No."

"Did you agree to marry him?"

"Yes."

"What does he do?"

"He is a surgeon, an *ajarn*. I am a nurse."

"Why are you afraid?"

"He does not understand Thai culture. I don't know what he will do to me."

"Has there been any indication that he would harm you?"

"No."

"Then I would suggest Buddhist practice," he said. "These are only thoughts, moving, fleeting things. Observe them as you observe the breath."

"Will he accept me as his wife?"

"I do not know."

"What can I do?"

"Practice dhamma. Understand the nature of suffering."

Ying listened.

"There is attachment and clinging. But everything is impermanent and unsatisfactory. Practice non-attachment. Use the breath and practice Buddhism."

Ying nodded.

"There are differences in cultures," Uttamo said, "but suffering is the same."

While the abbot in Tak Bai appealed to Ying and me as a defender of Thai culture, Uttamo, the forest monk, and *farang*, engaged her suffering as a Buddhist.

"I don't know if she is assuaged by this," I said. "But I hope so. We are on a journey that I began two years ago. I have accepted her and the somewhat outlandish circumstances of our marriage. But I do want her to be at peace."

Ying looked at me and then Uttamo and wai'd us both.

"Thank you," I said to Uttamo.

He said nothing, in another world it seemed.

I noticed his features. He had a large, "Jewish" nose, lop ears, and a nasal voice. He looked and sounded like a Jew. He was tall though, about six feet, a towering height for a Jew.

"I am a Jew too," I said to Uttamo.

He smiled with this and seemed to open up.

"I was formerly known as Robert Bender, originally from New York, but I moved to California where I worked as a physicist. I left the US in 1959 when Eisenhower was still President and did not return for thirty years. I went back just a few months ago to visit my ailing mother of 86 years."

"That must have been a trip," I said.

"I was glad to see my mother. My career path has been difficult for her."

"What interested you in Buddhism?"

"I had difficulties with my love life," he said, winking at me.

"Really?"

"Yes. But I came across some old Buddhist manuscripts and saw my life in Buddhist terms. I recognized the source of my pain as my 'desire' for things. I decided to leave the conventional world. I traveled overland through Europe and North Africa and into Asia."

"That was well before the backpack overland hippy era that began in the sixties," I said.

"Yes. It was unusual for the time. I arrived in Thailand after a year on the road and decided to explore my interest in Buddhism. I was running out of money. I did not want to return to my life back in the US. And so Robert Bender ordained as a Buddhist monk in Bangkok and became Uttamo. I lived in a monastery and traveled to Burma. I studied with a monk in Rangoon. I settled in Sungai Kolok where I have been for 30 years."

"Why here?"

"It was convenient. I remained an American citizen. Crossing the border and renewing my visa was a matter of going 20 minutes to Malaysia and back."

"Still, it is an odd place," I said.

"I spent the next 28 years living here in a shack with no running water or electricity. But in the last 2 years we have upgraded with electricity, water, TV, tape cassette, washing machine, refrigerator, and air-conditioning."

"Isn't that unbecoming for a monk? How do the local Thai Buddhists feel about it?"

"They were the ones who gave it to me. I have no money. They have been very generous through the years. They worried I was getting old."

"Why don't you live in a monastery?"

"Conventional Buddhist monastic life does not reflect true Buddhism. It is more local habits and customs. I prefer to live amongst the trees, insects, and wild life in the ancient tradition of the hermit monk, supported by alms from local Buddhists."

"So you can devote yourself to inner practice."

"Yes."

"Do you have many visitors?"

"Everyday from the local Thai who provide food and items and from

Westerners living or traveling through Thailand who visit out of curiosity or to learn about Buddhism."

I too was interested in Buddhism.

"What is the purpose of Buddhist practice?" I asked.

"To end suffering," he said.

"Have you been successful?"

"No."

"How do you end suffering?"

"By insight into the nature of suffering. Suffering arises from desire. You end suffering by killing all traces of desire."

He had acquired a significant following and reputation. "I have had pilgrims from many different traditions and faiths from around the world, including practitioners of Yoga, Hindus, Christians, Muslims, Jews and of course Buddhists."

"Really?"

"Yes, but I have yet to meet a Zoroastrian."

"You could market your hermitage in the jungle."

"It markets itself, only I don't charge."

We walked into town, going back over the same path we arrived on. We strolled past the small Muslim village.

"I have had no problems with them."

"That is odd since in addition to being a Buddhist monk you are also a Jew. And you live alone in the forest. The abbot in Tak Bai told us they have had serious problems and threats."

"I have had more problems with Thai heroin addicts. There is brisk drug trafficking across the border with Malaysia. I have had break-ins in my home by addicts looking for money or to steal some of my newly acquired householder items."

"Like your toaster or TV," I said laughing.

"Yes. Since then my Thai friends have placed locks on the door."

"So now you carry keys?"

"Yes."

"For Buddhist monks in Thailand, possession of things, let alone a home with household items under lock and key would be a little outrageous. But maybe for an aging *farang* monk, and a Jew, you are eccentric and old enough to get away with it."

"It would be scandalous for the average monk."

We walked past the monastery, skirted past the rice fields, dodged the muddy trail, and arrived in town.

I had to renew my visa. Uttamo accompanied me to the border crossing where I dipped into Malaysia for a half hour, got my passbook stamped, and reentered my beloved Thailand with a ninety day extension. I met Uttamo and Ying on the other side, and we walked back into town. I could understand Uttamo's choice in locating here, considering how convenient it was.

We went to the "Cheap Food Street," as Uttamo called it. He seemed happy to have someone to chat with, let alone a fellow Jew.

"How did you come to have your enclave with home, chalets, wooden pathways, pavilion, potable water, amenities, a sanctuary and retreat?"

"The local Thai built everything for me. It exists to serve those who want to spend time with me for meditation and discussion."

We returned and sat out in the *sala*, the open-air pavilion, and watched the insects crawl by.

We slept late. I meditated, read, and napped. Later we walked into town with Uttamo for dinner. He did not mind being with us or sitting down amidst the clamor and bustle of the "Cheap Food Street."

"Generally monks are not supposed to be in such places, especially at night,"

I said. They are supposed to be in their monastery or in the forest, chanting or meditating, not amongst the lay people engaging in worldly, crass things like earning a living and eating gluttonously."

"It is unusual," Uttamo nodded.

"No one seems perturbed that you are breaking the rules for a monk. It must be your status as the elderly, wise, and eccentric *farang* monk immunized from the usual expectations," I said.

"They are used to me," he said. "And I am used to them. We get along great."

We returned to the compound. He handed me some of his writings. All were handwritten in pencil.

"Why don't you publish them?"

"I prefer to practice dhamma."

"You give answers to common questions your many visitors have asked. It would be a perfect introduction to Buddhism. You could be famous."

"They're yours if you want them. I have no interest in becoming a renowned Buddhist scholar-monk."

We returned to our "chalet." The frogs were vociferous. Eventually I slept, finding their hysterical cadences somehow soothing. Ying slept instantly as she always did no matter the circumstances, an enormous talent I was envious of.

We made alms rounds in the morning with Uttamo before dawn. We walked through the railroad station where the stationmaster greeted him with a bow and a smile, past a small grocery where the proprietor offered some fruit for Uttamo's bowl, past many town folk, who received him respectfully and provided him with food.

Uttamo with Dr. Moss

"They seem to like you," I said, an understatement since they obviously revered him.

Uttamo stood at the market where the vendors displayed exotic Thai foods, fruits, and vegetables. The local Thai filled his large black bowl. He looked towards the ground, recognizing them with a slight nod as they wai'd him, dropped food into his bowl, and stepped back to wai him again.

"I admire this part of Thai culture," I said.

Uttamo mentioned later that the same people had been giving him food for the past 30 years.

"They are my family," he said. "They have taken care of me. I have seen their children marry and have their own. I have watched them grow old and die."

I read many of his writings. Some were bizarre, in particular his notes on women. He concentrated on their bad points so as not to be seduced by their desirable qualities, a kind of mixed logic. Some of his comments were not appropriate for a monk. Still this was a common Buddhist approach as one attempted the arduous task of killing desire.

"It is like the Tibetans who reflected on death and the decomposition of the body from decaying flesh to bones to dust, a somewhat morbid way to end clinging and desire," he said.

He wrote of "self," "emptiness," the nature of nirvana, rebirth, on the bodhisattva, and Buddhist doctrinal issues with the logic and clarity of a Talmudic scholar but obviously not for Jewish purposes.

"Buddhism," he said, "is non-theistic. There is no God, no supernatural force, no self or ego either. There is only a path for attaining freedom or liberation. In the end, it is an entirely solitary enterprise. There is no 'Shakti' or 'Shekinah' or Holy Spirit or angels or God, only one's diligent pursuit of wisdom through daily practice and dhamma."

"Buddhism says nothing about the origin of the world," I said. "There is no revelation or divine inspiration."

"It is liberating to be freed of such concepts."

That night, we stayed in his compound, enjoying the sounds and the food Uttamo shared with us.

We spoke of his return to the US a few months ago. "I had not been back since 1959. It was like a time warp."

"I could imagine."

"I had concerns about returning. I worried about the culture shock after living in Sungai Kolok for three decades, and what my family and friends would think."

"Appearing with shaven head and orange robes, I'm sure, was quite exotic."

"My mother was getting old and sick. She was considering putting me back in her will. She had taken me out after I became a monk and never visited. She also contemplated cutting my sister off, as they were not getting along."

"A minefield."

"She and her husband got a psychiatrist to declare my mother senile and unfit to change her will. There was a major legal battle over the inheritance."

"Money or dhamma?"

"My sister lost."

"So we have a wealthy forest monk?"

"Now I study impermanence by observing the stock market go up and down."

We spent a week with Uttamo. A respite of reflection, meditation, reading, not to mention good jokes and good food. The next morning we were up early, packed, and ready to leave.

"You are always welcome here," Uttamo said.

I kick started my motorcycle and we were off.

Chapter 30

We crossed the border into Malaysia at Sungai Kolok into the town of Rantau Panjang on the Malaysian side and rode over to Khota Bharu, the capitol of the Malaysian state of Kelantan, nestled in the northeast corner of the peninsula. It was an Islamic bastion and hub of Malay culture. It had some museums of note and a colorful market, but we did not dally. We continued down to Kuala Terengganu and to the coastal village of Marang where we spent the night at a Chinese flophouse called the "Marang Inn."

"I felt a sense of relief in leaving Thailand," I told Ying. "I've been there almost two years and loved it, but I was ready for other lands and cultures."

It was, perhaps, my curiosity at work, but it was more. I had grown too comfortable there. I understood the language and culture, was familiar and sympathetic to the religion of Buddhism, and now even had a Thai wife. But I had not embarked on this journey to stay in one place, as lovely and hospitable as it was. I wanted also to see if I could perform medical work in one of the major cities we would be visiting. I had been unable to arrange anything in advance, although I had obtained some leads.

The Muslim call to prayer from the local mosque awoke us at 4:30 AM. We relaxed the whole day. Marang was pleasant and pretty, a quiet town on the beach. The next morning we continued on the coastal road to Rantau Abang, the famous "turtle" beach where the large leatherback turtles come to lay eggs. Then to Cherating. The place was perfect. Beautiful beach, small, budget inns right on the sand, good restaurants and bars, and a laid back, easygoing atmosphere. We stayed at the Riverside Hotel for eight ringgit or three bucks. The next morning, we left Cherating and rode 150 km past Beserah and Kuantan, heading west through the center of the country to Temerloh enroute to the capital, Kuala Lumpur. Temerloh was one of the ugliest cities I had ever seen. There were some good Chinese and Malay food joints though. I broke my two-day fruit fast, vengefully gorging on fresh baked Chinese bread and cake at one of the many Chinese bakeries, irresistible, especially after two years in Thailand with its rice based diet.

We rode the next morning 130 km to Kuala Lumpur, the capital of Malaysia. It was clean, vibrant, and dynamic. There were parks, restaurants, and elegant Islamic and modern architecture. Skyscrapers mingled with Chinese flophouses, colonial styles, and austere, brilliant curving minarets pointing to the sky. It was a workable, even beautiful blending of the traditional and the modern. It had traffic but nothing like the madness of Bangkok or even New York. We stayed in Chinatown, the main budget area, in a place called the Colonial Hotel. It was a hotbed of foreign travelers and backpackers, including from Asian countries.

"This joint is definitely on the lower end even for us," I said.

"But at least it's cheap," Ying said, "and not too bad."

I took a shower in the communal bathroom and went to the room. I noticed that the walls were open at the top so you could hear everything in the next room. Our neighbors were partying, singing, playing loud music on their radio, and it was 11PM.

"Damn," I said to myself. "It's noisy. How am I going to sleep?"

I knocked on the door.

"Shut your radio off," I said. "I can't sleep."

A youth appeared who turned out to be Nepalese. He was a sturdy, muscular man with dagger like eyes and stern countenance.

"You do not order me," he said in thickly accented English. Several of his chums appeared. They also looked surly. They surrounded me. My slightly indelicate request for them to lower their radio had devolved into something else.

I learned later that there was a phalanx of about 16 of them who brought their wares down from Nepal and circulated between Kuala Lumpur, Bangkok and Kathmandu. After a hard day's work selling crafts and artifacts from Nepal at the local markets here, they congregated at this cheapo Chinese flophouse to party, drink, and play loud music, starting around 11 pm, exactly when I was going to sleep. I didn't realize that when I engaged one, I got them all. I also didn't know I was dealing with a traveling band of rowdy Nepalese gypsies, itching for a fight, probably soused or stoned.

"You do not talk to us this way," he said.

"You disrespect us," said another, who, I saw, carried a knife on his belt.

They advanced and backed me into a corner. I could smell the alcohol. The other problem was that I only had a towel wrapped around me, having just walked out of the men's communal shower.

Cornered by five of them, me in my towel and my gonads unprotected, Ying then appeared. She rushed over.

"Oh, hello, how are you?" she said, speaking Thai, sensing somehow that they would understand her, which they apparently did. She deftly inserted herself between my would-be attackers and me. "You speak Thai, oh, yes, I am Thai, oh, very sorry, please pardon my husband. He's antisocial. He didn't mean anything, please excuse us, we are so sorry," she repeated imploringly and with high feminine charm, almost irresistibly so.

They continued glaring at me, muscles taut, showing no signs of backing down.

"Oh, please, our mistake. We are traveling from Thailand. Very tired. Pardon my husband, he did not realize, I apologize for him," Ying said, keeping herself between them and me. I was more than happy to hide behind the skirt or, in this case, the towel of a woman, as she had just returned from the shower too.

The five of them backed off, and the tension was defused. They were not ready to push aside a petite woman. They stepped away, still staring at me. I would have had to fight the five of them, scrotally challenged, but for my wife who rescued me, making me even more scrotally challenged.

"Thank you Ying. You saved me," I said. "You were incredible."

"You have to be careful in these cheap hotels," she said. "You do not know who is staying here. Next time, don't be so stupid."

"Yes, m'am."

The next day we rode over to the University of Malaya.

"This is the oldest and most prestigious university in Malaysia," I said. "We will be meeting Dr. Prasad, the professor and Chairman of the Department of ENT."

"How did you learn of him?"

"One of the ajarns in Songkla gave me his name. I sent him a letter. He invited me to meet with him."

We waited a short time in his waiting room. When he came out he wore a white lab coat, shirt and tie, very formal and august, of Indian ancestry. He was older, perhaps in his sixties. We sat down in his office.

"Welcome to Kuala Lumpur," he said. He did not offer his hand or smile, and was curt, I thought.

"Allow me to escort you around our department briefly." We visited the wards. We quickly passed by the patients. There was no discussion. Nor did he introduce me to the nurses or other doctors. We returned to his office. He showed me pictures of cases he and his Head and Neck team had done, almost, I thought, a form of boasting, his way of saying, "We are quite capable of performing sophisticated surgery here." And, indeed, the cases were advanced. Afterwards, he asked, "What can I do for you?"

"I would be pleased to be of service as a visiting surgeon," I said.

"If you were to work here, your role would consist of nothing more than providing an additional pair of hands to assist me and others in surgery. You would not have a teaching position. Only a surgical or perhaps a research assistant."

"I see."

"We don't really need you and could not provide a stipend," he said. "It would be more in the manner of a chief resident or fellow. Something like an assistant for learning purposes."

"I am sure I would benefit from observing you and your team, but I would not be interested in that role," I said. Not after two years of head and neck boot camp in Thailand.

"I understand. Well then," he said, standing up, thusly ending our visit.

"He seemed arrogant," Ying said angrily as we left the building. "Even the chairmen of departments at major universities in Thailand will treat you better than this. He seemed to resent you."

"He was offended that a young American whippersnapper like me would have the gall to show up in my dungarees and flannel shirt and offer my services at this most esteemed university."

"Yes."

"But that was exactly what I had done the last two years in Thailand, although not in Bangkok, the capital of Thailand. Maybe there is a different attitude in a nation's capital city."

"He was still impolite," Ying said.

"He is probably accustomed to visits from other professors and chairmen from around the world, not undistinguished young Turks like me without a professorship from a major medical center."

We continued our sightseeing in KL (as Kuala Lumpur was called), drowning our sorrows in Chinese food. We visited the Friday Mosque (Masjid Jamek) near Chinatown. It had a pleasant, open, soothing atmosphere.

I sat down in the back against the wall. Ying rested her head on my lap.

In a moment, someone in Muslim garb, a Muslim prayer cap and gown, shouted and waved his fist angrily at us, saying, "You do not respect our customs. You cannot act this way. Get out of here!"

He glared as Ying and I stood up. Another Muslim man in street clothes who had just parked his motor scooter nearby came over in his motorcycle helmet and pacified the man.

"Okay, okay," he said, "they are leaving now, it is okay."

We walked out gingerly, put our shoes on, and thanked the man for coming to our aid. I realized, as I thought about it, that the act of Ying putting her head on my lap in a mosque would be unacceptable. I didn't think of it at the time. It seemed perfectly natural. But I had been careless and would not repeat that misstep.

We rode some 150 kilometers south through the pouring rain to Johore Bahru, the gateway to Singapore. It was a busy, heavily trafficked road, dangerous and unpleasant. There was not much in Johore Bahru with the exception of an incredible food market with hundreds of stalls offering delicious ethnic dishes. We feasted on Indian food, excellent.

The next day we crossed the causeway over the Straits of Johore into

Singapore. We found a budget hotel, locked the motorcycle, which had not failed us thus far, and toured the town. It seemed more traditional than Hong Kong the other modern Chinese city-state I had visited. It was clean and orderly, but a little colorless.

We bought tickets for Indonesia on Garuda Airlines. The hotel owners were gracious enough to let me keep my motorcycle there. I needed it to get back up to Thailand.

"When will you return," one of them asked.

"I don't know."

They shrugged and smiled. The next day we would jet off to Jakarta, Indonesia.

I felt now that we were stepping off the side of the planet, moving in new directions, truly unbound. I wanted to get back to my work but also enjoyed my new found freedom. Even though I had been abroad for two years, I had been working continuously. Now I was wandering with no responsibilities or schedules. My eyes were open to the wonders of the world and particularly the incredible array of cultures in Southeast Asia, as diverse a region as any. Still, I was not at ease with just being a nomad.

"We are traveling like tourists. It would have made sense if we had found work in KL."

"There is nothing wrong with traveling."

"But it is strange for me to go so long without working."

"It is good that you are obsessive, but you can relax and see the world too."

"I don't mind being a drifter. But I can't go long without working. It is not good for me. I don't want to lose my skills, my motivation, my whole purpose for being here."

There had also been a change in my relationship with Ying. I saw her through different eyes. Since our marriage, I had felt trapped by her. I recalled all that had happened in Songkla, Tak Bai, and Sungai Kolok. And then in Malaysia. I realized that my feeling for her had improved after that episode with the Nepalese gang.

"I haven't forgotten what you did in KL."

"I am your wife."

"Yes," I nodded. "My Wonder Woman."

She giggled. But then more seriously, she said, "there will be other times when I will save you. You will see. You may not realize this, but I am your protector."

Chapter 31

Indonesia seemed removed from the rest of the world, an archipelago of thousands of tropical islands draped across the Indian Ocean. It was the fourth most populous nation with more than 200 million and most of them crowded into only 7% of the total landmass, the island of Java where the capitol Jakarta was. The people were primarily Malay but there were many dialects and distinct cultures and groupings as you moved from island to island and even within the islands. Although nominally a Muslim nation, the largest Muslim nation by population in the world (although, oddly, it is the Hindu nation of India that has the largest population of Muslims), it was a softer version of Islam than one might encounter elsewhere and certainly in the Arab heartland. Perhaps it was a function of being cutoff from the rest of the world, drifting along in the Indian Ocean as the bejeweled chain of islands that it was, insulated from the great struggles and conflicts that crossed national borders elsewhere.

We landed in Jakarta and took a three-wheeled taxi, called a *bajaj*, to a cheap hotel. The traffic was horrendous. Jakarta was an urban nightmare with few redeeming qualities. With a population of ten million, it was squalid, over crowded, a magnet for the poor who came hoping to find work at very low pay. At least Bangkok had the Royal Palace, the Emerald Buddha and Wat Phra Keow one of the most beautiful temple complexes I had ever seen. Kuala Lumpur was in another planet all together. It was modern, diverse, and clean with great restaurants and traditional ethnic neighborhoods. Not so Jakarta. Here the teeming masses clamored and labored amidst the smog and dust of a city detached from order and beauty.

We left as soon as possible and took the train to Bogor 60 km south of Jakarta, relieved to get out.

"It reminds me of the way I felt getting out of Bangkok on the train to Chiang Mai," I said.

I liked Bogor right off, the perfect respite from Jakarta. It was much smaller and laid back and easy to get around. There were a lot of good restaurants serving up rice, tempeh, and peanut sauce.

We visited the botanical gardens, which was impressive. Also the Presidential Palace built by the Dutch. The next day we went to the "Punchak Pass," a very scenic drive between Bogor and the town of Bandung. There were resort villages and sprawling tea plantations along the way. We had lunch at a restaurant near the top of the pass, a refreshingly cool temperature compared with the tropical heat lower down. The owner of the hotel we were staying at in Bogor, a lady who was also a widow I learned, had arranged our one-day tour along with a couple hired hands and several other tourists.

The driver and guide cackled to me that she had never taken an interest in going with the tourists on the one-day trips.

"She has never come before," the driver said.

"Why is she coming now?" I asked.

He snorted and poked me in the ribs. He and the guide winked with lascivious grins and nodded toward the boss lady. I still wasn't sure what they were getting at. After lunch, while walking around the restaurant grounds and enjoying the view, I soon understood.

The boss lady ambled over to me with Ying in earshot, saying in accented English, "Can I speak to you Doctor."

"Sure," I said. And we walked off a ways.

"You a man. You a doctor. So I talk to you. Sometimes, you see, a woman has needs of man. I tell you because you a doctor, so you understand."

She sidled up against me and held my arm, a remarkable come-on, especially in a Muslim country, and right in front of my wife. She looked at Ying in sneering condescension.

"Stay with me Doctor," she said, pressing against me. "She cannot do for you anything. We have wonderful time."

I realized that the Indonesian brand of Islam was of a different order. I could not imagine this happening anywhere in the Middle East or even in Malaysia, which although relaxed by Arab standards, was still austere. Under normal circumstances a brief tryst would have been possible. But that was before. I lived under different constraints now. Ying quickly sensed what was occurring under her nose.

"Madame, please forgive me. I am flattered. Truly. But I don't think it is possible," I said.

I averted my eyes, not wanting a scene between my wife and her. The driver and guide, watching everything, gave me a fist pump, still laughing. Wonder Woman came over and reclaimed her property, and we continued on our journey.

The next day we bused to Garut, 63 km south east of Bandung, Indonesia's third largest city and capitol of West Java.

"We'll bypass Bandung. I don't want to see another grubby Asian mega-city," I said. "I think Bangkok and Jakarta jaded me."

Garut, as it turned out, possessed what we were looking for. It was small, high up in the hills with temperate climate, hot springs resorts and volcanoes, a common feature in Indonesia.

We bused to Bangor, a miserable, vertiginous journey and then boarded the "Orient Express" to Yogyakarta, the center of Javanese culture and Indonesia's most popular city, founded in 1755. The scenery during the train ride was spectacular.

"I realize how much more I enjoy train travel than buses," I said. "I don't get nauseous."

Two adorable Indonesian children kept us entertained the whole time. "Mr. Richard," they kept repeating, giggling, as we carried on together.

In the morning we toured this very traditional city. We rode a *becak*, a three-wheeled carriage with seats for two in the front and a bike in the back for the driver.

"My name is Achmah," the driver said, and he was as friendly as could be.

We went to the Sultan's Palace or "Kraton" within the old city, awash in markets, shops, and batik cottage industries, where they made the iconic decorative fabrics worn throughout Indonesia. The palace was still a functioning part of the government. Although the Sultan no longer held the power of that title, he was still the governor of the region. Traditionally garbed elderly men guided us through the lavish courts and pavilions. There were over 1000 palace guards or workers wearing batik tending to the rooms and halls. Hindu, Buddhist, and Islamic influences in the art and ornamentation reflected the synthesis of the three religions. There was a gamelan or traditional Javanese music performance, with its exotic, otherworldly bronze percussion ensemble.

The next day both of us were sick. Bad stomach cramps.

"Must have been one of the restaurants," I said.

We stayed in bed in our cheap hotel all day and read and slept. I was happy to have a bathroom nearby. By the next day we were better. We strolled around the old city once more. In the evening we saw *wayang* or traditional Javanese shadow puppet play of the *Ramayana*, the Hindu epic that describes the efforts of Prince Rama to rescue his wife Sita.

I had inquired about teaching hospitals in Yogya.

"I am anxious to get back into some medical routine," I told Ying. "I need to work."

The hotel workers advised me to visit the Dr. Sardjito Hospital, part of the University of Gadjah Mada. I contacted one of the professors of the ENT department there and Ying and I took a *becak* over to meet him. An ENT surgeon, perhaps my age or a little older, greeted us.

"Welcome," he said, shaking my hand. "My name is Sudomo Chandra. "Please sit down."

"I have been working in Thailand for two years. I have an interest in Head and Neck Cancer. I would be happy to visit and work in your hospital as a surgeon."

He did not seem at all perturbed at my offer to work in his facility, unlike Dr. Prasad in KL. His demeanor was warm and hospitable. But then this was not the premier teaching hospital in the country. Nor was it the nation's capitol. He introduced me to some of the residents and faculty and we made rounds.

There were large communal rooms with beds lined up army barracks style. The walls were concrete painted white. There were families around many of the beds, some sitting on the floor or on the bed of the patient and dressed in a manner that suggested they were from the rural areas, probably farmers and shepherds, not unlike other Asian hospitals.

"It reminds me of Chiang Mai, in the north of Thailand," I said. "The pathology here is impressive."

"Yes, this is typical. They come in at late stages. Probably as you saw in Thailand."

There were a fair number of large head and neck tumors. But there was more in the way of severe infectious disease including otologic or ear-related infection, in particular mastoid abscesses, which had been all but eliminated in the States. The severity of the disease indicated the usual problems of the third world, which was lack of access to health care, especially in rural areas, the absence of antibiotics and other medicines, and neglect. The ratio of patients to physicians was very high. People tended to delay seeking treatment until absolutely necessary, which may very well be at death's door.

"I had not seen as many severe infections in Thailand, although we had them. My first case in Chiang Mai was necrotizing fasciitis or gangrene of the neck. We wrote a paper about it. He required multiple debridements. We had to remove much of the skin and muscle of the neck with extensive grafting to repair," I said.

"We have terrible cases like that every day," Sudomo said.

There were several post-surgical mastoiditis cases on the wards with the familiar mastoid dressing around the operated ear and patients receiving intravenous antibiotics. The mastoid is the bone behind the ear and a thin layer separated it from the intracranial cavity. Severe infection there could lead to brain abscesses, meningitis, and intracranial thrombophlebitis or infected clots of large veins within the brain, all life-threatening conditions. There were also a fair number of acute sinus infections.

"Dr. Moss, you may be interested in this." He showed me a patient who was intubated, on a ventilator, and non-responsive. The skin of the nose was red and swollen. He was receiving intravenous antibiotics. "He has 'cavernous sinus thrombosis.' We have three such patients on our wards, but he is the worst. He may not survive."

This was an uncommon but often lethal infection that began in the sinuses or midfacial skin, invaded the orbit (eye socket) and ophthalmic vein, spread backward into the cavernous sinus, a large, intracranial vein with several cranial nerves and the carotid artery traveling through it, a deadly condition with a mortality over fifty percent. We had seen very few such cases in my residency. I recalled several in Thailand although my focus there had been head and neck cancer. It was more something we read about or feared as a deadly complication of inadequately treated sinus or cutaneous infection of the midface but rarely saw.

"It is amazing that you have three such patients on a random day when I am visiting."

"They come in frequently, even once a week," he said. "We have so much poverty and ignorance and superstition. Our patients often wait until it is too late. And then we can do little, especially for this."

He showed me the other two such patients. All in varying stages of extremis. Sudomo and his team had drained the abscesses where possible and administered intravenous antibiotics and heparin, a blood thinner, to prevent the clot from propagating further. They were very sick patients and their outcomes were uncertain. They were also fairly young, making it even more tragic. I felt again the urge to be back in this world, my world. The world of intolerable disease and dysfunction where I could play a role and push back against the misery.

The professor was gracious. We discussed cases. There was a small group of faculty, residents, and students accompanying us. I expounded as we walked from bed to bed, a typical grand rounds format. I was back in my element. I didn't realize how much I missed it.

"We would love to have you work with us," Sudomo said at the end of rounds on more than 70 patients. "We could learn so much. But I have no power to arrange a license for you. That would have to come from Jakarta. We are very small here. I have no influence with the medical board or the government. It would be possible only to teach as you have done today. You would not be able to do surgery. And I cannot provide a stipend or a place to stay. Or even a title."

"Would it be possible to arrange it in Jakarta?"

"You would have to inquire. But I don't know the regulations regarding foreigners working here, and I have no authority."

I wondered why it was so straightforward in Thailand? The system was more decentralized. Each University or teaching hospital was able to decide such matters on its own. No one had to seek permission from Bangkok.

"I am disappointed but very happy we had the chance to meet you. You've been very kind."

The experience had returned me to the realm of third world medicine, and I was grateful for that. But I hungered for more. I could taste it. Perhaps if I had made preparations in advance, as I had in Thailand? Or contacted medical centers in Jakarta? But I had not planned any of this, and I regretted it.

"There will be other opportunities," Ying said, sensing my frustration.

"I miss this. It means everything to me. I have to return to it. I can't keep wandering around like a gypsy."

We left the hospital.

"I should have thought about this," I said as we rode a *becak* back to the hotel. "We should have visited one of the medical centers in Jakarta or contacted someone in advance."

"But you could hardly stand Jakarta," Ying said.

"I don't know why I didn't think of working in Yogyakarta."

"We knew nothing of Indonesia or where we would want to stay and work," Ying said.

"We could have organized this if I had thought ahead. Yogya is a wonderful place and the opportunity to help as a surgeon with such overwhelming need would have been perfect."

"It may not have worked out. Every place is not the same as Thailand, as we saw in Malaysia. We didn't know any of this, and it is too late now."

"This is a lost opportunity, a major lapse in planning. I have to communicate with institutions before coming. I have to know in advance what the licensing requirements are. I must anticipate the prospects before I arrive, just as I did in Thailand. Then I can fulfill my mission. Otherwise, I am just another vagabond drifting from place to place."

Chapter 32

The next day we planned to visit one of the great sites of the world, only 42 km from Yogya, the vast Buddhist complex of Borobudur. Ranking with Pagan in Burma and Angkor Wat in Cambodia, Borobudur was one of the three great Southeast Asian Buddhist edifices. It was built within 50 years of the Hindu site of Prambanan, another incredible temple, which we had visited yesterday. The proximity of the two great sites and their roughly contemporaneous constructions suggested an easy alliance between the two faiths. This made sense since Buddhism emerged from Hinduism, and both were born of the fertile soil of India. Both shared an emphasis on inner reflection and contemplation, and promoted various mental techniques to harness the power of the mind for the purpose of attaining realization. What was also notable was the rapid disappearance of both religions in Indonesia with the emergence of Islam.

We approached Borobudur in a car on a single lane road. On a hill, amidst the trees and vegetation of the Kedu plain, Borobudur loomed large, an ethereal vision. Mt. Merapi, and other volcanoes, arose in the distance lending yet further drama to an already breathtaking vista.

"It is startling," I said.

Borobudur

It was the largest Buddhist structure in the world and possessed other-worldly grandeur and dimension. There were six massive square platforms capped by three circular levels that initially made me think of the Mayan ruins in the Yucatan peninsula in Mexico. Each of the levels were adorned with some 2,672 relief panels, many depicting scenes from the Buddha's life or prior lives (the "Jataka" stories) as well as of mythical Buddhist spiritual beings such as deities, bodhisattvas, apsaras, and others.

We ascended the stone stairs to each of the six square platforms, then the three circular levels up to the central stupa at the very top of the elaborate structure. The views from the top were also wondrous and exhilarating with Mount Merapi, visible in the distance rising as did Borobudur itself from the lush fields of the Kedu plain. We studied the bas-relief carvings at each of the various levels depicting scenes from the Buddha's life and prior lives along with remarkable renditions of mythic deities and bodhisattvas. It was hypnotic, a great moment and highlight in my travels through Southeast Asia. But there was a lesser, more base and ignoble aspect to the experience that Ying and I could also not ignore, noticing it as soon as we approached the lower level of this extraordinary edifice.

"I know you saw this and was as disgusted as I was."

"How could you miss it?"

Scattered throughout the temple complex were numerous curls of human turds littering much of the ground around the structure, and in and around the various Buddha statues and relief carvings that adorned the multiple levels of this extraordinary edifice.

"It is a deliberate display of contempt for the Buddhist religion and in the most disgusting manner," I said.

"It is not from dogs either," Ying said.

"No, they are human turds targeted precisely where it would be noticed to show maximal scorn for this magnificent structure."

What was also apparent during our visit at Borobudur was the incredibly flippant attitude and behavior displayed by local Indonesians. Many of the Muslim youths, who apparently had been taught that it was okay to do so, sat on the laps of the Buddha statues, irreverently leaning against Buddha images or with arms folded around their necks or over their heads or even sitting on their shoulders, posing for photos and yucking it up, truly shameful acts of disrespect.

"This is a place of pilgrimage for Buddhists, too, not just a tourist destination. It is like Mecca or Jerusalem. It should be respected," Ying said.

I nodded. "And if such behavior occurs here on our one day visiting it, then it most likely occurs every day."

"I warned you of this," Ying said bitterly.

I recalled the brisk reaction and anger of the Muslim gentleman in

Kuala Lumpur when Ying had rested her head on my lap in a mosque, an act that in retrospect was improper. However it was not deliberate. It was in fact entirely innocent and I think small in comparison to what I witnessed here today.

I wondered about Islam, its place in the world, and its ability to abide other faiths. Were there likely to be further clashes of civilizations between Islam and the other religions and cultures of the world. I was not sanguine about its prospects and wondered if Islam was capable of reforming itself as Christianity had done centuries before. If anything it seemed the forces unleashed by the Koran and the Hadith, the ongoing interpretation by clerics, its doctrines and history, indeed by Islam itself in its totality, worked in the opposite direction, glorifying as it did the purity of 7th century Arabia. Would there be an Islamic reformation, renaissance, and enlightenment as had occurred in Christendom?

"I doubt it," Ying said.

We traveled to Probolingo, the jumping off point for Gunung Bromo, also known as Mount Bromo.

"I have heard a lot about Mt. Bromo," I said. "It's an active volcano. Supposed to be one of the most thrilling spectacles in all of Indonesia."

We traveled to the town of Ngadisari, a small picturesque village with brightly painted homes and flowerbeds high up on the Tennger crater and right next to Bromo. There were actually two other mountains next to Bromo, Batok and Kursi. Further south was Gunung Semara, Indonesia's tallest peak and most active volcano. The whole area was incorporated into the Bromo-Tengger-Semeru National Park.

"Bromo" and "Semeru", of course, referred to the two mountains. But it was the "Tengger" part that intrigued me. The Tengger people or Tenggerese, were descendants of the Majapahit Hindu Empire. They fled to the inhospitable highlands in the 19th century when large numbers of Muslims immigrants arrived. Most though stayed and converted. This was a common pattern I suspected throughout the history of the world since the arrival of Islam some 1400 years ago.

"Yes" Ying said, "escape or convert."

"Or else face persecution as a second-class citizen or 'dhimmi.'"

It was an effective way of eliminating diversity and opposition and expanding a rigid ideology and religion. Those that emigrated to the Mt. Bromo area maintained their faith. As such, they were one of the few Hindu communities left in Java, numbering about 600,000.

We arose at 3AM to begin the ascent to the Bromo crater. We crossed the Cemoro Lawang or lava plain and climbed to the edge of the crater of this massive, heaving volcano just as the sun was rising over the horizon.

The view around us was spectacular. In the distance, there were lush, green fields nourished by rivers flowing down from the peaks. But then there was the unearthly, desolate beauty of the bare, rugged volcanic peaks themselves, of Batok, Kursi, Semuru, and others in the distance, the barren gravel plains and the *Laut Pasir* or "sea of sand," a vast grey volcanic layer surrounding us. It seemed to be not of the earth, although, of course, that was precisely what it was, only bereft of vegetation or trees or living things of any kind, something akin to the landscape of the moon or another planet. It was barren, bleak, uninhabited, and remote, hence its appeal and fascination. Ying and I were mesmerized by its fatal, grim splendor, as seemed were the others who had made the climb with us that early morning.

Turning towards the crater of Bromo itself, as we trudged gingerly over the thin edge of this smoking, belching caldera, some 10 km in diameter, was a glimpse into the center of the earth. It was a gnarled, twisted, contorted earth, darkly hissing and releasing noxious gases, white-saffron plumes of steam and sulfurous smoke, amidst a misshapened, seething, otherworldly bed of burning, glowing, crimson volcanic ash and stone. There were dark and sinister and deadly forces afoot in this cruel caldera, this bleak, wretched umbilicus to the fiery core of the planet. It was a reminder of some other era, a molten, searing, unlivable origin to this place, the earth, that humanity had settled on, living blithely and predictably on its verdant, docile, and fertile surface, ignorant of the overwhelming geologic exertions and temperaments that raged just below, held in delicate balance by myriad consents and managed strains and assertions, delivering some measure of stability upon which everything depended. We watched the red orb rising and sailing benevolently across the cloudless sky, over the outer edge of the caldera, enjoying this daily dance between sun and dependent earth. Looking down from our perch, on the outside of the crater, there were the ancient, stepped, folded patterns of lava, now frozen and encased in its final surge, like a timeless photograph taken eons ago, when Bromo last whipped itself into a frenzy of fire, ash, and molten rock, plunging forward from the craggy lips of the caldera, gushing outward from the enigmatic, brooding core of the earth.

Ying and I were smitten and moved by this memorable vision at Bromo. It was wholly unexpected. The experience conjured up a sense of wonder and odd reflections on life and the origins of the planet. It was removed from notions of history and religion. It was a wonder that life could even exist given the unlikely balances that the chaotic forces of nature were required to maintain for a stable, predictable platform for life to take root and develop. It seemed so unlikely an enterprise. And yet there it was. Perhaps in the end such moments suggested the existence of a great designer, a master clockmaker crafting this ultimate of timepieces, the finely tuned universe, orchestrating the cycle of life and death, of cataclysm and rebirth, of a small pebble orbiting in the darkness and the shifting moods of the sun upon which all our dreams and dramas were based, the wonder of life and of humanity.

"I disagree with the Buddha on this," I told Ying. "It is not random and accidental. There is a designer. A creator. I see Him in His creation. I embrace aspects of Buddhist practice, but I remain a believer in the God of the Bible."

Chapter 33

We continued back through Probolingo and then east along the coastal road to the town of Banyuwangi on the eastern tip of Java and the jump off for Bali. We had traveled the length of this most populous island of Indonesia. But I had been thinking of Bali since I arrived in Java. We enjoyed the many sights and landscapes of Java but Bali had an allure I could not resist, a tropical paradise with a storied and rich culture, exotic traditions, wondrous landscapes and coastline, fascinating villages and rural areas, and myriad temples and statuary. It was here where the remnants of the ancient Javanese Hindu Kingdom survived, maintaining its way of life, culture, and faith.

We spent the night in Banyuwangi and took a *bemo* (public minibus) 8km north to the town of Ketapang, the port for the ferry to Bali. We bought our tickets and boarded the ferry for the 45-minute journey across the Bali Strait.

We got off the ferry in the town of Gillimanuk in Bali. We boarded a *bemo* to Denpasar, the capital of Bali. It was a dizzying journey, shuttling through the hills and valleys often at high speeds, the driver stopping and starting to pick up and drop off passengers, barely avoiding the donkey carts, cattle, goats, chickens, pedestrians, vendors, bike riders and other vehicles, typical third world chaos on the narrow roads.

"Pure craziness," I said, shaking my head.

Ying and I were situated in the back of the bus. The back door was left open for passengers boarding and disembarking. The most memorable part of the two-hour journey was when I noticed Ying turning a shade of pale green as the bus driver raced along at breakneck speed, curving, dodging, and barely flying off the road. I saw her eyes cross and beads of sweat forming over her brow. Wonder Woman was getting queasy.

"Ying, are you okay?"

She mumbled something, barely audible.

"Get up!" I shouted. I rushed her to the open door. "Lean forward. I have you."

I held her by the waist as she promptly heaved her breakfast. With the bus hurtling at 100km per hour, the vomit slammed back into the bus, showering three locals who were sitting behind us. She continued vomiting large amounts of spew all of which flew back and peppered the poor Indonesians. I could scarcely turn around to apologize, intent on holding on to Ying as she continued upchucking. After finishing, she returned to her seat and promptly fell asleep. I turned to the Indonesians, coated in puke, as they cleaned the chunks and stains of vomit from their shirts, arms, and faces.

"I'm very sorry," I said.

It was deeply embarrassing.

When we arrived in Denpasar, we quickly arranged bus tickets for Ubud, which was in the mountains north of the capital. I didn't want to stay in the big city, although by big-city standards Denpasar wasn't too bad. Nor did we go to Kuta Beach, the main tourist area in Bali, full of western tourists, restaurants, hotels, great surf, white sand, and partying. I preferred to avoid big tourist destinations, mainly because the whole experience of travel lost much of its exoticism and romance with thousands of westerners around.

"Do you want to stay on the beach, Ying?" I asked.

"No," she answered.

We boarded the bus and made the 40-minute journey to Ubud, the cultural center of Bali, a wonderful place to see traditional Balinese arts, dance, music, and crafts of all kinds. It also boasted excellent restaurants. There were wonderful places to walk including a "monkey forest," along with many spectacular ravines, rivers, forests, exotic Hindu temples, and terraced rice fields. But it was also the lifestyle of the people, their manners and expressions of faith and worship that intrigued. There was a reason Bali and especially Ubud and surroundings were as popular as they were. It was a feast of the senses, all senses, and of the mind and spirit.

We found an inexpensive inn or homestay as they called it. It was a nice room with a view of the inner courtyard, a reflecting pond, fountains, and Hindu icons. There was burning incense, a very quiet atmosphere, and the ubiquitous *canang sari*. These were tiny offerings consisting of leaf trays with flowers, rice, and cookies, and burning incense sticks. The people sprinkled them with holy water three times a day before meals and placed them in front of their homes, work places, hotels, restaurants, and temples throughout Bali.

It seemed as if the Balinese lived their religion, with every part of life immersed with Hindu rites and practice. It created a peaceful environment and certainly an appealing one from my perspective. I reflected on the oddity that this little pocket of Hindu culture and religion could endure on this tiny island in a sea of Islam. The Majapahit Kingdom, which had dominated much of Indonesia and particularly Java, had condensed down to this nucleus, a distant cry from its former splendor. Its survival was probably an accident or function of geography more than anything else being as it was a small island. Yet most of the other islands of Indonesia, some smaller than Bali, were Islamified. Whatever the accidents of fate or chance, it was fortunate that history had seen fit to protect this single enclave of Hindu life on the Indonesian archipelago in the Indian Ocean.

Ying too delighted in the soothing atmosphere. "It reminds me of Thailand," she said.

Yes. But as an island it was more insulated and protected, able to evolve and maintain itself with little interference, almost like a living time capsule. It was a pure, distilled form of Hindu life and practice, probably very distinct even from India where Hinduism originated. I was hooked before I had even unpacked.

We walked through the town. There were many tourists but still a lovely ambiance. Many of the locals dressed in traditional attire. They placed their leaf tray offerings with burning incense before their homes or businesses. They performed a kind of ritual gesture as they went about their devotions. There were many restaurants. Examples of Hindu sculpture and imagery abounded on streets and corners. We walked to the Monkey Forest, with thick, dense rain forest-like vegetation, tall trees with tendrils descending to the earth, and small streams and rivulets roaring and gurgling, the sound of moving water omnipresent. Then there were the monkeys who were amusing, enchanting, and sometimes aggressive, quite accustomed to the many tourists that visited and eager to plead their case for food.

We crossed the "Dragon Bridge" over a ravine with elaborate statuary and sculpture. From there we visited the "Goa Gajah," or "Elephant Cave" with a cave that dated back to the 9th century, the entrance of which was a large demon's mouth. Later on towards the end of the day we saw the Puri Saren Agung or Water Palace, formerly the palace of the kings of Ubud. This was an ornate, dazzling complex of royal buildings, dwellings, walkways, staircases, ponds, bridges, and fountains adorned with elaborate cosmic Hindu sculpture and carvings that was truly breathtaking. In the evening there was a performance of Balinese dance and music with female dancers dressed in colorful golden and green traditional apparel with lovely, stylized gestures and movement that reminded me of performances I had seen in Thailand. Perhaps the roots were related, emanating from Hindu India and often depicting great Hindu epics such as the Mahabharata, the other great Sanskrit epic of ancient India, or the Ramayana. With the traditional gamelan orchestra and the backdrop of water, lily pads, and the stunning statuary and sculpture, set against the velvety black sky, it was as transporting an experience as any I have had.

After a couple days touring Ubud, Ying and I were ready for the road to see more of Bali. We rented a motorcycle, which was wonderful.

"I feel like I am back in Thailand, reunited with my motorcycle and freedom," I said.

Hindu Temple, Bali

Both of us were impressed with what we had seen in Bali and understood its standing in the world as one of the great island destinations. It had fantastic scenery, fascinating culture, wondrous temples, forests, mountains, beaches, and excellent food, and so we were eager to see more. It also seemed very safe and friendly here. The atmosphere was congenial. As someone on a journey of medicine and healing, I saw also the religious influences that could promote such curative restoration in an alternative form. Hinduism and Buddhism, both mystical creeds with a strong emphasis on meditation and insight, lent themselves to such an enterprise. Might there be a possibility of a fusion of the two worlds? Of medicine and meditation. Of healing medically and spiritually. Of faith, meditation, and prayer, of proper diet, exercise and lifestyle, of breathing, reflection and concentration, merged with the antidotes, potions, and surgical incursions of modern Western medicine? Surely there was. Just being here in Ubud and visiting its many temples and forests or even just walking on the streets with the inhabitants in traditional dress, preparing offerings, performing rituals, reciting prayers, provided healing. At what level healing occurred, whether it was at the cellular, biochemical, hormonal, immunological, or neurological, or some fusion of all of these curative pathways, I could only guess. What were the precise mechanisms of therapy and restoration? I did not know. I was certain there was an elaborate "healing" literature available to answer these questions, but I imagined that there was more to restoration and repair than this pill or that procedure as vital as those ministrations were.

I wondered again about this Hindu preserve, how it had survived the Islamic wave. I was not sure why the Muslims had spared Bali? Generally, their interests were global in nature. Particularly towards a religion like Hinduism, which with its iconography, temples, gods and goddesses, graven images all in the Muslim view, were pure blasphemy, as antipodal a religion from Islam as could be imagined. Yet, for various historical reasons, Bali had been spared and so we were able to enjoy this small Hindu island sanctuary, rich in culture, art, and natural wonders.

I did not feel here the conflict over not working as a surgeon, which had reached a crescendo at the hospital in Yogyakarta. The pain of that oversight still burned but was submerged in the flowing resonances of mystical Bali. I was taken by the mood and milieu here. I saw it as part of the journey, not mere tourism but something of a curative nature. It lent itself to internal flights, which were self-sustaining. I immersed myself in the emerald meadows, churning waters, and numinous rites of Bali, allowing it to illuminate me in subtle ways. I did not abrade myself as much over my forced marriage, which I reflected on, as much as I tried to suppress it. I questioned how I had allowed the situation to progress as it did. How I had failed to recognize and take actions to counter the obvious direction we were moving towards back in Songkla. Women had powers that transcended men's. They were designed to overwhelm our natural defenses. Yet, I had always navigated deftly around them. But Ying designed the perfect snare. She was skillful. And since beginning our journey together, I saw how capable and insightful she was.

We motorcycled to the district of Bangli where the famous Pura Kahen temple was located. At every turn there were jade pastures, dense forests, lush mountains, sparkling terraced rice fields with scrawny men riding ploughs pulled by teams of oxen or donkeys, the stepped fields of rice glistening like a thousand mirrors on the sides of the hills, changing with every twist and turn of the road. "This is magical," I said, as we rode past.

There were evanescent teardrop villages with thatched roofs, scantily clad children pealing with laughter, their voices like small clarinets. Women in colorful Balinese garb ambled gracefully on narrow dirt trails with large baskets of fruit and other offerings balanced perfectly on their heads to bring to temples. Small canals and rivulets fed the ploughed fields, glittering and noisy with fresh gurgling water from the mountains and heavens. Above this panorama, the enchanted canopy of turquoise sky and tumescent ivory clouds spread itself like a garment while the canary sun illuminated the painted fields and the copper earth of Bali. Yes, it was paradise here.

We rode to Tirtaganga. This was the famous water palace built by the Raja or King of Karangasem in 1948 near a natural spring at the foot of a hill. Tirtaganga literally means "water from the Ganges," the sacred river with various pilgrimage sites in India for Hindus. Hence it was also revered for the Balinese. It was a network of fountains and pools placed within a lavish garden with many stone sculptures and statues. There were gardens, stone walk ways, shrines, and temples. In the center of the palace was an 11-tiered fountain with many carvings and statues. In the background were the hills and mountains and the finely chiseled terraced rice paddies glinting in the afternoon sun. I swam in the pool. It was refreshing and peaceful. I walked around in a batik sarong, going full native.

"You could be an Indonesian," Ying said, laughing.

We rode to Lovina Beach and stayed a few days. It was relaxing. We went on a day trip to Singaraja to see the waterfalls. At night we had dinner by the beach and watched a traditional Legong dance with the mesmerizing, intricate finger gestures, complex foot movement and intense facial expressions of the performers. There was a Buddhist monastery nearby, named Brahma Vihara Arama, which we visited. Ying wai'd the Buddha images. She felt most comfortable in the confines of her native religion. We sat and relaxed here. I too felt very comfortable in the Buddhist milieu, very much at home.

"In the end, I am a Buddhist," Ying said.

"In the end, I am content within the Buddhist world, but I will always remain a Jew."

"As you should."

"But I admire Buddhism."

"I know you do."

"But there are inconsistencies."

"I want to hear."

"The doctrine of 'non-self.' I don't believe 'self' or identity is an illusion. There is a spirit or mind beyond the body. The spirit expresses itself through the body but exists apart from it. We are more than complex chemistry sets. The Buddhist goal of ending desire is also impractical. Humans were meant to desire things.

"Yes, we do have desires," Ying said, smiling and pressing against me.

I laughed. "Right. We do."

"Go on *ajarn*," she said mockingly.

"Are you making a point about desire?"

"Yes," she said. "Go on, *ajarn*."

"'Okay. Let me concentrate," I said, still laughing at her efforts to distract me.

"I'm waiting."

"'Desire' drives individual achievement and is critical to human progress," I said.

"But you can be less attached while pursuing worthy goals," Ying responded.

"True, nonetheless the message can be confusing. We should encourage worthy 'desire,' understanding its necessary role in improving life when properly employed."

"Okay, *ajarn*, sounds like a reasonable 'Buddhist' balance," Ying said smiling.

"Ending suffering is likewise implausible. Suffering is often necessary and unavoidable. It can also be transformative and uplifting," I said. "But on balance, the reflective life advanced by Buddhism is beneficial as is its message of moderation."

In the monastery, there were numerous golden Buddha images and stupas not unlike Borobudur. Yet the style was Balinese. Near by were the Banjar Hot Springs. It was as wonderful a combination as could be imagined. The hot springs were located in a luxuriant garden with stone-carved mouths pouring water. The temperature of the waters was pleasantly warm.

The ride from Lovina Beach to Bedugul in the mountains was wondrous. It was a winding road with no traffic and stunning views in every direction. There were mountains, lakes, rivers, terraced rice fields, fertile valleys, and then lovely Lake Bratan. The scenery along the way made me think of a Greek Island but by now I felt as if Bali had surpassed all that. Between the scenery, culture, temples, and people, all packed into one small, accessible island, Bali was as good as it got and deserved its great world reputation.

We returned to Ubud, relaxed a couple days there. Then we went to Padangbai, the port for the ferry to the island of Lombok. It was a two-hour journey across Lombok Strait to Lembar Harbor.

Chapter 34

Lombok was mostly Muslim but about ten percent was Balinese Hindu. It had the three small "Gili" islands just off shore, which were being discovered by backpackers but otherwise off the beaten tourist path. They were undeveloped with no resorts or hawkers and magnificent coral fringed beaches. I had heard about it from other travelers, and so we planned a short stay.

From Lembar we took a bemo to Pemenang about 50 km north. Then a short cidomo ride (horse drawn carriage) to the port of Bangsal. Then we took a public boat to one of the three Gili islands known as Gili Trawangan, the largest of the three. The boat ride over took a half hour and was itself wonderful. The waters were clear and lustrous and the small islands in the distance lush and verdant. The sky was deep blue, to match the sea, cloudless and startlingly beautiful. We found a simple bungalow on the beach.

I had noticed that the proprietors were aggressive in tone. I did not want preconceptions about Muslims to influence my perceptions, especially now, coming after nearly a month in Bali with its enchanting Hindu culture and rhythms, which I already knew I was partial to. Nor did I want it to intrude on what was otherwise a magnificent setting and destination.

"The beach is incredible. I am feeling more comfortable with you Rick. I did not trust you before. I know that you resented me for what happened."

"It was not the ideal circumstances for a marriage."

"I was so emotional. We got involved romantically. I never thought about you and your concerns. I felt I could not live without you, and so I took drastic measures. I was not myself. Something happened. I could never have lived with the shame if we had not married. But I know Western culture is different. Maybe your way is better. But I could not have gone on."

"If you were a Western woman none of this would have happened. We would have gone our separate ways, just a brief affair. I did harbor resentment. But I felt you would have ended your life if I didn't marry you. And I couldn't live with myself if I allowed that to happen."

"My family has worried about me since we left Thailand. And I worried too."

"You didn't really know me, even though you had decided you had to marry me."

"Yes, I know it doesn't make sense. But I know you better now, Rick."

I looked at her and smiled.

"Thank you, Rick."

And I thought about this whole matter of my wife and me. Did I betray myself in accepting the demands of Thai culture, the Mattanyukul family, and Ying? Yes, I had. Had I been weakened and damaged by this affair? Yes. I had been compromised. The ramparts had been breached. Yet I did not see myself abandoning her. I clung to some mystical notion that a higher purpose, unseen as yet, had been served. I did not know what it was. The mixing of the bloods? The coming together of disparate peoples and cultures for some end? Perhaps it was something I would come to understand only in years, even decades to come. Why marry her over the many other accomplished and devoted women I had met? Her appearance in my life and the sudden, life-altering, and weird circumstances of our relationship and marriage were a thunderbolt across my path and career. I could not explain it rationally, indeed because it was irrational, an elaborate web I had chanced into.

We kissed, held hands, and explored the magnificent shore.

The sand was white powder, the waters turquoise and clear. There were long sweeping bays, palm fringed, coconut laden, and rich. Just offshore were polychromatic coral reefs with iridescent fish darting past. We had avoided the crowded beaches of Bali but this destination was different. It was laid back and sparse. The owner of the bungalows served food, which was medi-ocre but acceptable, and so we were content to simply stay on the beach and relax. The water became very deep just a short distance from the sand. There was a current below the surface that you could ride, observing the coral and fish as you drifted by underwater. It was blue, clear, and luminous through to the sea bottom. At a certain point you would come up and swim back so as not to go too far or wander back up the beach and repeat the cycle. I did this for several hours each day, rare for me. It was as delicious a way to idle the time as any. I accepted this brief respite from life. I realized this too was "life," just not the one I had been used to all these years. I had always been on the move, planning, working, preparing. Even when traveling. The idea of doing nothing was alien, let alone just floating along on a current, observing the coral, the seabed, and small gleaming flickering fish darting by. Yet, I could use more of this. Lurking in the background though was my wish to return to my work, my reason for being in Asia in the first place. I could not say I felt guilty for this sinful wandering of the last several months. Only that I did not want to stay away long from my purpose for being here: the battle against third world disease. Ying had joined in my little crusade, a band of two. But now we were floating on the azure waters off Gili Trawangan by the island of Lombok in Indonesia.

"You will be busy again soon enough. You have worked your entire life,"

Ying said. "But you cannot stay away forever. I know that. You will have to return, and we will."

When she began using the first person plural, "we," it bothered me. I always worked alone. "I" suddenly become "we." Lately, I found it less vexing. What had become of me? My internal immune mechanisms had been breached. Yet no alarms had sounded.

One of the days there I became very ill with explosive diarrhea. Instead of lounging on the beach, I stayed within a few feet of the primitive squat toilet we had in our small hostel. It was here that I discovered the wonders of Imodium. A fellow traveler in an adjacent room offered it to Ying when she told him of my travails. I took two. It was miraculous. With my stomach settled, I quickly returned to my hammock and immersed myself again in the ivory beaches, gentle breezes, and the hypnotic waters arrayed before me like satin.

We spent nearly a week there. Then we returned to Lombok. Took the ferry to Bali. A bemo to Ubud. It was crowded with western tourists.

"I am weary of the tourist trail," I said to Ying. "I am ready for reality, for work, for medicine. It is good to travel. But there is something frivolous about it. I prefer to *live* in a place not just visit. And to work and continue my mission"

"I know you do," Ying said.

"I understand the curiosity of travelers. I am one of them. But there is something more that I am seeking."

Chapter 35

We spent my birthday in Ubud. Enjoyed more of the sights. Then we flew from Bali to Singapore and back to the hotel where I had left my motorcycle. When I saw the chrome and steel of the old bike, after more than two months, I was beside myself with joy.

"I have never felt so happy to see a machine," I said excitedly. "I feared the worst. That it might have been stolen or damaged. That parts may have been taken. But here it is, safe and sound. That's our horse. Our freedom. It's everything. I missed it."

Ying said nothing, observing me with amusement. After greeting and thanking the owners of the hotel who had graciously allowed me to park it here, I unlocked it and kick started it and lo it miraculously revved up instantly. The sound of the old motor still cycling though, sputtering and noisy, were as sublime to my ears as any symphony.

"Pure bliss, as close to enlightenment as I will ever get. Is it possible to attain nirvana through love of one's motorcycle?" I asked.

Ying hopped on and away we went, touring Singapore and feeling the adrenaline rush of gunning my Honda 125 once more, the iron steed that had carried me so many thousands of miles to remote and dangerous locales, exotic villages, and capitol cities.

The next morning we left Singapore and rode into Malaysia. In two days we were back in Kuala Lumpur. I was in heaven. We went to Chinatown to eat. I loved their iced soybean drink. And then the various stir-fried dishes with tofu and vegetables, all fresh and delicious, cooked right in front of you. It seemed so civilized here. Sophisticated. With a high standard of living. I felt stronger now as if Indonesia had sapped my strength.

"I think you miss the good food here and in Thailand," Ying said.

It seemed that if a nation could not sport a decent plate of food, and Indonesia, in my travels, notwithstanding the magnificent temples, scenery, and other cultural points of interest, often failed in that capacity, then the nation or culture just didn't have it together. Perhaps it was a new approach for measuring the likely success of an emerging nation – the ability to produce good quality food in every town and village, indeed every street corner, as I knew they could in Thailand, Malaysia, and Singapore. If it could not, then there were likely to be other deficiencies.

"Indonesia was substandard."

The next day we were on the road again. We rode 200 km north to the town of Ipoh. This was a busy and prosperous Chinese town with excellent food and impressive colonial architecture. We spent the night and continued the next morning to Penang, an island just off the coast of Malaysia and connected to it by a 10km bridge. It crossed the south channel of the Straits of Melaka, and it was truly exciting to ride our motorcycle across the vast expanse with the sea on either side as we entered into Penang. This was the oldest British settlement in Malaysia and a popular tourist destination because of its beaches and historic Georgetown. I had been here before to renew my visa for Thailand. It too seemed very "Chinese," hence vibrant and thriving. It too had superb food, something I no longer took for granted. Our interest here though was not so much to visit Penang or renew my visa for Thailand, which I would do later, but to board the night ferry to the Indonesian island of Sumatra.

"I know that Indonesia has weighed on me," I told Ying, "but with Sumatra so close, a mere budget ferry ride over, it's hard to resist. Just the sound of the word, 'Sumatra', stirs the imagination."

And so we arranged our tickets and took the 10-hour night journey across the Straits of Melaka. It was not a wise choice for us to stay down in our little cabin in the hull of the boat. Ying, prone to motion sickness, was quite ill. I had her come up to the deck. The cool air and velvety black sky dotted with twinkling stars comforted her. I made out the constellation *Orion*, the legendary hunter and son of Poseidon, God of the Sea, appropriate on this sea journey.

"Thank you, Rick. I feel better." I caressed her forehead. And she fell asleep, her head on my lap. I gazed out at the wondrous canopy above, peace descending upon us as the ferry plied the dark waters. I felt more protective of her, the two of us, it seemed, gradually merging as one.

In the morning we arrived in the port at Belawan, then took a 40-minute bus ride to Medan.

Medan was the capitol of the province of Northern Sumatra. With a population of more than 2 million, it was Indonesia's third largest city.

"It's as dirty, noisy, and unappealing as Jakarta," I said.

Smoke-belching motorcycle becaks assailed us as we left the bus station, trying to get us to go to one hotel or another. We spent a single night in Medan and ate at a small dive just down the block from our cheap flophouse. It was a primitive looking place and I thought somehow that it might give us a flavor of the area. We ordered a simple rice dish. While waiting a number of male locals gathered around our table, sitting in chairs or tables on all sides of us. I noticed them staring at us. I wasn't sure what the matter was, but the hostility was palpable. And the glares were threatening. I looked at Ying who kept her eyes down. Perhaps, they didn't appreciate a woman in their midst? I knew what would have happened if she been unescorted. The small white bowls of unappetizing rice and stringy vegetables appeared but the staring did not relent. We ate quickly and left the grim place.

"They would have raped you if I was not with you," I said. "And they were just about ready to do it anyway. You can never go alone to places like this. Even when together we should avoid them. That was a close-call."

Of all the remote places of the world, with the possible exception of Timbuktu and Borneo, there was probably no place that conjured a sense of isolation, mystery, and adventure more than Sumatra. Although I realized how important it was for me to return to my medical work, the proximity of so far-flung and outlandish a destination was too great a temptation.

Sumatra was the sixth largest island in the world, 2000 km long, but it was not our intention to explore all of it. Rather, Ying and I had alighted on a single objective. To visit beautiful Lake Toba, which was close to Medan.

"We are not tramping across Sumatra like we did Java. But I have heard that Lake Toba is worth seeing, and it is nearby."

We boarded a bus to the town of Parapat on the eastern shore of Lake Toba. The next morning we boarded a ferry to the island of Samosir in the middle of Lake Toba. It was as dramatic a setting as any I have seen.

Lake Toba rested in the caldera of an immense volcano that collapsed in on itself after a massive eruption some 100,000 years ago. The flooding of the crater created the largest volcanic lake in the world. It was 100 kilometers long, 30 km wide and 505 meters at its deepest. The explosion that produced Lake Toba, known as the "Toba Catastrophe," was believed to have been a climate changing event and the largest eruption on earth in more than 25 million years. It killed most human populations at the time and led to a volcanic winter with drops in temperature of 3-5 degrees C. In the middle of the vast blue expanse of Lake Toba was the island of Samosir, some 45 km long and 20 km wide, roughly the size of Singapore. It was the center for the Toba Batak people who were mostly Protestant Christians, which I thought was odd.

Surrounding the lake were mountains, ravines, and beaches. The temperature was refreshingly cool. It was lush and green, almost like a rain forest. The homes along the water's edge showed the traditional Batak architecture, rectangular structures with the angular, scalloped roofs. We arrived in the village of Tuk Tuk on the island of Samosir, and stayed at a simple homestead, the "Romlan," with fantastic views of the lake and surrounding verdure. The next day we explored. We walked around the village, met the locals along with fellow travelers. Although Lake Toba was part of the backpacker itinerary, it was much less crowded than Java or Bali, and so it was easier to enjoy the local people and culture. It was strange to see churches in Indonesia.

"It seems as if the non-Muslim religions in Islamic nations survive best in the more remote areas, either islands or rugged mountains, like Bali or by Mount Bromo or here," I said.

After several days of relaxing and doing nothing, we rented a motorcycle and toured the island. It was beautiful and transporting. But many of the locals were aggressive in trying to sell their wares or souvenirs, an ongoing battle in Indonesia.

"I know they are poor and need money, but I've had enough of it already. It was never this bad in Thailand."

The time here was otherwise pleasant. The scenery was spectacular. The food was decent. The locals were generally friendly. After almost a week, we left Lake Toba, took a bus to Medan where we stayed for a night. I was pleased that we had managed to include the forbidden island of Sumatra in our voyage. But I knew that I had no appetite for more.

"I am ready for something else. As a tourist, I'm spent."

The next morning we boarded the ferry across the Strait of Melaka back to Penang. The next morning I arranged my visa at the Thai consulate. Then we crossed that same magnificent 10 km bridge over the waters of the south channel onto the Malay Peninsula. We rode through the mountains to the town of Grik, a superb ride. The next day we motored to Rantau Panjang over the Golok River and into Sungai Kolok, Thailand. I was relieved beyond measure. I was truly happy to be back in Thailand. Somehow I felt as if I was home. I immediately sensed the friendliness and openness of the Thai people. How easy going and welcoming they were.

"I love this country," I said.

We rode to Uttamo's sanctuary. He was as delighted to see us, as he was surprised. He showed us to our little bungalow amidst the swamp and jungle and dense overgrowth and we rested.

Chapter 36

We spent a few days with Uttamo. We spoke of Buddhism and other religions. I described some of my experiences over the last few months, particularly in Indonesia, where there was a confluence of powerful religious traditions at work, of Hinduism and Buddhism that went back centuries, one layered over the other, and then the final layer of Islam that had consumed them all. There were architectural vestiges of those earlier great faiths, particularly in Yogyakarta at Borobudur and Prambanan, and other cultural manifestations such as the dance and puppet theater and other depictions of such Hindu classics as the Ramayana epic, but as living religions with active faith communities, other than Bali and the tiny community of Tenggerese at Mount Bromo, they had vanished never to be seen. What could account for such a monumental loss?

"Did the local Hindus and Buddhists flee or simply accept the inevitable and convert, as much of the world had done over the last 1400 years before the might of triumphant Islam?" I asked. "And why had it not occurred in Hindu India, itself invaded by marauding Muslim armies and a long history of Muslim domination? What forces had preserved Hinduism in India but not in Indonesia other than Bali? And why had Buddhism vanished in both, including in India, the land of its birth? Will Buddhism survive here in the south of Thailand, or will it go the way of Buddhism in India and Indonesia?

"It will not survive in the south," Ying said. "Thai Buddhists are already moving out. I have seen the changes through the years."

"Perhaps it was Buddhism's openness and dearth of formal structure or hierarchy within the general population that accounted for its lack of resilience in the face of aggression by other faiths? I remember the abbot of the temple at Tak Bai who spoke of the difficulties of surviving in a Muslim environment."

"As a monk," Uttamo responded, "my focus is on the practice of Buddhism. It will be for the lay Buddhists to sort out the fate of Buddhism in the south or elsewhere."

I had identified with Buddhism and felt concerned with its lot. My friend Uttamo, a Buddhist monk of more than 30 years, was not.

He had a copy of the Old Testament that I was perusing. In it I had seen a picture of Adolph Hitler. On the back of the picture Uttamo had written, "In order to believe in the Jewish God, protector of His chosen people, you would have to believe that God used Hitler as his rod of wrath for Jewish misdeeds. It is impossible to believe in such a God."

"I believe in the practices and teachings of the Buddha," Uttamo said after I read aloud his inscription, "which teach not the existence of a perfect God but in the ability of man to perfect himself." He then added, "But I found nothing in the Old Testament that refutes the Buddhist Bible."

"How can that be," I asked. "They are completely different traditions."

"'Love thy neighbor as thyself.' 'You shall love the Lord your God with all your heart, with all your mind, with all your being.' 'God created man in his image.' These are all from the Jewish Bible. If we are created in God's image than God is within. In the end, its teaching leads to emptiness and wisdom, no different than Buddhism. At the esoteric, spiritual level, the two paths converge."

Uttamo was also referring to the "Tipitaka" or *Pali Canon*, what he also termed the Buddhist scriptures or "Buddhist Bible." Uttamo was not ready to dismiss his birth faith although he obviously had devoted his life to another. But this did not prevent him from arguing against the existence of an eternal soul.

"If you are conscious after death, conscious of what? And through what medium? The eyes, ears, nose? What are the modalities of awareness? They are all dependent on conditions, which are impermanent and therefore unsatisfactory, subject to change, decay, death, and suffering."

He wrote extensively on the differences between Mahayana and Hinayana or Theravada, which was the type of Buddhism practiced in Thailand and by Uttamo. They were also referred to as the "Greater and Lesser Vehicles," a not complimentary nomenclature for the Theravadins, hence not used by them. Mahayana was common in northern Asia, Hinayana (Theravada) in Southeast Asia particularly Burma, Thailand, and Sri Lanka.

Uttamo's writings were erudite and scholarly. He had many followers from around Thailand who sought his counsel. Yet he refused any acknowledgement of achievement or status. Later, he regaled us with a host of hilarious stories in light of his being a Buddhist monk.

"I was studying in a Temple in Burma and was given a bed filled with bed bugs. I found bug spray and committed mass genocide against them. The other monks chastised me. But I returned later with the bug spray, when no one was looking, and finished them off."

"Would you kill a mosquito that was pestering you during meditation?"

"Yes!"

He mentioned that he longed for something exotic in his alms bowl like a McDonald's hamburger.

We discussed Kundalini Yoga, to which he said, "No one has ever discovered a chakra." He provided me with his stock answers for why he became a monk. "I couldn't find a girlfriend, I like orange robes, and I enjoy the 'holier-than-thou' feeling I get from being a monk."

He spoke of growing old. "My tits are getting bigger. I need a bra. My muscles sag. My joints ache. I have wrinkles. It's awful." He showed me a "Kung-Fu diploma" he said he received from the most famous Kung-Fu school in China. "I graduated with honors because I could levitate longer than other members of my class." When I chuckled, he said, "Pra Uttamo, not very religious but a million laughs."

After several days we left. I revved up my motorcycle. Uttamo told me not to forget about surgically pinning his ears back. He had noticeably protruding ears, "Dumbo ears," he called them. This was an operation known as an "otoplasty." "They've bothered me my whole life," he said.

"But you're a monk."

"Never mind. I want you to pin them back."

I laughed.

"And don't forget my eyelids."

"You're a funny Jew, Uttamo. We'll make arrangements when we return to Hat-Yai."

Chapter 37

We drove to Narathiwat. Then to Hat-Yai. It was strange but reassuring to be back in Prince of Songkla University with my old colleagues. I had contacted Kowit a few days earlier, and he let everyone know that I was returning. I was glad to see the familiar places and people I had worked with so closely not long ago. I spoke with Dr. Sumet who welcomed me back.

"I already spoke with the university and made all of the arrangements."

Kowit, my helper and confidante, welcomed me as well.

"Welcome, Ajarn," he said, waiing me.

Ying was accepted. She was my wife. She had been a student and then a nurse at the hospital. It was as if we had always been married. The strange and sudden turn of events surrounding our relationship was not raised. We stayed in my old quarters. I wanted to get back to work seeing patients and operating. My colleagues accommodated me. I wanted to heal again, and through healing others, heal myself.

The next day I saw an elderly female patient with Dr. Vitoon. She had a massive "glomus" tumor of the internal jugular vein that reached up to the base of the skull, a very vascular tumor, always a difficult case as they bled so much.

"We will have to split the mandible to gain access," I said to Vitoon.

I was delighted to be back with the typical advanced cases I had come to know and expect here in Thailand.

I had been away for several months since my journey to Malaysia, Singapore, and Indonesia. I had visited a few hospitals along the way and seen some terrible cases that one day in Yogya but had not operated.

"Now that we're back, the first case is no simple or straightforward head and neck case. This is a large, nasty tumor."

I saw now that the wandering life was inadequate for me. I needed more than simple tourism. I had to be immersed in the life and culture of the place. To experience it as a stakeholder and serve some purpose beyond tourism. Visiting and touring were fine, but did not satisfy me. As much as I enjoyed what I had seen these last several months, it was insufficient. I needed to be working, as a physician, and, hopefully, as a healer. I saw a convergence of medicine and spirituality. It seemed that the one required the other, the two threads joined. The operating room was my temple, my

Buddhist sanctuary. My surgical instruments my sacred tools. The nurses and doctors my *sangha* or clergy in the path to redemption. And so I eagerly, even impatiently awaited the next day, a quite challenging and difficult case, not ideal for someone who had not stepped into an operating room in four months, but it was what I needed.

"I am looking forward to this," I said to Ying. "I am glad we are back."

Ying and I arrived in the operating room with Vitoon and several residents. The patient was already asleep, the tube threaded down her airway, into the trachea, moving oxygen and carbon dioxide in and out of her lungs. She was a frail, old lady and I did not relish doing what I would have to do to her. It seemed improper to subject her to this, to inflict such a grave insult and invasion on so aged and feeble a patient. But there was no choice. The tumor would otherwise continue to grow and ultimately invade the base of the skull thus penetrating the intracranial space making it impossible to remove.

Her neck was extended and turned to the left. She was prepped with brown betadine solution and swathed in sterile green drapes with Thai lettering on them, leaving only the right side of her neck and face exposed. All else was covered. The operating room lights were adjusted and aimed directly on the surgical site. Residents, medical students, and nurses gathered around to observe. Vitoon and I stood opposite one another on either side of the patient's neck. The operating room nurse was ready with the surgical instruments. Two residents had joined us. The anesthesiologist ventilated the patient, tending to her vital signs, oxygen levels, and EKG, administering medicines to maintain her vegetative functions and keep her in the deep sleep that allowed us to commit odious but necessary surgical violence to her neck and face. Surgery was controlled assault, an insult and invasion of the body done with surgical precision, but a form of controlled violence just the same to wrest the individual from the ever-tightening grip of a disease or tumor that in this case would ultimately be fatal. I was delighted to be back in this universe, in the realm of healing where the mind, spirit, and hand joined seamlessly to restore and protect, to render health, indeed to heal. It was with these instruments, these weapons, these fellow soldiers and warriors that we engaged in mortal combat, in just war. This was the arena, the theater, in which I operated and flourished.

I drew a line with the surgical pen for the incision in the neck that I would extend later through the middle of her chin and lip in order to split the jaw in the middle. Vitoon grasped the knife, a #10 blade, and made the initial incision in the neck as I put tension on the skin to allow for a clean cut. After the incision, Vitoon did something that I thought was strange but understood, indeed preferred. He promptly handed the knife to me.

A glomus tumor was not a typical tumor. It was composed of proliferating blood vessels that bled readily because the vessels were thin walled, lacking as they did a "muscular" layer around the delicate and friable endothelium or inner layer. Lacking a thick muscular coat, any manipulation or grazing often lead to profuse bleeding, difficult to stop. Typically, the patient would have also had preoperative embolization of the vascular supply, tiny beads shot into the tumor through the feeding vessels to clot them off and minimize bleeding. But that was not available. By handing the blade to me he wanted me to take responsibility for the case, which was what I wanted.

We fully exposed the tumor in the neck. It was an ominous, frightful thing, pulsing away with each beat of the heart, like a small, clenched fist, it almost appeared to be laughing at us, daring us to invade its fortress domain, knowing the firepower it possessed and the foolhardiness of attempting a direct frontal assault. I also saw and knew from the preoperative CT scan that the tumor extended up towards the base of skull and could not be properly exposed without splitting the mandible and swinging it laterally. I extended the incision up through the middle of the lower lip and then used an oscillating saw to split the front of the mandible in a stair step fashion, cut along the floor of the mouth. I ligated the salivary duct of the submandibular gland, which normally would have prevented moving the mandible outward. We cut the muscles of the floor of the mouth and towards the back of the throat laterally and swung the mandible thus exposing the superior aspect of this pounding heap, seething and throbbing as it did. Now we began our direct assault on the mass. We separated it from the surrounding tissues. Peeled away the carotid artery. Tied off vessels feeding it. Exposed the jugular vein above and below, ligated the vessel, isolated the mass, freed all attachments, and removed the now docile, tamed devascularized glomus tumor and tossed it into a metal bowl. Pictures were taken.

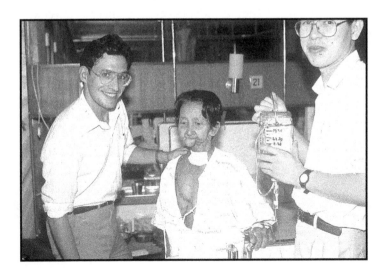

We reassembled the ladies jaw, face and neck, and she was sent to the recovery room in stable condition. Vitoon and I, all smiles, shook hands.

"Excellent, Ajarn," he said.

I was back in my world.

A few days later I had an unusual visitor. It was Uttamo in full regalia, in orange robes and sandals and shaven head who had taken a train from Sungai Kolok to visit me in Hat-Yai. We arranged to meet him in the ENT clinic. I was with Dr. Sumet, the chairman of the department.

"I am unhappy with my ears," said Uttamo, as unorthodox as always. "They stick out and I don't like them."

He had mentioned this right before we left Sungai Kolok, but I didn't think he was serious. I was amused. Dr. Sumet less so.

"I also don't like my eyelids. They sag."

"Anything else?"

"I have a deviated septum and can't breathe through my nose."

This, at least, was an acceptable medical condition.

All of this I found so unexpected and atypical as to be hilarious. In a place where patients with severe and deadly ailments appeared daily in our clinics by the hundreds, such concerns seemed patently frivolous. There was a place, of course, for cosmetic surgery, generally done in private clinics or surgery centers, paid in cash by the patient, not insurance companies or the government. But what was really out of place and bizarre, of course, was that Uttamo was a Buddhist monk, a revered monk who had donned the orange robes and until recently at least assumed the quite stringent behavioral codes and deprivations that went with such a commitment. If all things were impermanent and unsatisfactory, if desire led to suffering, if emptiness was the goal of Buddhism, why would one care about the appearance of one's ears or eyelids? And why should Thai lay people support such an individual as they obviously did. In a nation like Thailand, which revered Buddhism and its clergy, and the Buddha himself, this came close to scandalous. Buddhism in Thailand, like all religious hierarchies and structures, had had its share of improprieties, transgressions, and misconduct. Although not nearly as egregious as other outrages, this would nonetheless raise eyebrows.

Sumet was having none of it.

"You are a monk," he said.

"But I always disliked my ears," Uttamo responded as if that were a winning argument.

"We have many very sick patients here. And you are a monk."

"My eyelids are bothering me too," Uttamo added with no visible evidence of self-doubt in his request.

"But you wear the orange robes. You are a monk. It is not proper," Sumet fired back.

Sumet, of course, was right. At the least, Uttamo should have removed his orange robes and come as a civilian, knowing the consternation it would bring. It almost seemed like an "in-your-face" behavior for some, perhaps, unconscious reason. I had not promised Uttamo anything but I thought I could resolve this in a way that would be acceptable to Sumet.

"It would be valuable, Dr. Sumet, for the residents to see how to repair lop ears since they may have to do it with other patients. Especially young children who may experience ridicule because of their ears. It is a procedure ENT surgeons would be expected to know," I said.

This seemed to resonate with Sumet because of the potential teaching value. Since the focus at the Prince of Songkla University Hospital was serious, often life-threatening disease, which presented in great abundance, scarce attention was given to less urgent but nonetheless important conditions like this.

"Also, it would be useful for the residents to see a blepharoplasty to understand the approach and surgical anatomy of the eyelids," I added.

Here too Sumet nodded.

"Okay," he answered, shrugging his shoulders. "But it is very peculiar for a monk to have his ears pinned and his eyelids lifted. But there would be benefit for the other doctors to see this."

He looked at Uttamo with something of a glare and left. He did not wai him, virtually unheard of in Thailand.

The next day we operated on Uttamo. There was a large crowd of residents and students and even other faculty members including Sumet who wanted to observe the procedure. Together with a resident, we pinned back Uttamo's ears and lifted his eyelids and repaired his deviated septum. It went well. He was bandaged and sent to recovery and then to the wards where Ying and I and the other doctors visited him.

On the second post-operative day, the residents were across the room doing an emergency bedside tracheostomy on a patient. I thought it was a strange juxtaposition. A man nearly suffocating from a large tumor of the larynx obstructing his airway, undergoing an emergency tracheostomy, and just as stoic, mind you, as could be. He moved nary an inch while two ENT surgeons slashed through his neck, cut open his windpipe to secure his airway and prevent him from choking to death. On this side of the room sat Uttamo and his pinned ears.

The next day we removed the dressing from around his ears. They looked good. Pinned back. Symmetric. No longer sticking out. We brought a mirror. The old monk was pleased. His eyelids were still puffy from the surgery but were fine. And he was breathing better through the nose after the septoplasty. A couple days later we saw Uttamo off at the train station. He would arrange for someone in Sungai Kolok to remove stitches. I smiled as my idiosyncratic friend ascended the train.

"You're a funny Jew, Uttamo," I said, as the train pushed away. Ying and I wai'd him and waved. I would miss him, peculiar and eccentric as he was. Even as I smiled in thinking of him, I recognized that my good friend had to be troubled, at least in some way. To dedicate one's life to the study of impermanence in a forest having given up all worldly comforts and then want at the age of sixty one's ears pinned back was an unbridgeable chasm from a Buddhist perspective. Perhaps, I wondered, if his entire life as a monk in a jungle in Sungai Kolok was an escape from some inner turmoil or disappointment from his past in the States, as a physicist, as a Jew, as someone hurt in some way. I believed that Buddha's first noble truth of suffering was active in my accomplished Jewish-Buddhist mentor, Uttamo, whom, regardless of his contradictions, I still respected. He embodied an odd convergence of the sublime and the ridiculous, the spiritual and the mundane. But I would always see him as friend and guide. Like me, and everyone, he was on his own healing journey.

Chapter 38

There was a winding dirt-gravel road out of Hat-Yai that I often traveled with Ying on my motorcycle. It looped through a number of small villages in the hills and valleys of the area. There were streams and lush forests, rolling wooded fields, and rice paddies, an idyllic escape from the traffic and noise of Hat-Yai. On one such journey, I turned left to follow an even smaller road for about a half-kilometer. Another short turn and the road opened into a large temple courtyard known as *Wat Satchatam* ("The Truth").

"I have driven past before but never stopped," I said to Ying.

We parked the bike.

I noticed the monks in orange robes with shaven heads practicing various forms of meditation, including walking meditation, where the monks filed barefoot back and forth silently and in solitude, often for hours, as if absorbed in the moment. It seemed intended to discipline the mind and prevent it from wandering as the mind inevitably did, to experience each moment in its fullness. I enjoyed observing them practicing that and other meditative techniques. My enthrallment was not passive though. I wanted to join them.

"It would be a fascinating to experience this," I said to Ying.

I had great respect for Buddhism and wondered if this was my chance to immerse myself in Buddhist practice. I had the time and there may not be another opportunity. Yes, I wanted to get back into medicine, but I did not see a conflict. It was a merging of the two. The profanity of disease, the insult of surgical intervention, with healing and spiritual practice. The two paths merged.

"I have been so close to Buddhism these last two years, but always admiring it from a distance, visiting temples, enjoying the beauty of the art and architecture, the iconography and Buddha images, observing the monks as they set out each morning for alms," I said. "I am drawn to this."

"It is a part of you. And you have studied it. You and Uttamo had the most detailed conversations."

Buddhism, as I saw it, through readings and discussions, was a practice intent on mastering the mind and grasping reality. It used proper understanding and techniques to break the world down into its component parts, acquiring insight into the nature of reality for the purpose ultimately of liberating oneself from suffering. There was nothing about it that offended me.

We walked through the temple grounds and visited the monks and spoke with some of them. It was a peaceful atmosphere.

"I am not new to eastern practice," I said to Ying. I spent seven years in a yoga ashram in my college and medical school years. We did Kundalini Yoga. We tried to 'awaken' the 'chakras' and create a 'flow of energy.' But I prefer the austere approach of Theravada Buddhism, Thai-style Buddhism, absent chakras, flows of energy, and the rest, a direct assault on the mind."

We got on our motorcycle and rode home.

I spoke with Ying later in our apartment.

"I have had a long interest in Eastern religions, but I never thought seriously about entering a Buddhist monastery and becoming a monk."

"Most Thai men ordain. Even the King of Thailand ordained. But we are married now. And you are just getting back into medicine," Ying said.

I returned to the ENT department for the week, making rounds, seeing patients with the residents in the clinic, and doing surgery. I was not on salary and so I had latitude in my schedule. On the weekend, Ying and I visited the temple again. I met with various monks and, in particular, the head monk of the temple, *Phra Maha* Jaroon or *Ajarn* Jaroon. He seemed right off to be a charismatic individual and spiritually accomplished. I sensed a presence and power in him. His mind and energy were focused and concentrated. He seemed to be in constant meditation, aware of the breath, the mind still, and yet able to carry on a conversation. He was committed to the practice of *"sa-ti"* as he called it, awareness at all times, or mindfulness.

"What do you do all day," I asked.

"Practice dhamma," he answered in Thai.

I believed him. I felt as if I were experiencing it. He was actively engaged in the practice of mindfulness or *sati*. He was my age and we had, I felt, an immediate affinity. Ying explained to Jaroon that I was a surgeon at the University.

"He has been here for two years, *ajarn*. He does surgery and teaches. He helps Thai people. He makes very little money. He is from the US." I noted Ying's pride in saying this, which I appreciated.

Jaroon nodded approvingly sensing perhaps that someone who had devoted himself with the kind of intensity required to become a surgeon could probably deploy the same dedication to the practice of Buddhism. And the prospect of having such a student in his ranks intrigued him. I wanted to work and learn from him.

We left. I thought about my deep interest in ordaining at *Wat Satchatam* under Jaroon. I was consumed by it. We visited again the next day. While walking amidst the temple grounds with Ying, I wanted to tell her of my intention to ordain and enter the monastery. I understood fully the ramifications in a young marriage. I wasn't sure how she would take it.

"I'm going to ordain with Jaroon for six months," I said.

Ying looked at me. "It will be good for you and you will bring honor to my family."

"You understand what this means."

"Yes."

"I was not expecting that answer. I want to thank you." I was relieved.

"I knew you wanted to. I will not stand in the way of my husband studying Buddhism. That would not be good karma. You're a funny Jew, Rick."

We both laughed, remembering Uttamo.

"We cannot have relations."

"I know that."

"All physical contact, even simply touching or holding hands or looking into each other's eyes is forbidden. No signs of affection are allowed."

"Maybe you will calm down a little." We laughed again. "You will be more focused and humble. You will learn alot as a monk."

The truth was that I could not stay away from my work as a surgeon that long. I had only said six months to see her reaction. It would be less than that for I was committed to returning to medicine soon, although I did not divulge that. That she had accepted the proposal with such equanimity impressed me.

"You accommodate me in everyway."

"I am your oriental wife, *ajarn*."

That evening, as the soft glowing twilight moved swiftly to velvety darkness, the sultry tropical air cooling with the night, and the sounds of the forest, the crickets, katydids and frogs resounding in the stillness, I knelt with hands pressed before me in a deep wai before someone I already considered a friend and confidante and Buddhist teacher, Ajarn Jaroon, who sat on a platform cross-legged in his orange robes, resplendent and of noble bearing, his head and face luminous and intent, the fullness of his presence and concentration in the moment even more pronounced than before.

He seemed truly to glow with spiritual fire and purpose. He lived Buddhism in his every breath and moment, as pure an exemplar of Buddhist teaching as I had ever encountered, someone who inspired me with his towering presence beyond any words he may have uttered. If not a living Buddha or an *Arahant*, one who had attained enlightenment, he had come perilously close to that mystical, electric realm that had been written about and described but few if any had ever entered or knew intimately beyond the intellect. But there I swore he dwelled. I acknowledged within myself his presence, recognized his attainment, sensing intuitively but with unfailing certainty that this obscure monk in a forest temple outside of Hat-Yai in southern Thailand dwelled amongst the saints and deities of Buddhist lore.

He embodied Buddhist teaching by his presence and manner and gesture and grace, was an incarnation of Buddha-nature, a critical link in the great patrimony and lineage that traced back through the eons, through the Himalayas and Tibet and China, to Japan and Korea and beyond, through southeast Asia and India, through the millions of souls who embraced its teaching, ultimately linking to the Buddha himself.

I felt myself blessed and supremely fortunate to have happened upon him and knew that he was not an ordinary monk or man but someone who navigated at will between the two planes, moved easily between the two spheres, between the worldly and the sublime. As he began the evening meditation and chant and my ordination into this esteemed spiritual community, he had fully engaged himself in the wisdom and power of Buddhist practice, which was full awareness in the moment, of self mastery, of wisdom and insight into the nature of reality, the killing of ignorance, the slaying of defilement, and the banishment of suffering. Around me were the other monks of the temple, all sitting, hands pressed together, quietly chanting ancient Buddhist prayers.

There were several lay people present, men and women who assisted the monks. There was also a single nun, an elderly but spry Thai lady also with shaven head but in white robes, as women were not permitted to become monks and so could not wear the orange robes. There were dozens of candles flickering and sticks of incense burning before the various Buddha statues. The shadows moved and shifted stealthily across the yard.

Ying knelt behind me also with hands pressed tightly, head bowed as she listened to the hypnotic chants of the monks echoing in the stillness of the dark night. The atmosphere was charged. Even magical and otherworldly. I was delving into a wondrous pool that was clear and lucent but mysterious and profound. I unwound my mind in the flowing cadences of the incantations, carried by a light breeze that moved surreptitiously amidst the trees and foliage that surrounded us, wrapping and lifting me in a protective curtain of wondrous sound. My senses were alive and riveted. Each ephemeral moment an eternity. I was elated and moved as I passed from one world into another, from the lay householder to the Buddhist monk, piercing a thin invisible membrane that divided the two realms, the ordinary into the transcendent, from daily life to the dhamma.

I was now the recipient of an ancient tradition that began 2500 years ago in India, a spiritual enterprise begun by a single man, a prince of a local kingdom, Siddhartha Gautama, who left his comfortable life to pursue wisdom and end suffering. He developed a teaching and a path that became the great world religion of Buddhism, handed down and spoken of from generation to generation, preserved and tended to as something sacred and exalted for centuries on end, flowing through time to this moment, in this forest temple to be uttered by Jaroon and received by me. I saw it in the same light with which I grasped the Jewish tradition, a long continuum through time, a chain of being, a great wisdom tradition that crossed the long trains of time and space, through every continent and era to arrive here and now in this place and moment. It possessed the weight and force of the centuries, and the millions upon millions of lives over two thousand years spent studying, living, and practicing it.

The Pali chants I was listening to and would soon repeat myself were the essence of Buddhism, its central theme and inspiration. They referred to the *Triratna* or the Triple Gem of Buddhism, also known as the Three Treasures or Three Refuges. These were the Buddha, Dhamma (Dharma, in Sanskrit), and Sangha. *Buddha* referred to the historical founder of Buddhism, the Enlightened or Awakened One, Siddhartha Gautama. It could also be interpreted as "Buddha Nature" or the highest spiritual consciousness that lived potentially within all beings. *Dhamma* referred to the Buddha's teachings but could also represent the Eternal Truth revealed by his teaching or the path to enlightenment. *Sangha* was the community of enlightened beings that were present among us to assist us in our paths to enlightenment but also the community of monks ("bhikkus") and nuns ("bhikkhunis") and all individuals who had devoted themselves to Buddhism and Buddhist practice.

Jaroon guided me through the recitation of the *Triratna* or Triple Gem of Buddhism. I repeated in Pali the chant that I had been listening to for the last 20 minutes here in Wat Satchatam and that was uttered in temples throughout Thailand and the Buddhist world.

Buddham saranam gacchami. (I take refuge in the Buddha.)
Dhammam saranam gacchami. (I take refuge in the Dhamma.)
Sangham saranam gacchami. (I take refuge in the Sangha.)

I spoke these words alone, my words piercing the soundless night, the unruffled air, the looming darkness with dancing shadows, flickering candles, and folding aromatic plumes of burning incense, orange robed monks around me, my wife behind me, Jaroon before me, a dream, a vision, unreal and lovely, and they echoed within me as a wave. Jaroon, the monks, and now I continued the chant into the night. At the end, Jaroon handed me my robes. I donned them. I now lived in a parallel universe. I had pierced the thin veil that divided the world and dwelled in another land. One of the monks showed me my abode. A wooden floor, thatched hut, with a thin mat and a net, in nature's bosom, in the forest with the trees and the flora and the insects and animals that inhabited this parcel of jungle, my neighbors. Here I would sit, sleep, live, and practice.

Chapter 39

I woke the next morning at 4:30. I strolled slowly back and forth with hands cupped together just below my navel, alongside my forest hermitage, absorbed in "walking meditation." The wildlife was raucous. A symphony of insect and animal sounds and crisp sweet-sounding birdsong echoing back and forth, a chorus of nature, a conversation amongst the denizens of the local community. There were also snakes here. Some reputed to be poisonous and seen occasionally traversing the narrow dirt path that I must walk to get to the main courtyard. In my sandals with exposed ankles, ambling quietly back and forth, I felt exposed. Every sound or movement was a threat or lurking danger. I must quiet my mind. Let thoughts come and go without attaching. Follow the breath. Feel the movement, nothing more.

At 5:30 AM, I "binta-bahd" or go on alms rounds with Jaroon. We each carry our wooden bowls and walk barefoot along a dirt path, over a creaking wooden bridge that traversed a stream towards the village. The sun was rising. The air warming. The early morning light wrapped around us like a garment. The heavens spread forth as a curtain. The dense forest surrounded us. Workers trudged off in sarongs or dirty clothes to the rice fields and rubber trees. We visited the simple homes and we were greeted. First an old lady. A young girl hid behind her dress looking at us bashfully. The lady spooned rice into our bowls, stepped back, knelt, wai'd us, smoothed her hair back, the Thai gesture of respect. There was light conversation. Her face was wrinkled, smiling, and lovely. We continued on our way. At every home and along the road we were greeted by the local people who awaited us, ready to give us food. More commonly it was women, often elderly but not always. Some lifted the food up to their head as they knelt and bowed as if to elevate it as an offering before placing it in our bowls. The food was often wrapped in a plastic bag or a banana leaf. The villagers were polite and deferential to us. Jaroon introduced me.

"He is a farang," he said in Thai.

They smiled and bowed.

"We appreciate that you want to learn about Buddhism," one lady said to me in Thai. "We have never had a farang here before." She wai'd me.

I almost wai'd back but stopped realizing that monks do not wai lay people.

"In some of the forest temples in the north," Jaroon said to me later, "there are many westerners but not here in Hat-Yai. So it is unusual."

Giving of alms was essential to the laity. This act of devotion each morning was their vision of what a good Buddhist should be. They did not meditate or study deeply about the nature of Buddhism, the teachings and practice. For them, Buddhism was this simple act of devotion each morning. This provided some religious compensation for them, to make "merit" and have paid back the monks and the Buddha for having undertaken the difficult road of spirituality and renunciation. The lay people and society as a whole were also the beneficiaries of that dedication, as the monks were there to provide them with spiritual counsel and guidance as the laity provided them with food, other items, and financial contributions to support them.

We continued on our way, receiving food offerings from the lay Thai, filling our bowls. We returned to the temple where the lay devotees that associated with every temple in Thailand arranged the food and prepared the meal for the monks. We sat and ate in silence.

The next morning Jaroon woke me at 4AM. "Yome" (the name monks use for beginners), he called out. "Wake up! You are missing the very best part of the morning. THIS is the time for meditation," he said exuberantly. For the next two hours, I trudged, as Jaroon instructed, like the best foot soldier, back and forth, in front of my hut, mindfully following the "in-breath and the out-breath" in walking meditation. Then, at six, alms rounds again. Breakfast. Then a second meal before noon. Monks could not eat after noon, although they could drink.

I sat cross-legged with the monks and nuns, eating the food offered this morning from the local village. As I reached over to grab a spoonful of the clotted cow's blood marinated in hot green curry I heard the admonishing but friendly voice of Ajarn Jaroon: *"Sati!"* he said and then repeated with solemn emphasis: *"Sati."* Mindfulness. After a pause he took a long, deep breath, filling his lungs and slowly, even gracefully, exhaling. Seeing this grand display of *"sati"* in action, I felt compelled to respond in kind. With my spoon hovering only inches above the green paste of curried cow's blood, arm stretched outward, back hunched over and face nearly buried in a bowl of rice, I too reached deep down into my solar-plexus and sucked in the spicy air. I then released the breath slowly. I looked up at my teacher. He smiled approvingly, *"Sati,"* he said softly. He then returned to his food.

"Sati" was a very important word in Buddhism and especially at Wat Satchatam. It was Pali for mindfulness. Maintaining *"sati"* throughout the day, in any and all activities, was one of the eight cardinal "paths" of Buddha's "Eight-Fold Noble Path. It referred simply to being aware of yourself, feeling your body, being mindful as it were, all of the time. During the day, Ajarn Jaroon could be heard advising *"Sati"* to monk and layperson alike.

I sat in the meditation hall with some 20 lay devotees and a handful of monks and nuns while Ajarn Jaroon guided us through a meditation exercise. He was amiable enough, yet his manner and bearing suggested more nobility than humble monk. While attentive to the audience he managed to remain attuned to the subtle modulations of his own psyche and body, as if checking over with his mind the precise physiologic weave unfolding within himself and particularly the cyclical rhythm of his own breathing. Locals and monks alike had mentioned to me in hushed tones that he had *Saksit* ("spiritual power" in Thai). I had felt this from the beginning.

During my stay, Jaroon permitted me to do some writing and I managed to prepare a few articles for the Bangkok Post and the Nation, two of the main English dailies in Thailand. He was also content to have me read books on Buddhism, in particular from the *Tipitaka* ("Three Baskets") also referred to as the Pali Canon or what Uttamo called the Buddhist Bible. It was the collection of Pali language texts that comprised the scriptural basis of Theravada Buddhism. But he frowned on routine leisure reading.

"Use your time here wisely," he said. "Practice dhamma. Practice *sati*. Mindfulness. This is the basis for all spiritual attainment. You must discipline the mind and remain engaged in each moment. With that discipline will come intuitive wisdom and insight into the nature of things."

I read and Jaroon explained further the basis of this practice, which has come to be known as the Thai Forest Tradition or Vipassana (Insight) Meditation. Through insight into "the way things are" one could reach liberation or enlightenment by knowing intuitively the three "marks of existence" or *tilakkhan,* which referred to *dukkha, anatta* and *anicca* or suffering (unsatisfactoriness), impermanence, and non-self.

"There are the Four Noble Truths," he said, "and the Eight Fold Noble Path, but the foundation is the practice of *sati*. With *sati* comes insight into the reality of impermanence."

There was a nun in Wat Satchatam, whom was called *Mae Chee,* a colorful figure and accomplished in her own right. She wore the white robes of a nun and sat on her platform inside a net meditating for hours without budging. She was 57 years old, used to sell goods in a local market to earn a living, but then left her family and three children five years ago to live here and become a nun. She also made medicines out of various herbs and plants for an array of ailments and purposes such as hemorrhoids, constipation, menstruation, muscle and headaches. She was a fortuneteller and palm reader. She predicted lottery numbers and claimed to turn unlucky people into lucky people. One day an older monk was sitting before a fire he had started, chanting and gazing at the blaze. The monk was chanting softly, rubbing his fingers together while Mae Chee studied the flames.

"Have you seen anything yet," the monk asked Mae Chee in Thai.

She was trying to discern a lottery ticket number within the raging flames.

"Go faster," she said to the monk, which meant to rub his fingers more quickly.

"Anything?" the monk asked.

"I still cannot see the number."

"Look at all sides of the fire. Then you will find it."

She moved around the flame looking for the number. Then she gave him two *saksit* (power) coins, and he began rubbing the coins between his thumb and first two fingers.

"Rub the coins as fast as you can. Then I will see the number."

This continued for a half hour.

"I see it now," Mae Chee proudly declared. "It is number 511."

She later gave the number to a layperson in the community that had asked her to divine the right number for an upcoming lottery. It was wrong, which was predictable. But no one cared. She had a good record. When she got it right, she received money and gifts.

Mae Chee

I brought this up to Jaroon. He laughed.

"It has nothing to do with Buddhism, but I permit it. It is the local culture and I cannot fully dismiss the superstitions of the people around us, even though it is not Buddhism."

"It could be corrupting," I said.

"Yes, it can. It is a common problem with Buddhism in Thailand. We have many scandals. Buddhist temples are often more like social or psychological counseling centers than places of in-depth Buddhist practice. Monks have to help those with serious mental or social problems."

"Like churches in the US."

"Even in Wat Satchatam, a forest temple devoted to serious Buddhist practitioners interested in insight or Vipassana meditation."

He told me that one of the monks had grave family problems and so joined the temple to help him learn to cope. There was a darker skinned Thai fellow who was a killer from the province of Satun. The older monk who assisted Mae Chee in fortune telling, other than chanting, had not spoken a word in years. Another odd-looking, pudgy fellow with a kind of webbed neck and thick glasses was almost comical in appearance. He chose to live in a hole exactly two meters deep and two meters square. Inside his subterranean abode he had jugs of ancient Chinese medicine he had made including a mushroom juice mixture that he produced from the local forest. He also had a virtual pharmacy of homemade remedies for a variety of ailments including memory loss, insomnia, and mood swings. He had something for colitis, depression, and joint pain. He insisted I try one curative to reduce libido, perhaps useful for monks.

"This helps you not think of women," he said.

I declined.

Jaroon understood Buddhism intellectually but also practiced it, a perfect merging. When around him I felt myself in the presence of someone fully engaged in Buddhist exercise. He observed each moment, not one jot escaping his notice, the deluge of sensations and thoughts, witnessed and noted as they drifted by. That was his work, his life, what he described as "practicing dhamma."

"Don't think, better to feel the body. Nothing else," he said to me one sultry afternoon while sitting in the courtyard. It was a splendid day. Hot but pleasant. The monks practiced walking meditation or else rested in their simple dwellings. The lay assistants cleaned quietly in the kitchen. The temple dogs settled in for a lazy afternoon. A light breeze stirred the leaves and branches of the towering trees and foliage. There was so much here in each moment. Here and everywhere.

"When I am back in my world as a surgeon, in the operating room, seeing dozens of patients each day in the clinic, can I still practice as we do here?" I asked.

"Yes, mindfulness. *Sati*. Feel the body, observe the breath, at all times."

"I find it hard to maintain focus here in the temple with nothing to do but meditate. How can I do it when I am busy and preoccupied with my work and life?"

"Dhamma must become bigger and bigger. And the world smaller and smaller. Until there is only dhamma. Grasp or cling to dhamma. Don't cling to the world."

"There are so many problems in my life," I said.

He gazed across the courtyard in a state of contemplation, his norm it seemed. "You cannot correct the outside, only the inside. *Sati* at all times. Mindfulness. The world is an imperfect place. It can never be perfected. Only the mind can be cleansed and perfected. Through the practice of mindfulness."

I nodded and practiced the technique myself.

"See the mind, thoughts, feelings. See the emptiness of mind. Practice dhamma. Every day. Every moment," he said.

"I want to return to my work as a surgeon, yet I love this life. I want to perfect myself, to discipline the mind, but the distractions of the world are great."

"But within each moment there is only mind. Where is your mind? Your heart? There is only this mind, this body, this moment. Study the mind, study self. Embrace this moment and nothing more," he said.

"It is simple. Yet hard."

"Kill defilements or defilements kill you. Either the world consumes you or dhamma consumes you. Either the world becomes bigger within us or dhamma. Cling only to dhamma. Abandon yourself to dhamma," he said.

I saw only wisdom emanating from my friend Jaroon. And the over-whelming presence of a man who had attained a level of self-mastery that was astonishing to observe. A man who truly had abandoned the world to embrace the dhamma, who was alive with dhamma well beyond the intellect but at the level of perception, intuition, and the unconscious, who's entire being emanated a charged, fully engaged awareness of non-self, dhamma, and each eternal moment.

I wondered if I could use the term "enlightenment" to describe him but never asked. Perhaps it was not a term to use since the effort of enlightenment was ongoing and needed to be maintained, *sati* stable, fixed, and enduring. Once attained, I imagined, one would never depart from its brilliance or splendor, would never imperil it, and hence preserve and protect it as some-thing precious and rare – else fall away and lose oneself again to temptation and attachment. Or, perhaps, enlightenment, like healing, came and went, was not fixed or static, and always at risk. In either case, I felt that I was in the presence of such an individual, an enlightened being, an *arahant* or living Buddha, someone who had perfect wisdom and compassion and no longer subject to rebirth. What the Mahayanists or Tibetans might refer to as a *Bodhisattva*. I reconsidered my cynicism towards the attainment of enlightenment. Jaroon was a living example. It was possible, I now realized. I had witnessed it. It gave me hope in my own spiritual journey.

Jaroon

"There is only meditation. Each moment, whatever you are doing, is a meditation," he said. And so it seemed for him. For whatever we were doing, he was present in full, his entire being alive, aware and attentive to the moment.

I spent three weeks with Jaroon and the other monks. I could easily have spent six months or perhaps a lifetime. Ying had been patient but was pleased that we could be together again. I had not told her how long I would remain in the temple. Perhaps, because I did not know.

"I missed you," she said. She wai'd me.

"I am happy you let me do this."

Jaroon had become a friend and spiritual guide. I respected him. I also found that he had contracted malaria, which was not surprising given his life in the forest. He was on medicine for it and was quite anemic. He looked pale I thought, but he remained vigorous.

On the day that I left, I returned my robes. Now it began. It was remarkable to return to this world. All the activities and diversions of routine life were available to me again. It was exciting and a relief. Yet I knew what I was relinquishing. The stillness and serenity of the monastic life, the freedom from the very things that now seemed so enticing. The Buddhist life was constraining yet liberating. It was freedom from the endless pursuits and plans and desires of mundane existence. It was the experience of the mind in the moment and nothing more. It was emancipating. Yet I remained driven to return to my medical work. I could not delay that any longer. Perhaps the practice of medicine was my walking meditation, helping those in need in some of the poorest countries in the world, my path to salvation and realization. I would maintain the Buddhist practice of *sati* in the real and often painful realm of third world medicine and surgery. I would take the lessons of my good friend and teacher, Phra Maha Jaroon and endeavor to integrate the two.

I also stopped in to bid farewell to my colleagues at the ENT Department at Prince of Songkla University. Dr. Sumet had generously allowed me to stay in my old apartment.

"I am impressed that you spent the last three weeks in a forest temple. I am Thai and I have never done that," he said laughing.

He and my other friends and colleagues wished Ying and me well.

The next day, Ying and I rode the train up to Bangkok. We booked two tickets to Kathmandu, the capitol of Nepal aboard Biman Airlines, the national airline for Bangladesh. The thought made me nervous. Did Bangladesh even have a national airline? Floods and typhoons maybe but an airline? But no matter. The next phase of my journey would begin as we prepared to venture to the Himalayan Kingdom of Nepal.

V. Nepal

Chapter 40

October 16, 1989

The plane soared high over the flat wetlands of Bangladesh in transit to Nepal. Lacing rivers and estuaries, interspersed with vast green fields, saturated the landscape. All of a sudden, I noticed the plane seemed so much closer to the earth. I hadn't felt the plane begin its descent. What was going on? A Biman Airlines special? I looked around outside the window and realized that, in this case, the earth had come up. We were entering Nepal and flying over the foothills of the Himalayan Mountains, the tallest mountain range in the world. Nepal, a small landlocked nation sandwiched between the two Asian giants, China and India, sat right in the heart of the tallest part of the range. Mountains filled the view from the window as we landed in Kathmandu.

I had been invited to visit the Tribhuvan University Teaching Hospital in Kathmandu by a local ENT doctor there named Rakesh Prasad. Unlike Thailand, no provisions could be made for me. Although I could hardly save money in Thailand, at least accommodations and a small local wage had been given. In Nepal, an extremely poor country, there was no such allowance. My personal funds were running low, and Ying and I would be on a tight budget. Not to worry, as the friendly letter from Rakesh mentioned, "You will find living in Nepal very inexpensive." I hoped so. Still, shrinking funds notwithstanding, I was very excited about this next phase of the journey. Nepal was one of the most beautiful countries in the world, and I was going there to work, teach and perform surgery on poor, neglected patients. I was young, without ties or responsibilities, and could offer something that was vitally needed. There was nothing else I would rather be doing.

After our arrival, we passed through customs, changed money, and walked out of the airport. We were instantly besieged by an army of cab drivers offering rides to "good, cheap hotels" in town. A middle-aged man with a Nepalese hat, who looked and sounded exactly like Nehru, the first Prime Minister of India, finally whisked us into a car. It was almost uncanny. He spoke in gentle, fatherly tones, reassuring us that he had a fine, inexpensive hotel that he was certain we would enjoy. Along the way, "Nehru" pointed out small temples and other sights, and referred to Ying and I as "little brother and sister." Although I knew Nehru was a "hotel tout," that is, someone paid a commission to lure people to a particular hotel, Nehru had a way about him that made you feel ashamed to even think of not choosing his hotel. We arrived shortly at the "Paramount Hotel" in the center of town. The ceiling was low, there was no heat, and the shower was ice cold. You could hear footsteps from three floors away and children crying in the next building. It was cold, dark and noisy, but at one hundred rupees a night (about three dollars), Nehru was right. It was a deal.

Ying and I dumped our bags in the room and ran up to the roof for a view of the city. In the distance, we could make out the magnificent snow-capped peaks of the Himalayas, hovering silently amidst the clouds. Kathmandu nestled in the shadow of these powerful giants, cut off, until recently, from the rest of the world. The city spread out in all directions in the center of a broad valley near the foothills of the mountains and was laced with intimate, labyrinthine streets and alleys. Ornate and grand temples and shrines were visible in the distance.

"What an amazing place," I said. "I can't believe we're here."

We ran down to the streets below like two excited kids to find Kathmandu in full medieval fervor. The place was a blur of movement and activity. Just outside our hotel was a rusty old water pump with a long line of Nepalese waiting with wooden buckets in hand to fill up and carry to their homes. Flamboyant mountain people dressed in colorful garments, balanced large sacks on their backs or huge jugs of fresh milk. Some of them led cows or families of goats along with a whipping stick, controlling them with a strange, piercing sound they made with their throats. Teams of oxen crowded the narrow dirt roads pulling large rickety carts that crashed forward on their wooden wheels over the uneven paths. Miniature stores lined the streets, some the size of closets, where the owners sat on small platforms, cross legged like monks, carefully surveying the traffic, displaying their ware of grains and polychromatic spices, freshly made yogurt, dhal (a kind of lentil), vegetables, figs, apricots, raisins, and a profusion of nuts. Butchers hacked away at huge slabs of beef that hung in your face or lay on the dirt floor with flies buzzing around.

Vendors hawked traditional garments, ornaments, religious artifacts, Tankas (paintings of Tibetan Buddhist deities), jewelry, ritual instruments, and bowls. There were necklaces carved from the bones of yaks studded with turquoise or other semiprecious stones. Peddlers displayed Tibetan flutes made from the femurs of monks, or ritual prayer bowls decorated in silver formed from the actual skulls of powerful saints. Tailors sewed religious symbols on jeans and shirts in brilliant golden thread for a couple of dollars.

Tibetan Buddhist and Hindu temples and iconography abounded with ornate and sometimes erotic carvings and sculpture. Buddhist devotees circumambulated the large white domed-shaped stupas or shrines, turning prayer wheels, lighting incense and candles, or whispering invocations. Monks and sadhus passed by, dressed in red or purple or orange robes, some with their foreheads covered in colorful pigments, chanting mantras, posing for pictures (for a fee), fingering beads, or spinning hand-held prayer wheels.

"It is another world," Ying said.

I nodded. "A vision from the past."

Everyone seemed to be in a hurry, oblivious to the world about them, locked into their little worlds, where life moved in the same centuries old patterns and rhythms. The atmosphere was charged with a deeply religious or spiritual quality, yet simultaneously secular, material, and wildly chaotic. There was no inconsistency or dichotomy. The religious and the secular seemed to merge without seams or borders, one immersed in the other, rendering everything, including the most mundane activities with a sanctity or religiosity.

"I love the disorder," I said.

The city seemed to be in miniature. The streets, homes, and stores, even the people, were small and intimate. It was vital and alive, almost in a fever, yet old and harkening back to the ancient ways. It was a storybook village, an intense and beautiful pageant, a window through time, where you could smell, taste and feel the presence of the past in every corner and alley. The people still reveled in their traditions, moved freely and comfortably within the confines of their culture, spoke, thought and acted based on age-old customs and beliefs, and yet, still managed to absorb, without missing a step, the inevitable intrusion and disruption of the West.

There were also sundry novel and peculiar characters inhabiting Kathmandu, holdovers from the old hippy days that gathered here. Kathmandu was one of the main destinations on the Europe to Asia overland backpacker trail, a major stomping ground for budget world travelers, along with Kabul in Afghanistan, and Goa in India, that had emerged in the sixties and seventies and persisted to this day. Kathmandu definitely had its share of western freaks, new-age types, neo-Buddhists, spiritualists, druggies, radical vegetarians, old fashioned hippies, and strung out down and outers.

"We will not avoid Westerners," I said. "I guess we are all drawn to the same thing."

Nepal, like Thailand, had definitely become a trendy hotspot on the international tourist circuit. I was not particularly fond of the multitudes of tourists, and, hypocritically, I suppose, wished they would somehow disappear. I worried about the impact of these hundreds of thousands of westerners on the traditional culture as well as the environment. "I wonder if the system can endure all this," I said, "without a breakdown somewhere." Despite the resiliency of their traditions, sooner or later, something had to give. Like it or not though, they were here to stay. "I only hope they will keep their ways and traditions and not lose everything for the sake of foreign revenue," I said. "Maybe they will find a way."

"I hope so," Ying said. "We have gone through this in Thailand."

"When you lose your culture, you lose everything," I said.

I saw tourism as something of a kiss of death.

That first day we took a walk to Durbar Square, the center of old Kathmandu. From there we headed west to Swayambhunath Stupa, also known as the "Monkey Temple" as there were dozens of "sacred" monkeys present, living within its sanctuaries and holy places. Visible from a distance, it beckoned like a shining light with its massive white dome and golden spire atop a wooded hill. It was a landmark of Kathmandu, possessed of much historic and religious significance. "We'll make a pilgrimage," I said to Ying.

There was a staircase of some 365 steps leading to the main platform. Upon scaling the final steps, we were met by the largest *vajra* ("dorje" in Tibetan, a thunderbolt scepter, a Tibetan Buddhist "Tantric" energy instrument) I had ever seen. "Incredible," I said. "I have seen smaller dorjes you can hold in your hand but never one the size of a person."

Vajra was a Sanskrit word meaning both thunderbolt and diamond. It possessed properties of both. A diamond was indestructible. A thunderbolt contained irresistible force. The vajra was a ritual knife or scepter with a ribbed spherical head. It was used in the spiritual traditions of Buddhism (Mahayana or Vajrayana), Jainism, and Hinduism and represented both resolute spiritual determination and vigor. Vajrayana Buddhism was one of the three major branches of Buddhism (along with Mahayana and Hinayana, the latter also known as Theravada). It could be translated as the "Thunderbolt" path or the "Diamond" path. Vajrayana Buddhism was also referred to as "Tantric Buddhism" because of the use of the various "tantric" or ritual objects such as the vajra (dorje) or ghanta (bell).

"I took Tantric Yoga classes," I said, "when I lived in a Yoga ashram in Bloomington, Indiana as an undergrad and later as a medical student. The vajras are said to be able to cut through layers of ignorance like a knife."

I suspected there were similarities in its use between the various Tantric schools. There were other giant vajras spread throughout the complex.

"There is a big difference between Tibetan and Thai style Buddhism," I said. "You would never see this in a Thai temple. It is alien to the Thai tradition."

"I have never seen one before," Ying said.

"I like the pageantry of the Mahayana or Tibetan style," I said, "but it is very different from Thai Buddhism. It is amazing to see how Buddhism evolved as it made its way from India to the rest of Asia with all of the variations. I remember 'Pure Land Buddhism' in Japan when I lived there as a medical student. There you recite the Buddha's name and pray for deliverance, almost a Christian form of devotion. It is a far cry from the self-mastery and insight of the Theravadins."

There were many Buddhist innovations in its 2500-year history. The Mahayana and Vajrayana (Tibetan style) not to mention Zen and other variants were dramatic adaptations that evolved through the centuries.

"I ordained as a Theravadin at Wat Satchatam. I believe it is the best path to wisdom in the Buddhist tradition. But I am attracted to this as well."

We clambered up to the main level. There were other shrines, painted deities, sanctuaries and religious objects dispersed throughout the temple complex but the dominant structure was the conical white dome with the golden cubical above it with the Buddha's eyes painted on each side, gazing out serenely in all four directions of Kathmandu valley.

Monkey Temple

"I am content in this Himalayan kingdom," I said. "I like its openness and chaos. It is spiritual pandemonium. Hindu, Buddhist, and all the various schools of Buddhism. I wonder if they have any Hassidic Jews here?"

Ying didn't know much about the different Jewish movements but seemed to know this. She laughed. "You mean the funny ones with the black hats and long sideburns?" she asked.

"Uh huh."

She giggled again.

"Pretty good, Ying, I didn't think you would get that."

"I saw something about them on TV. It was a program about Israel," she said.

We walked back to our hotel. It was, I felt, an auspicious beginning to our work in Nepal. I wanted it to succeed. I wanted to enjoy this amazing country and do some good.

Chapter 41

Dr. Rakesh Prasad was an Otolaryngologist on the faculty at the local teaching hospital. I had contacted him before, and we arranged to meet at my hotel. I wondered what he thought when he poked his head into my small, dark room to find me sitting on my bed, unshaven, dressed in sneakers, dungarees and a raggedy Nepalese sweater. Somehow, I imagined, I didn't quite fit the image of a cancer surgeon. Rakesh was in his mid-thirties, plump, conservatively dressed, and appeared prosperous. He extended his hand, ducking under a low-lying beam as he greeted me with some curiosity.

"So you are finally here after all this time," he smiled. We had first communicated by mail more than two years ago when I lived in San Francisco. I had told him I would get here - eventually.

"Yes, it's been a while since that first letter. I had a little stopover in Thailand. But it was useful. I made all my mistakes there so I would be ready for you."

He laughed.

We walked outside together, towards "New Kathmandu," the modern, recently built part of town with regular streets where his car was parked. We arranged to meet there tomorrow to go to the hospital. He apologized for not being able to pick me up at my hotel, but the narrow crowded streets of old Kathmandu could scarcely be navigated by car.

We arrived at the Tribhuvan University Teaching Hospital the next morning, the main, if not only, referral hospital for the entire country. It was built by the Japanese a few years ago, at a cost of three million dollars and was surprisingly modern and clean. We entered through the Emergency room, turned right and headed down a narrow corridor for the Ear Nose and Throat clinic. As we passed, I noticed pictures of the King and Queen of Nepal hanging above the entrance. It reminded me of similar photos of the King and Queen of Thailand. I had already learned though, in my short time here, that the royal family of Nepal was not nearly as popular as their Thai counterparts.

The hall was packed with Nepalese, filling the benches, sitting on the floors, standing, all waiting to be seen by the ENT doctors. As we got closer to the clinic, the crowd only thickened. Scores of Nepalese pressed so tight you could hardly budge. We arrived at the door and encountered a Nepalese soldier dressed in a green uniform and beret and carrying an old musket. He looked me dead in the eye, held his musket in my face and indicated in no uncertain terms that I was not getting through the door. "Whoa, what's this all about," I said to Ying. I looked for Rakesh. I had lost him in the crowd. It dawned on me that as far as this soldier was concerned, Ying and I were two more locals in the throng waiting to get in. "He thinks we're patients," I said. I had dark hair and complexion and looked like any other Nepalese or Indian, while Ying, with her small size and oriental features, could easily have passed for a Tibetan. Considering the huge crowd, I could understand the need for this sort of thing. Fortunately, Rakesh appeared, and the soldier immediately allowed us to pass.

Inside the clinic it was no less crowded. There were individual booths set up where the doctors and residents were examining the patients. Off to the side was a room where Rakesh and Dr. Amatya, the chairman of the department, could examine the patients privately. Rakesh escorted us to the private room where we encountered a short bespectacled man, in a blue suit and tie examining a patient. He was impeccably manicured, scented, and groomed, and appeared as dapper as any man I have ever met. Dr. Amatya, recognizing us immediately, looked up from his patient and was utterly beside himself in welcoming us to his little kingdom in the mountains.

"Dr. and Mrs. Moss?" he began, in very polished tones. "Please, please, sit down, sit down. Make yourselves comfortable. I am so happy to see you. Let me get you some tea. Some coffee. Some donuts. Welcome, welcome."

In seconds, one of the nurses, chubby and matronly, appeared with two steaming cups of tea. "Drink, please be comfortable. I am so pleased you are here. Some donuts?" Before I could say yes or no, two tiny deep fried donuts appeared. "Eat, eat, you must be hungry, please eat. It is so good to have you. We have so many patients and so many cancer cases. By the way, how was your trip?" I was amused at Amatya's ability to shift gears. "We are fine, thanks."

"Good, good," he responded, pausing for an instant to catch his breath. "You see, Dr. Moss, our problem is we lack experience with the cancer cases. We all do our best, but it is not enough. It will be so good of you to help us. We have saved cases for you, some of them are very late stage. I hope you won't mind. We will make rounds together, and you will have a better idea. But please, finish your tea. Another donut?"

Ying and I were led to the wards by a small contingency of Nepalese doctors, including Rakesh, Amatya, a young male resident with the auspicious name of Dharma, a beautiful intern with long black hair that ran down below her knees named Bi-pu, a senior resident, Prasad, tall, dark, and thin, somewhat ghostly looking, and others. "Welcome, Dr. Moss, I will be happy to take you around," said Dharma.

The wards consisted of large communal rooms with about twelve beds lined up army style in each. At the entrance to each ward there was the familiar Nepalese soldier with high black rubber boots, beret, ruffled, green uniform, and American civil war musket. After recognizing us, the soldier let us pass, usually accompanied by a good, stiff salute. The nurses on the wards wore traditional blue uniforms with lovely bonnets and eagerly followed us around as we went from bed to bed.

One of the first patients I met was an eight-year-old boy, who, on first glance, appeared perfectly normal. He was lying on his side and was roused from sleep by a concerned father as he saw us approaching. The boy sat up sleepily, and, as the doctors turned him around, I could see that rather than normal this young boy had a large tumor that had completely bulged the left eye out of its socket. The eye, already showing signs of exposure was swollen and red and beginning to cloud over.

"You see what I mean," Amatya said, almost despairingly, "we are not sure what to do with this poor boy, he is so young. And the tumor is so close to the eye."

"I see."

"What do you think?"

"Do you have a CT scan here?"

"Excuse me, Dr. Moss?"

"A CT scan."

"Uh, no, Dr. Moss, we do not have such equipment here," Rakesh cut in. "We would have to send him to New Delhi for that, sorry."

"Uh huh. I understand." I was not surprised. I imagined there were more pressing needs in the Himalayas than a CT scan.

"I'm afraid there are many things we will not be able to provide you with. I hope you will not mind," Amatya added.

"We'll make do." I felt a little uncomfortable operating on a kid like this without knowing exactly where the tumor was arising from, or how extensive it was, but if I waited, he would lose the eye. I quickly made up my mind. "He probably has a tumor in the ethmoid sinus, and it's invaded the orbit. We'll have to approach this through an extended Lynch incision. We can operate as soon as you can get him ready."

"Fine, sir, I will arrange it," Dharma answered. I liked Dharma. He was attentive and eager to learn.

"Great."

We continued on to the next bed to find a middle-aged man who looked fine until he opened his mouth. Using a tongue blade and penlight, I identified a large beefy cancer that had completely devoured the poor man's palate. The tumor had also spread into the man's lip and the undersurface of his cheek and nose. He kept a gauze pad in his mouth to absorb the constant oozing of blood.

"We operated on him a year ago, but unfortunately the tumor has come back. He waited too long before seeing us. Now it is so large." Rakesh said.

"He'll need surgery."

"We will arrange it, Dr. Moss," Dharma said.

We next came to the bed of an elderly woman who had the left side of her face and head wrapped in a blood stained, dirty bandage. She was old and gnarled and crying from pain. Slowly, layer-by-layer, one of the interns removed the dressing. As the last layers of gauze came off, I noticed a foul odor. As they turned the patient toward me, I could see where the smell was coming from - a large festering cancer that had eaten the skin off the side of her face, eye and forehead. Her left eye dangled in the center of this rotting mess, like a shriveled, dried out onion, and the bone of her skull was exposed and partially digested. If I pushed in hard enough, I probably could have touched her brain.

"Do you have a neurosurgeon here?" I asked.

"There is one, but he is in another hospital. It is very difficult to get him. He is the only one in the country," Rakesh answered.

"We'll have to speak to him before I do this case."

"That may not be possible, but we will do our best. We have tried to contact him before."

"To take this tumor out you're going to need a neurosurgeon."

"I understand, but it may not be possible, Dr. Moss, he is very busy."

"If not, you could possibly give her radiation for palliation. You'll have to clean it up a bit first."

"I'm afraid we cannot offer that either."

"Why not?"

"We don't have radiation. The Japanese are thinking of buying a machine for us, but until then we have nothing.

"No radiation in the entire country?"

"No."

"Then we may not be able to do anything for this lady," I said.

"I understand. Unfortunately, that is not uncommon here."

I understood it too. This was life in the third world, and patients often had to be abandoned to their fates. There simply wasn't the resources or expertise necessary to help everyone.

We started to move on to the next patient when the old lady suddenly leaped from her bed and grabbed my arm. It was remarkable to see this dying old woman move with such speed. She cried and moaned while clinging to my arm, and I could see the tears forming from her one good right eye, while the other hung freely in the air, dripping pus and cloudy, yellow serum. She fell to the floor and held onto my legs. I watched her head bobbing up and down as she sobbed, appealing to me to help her. The doctors slowly lifted her from the floor and returned her to bed. She remained unconsoled and tormented. Cancer had pushed her body beyond the pale, and there was nothing we could do for her.

The next patient was a man who lay curled up on his bed like a fetus. The doctors sat him up. He was drooling and groaning and appeared in great pain. He did not acknowledge me or anyone else, keeping his eyes closed as if he could block out the pain by shutting his eyes tightly. Dharma had him open his mouth, and held his cheek to the side with a tongue blade. "Open wide," Dharma said in Nepali as the man winced even with this small effort. A large cancer had encased half of the man's tongue and throat like a bed of concrete. The man's son, speaking in Nepali, explained that his father had not slept in months because of the pain. "Since the thunder entered his mouth," Dharma had translated from the son's own words. "We can operate on this one. He'll need a Commando and a flap. We'll have to take most of his tongue and jaw. This will be a good case. You will learn a lot," I said. (A "Commando" was the resection of part of the tongue, jaw, and the lymph nodes of the neck, a major operation.)

We continued through the wards examining patients and discussing cases. Each patient seemed to be more extraordinary, advanced, and grotesque than the last. The final patient we saw was a man from a remote village in the mountains. He spoke only a dialect of Nepali and wore a hat low down over his forehead. What was immediately apparent on meeting him was that he was missing his entire upper lip, cheek, and palate. As with so many other patients I had encountered in Asia, he was remarkably nonchalant about his rather repulsive condition.

"I think he had a bad infection as a child. Probably from malnutrition. It destroyed his upper lip. It is common here," Dharma said.

"And he only came now?" I asked.

"Yes, Dr. Moss, that is common too," Dharma replied. "As you see, we have a problem with our patients neglecting themselves. But this man has been in the hospital awaiting your arrival for more than a month. He comes from a remote village. We have been saving him for you."

"He's been waiting more than a month?"

"Yes."

"Why?"

"He lives in the mountains. It would take weeks to go and come back." Amazing, I thought to myself.

I examined the patient, looking at the large hole between his lower lip and nose - just empty space. You could look directly into his mouth and sinus and see the fleshy parts of the inside of his nose. Otherwise he looked great. Or so I thought. I took off his hat. What I saw looked even more hideous than the missing lip. Half of his forehead had been completely crushed in as if someone had taken a sledgehammer to his head. The patient smiled in his own peculiar way at the look on my face.

"How'd this happen?"

"We are not sure. He was not disturbed by it so we did not inquire. He did say he has had it all his life, as far back as he can remember and thinks it may have happened when a cow stepped on his head."

"And you didn't mention it to me?"

"Sorry, Dr. Moss, but he was not bothered by it. Our people live with so many things."

"I see."

"But he did want his lip fixed. He said he wants to kiss his wife," Dharma smiled. Shy laughter rippled through the crowd. I somehow found it odd that he would have a wife.

"We can definitely help his lip but find out about the forehead. If he wants to kiss his wife, we may as well make him look good while he's doing it." Dharma spoke in Nepali to the man who listened carefully. His eyes suddenly lit up, and he began nodding excitedly.

"He would like that done too," Dharma announced proudly. "He has been this way all his life, and did not know it could be fixed. He is very happy you have come."

"Good, let's do it next week."

Chapter 42

On the way down the stairs of our hotel, I was stopped by a balding, burned out looking hippy type, who was probably in his mid-forties, but could have passed for sixty. He was pale, thin, and exhausted. I never met the guy before, but he seemed to know me.

"Hey man, I heard you wuz livin' here. I heard about your work, man, it sounds really interestin', y'know." There was no mistaking that accent - another New Yorker in Kathmandu. "I'm here in da same hotel, for cryin' out loud, whaddaya dink about dat?" There could be nothing more incongruous than a thick New York brogue in Nepal.

"Huh?"

"Your work, man, your work. I wanna tawk to ya about dis work you're doin'."

"Sure," I answered, "No problem. How'd you hear about me?"

"Dese Nepalese guys downstairs told me."

"What'd they tell you?"

"All about you, man. What you're doin' in the hospital here."

"What did they say?"

"You're a regular friggin' healer, man, that's what they told me, for chrissakes. Dey come in sick n' you cure 'em. "

"Are you in medicine?"

"No, but I'm interested."

"How so?"

"I'm interested in anyone doin' somethin' good - and different. 'Cause dat's what I've been doin' the last seven years."

Ying started down the stairs. "We're going out to eat now, why don't you join us?"

"Cool, man, let's go."

We went out to eat. Ted Abramowitz, my newfound friend, was something of an aging hippy although not exactly.

"I came of age in the sixties," he announced proudly. "I'm forty-four years old, Jewish, from New York. I used to be a chemical engineer." Somehow he made me think of Uttamo, also Jewish, from New York, and a physicist in his former life. "I was raised by my aunt. She died seven years ago and she left me eighty thousand dollars. I quit my job and spent the next seven years traveling through Asia and Africa living off the money my aunt gave me."

"Where'd you go?"

"Where didn't I go? You can cover a lot of ground in seven years of continuous travel, no work and no kids."

"I may need to try that some time."

"I had incredible adventures, all sorts of close encounters and narrow escapes."

"Really?"

"Oh, yeah. I've been sick with yellow fever, malaria, and every form of dysentery known. Especially in Africa. Really backwards there. I lived hand to mouth, went completely native. I avoided all forms of luxury or creature comfort in the poorest countries in the world. I was living the dream, man."

We laughed.

"Why not indulge a little."

"Wasn't into it, man. I wanted it straight, just like the locals. No different. I wanted to become one of them."

I nodded. It was a kind of Uttamo story albeit very different. I liked his wackiness and intensity.

"But the endless movement has taken a toll on me. I haven't been home in seven years. I am dizzy and worn out. I feel like an old man, really beat up. And my funds are running low. Can't live off my beloved auntie forever."

"Right."

"But there's no doubt about where I want to be. Right here in the third world. It's where I belong, with the natives, poor and run down, barely surviving day to day. That's me, man. It's reality. I would just as soon starve to death on the streets of Kathmandu than consider the option of returning to my former life. It's a matter of honor. Of not selling out my vision."

"So you won't return home? Even if you get sick?"

"Never. That world is dead to me. It's artificial, synthetic, make-believe. It's without substance or meaning. It's better to live and die here among the natives who understand life so much better. Besides, dying wasn't the point. It was how you died and where. There's more dignity in dying of starvation or cholera in the mountains or in a forest or on an abandoned dirt road somewhere than in a hospital with tubes and IVs and monitors back in the states."

"I like it, and I understand you fully. So you're never going back?"

"No way, Rick, no way. I'll never go back. I'd rather die."

"Why not return, make a little money and get back on the road later?"

"Because I couldn't do it. I left that life already. I'm not interested in going back. It doesn't matter to me."

"What about your health?"

"It doesn't matter."

"What about your life?"

"I don't care about that either. What does my life mean? What does it matter if an animal dies in the woods? Most people are lookin' for places to live, or settle down, to lead their lives, but me, I'm not lookin' for a place to live, Rick, I'm lookin' for a place to die."

He was a weird guy. But our lives and philosophies converged. He seemed very Asian or perhaps American Indian. "Where do you want to die?"

"Africa. I wanna die in Africa. I'm goin' back 'dere next month."

"Why Africa?"

"Cause that's where it's at. It's raw out there in the jungle. Naked, clean and wild. When you wanna feel your heart beating, dat's the place."

"To die?"

"Yeah, to die. Maybe. We'll see, Rick. I'm not sure yet. I'm gonna buy a horse when I get back there and look around."

He was strange, Ted was, but I liked him. One look at him and you knew he'd gone off the deep end once or twice, but he still had a clear perception of what was important to him. He also wanted to observe me in the operating room. "I can still get into what you're doing, Rick, it's good. Especially out here in the boonies. "'Dat guy in the hotel told me about you. I can take pictures if you want, help you out in some way. It's something I never saw before. I'd love to watch. Whaddaya think?"

"No problem, Ted, I could use a photographer."

"Hey, dat's great. I'm really lookin' forward to it."

And so it went with our evening, talking until late, stopping by the Baker's Café, one of our favorite haunts, for some homemade apple pie, listening to crazy Ted go on about his adventures, but somehow taking great interest in my own odd career as well. Ted would accompany me frequently to the operating room during my stay in Nepal, and we became good friends. For some reason, the idea of helping me in my work seemed important to him.

Chapter 43

It had been a long day in the operating room. We had operated on two cases and still had to do the man with the missing lip and the crushed forehead. The first patient was the eight-year-old boy with the tumor in the eye. The second was the man with the tongue cancer. Both cases had gone well but had taken time. It was five PM, and the anesthesiologists were unable to stay for the final case. I didn't feel like starting another major case at this late hour, but I didn't want to disappoint the patient. There were so many other urgent cases to do. We could have operated seven days a week and still not take care of the backlog. I would have to operate on him today; but because the anesthesiologists had to leave, I'd have to do it with him fully awake.

Fixing the lip under local anesthesia did not present a problem, but I was concerned about the forehead. To repair the forehead, I would have to take bone from one part of the skull, and move it into the area that was crushed. That meant using a drill, hammer and chisel on the poor guy's head while he was fully awake. There was no neurosurgeon in the hospital in case I got into trouble. What if the patient moved or the chisel slipped? What if I accidentally got into the guy's brain? Lots of things could go wrong with this case, and I was doing it alone.

The patient was brought to the operating room table, and his head was completely shaven. I injected the scalp with Novocain to numb it. The nurses painted the head with brown iodine solution and placed sterile towels around the surgical field. His head sparkled like a fragile brown egg in the bright overhead lights. I drew a line with a marking pen over the top of the head, from ear to ear, where I would make the incision, and took the knife. In one swift movement, I pressed knife against human scalp and cut long and deep and retracted the scalp out of the way exposing the underlying white bone of the skull. I looked at the crushed bone where his forehead used to be. It was completely smashed in from a decades old event now lost to memory. I then exposed the part of the skull where I would "borrow" normal bone in order to reconstruct the forehead.

I asked for the drill.

The only working drill in the hospital was an ancient orthopedic contraption used for amputating legs. It had all the precision of a jackhammer. I picked it up. It was very heavy. I had to use both hands to lift it. I was accustomed to a small, precise mastoid drill for microscopic ear surgery, which you could hold with your fingers like a pencil. Unfortunately, that drill was under repair, and they did not have a replacement. Ying, who was assisting, looked at me nervously. Even New York Ted, who had been carefully observing and taking pictures, clammed up. Every eye now focused on this big drill poised precariously over the man's shiny skull.

"Turn it on."

It turned just like a cement mixer, slow and noisy. I brought the rotating steel burr down on human skull. I felt the bite and torque of the drill as the burr began grinding into bone. I had to use all my strength just to keep the drill in proper position. I felt very uncomfortable. White bone dust began building up. I called for irrigation.

Dharma, nervous by nature and clearly out of his depth here, began dripping water from a syringe to keep the bone from heating up.

"Suction."

The burr continued grinding away.

"Aaaarrrggghhhh." The patient began fidgeting. Dharma shouted at him in Nepali to hold still.

"Dr. Moss, he only wanted his lip fixed, maybe we should stop?"

"Don't worry Dharma. Keep suctioning."

I continued drilling. "Damn, this drill." It was overheating. I had to stop for a minute.

My mind drifted. What if I screw up here? He's lived this long with his crushed forehead, why did I have to start fooling around now? There was no neurosurgeon, and I was using an orthopedic cement mixer on the skull. The room was tense and doubts surfaced in everyone including me.

I started the drill again.

Crap! A jet of bright red blood spurt out from the skull and pooled around the head.

"Ohmigod, Dr. Moss, he is bleeding. It's the brain! I told you, Dr. Moss, I told you! We must stop now! He only wanted his lip fixed!" Everyone froze.

"Bone wax." Dharma nervously shoved a large glob of wax in my hand. I pressed it hard against the skull, and the bleeding stopped instantly.

"Just a little bleeder, Dharma."

Dharma was sweating profusely and shaking. "Ohmigod, Dr. Moss. Do we have to do this?"

"Chisel."

I had drilled out the outer perimeter of the graft, creating a kind of trough around it. I now needed to slice through the middle layer of the skull with the chisel, to split the outer half of bone from the inner half, creating a "split thickness" bone graft. The middle layer of skull bone was a natural cleavage plain between the inner and outer cortex. I would leave the inner layer in place, while chiseling out the outer layer to graft and restore the contour of the crushed forehead. I handed off the cement mixer. Ying passed me the chisel. There was dead silence in the room. I wedged the chisel in the right position in the man's skull.

"Hammer."

I pressed the chisel into the bone at just the right angle to drive it in. No one budged or spoke. Everyone was wondering why I was doing this. Why didn't I leave well enough alone and just fix the damn lip? The nurses were anxious. The doctors were tense. Even Ying was worried, wondering whether her husband was about to screw up. Dharma was out of control. His pupils were dilated, and sweat was dripping from his brow. Only Ted, the aging hippy, kept his cool, but then he wasn't holding the chisel.

I raised the hammer with my right hand, while holding the chisel with my left.

"Tap tap tap." I carefully banged the chisel into the man's skull.

"Aaaarrrggghhhh." The patient was moving. Dharma begged him to hold still.

"Tap tap tap." I circled around the bone, trying to gently nudge the outer layer free.

"Tap tap tap." The chisel went deeper into the bone. "Tap tap."

"Aaaarrrggghhhh." The patient was feeling it. The Novocain did not work on bone. Dharma nervously pleaded with him.

"Tap tap."

"Aaaarrrggghhhh."

There was more bleeding from the bone. "Shiva protect us," I heard Dharma praying underneath his mask.

"Tap tap."

"Aaaarrrggghhhh."

More bleeding. "Suction. Quick!"

"Tap tap." A lot of bleeding. "Hurry up with the suction!"

"Yes, Dr. Moss, Ohmigod!" Blood was spilling out over the edges of the bone, drenching the towels around his head.

"Tap tap." Everyone in the room was nervously praying to their respective gods. I wished the damn bone would come apart the way it was supposed to.

"Tap tap." I continued to delicately nudge the outer half of bone.

"Tap tap. Cccrrraaaaaacckkk." The entire room instantly froze, convinced that something terrible had happened. I twisted the chisel at an angle, rotated it up and back, shimmied it in just a little deeper, and, as if by magic, a perfect split thickness bone graft popped out of the man's skull. I held it up and gazed at it.

In that single instant, the atmosphere in the room moved from utter darkness and despair to lightness and joy, as if some terrible catastrophe had been miraculously averted. Ted began snapping pictures. Ying smiled quietly. Dharma was beside himself in pleasure and relief. The nurses were chatting cheerfully like birds, and the students and residents eagerly poured in over the patient to have a look. Everyone seemed completely transfixed with this small piece of bone, admiring it with the same sort of reverence reserved usually for articles of religious significance.

I wired the bone into the crushed forehead and then closed the scalp incision. Soon after we reconstructed the missing upper lip. When we were done the patient looked like a human being again.

"Thank you, thank you, Dr. Moss. It is absolutely beautiful," Dharma said.

Chapter 44

Ying and I hopped a local bus to Pharping, a small village in the mountains near Daxinkali, a Hindu temple dedicated to the wrathful goddess Kali, incarnation of Shakti, wife of Shiva the destroyer, nineteen miles from Kathmandu. The bus was already packed with Nepalese and noisy with the sounds of animals, chickens, ducks and goats. "What a scene this is," I said to Ying. "I like sharing a bus with animals."

"But I don't think it will be a happy voyage for them," Ying said.

Every hundred feet or so the crowded bus would stop for yet another pilgrim, carrying or dragging an animal heading for the same destination. When we got to Pharping, the bus completely emptied, and everyone walked about a mile on a narrow dirt path, traversing lush yellow fields of wheat and carrying or herding their animals innocently along. It was an oddly serene pastoral prelude for what we were about to witness. As we approached the temple, long lines of pilgrims formed, numbering in the hundreds, each carrying a chicken or duck or pulling a goat along with a rope.

Once inside the temple, we could hear the screams of animals, especially the goats, echoing in the temple enclave. "This will be something to see," I said.

The temple had been carved in rock on the side of a hill and had a large stone altar dedicated to the angry goddess, Kali. There were two gates for the pilgrims and their animals to enter the temple, and the ritual priests were hard at work.

One by one, the devotees passed through the gates to hand the priest their animal. The animals all seemed so docile and agreeable, right up until the final moments when the harsh recognition of sudden violent death crowded their small minds, and the instinct for life took over. Holding the animal in the direction of the altar, and clasping a long sharp knife, in one swift stroke, the priest sliced the clucking animal's head off and sprayed the spurting blood at the altar wall already blood stained and dripping, covering it with the same dark red liquid. The head of the animal fell to the ground, while the two carotid arteries pumped rhythmic red plumes, like small fountains, from both sides of the animal's neck until the twitching body of the animal emptied itself. The lifeless carcass was then handed back to the pilgrim who left the sanctuary satisfied that he had performed his duty

228

and comforted in the knowledge that the goddess Kali would look upon him favorably. "Perhaps, it was not unlike this in the ancient temple in Jerusalem," I said. This cycle was repeated over and over for hours, with hundreds of animal sacrifices performed before the morning was over. The floor of the temple was littered with the heads of animals. "I prefer the Tibetan use of 'sacrificial' incense," I said.

The goats represented a major sacrifice, saved for special occasions and felt to augur especially good will from Kali. Two men were needed to hold the neck back and control the animal while the priest, using bold, violent thrusts, sawed the front of the neck open. Two red fountains spurted from the cleaved neck against the sacred altar five feet away while the dying animal struggled and screamed helplessly for its life, gasping and jerking convulsively, red mist spraying from its severed windpipe, its last panic stricken moments of life passing rapidly. The priest kept cutting right through the back of the neck and spinal cord, completely amputating the head, which tumbled towards his feet, rolling a distance and coming to a halt, its eyes still open with the terror and fear of its final seconds. "It is brutal, isn't it," I said. Ying agreed, shaking her head with disgust. The animal's lifeless body, after painting the altar wall with its blood, fell to the ground twitching and bleeding, to be dragged off for boiling and butchering at a station a few levels below. The head of the goat was carried off, placed by a minor altar at the side of the temple, painted with a red pigment between its eyes, a lit candle set atop its head, and burning incense sticks placed around it.

"Kali must be appeased," I said.

"But it is primitive, don't you think Rick?" Ying asked. She was very forthright, which I liked. "We do not do such things in Thailand. We release creatures like birds or fish to gain merit, but we do not sacrifice them. It is very strange to me."

"It is backward," I said.

"I know it is interesting to watch, but it is the opposite of spirituality. You don't need blood sacrifices to appease God. If God created all creatures than how do you gain merit by sacrificing them?"

"I agree."

"The Muslims do the same during their holiday 'Eid,'" she continued. "I grew up with this in the South of Thailand. We did not respect it at all. It is primitive. We do not accept such barbaric practices. We avoided their neighborhoods and villages during this time. We didn't want to see their 'sacrifices' for God. It is not godly at all. It is appalling. How can sacrificing an animal help you or please God?"

Chapter 45

The word spread quickly through the town of Kathmandu that there was an American surgeon visiting who was doing cases. Before long, I was receiving requests from many of the local doctors at the university hospital and other hospitals as well, to see their patients. Local people, expatriates and members of the diplomatic community also heard that I was in town and called, wondering if I could see them or a family member. The westerners usually had more routine ENT concerns than the local Nepalese who tended to ignore their medical problems until the last moment. It was always interesting to observe the different complaints the locals came in with when compared with their more pampered western counterparts. In either case, I soon became quite busy with a variety of calls and requests.

Many of the diplomats and other westerners who came to see me usually offered to pay, but I invariably refused. Having come to Asia only after completing my training, with no private practice experience, I had no idea what to charge. More importantly though, the fact that I had been working more or less for free the last two years, made me feel uncomfortable taking money. Perhaps foolish, but I wasn't used to it, and though I could have used the money and probably should have accepted, I never did. Instead I saw everyone for free, which, of course, did nothing to slow the incoming calls and requests. I did not know how to "monetize" my work. It seemed alien and inconsistent with my goals.

One day, I received a request from an elderly American woman, who had lived in Nepal the last twenty-five years working for the Peace Corp.

"Would you be able to come to my house and see my mother? It is very difficult to transport her. She is ninety years old and in a wheel chair. She is having trouble swallowing."

Ying and I went over, and I examined the mother. Finding nothing wrong, I reassured them and suggested more of a soft diet with liquids.

"Thank you, doctor," the daughter said. "I'm delighted you didn't find anything. I feel much better. How much do I owe you?"

"No problem. I'm happy to see your mother for free."

"You can't work for nothing. You came to my house, which was very kind of you since it's impossible to move my mother. Please, let me give you something."

"It's fine, ma'am. Don't worry."

"I insist."

"I would have no idea how much to charge."

She shoved fifty dollars into my hand. "Take it. I can pay you. I will not hear another word of it."

I reluctantly accepted, although I felt very awkward.

"You are an ass, Rick," Ying said as we left her home. "Of course you should charge for your services. You spent fifteen years studying to be a surgeon. Why should you work for nothing? You have a right to be compensated."

"It seems contrary to my mission."

"That is truly ignorant." I looked at my Chinese wife, a member of an ethnic group known for its business expertise, not unlike the Jews, and smiled. "I mean it," she said testily. "You don't have to be a beggar forever. You are allowed to earn a living."

"It is difficult for me to accept money."

"Have you ever thought that it is might be important to your mission? That by charging money from those who can afford it, you can serve the needy longer. That maybe you can have a career here, earn money, help the poor, and live in Kathmandu, since you love it so much?"

It was another fortune-cookie moment, like the one I had in the Chinese restaurant in New York, only in reverse. "Do not forsake your dreams for material security," the original fortune cookie message had read. Now it was, "Do not forsake material security or you will *lose* your dreams." But the lights did not go on. I did not see the business opportunity that existed in this impoverished but amazing land, a land I would have been happy to dedicate my life to. Here was a way to merge the two paths, the temporal and the noble, the worldly and the sublime, the one sustaining the other. But I saw only the latter and was blind to the former, not recognizing its urgency. I did not appreciate that business and income were not crass or vulgar but essential and virtuous, for the good and decent depended on it.

"I don't know how to turn what I do into a profitable business, Ying, and I don't want to start."

Ying scowled. "You are a fool!"

Chapter 46

One weekend we walked over to Pashupatinath, one of Nepal's most sacred temples in the eastern outskirts of Kathmandu. It was dedicated to the Hindu God Shiva and located on the banks of the Bagmati River. "It's on the other side of town," I said to Ying. "It is holy to the Hindus. We saw the Monkey Temple and now we have to see this."

Elderly Hindus came here in the final weeks of their lives to die and to be cremated on the banks of the river, their ashes scattered in the sacred waters of the river to flow downstream to merge with the holy Ganges River. Hindus from Nepal and India arrived here to worship and to die.

"A temple for dying," Ying said.

It was a temple of death, with an atmosphere of death, where the spirit of death moved freely in every corner and bend, where every ritual and shrine was imbued with death. This was where the Hindu faithful came to die.

"It is the other side of the ledger," I said.

Intrinsic to birth and life was dying and death, the inevitable outcome of life. One made sense only with the other. One was incomplete without the other. Life and death required one another to be meaningful and were empty without it. One had a fixed allotment of time, no more. Some had more, some had less, but in the broad sweep of time, of eons upon eons, of eternities and infinities, of epochs upon epochs, each life was a shadow, a turning of a page, over in an instant. One had to make his way in that brief interval, learn his truths, elevate and better what he could in that narrow sliver of time.

As we viewed the temple we could see the funeral pyres burning, the flames and smoke rising into the atmosphere, the bodies of the deceased consumed in fire, accompanied by incense and prayer. "It is an impressive sight," I said. "They are realists, the Hindus. They know how to live and to celebrate life. But they also know how to die."

"It is like our Buddhist funerals in Thailand," Ying said. "We understand the role of death in life."

"It is better to die this way, in the way of your faith, in a sacred temple before a sacred river. Where you can reflect and prepare yourself spiritually before the end. Rather than in a hospital bed or nursing home."

"The less modern countries have a greater wisdom beyond science and technology."

"Yes, they do," I said.

We continued walking.

"I think the Christians with their emphasis on the afterlife and heaven, miss the significance and even beauty of death, how critical it is to a life well lived."

"The Hindus and Buddhists know about this," Ying said.

"And so do the Jews. This reminds me of our Yom Kippur service for the dead. There is a profound acknowledgement of death, of our small, limited lives in the canvas of time."

We spent an hour wandering through this temple of death and dying, a sacred Hindu complex where death drifted here and about with the flames and smoke and ashes of the dead. It was here where life and death courted one another, intermingled and merged, swirled and separated like the grey clouds billowing from the smoldering bodies, where death was not rejected or feared but accepted and embraced.

"There is a lesson here also for those who care for the sick and dying as both of us do," I said.

Chapter 47

I heard a knock on the door of my room at the Paramount Hotel. I opened the door to find Ted standing in the hall. "Hey, Rick, 'dere's a big crowd waitin' for you in the lobby," he said. I hurriedly put on my clothing, splashed some water on my face, and ran down the stairs, unshaven and ungroomed, wondering what was going on. When I arrived, the sight of about twenty scruffy Nepalese in traditional clothing, waiting patiently in the small, poorly lit hotel lobby greeted me. I recognized one man, the father of a teenage boy I had operated on recently, who stepped forward and clasped my hand warmly.

His son was a young man of about seventeen years who had crushed his voice box and windpipe in an accident more than ten years ago. Because of the damage to his larynx, he had been unable to speak since the injury and had to wear a tracheostomy tube to breathe. I examined the boy carefully several weeks ago, looking down his throat with a scope while under general anesthesia in order to assess the severity of the obstruction. I informed the family that I could operate on him, explaining that I should be able to remove the crushed part of his windpipe and voice box and create a normal airway. After the operation, things had gone even better than expected. I was able to remove the trache tube, and although hoarse, the boy's voice had returned. The father listened happily as his son spoke for the first time in years.

The father, who did not speak a word of English, was thanking me in his native language. He introduced me to all of his friends and family, none of who spoke English either, and each thanked me in Nepali with the same warmth as the father. His wife, a short, chubby Tibetan woman dressed in a shawl, smiled shyly and bowed to me. His other children also bowed, dropping to their knees, and touching my feet with their foreheads. They even brought a Tibetan monk along dressed in purple robes and carrying a prayer wheel who uttered prayers and blessings. The father then gave me a small gold replica of the Hindu temple Pashupatinath contained within a glass case, which Ying and I had just visited. After greeting everyone, I posed with the father, while Ted snapped pictures. As the photos were being taken, I heard some animal sounds coming from behind a few of the family members standing by the entrance of the hotel. I looked around, wondering if I was hearing things. Farm animals in a hotel? At that moment, one of the father's relatives stepped through the hotel doors carrying a beautiful baby goat and a fat white chicken in his arms. He walked directly over to me and promptly placed both of the animals in my arms. "This is for you, Dr. Moss," he said in broken English. "The family is very appreciative to you for helping their son." I held on to these two animals as they wiggled nervously in my arms, while everyone smiled and giggled. The father, with a big proud smile on his face, indicated through a translator that the chicken and goat were gifts.

"He wants to show his appreciation for your kind offering," another said, translating in broken English. "He has not heard this son speak since he was a child. These are his best young animals, and he would be grateful if you would accept them."

"I am honored," I said, as I wondered what I was going to do with them.

Chapter 48

We took a bus 40 km southeast of Kathmandu to Namobuddha, another important Buddhist pilgrimage site. The Namobuddha stupa honored the site where a young prince (some accounts cite the Buddha himself) happened upon a tigress close to starvation and unable to nurse her own cubs. Overwhelmed by sympathy, the prince offered himself to the tiger as food so that she may be able to feed her cubs.

I had heard of this story before, a remarkable account that spoke of the compassion that stood at the heart of Buddhism. We entered the temple. The main stupa was white, conical, and vast with a multi-tiered circular tower and crown made of copper, with Tibetan prayer flags tied to the copper tower and wound outwardly around it. The monastery was a stunning structure made of sculpted wood, painted red and white, with ornate golden roofs and towers and smaller stupas. It was a place of serious practice and worship and there were many Tibetan monks and lay followers present. There was also more detailed information about the narrative of the prince/Buddha who sacrificed himself for the sake of the tigress. One of the Tibetan monks introduced himself to us.

"Welcome to our monastery," he said.

He wore purple robes and sandals. Tall for a Tibetan, he possessed much dignity. He spoke English well with only a slight accent. I imagined he had spent many years as a monk and held a senior position here within the temple. I was interested in the story. He was happy to accommodate me.

"The perfect Buddha, in a prior life," the monk began, "was one of three sons, princes to a King who ruled over a small kingdom."

I thought here of the differences between the Mahayana and Theravada. The Mahayana accepted the notion of many Buddhas or enlightened ones, while the Theravada believed in the one historical Buddha to whom they paid great homage. I felt the Mahayana version diminished the significance of one of the giants of history, the Buddha, who created one of the great world religions. It also opened the door to all sorts of speculation and myths since one could fabricate any number of Buddhas. But I was content to suspend judgment and hear the story.

"One day," the monk continued, "the King, Queen, and the three sons went on an outing with their ministers and servants. They came to a place of great beauty and set up an encampment. The three young princes explored the area. They found a den in the woods and discovered a tigress sleeping beside her cubs. The two older princes, both warriors, prepared their bows and arrows and readied to kill the tigress. The younger prince stopped them, saying that it was wrong to kill. He also noticed that the tigress was not able to move, for she had just given birth. She also feared that if she left her cubs to hunt another animal might harm them. Tortured by hunger, she lay on the earth unable even to raise her head. The young prince asked his brothers what kind of food would the tigress eat. They told him it would have to be the warm flesh and blood of a recent kill. The young prince realized that he would have to kill another animal to save this one. He tried to arrive at a solution. He and his brothers walked back to the encampment when the young prince told his brothers that they should go on and that he would return later. He walked back to the den. The tigress was still there, unable to move. He touched her face, but she was so weakened she could not even bare her fangs. He took a knife and began cutting his body to draw blood. The tigress licked the blood. Then it stood up and with a roar, pounced on the young prince, devouring him."

It was an amazing story, gruesome to contemplate but inspiring in a way.

"The young Buddha," the monk said, "in a prior life, sacrificed himself to save the tigress and her cubs. It was the ultimate sacrifice."

"I like its message of compassion," I said. "It took tremendous courage. But it seems unrealistic. I don't know that I would be up to that challenge."

"Of course you wouldn't," Ying said, "it's a fable."

"It flies in the face of one's natural instinct for self-preservation. Not to mention avoidance of pain and a grisly death."

"It is a difficult story," Ying said. "I don't agree with its message."

"When you contemplate it," the monk said, "it says many things. It speaks of compassion. But also great valor. There is also the message of impermanence and suffering. And escaping samsara or rebirth. Through practice, meditation, and compassion."

"Respectfully," Ying said, "it is foolish."

I was not sure where this sat within the context of my world of medicine, of healing, of the spirit, of medical work in the third world. Our patients offered themselves up not to be sacrificed but to be healed. But their suffering was a form of sacrifice, as was their willingness to submit to our brutal interventions, to heal and redeem them, and redeem ourselves.

Chapter 49

Nepal was a country with limited resources, and so it was not uncommon for patients stricken with advanced disease to go untreated. Those with cancer or other life threatening illnesses simply died of their disease at home. For cancer patients who were able to have surgery, the treatment was still incomplete because there was no place to give radiation. In a place where people generally died of infectious disease, diarrhea, malnutrition, and other common third world maladies, radiation, chemotherapy, and other routine cancer treatments and technologies were luxuries that could not be afforded nor even available.

"There is no funding for such things," Dharma said one morning as we made rounds. "We are very poor. Especially chemotherapy, which is expensive and experimental. But also radiation, which is critical for head and neck cancer. Most of our people die of other causes. We are behind in so many things. Without the Japanese we would not even have this hospital."

"It will take time for Nepal," I said. "It is landlocked between India and China and dependent on them. Your economy scrapes along. Mainly tourism, which at least helps."

"But with time, it can improve," Ying said.

"Yes," I said. "In a short time Thailand has made great strides. Think about Japan and the four Asian Tigers." This was a reference to the newly emerging Asian economic powerhouses, South Korea, Hong Kong, Taiwan, and Singapore. "Twenty or thirty years ago they were backwards and impoverished. Now they have modern economies, good health care, and a high standard of living."

"It is possible," Ying said.

"It will be slow," Dharma said. "In the meantime, you must cure them with surgery, Dr. Moss. We have nothing else to offer our poor patients. And then teach us to do what you do so we can continue your work."

"It is my pleasure, Dharma," I said.

Dharma was very earnest. I understood his frustration. He wanted to do more. His words were also a great inducement for me. This was my nirvana. If I could spend a lifetime in Nepal, doing this and nothing more, I would, and it would be a glorious life. I loved it here. I loved the culture, the religions, the picturesque villages, the vibrant people, and the wondrous scenery of the Himalayas. Ying too was at peace here. But as so often occurs, it was a question of money.

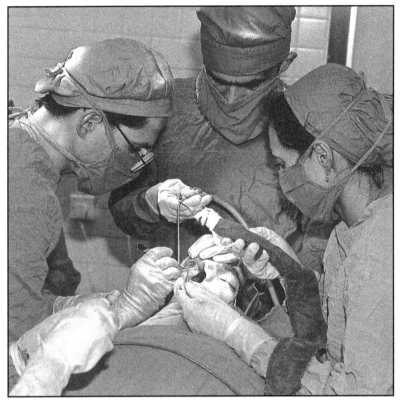

Dr. Moss operating, Bi-Pu assisting, Nepal

Ying pressed me again after our discussion with Dharma. "Why can't you see the possibility here? Why are you opposed to making money? To join with the ENT doctors here and have a life? With Rakesh or Dr. Amatya. They would love to have you. You could live in Kathmandu. You can continue the charity work and earn a living. What's wrong with that?"

"It is alien to me."

"Without money your mission will end. What will you live on?"

"I'm interested in the purity of work, of giving and healing, not about compensation. As a Buddhist, I thought you would understand that."

"You sound like some idiot college radical."

"It's not political."

"You are like a child when it comes to money."

"You do not know me."

"There is nothing immoral about getting paid for your labor especially by those who can afford it. Then you can continue your mission. You are blind and arrogant. You can have it all but too stupid to realize it."

"I will continue this life as it is. I can do no better than the exact life I am leading."

Chapter 50

I was performing a cancer resection on a patient I had seen on one of my first days in Nepal. He was a man in his fifties who had a large, infiltrative cancer on the left side of his tongue. It had invaded deeply and extended over to involve the mandible. Like so many others, he had neglected it until he could stand the pain no longer. Only then did he seek treatment. He had heard that I was visiting and had come down from his village. I met him at his hospital bed while making rounds with Dharma and the residents. He could barely open his mouth, but enough so I could see the large tumor.

"He chews betel nut," Dharma said. This was a known carcinogen, a common habit in Nepal.

"It's cancer," I said. "Let's operate."

We performed a left neck dissection, removing the lymph nodes of the neck, split the lip, raised a large cheek flap, exposed the mandible, sawed through it, and resected half the tongue, along with the mandible and part of the neck, the "commando" or "tongue-jaw-neck" procedure. Both of these names, I liked. They possessed a martial, bellicose quality. This, among other cases, we did on a weekly basis. They were important operations and provided teaching value for the faculty and residents.

The anatomy, as always, was striking, reflecting, I felt, the genius of the creator who fashioned, in His way, this instrument, the body, integrating perfectly form and function. We tracked the anatomy, peeled away the layers, revealed the underlying contours and vital structures, admiring the weave of the interlocking muscle, nerve, artery, and vein. We noted the enveloping gossamer sheathes, the tiny oval shaped lymph nodes and the silken, flimsy curtain of lymphatics they rested in. We gathered them fastidiously, swept them upward, guarding them, our harvest, jealously. We left not one behind, carrying, as they may, microscopic malignant cells that had burst forth and spread like virulent spores from the primary tumor in the tongue, our target in this extended ritual of surgical violence. The pearl white of the jaw was sacrificed, it's shape and delineation, anchored to sinew and tendon, shattered and broken of necessity. The tongue was also conceded, this remarkably agile and adept structure, fluid and precise, a nimble fist of muscle, able to reform and mobilize itself as swiftly as the hand or voice, crucial to speech and swallowing, compromised and undermined by cancer. But we divulged in the end, like sculpture, the hidden silhouette and design of the body, its mystery and grandeur. I reveled in my good fortune to have trained in its secrets.

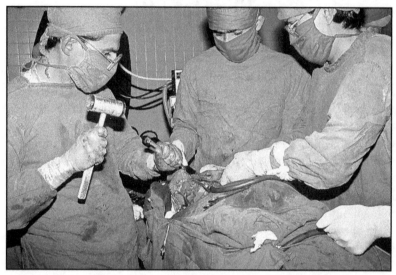

Dr. Moss operating, Dharma assisting, Nepal

What was left now was the reconstruction of this horrendous defect, deliberately created in the process of removing the tumor, a massive breach that now existed between the neck and throat, referred to medically as a "fistula," an unsustainable condition that required our attention. It was at this time that several guests entered our theater, the operating room, to share notes and observe. In particular, one individual I already called friend as well as colleague, a robust, fiery sort from Morgantown, West Virginia by the name of Dave Fogarty, a plastic surgeon. Dave was the team leader of an expedition of healthcare workers from the US associated with the organization *Interplast*, a group based in Palo Alto, California that sent teams throughout the developing world to perform reconstructive surgery, congenital defects mainly, in particular cleft lip and palate although not limited to that. It enjoyed an excellent reputation, bringing the very best of medical care from the US to underserved areas.

I had never heard of it before, but that meant nothing. I was my own one-man healthcare expeditionary force, living in my own bubble, cognizant only of the day-to-day universe of third world medical disasters as I encountered them, my wife, my colleagues here and elsewhere, my desire to cut and cure, my fascination and obsession with the local cultures and religions, and, of course, my eternal lack of funds. That reality necessarily impacted the rest, but we would somehow manage at least for now until my small pot ran dry. But living in three dollar a day hotels and eating street food like the locals helped. I wondered how things would have been different if I had joined some international organization that provided basic assistance, a stipend, health insurance, travel expenses, and the like. No doubt it would have been easier. But then it would not have been me. I was fated by disposition and nature to proceed as I had, independent and disorderly, whatever the constraints. But the two methods now crossed here in this operating room, at the Tribhuvan University Teaching Hospital, built just a few years ago, thank God, by the Japanese, in Kathmandu, Nepal.

"Well, well, what have we here?" thundered Dave. He was in scrubs and wore a mask that hid only part of his trademark red beard.

"Oh, just this little defect," I quipped.

"My, that's a major league defect in my book," he said admiringly. "How are you going to repair it?"

Dave had a wife and seven kids, two of them adopted, including a girl from Honduras and a black son from America. He was a big man, large in many ways including girth, height, and spirit. He laughed heartily and had a booming voice. And then there was that flaming red hair and bushy red beard. Looking at the man, hearing him speak, you would not be surprised to learn that he came from the hills and backwoods of West Virginia. You would probably not guess however that he was a physician, let alone a highly skilled, world-traveling plastic surgeon that spent large chunks of time every year doing exactly what he was doing here in Nepal.

"In your honor, Dave, we're going to try something different," I said. "Usually I go with the pec-major, but today we're going to use the temporalis myofascial flap. Perfect for these posterior defects. I also want my friends here to have a few different options."

The "pec-major" was a big muscle-skin flap from the chest and an excellent and reliable choice for head and neck reconstruction. The temporalis flap referred to the temporalis muscle, convenient to the head and neck, located as it was on the side of the head. It was in the same surgical field and was also an excellent approach.

"I did a few of these in southern Thailand. Even wrote a paper on them."

"I wanna see this," said Dave in his twang.

The *Interplast* team included another surgeon, two anesthesiologists and a couple of nurses and support workers. I had watched Dave and his co-workers repair a cleft lip and a burn injury patient yesterday. He told me he had been with *Interplast* for years. "I go out every year for at least three months, two weeks at a time. I love it. I'm with the university so I can swing it. My wife puts up with it. It's also great for teaching our own residents and faculty. They can see more in two weeks here than they could in five years back in the states."

Here was a man after my own heart. He had figured out how to combine two lives. One being an intrepid surgical apostle, scurrying about the planet to long-suffering regions in search of dragons and beasts to slay with his surgical sword. Yet he also returned home after each such laudable jaunt to wife, kids, employment and suitable compensation. He could still build his castle, enjoy the security of benefits, holidays, insurance, pension and the rest. The full catastrophe as they say. I had only managed the one. Mine was the healthcare saga that never ended. I envied the ability to combine the two. In some remote corner of my cerebral cortex, buried within a jangle of nerves and synapses, I recognized a wish for some measure of the stability my friend Dave possessed. Yet the thought of returning "home" (a concept that meant less and less with time) to the states to begin a householder's life replete with home, mortgage, and practice was insufferable. I no longer fit in that world anymore. I was free and unruly. My home was here doing what I was doing.

"You've got a good life, Dave, a nice balance," I said.

"You've got one helluva life yourself, my friend," he answered.

I had shown Dave some of my articles published in the English dailies in Thailand. After reading them, he said, "Stop operating and just write. Heck, anyone can do a neck dissection but man you've got talent." I appreciated his kind words but did not take his advice.

I made a horizontal U-shaped incision in the left side of the head, exposed the temporalis muscle, elevated it off the side of the skull, preserved the blood supply, excised the midportion of the zygoma or cheek bone to allow room for the flap, tunneled it into the mouth, sutured it in place, closed the defect, separating mouth and neck once more. This tidy little flap had allowed us to achieve something that in a way was miraculous, at least a secular miracle. We closed the enormous hole in his throat that would have drained torrents of saliva not to mention food and liquid down into the man's neck, bathing critical structures including the great vessels, the carotid artery and jugular vein, with infected material, a potentially lethal complication that would have prolonged his recovery by weeks or months. If all went well, thanks to the flap, he would be eating within a week and out the door and back to his village. We set upon closing the incision like tailors, the soft tissue and then the skin, stitching the edges together neatly, fashioning seams, restoring harmony to the besieged man's head and neck once more.

Dharma, the residents, students and nurses were giddy with the outcome. They had witnessed a first today like other things we had done in Nepal. They could now manage the resection and repair of major head and neck tumors with a number of reconstructive options. It was a good day's work.

"That was great my man," said Dave. "A beautiful case. Let me know if you ever want to join us. I'll give you my card. Give me a call. I go out three months a year, every year without fail. Be great to have you. But don't forget about writing. That's your real talent, man. But that was a helluva case."

I loved this guy. Bushy red beard and all. "I will, my friend," I said. "Thanks."

Chapter 51

Ying and I wanted to visit Tibet while in Nepal, bordering as Nepal did that fabled land of the Dalai Lama, of the Tibetans and Tibetan Buddhism. I had many Tibetan patients since coming to Nepal and had visited several Tibetan temples. As a student of Buddhism, I was curious. Tibet was the fount of Vajrayana Buddhism, of Tantric Buddhism, of the vajras, of the thunder and diamond path. Lhasa was this mysterious land's ancient capitol in the northern Himalayas and sat on the banks of the Lhasa River, a tributary of the Brahmaputra River. It was known as the Forbidden City until the 20th century because it was closed to foreign visitors. Lhasa was the seat of the Dalai Lama until 1959 when he and nearly 100,000 Tibetans fled into exile in India with the invasion of Tibet by the Red Chinese. "If we can get into Tibet, we're going," I said excitedly to Ying.

"It won't be easy," she responded. "There is turmoil there."

Tourist agencies in Kathmandu promoted treks to Tibet. The journey was about 1000 km overland, most of it in Tibet. The first 100 km or so in Nepal. "You pass through the north face of Mount Everest base camp," I said, "the Tibetan cities of Sakya, Gyantse, Shigatse, and then into Lhasa. We'll see many of the important Buddhist pilgrimage sites."

The Red Chinese under Deng Xiaoping (who took over in 1978 after the death of Mao) were opening their country to free-market economic reforms and to the West in general, but Tibet, I realized, was different. Tibet was something of a *cause celebre* in the West and the Chinese resented it. They considered it meddling in their internal affairs.

"When China fell to the Communists under Mao in 1949," I said, reading from a brochure I had picked up, "it prepared to incorporate Tibet into China. There were negotiations between Tibet and the new People's Republic of China, which failed. The People's Liberation Army (PLA) entered Tibet in October of 1949."

"I am sure the Chinese took advantage," Ying said.

"Negotiations continued and in 1951 a forced agreement was imposed upon Tibet. The Tibetans were made to accept China's view of the two nation's common history. It authorized China's rule over Tibet and the PLA presence in Tibet."

"It is not surprising."

"Tibetan militias formed over disagreements regarding land reform measures imposed by the Chinese government," I said. "The uprising spread to Lhasa in 1959 and the Dalai Lama fled. The Chinese government dissolved the Tibetan Local Government and ended any autonomy they may have had."

"Shameful."

"It is estimated that 1.2 million Tibetans, or one fifth of the population died as a result of China's policies over the next 20 years," I continued reading. "More than 6000 monasteries, temples, and other cultural sites were destroyed and pillaged."

I shook my head. "I despise Communists in all their shades and variations. Bloodthirsty, fascist bastards. Socialist. Communists. All the same crap. Mao was as bad as Stalin, or worse. Pol Pot, Castro, Ho Chi Minh, and the rest."

"They are also moving ethnic Chinese into Tibet," Ying said.

"To make Tibet a Chinese province, basically," I said.

"With their large population," Ying said, "they will overwhelm Tibet."

"I read in the local paper that there have been demonstrations in Lhasa lately against the Chinese."

"That will make it difficult to get in."

It seemed strange to go to the Chinese embassy to arrange a visa for Tibet. Tibetans had a unique culture and religion. Surely, they should be autonomous and separate from Red China.

"It would be tragic," I said, "if this ancient culture were lost to the world. It reminds me in ways of the Jewish people. We were displaced and homeless for centuries, not to mention hated and persecuted, replete with expulsions, pogroms, and the Holocaust. But the Jewish people were able to maintain their civilization and religion. After 2000 years, we miraculously found national expression with the founding of Israel in our ancient homeland in 1948. Perhaps, we have something to teach the Tibetans about maintaining their culture and faith in the face of oppression, and in their diaspora."

"It is a good comparison."

We entered the Chinese embassy and walked over to the visa office. It was a large, drab, mostly empty room, Maoist chic, I supposed, grey and dreary, save for a man sitting behind a charmless steel desk. No capitalist-dog embellishment for our socialist friends here at the Chinese embassy. He sat, facing us, unsmiling, his hands folded together on the desk in front of him.

"Hello," I said, "we are interested in visiting Tibet."

He slammed a fist down on the desk. "It is China!" he shouted. "Not Tibet. You want to visit China."

"Oh, right," I said, realizing my unintentional slip. "Yes, China, but to... Tibet."

He slammed his fist again. "China, not Tibet!" he shouted. "You are not going to Tibet. You are going to China!" He glared at us. I wondered if this was some game the comrade played with all Western tourists since he had to know what our purpose was.

"Well, we would like to go to China but to, uhh, well - what do I call it?"

"The Tibetan Autonomous Region," he said more calmly. So this was the magic phrase. Although I knew there was nothing autonomous about it.

"Uh huh. Okay. To the Tibetan Autonomous Region," I said.

Now he smiled. He had me where he wanted, and, I was sure, every other Westerner who came to his desk seeking a visa. Basically forcing us to repeat the Chinese propaganda that Tibet was and always had been an integral part of China.

"So, sorry," he said. "Impossible. Westerners not allowed. Much unrest. Try next month, maybe possible." He smiled like a typical bureaucratic schmuck knowing this was going be the result of our visit today no matter what I said.

Ying and I looked at each other. Tibet was not going to be in our itinerary. I did not like the smirking bureaucrat. "Thanks for nothing," I said."

We were out the door.

Chapter 52

"I want to go to the Central Jail," Ying said.

"What?"

"The main jail in town," she said. "It's called Kathmandu Central Jail."

"What for?"

"The owner of the hotel told me there were two Thai monks there. He didn't know why, but I thought we should visit them."

I spoke later with Rakesh. "Yes," he said, "it is our largest prison. It holds hundred of prisoners. The conditions are not good. Many are foreigners in for smuggling drugs. It is the largest contingent."

"Really?" I said.

"Yes. Kathmandu used to be a major hippy center with lots of drugs. My father used to say, 'these hippies and their drugs, they are destroying Nepalese values.'"

Kathmandu was famous for many things. It was a major Hindu and Buddhist hub with sacred sites and temples throughout the city. It boasted the tallest mountain range in the world with outstanding scenery. And now, I learned, it was a famous stoned-out hippy haunt on the overland, backpack trail with a notorious international drug scene.

"Its heyday," Rakesh continued, "was in the sixties when marijuana, opium and other drugs were legal. We had government-run hashish shops. So many western hippies here getting high. There was a little street just south of Durbar Square where they hung out named 'Freak Street.'"

"I've run into some of these characters since I've been here, but they're much older. More like aging hippies. But I didn't realize it was such a scene. I used to encounter these types in Haight-Ashbury in San Francisco when I lived there. Burnouts from the hippy-era trying to relive the glory of the sixties. Or perhaps they never left it. I met them in the East Village in New York and even in Woodstock when I lived in upstate New York."

"You can still hear local Nepalese groups," Rakesh said, "in the Thamel district playing psychedelic music by Jimi Hendrix and Jim Morrison in some of these rundown, hippy bars."

"Wow."

"It was quite the scene here, hippy culture at its best."

"What happened," I asked.

"In the 70s, drugs were made illegal. Instead of hippy tourism, which we really did not embrace, there was a push for the more respectable "trekking" and cultural or religious tourism. It is much better."

"I agree."

"But it has not stopped the drugs. It is just less of a spectacle. Also, now, in addition to marijuana and hashish, you have harder drugs like heroin and cocaine. Heroin dealing was made lucrative. It became a big racket and scandal in Nepal with members of the royal family and other elites involved because of the money. There are many drug traffickers and users from around the world who still come to Nepal and many of them wind up in jail. I heard recently that more than half our prisoners are foreigners in for drug smuggling."

So, two Thai Buddhist monks landing in jail in Kathmandu began to make sense.

Ying and I walked over to the Central Jail. It was 5 PM. This was visiting time. There were about 200 prisoners. We let one of the guards know we wanted to see the Thai monks. He knew right away whom we were talking about. I wanted to make sure they showed up. It was quite a scene. Dozens of people were waiting for the prisoners. For many it was a routine. There was an American lady, perhaps in her forties who came to visit a particular prisoner. She was overweight, disheveled and appeared anxious.

"I come here everyday to see him," she said. "He's an Aussie."

"How long have you been coming," I asked.

"Three years."

"Did you know him before he was in jail?"

"No."

"How'd you get to know him?"

"Someone told me about him."

"You came to visit?"

"Yes. And I never stopped. I have not missed a day."

She was not an attractive woman. I had not yet seen her *beau ideal* and so did not know what he brought to the table. Was she smitten by him? And was he smitten by her or merely taking advantage of her kindness? Who knew what propelled her to this degree of devotion.

"How are the conditions here?

"Terrible. They have no rights. Three bowls of rice a day with tiny strands of meat. And lice. The cells are dark, tiny, and cold."

"How much longer before he gets out?"

"Another two years."

"Wow." What a loss for the man, I thought. All for drugs, I wondered?

She was carrying a bag of food items and some toiletries.

"What's he in for?"

"Drugs," she said. "But he was set up. It was planted on him."

The prison door opened. There was a large space that quickly filled with prisoners behind the metal bars that separated us from them. Suddenly, there was tremendous commotion and movement and activity. Everyone shouted past each other chaotically, from one world to another, from the world of freedom to the world of imprisonment and back, prisoners and visitors lapping up hungrily the precious moments together. Some laughed and were joyous, others cried and rended garments. The emotions were high. The atmosphere intense. Several Nepalese prison guards with the same green uniform, beret, black boots and civil war era muskets I had seen in the hospital were present. The Aussie was robust and tall with dirty blonde curly hair. I figured late twenties. A good-looking lad. The woman was beside herself. "Oh, it is so good to see you," she shouted emotionally. "I brought you some food and things." She tried to give it to him but the guard stopped that. He took the supplies and hopefully would give it to him later. "Oh, you're such a dear, sweetie, really, just heavenly," he said with a thick Australian accent.

They chatted a few minutes. Mostly she gawked at him breathlessly. They were not allowed to touch or kiss. The guard ended it. The time allotted for visitors was brief.

"I'll see you tomorrow," she said.

"I'll be here," the Aussie said jauntily. "Look forward to it, love. You're a dear. Thanks again." He seemed surprisingly at ease in his bizarre world.

The lady waved as tears rolled down her face. The young man turned away and walked back into the prison.

The two Thai monks appeared. They stood stiffly behind the iron bars. They gazed at the ground. They both wore their orange robes and had shaven heads. I thought this was odd. Were they allowed to wear the sacred robes in prison? They were gaunt and awkward. One was taller than the other. Ying wai'd them, which made them more uncomfortable, yet any Thai would do the same given their respect for Buddhism and Buddhist monks. Even behind bars.

"Sawadee ka, Ying said sweetly. They spoke in Thai. I could make out most of it. "How long have you been here," Ying asked.

"One year," the shorter one said.

"Why are you here?"

"Drugs."

I was amazed at this admission. I thought he would be embarrassed. Ying went no further with it. "What is it like here?" she asked.

"Very bad," the taller one said. "Always hungry. No space. Very cold at night."

"Can I help you?"

"I have family in Thailand. I need to contact them," the shorter one said.

"Write their name and address," Ying said. One of the guards was kind enough to furnish paper and pencil. "I will take it to the Thai embassy. I am a nurse. This is my husband, a surgeon from America. I will try to help you."

For the first time their faces opened up. "Thank you very much," they both said. The shorter one wrote down the information in Thai and handed it to the guard who then handed it to Ying. As per Thai tradition, monks could not hand something directly to a woman.

But there was a problem here that Ying now addressed.

"You must remove your orange robes," Ying said directly. For anyone who understood Thai culture, monks wearing orange robes in prison was scandalous. Still it was courageous for a Thai woman to challenge them this way. I wondered which was her main reason for visiting them – to help them or defend the honor of Buddhism. Or both. She continued. "You cannot wear the robes when you are prisoners."

This angered the monks. They glared at Ying threateningly. "You have no right to speak to us this way," said the shorter one.

"You are in prison because you have smuggled drugs for profit. And still you wear the orange robes. You bring shame to Thailand and to Buddhism. You should know better. You should not wear these robes!" she said defiantly.

The two monks paced and spat and scowled. They had the idiotic notion that they were entitled to wear the robes despite what they had done and where they were.

"We are monks. You are Thai. You are a woman. You do not show proper respect," the short one said bitterly.

"No one will help you," Ying said indignantly. "The Thai ambassador and the embassy will not assist you. They will be angry with you. You disgrace Thailand and Buddhism. You are prisoners now. You must take off your robes and wear prison uniforms. You are not monks any more. Then we can help you. But not now. You do not deserve our help, and you do not deserve to wear these robes."

They continued to mutter and fume and glower. She did not relent. I have never been prouder. They left us. Ten minutes later they were back in prison garb. They had given the robes to the guards. The Thai embassy staff would pick them up later. They wai'd Ying, an incredible admission of guilt and expression of repentance.

Ying took the information to the Thai embassy the next day. She spoke with the Thai ambassador. They promised they would visit and help them. They had heard through channels about Ying's demand that they remove their robes. They were pleased. I suspect it helped the prisoners' cause. We never found out what happened.

Chapter 53

Toward the end of my three months in Nepal, Ying and I decided to take a week off and go "trekking," or wandering through the mountains, probably the single greatest attraction in the country and the primary reason for its popularity with tourists. But we would do it with a twist. We planned to trek through the Himalayas on a motorcycle.

Rakesh managed to borrow a motorcycle for us from his nephew and then arranged to get us enough gas for our journey, not a simple task in Nepal as gas was rationed due to a crippling trade dispute with India. Since there were no gasoline stations up in the Himalayas, we had to carry our own gas with us to make sure we had enough to get back. We filled up two large containers, placed them inside a large traveling bag to conceal them and strapped them to a rack behind the seat. "That's to get us back home," I said. We also rented "goose down" sleeping bags, heavy down coats, thick Nepalese stockings, gloves and scarves, all guaranteed to withstand anything the Himalayans could dish out. "That should do it, I hope." We strapped our belongings down tight in the back and began our journey.

We drove along a curvy road to a small river town named Trisuli and spent the night in a dirty hotel. There was one decent restaurant in town where we ate soggy noodles and listened to a German couple complain about the lice they had acquired the night before in the same hotel we were staying in. Ying and I looked at each other. When we went back to our room, we checked the bed carefully. No crawly things. I didn't care. "I'm not sleeping in that bed," I said. We spent the night in our clothes on the floor.

The next day we set out on an unpaved, gravel road to Dunche, a small mountain village. This town was more of a tourist center and had better food and hotels. Just outside our room, in the distance, lay the majestic Lantang mountain range. The following morning we planned to travel to a tiny village called Syabrubesi, which was located at the base of a deep valley, nestled amidst tall peaks, from where we would begin our motorcycle trek into the heart of the mountains.

The road leading to Syabrubesi was a curving narrow dirt path, littered with stones and debris. Most of the way, the path ran alongside a steep ravine with a precipitous incline that fell sharply into the valley below.

We could tell that no one had driven a motorcycle here before, because the cows that we encountered seemed terrified of this strange iron beast as if it were their first time seeing such a thing. At one point as I rounded a blind curve, we came upon a large black cow with two calves behind it. I immediately stopped the bike as the huge animal tensed up at the unexpected sight of our motorcycle only yards away. Rather than run away in terror, this powerful beast came hurtling at us. My own animal instincts for survival engaged. I turned the gas throttle up as far as it would go, pulled in the clutch, revving the bike up to 70,000 RPMs and let out a blood curdling samurai scream. "Aaaaahhhhhhhh." With my lungs strained to the point of ripping, my mouth thrown open in terror, and every muscle in my body tensed and shaking, I felt my life condense into a single instant. At the moment before impact, with the animal charging, its eyes panicked and fierce, its body poised to kill, the engine roaring, my horrendous scream shattering the stillness, violent death beckoning, the miraculous occurred. The terrified creature broke and ran. "I can't believe it," I whispered in awe and disbelief. I had seen the angry face of savage death up close. Instead of a terrible collision sending us hurtling down the side of a cliff, Ying and I were left safely in the quiet majesty of the mountains. I heard the baying of the wind in the distance and the flow of a small brook behind me. My breathing calmed as I watched the frightened cow and two calves scurrying up a dirt trail. I was a foot away from the edge. I turned to Ying, who, with eyes closed, was rubbing her thumb and forefingers together, reciting Buddhist prayers. "That was a close one, honey," I said. "Praise Buddha," Ying said. I looked down the side of the mountain. "Whoa. We never would have survived." We continued on our way to Syabrubesi, to spend the night with a Tibetan family. We listened to the sound of the river and went to sleep in our cold dark room illuminated by candlelight.

The next day we began the most magnificent part of our journey. We traveled along the edge of a mountain, crisscrossing up, up, endlessly up, until we approached the level of the glaciers in their icy diamond brilliance. At every turn the vista changed, the mountains transforming themselves before our eyes, as we viewed them from one angle or another. We traversed a pass, ascended or rounded a bend, only to come upon another ridge of glacial crowns and ravines. They were imperious and regal, grand and indifferent. The metallic grey of the mountains pierced the canopy of the sapphire sky. The cold wind howled and bit, blowing silver plumes of snow from the grizzled peaks, communing with the lucid sunlight, the rarified air, the saturated color, and the crystalline frigid lattice of the summits. We drove slowly, never stopping, hypnotized and transfixed by the towering expanse, the fierce, barren beauty and frozen clarity of the Himalayas.

"This is ecstasy," I said.

At one point in our journey the bike stalled. Somehow, I had never considered what I would do if the motorcycle died. I had no mechanical ability nor did I have any tools. Suddenly, the harsh reality of my own human frailty pitted against the merciless elements of these great giants came crashing in. "It gets cold at night in the Himalayas," I said, looking at Ying. To make matters worse, at that very moment, four rough looking mountain men just happened to appear as they clambered up onto the dirt road from the valley below.

"Holy crap," I whispered under my breath. They stood gaping at us as surprised to see us as we were to see them, dressed in bright woven garments, sandals and woolen hats, and all carrying, as it happened, long sharp, curved knives that dangled from their belts. I started to wonder about these guys. Here was a golden opportunity for them. There was my wife, my motorcycle, my gasoline, camera, wallet, watch, traveler's checks, money, credit cards, and here were these four mountain men with long knives and no one else around. Would anyone ever find out what happened to Dr. and Mrs. Moss?

They were friendly. They looked at me, Ying, and my camera, shook my hand and laughed heartily. They studied carefully, as if looking at something from another planet, the flashy engine and chrome of the motorcycle. They laughed and chatted amiably among themselves. I got them to pose for a picture. They laughed more. "Thank you," I said. They smiled. I wondered if they had ever met a westerner before. With the mountain men watching attentively, I turned the key, pumped the throttle and kick started the motorcycle. The gods smiled on us again, and the motorcycle started up. Ying hopped on as we bid our friends farewell and continued on to the border of China to a tiny village called Samodang. After that the road simply stopped. Ying and I had followed the road to the end, and we could go no further. "After this, we fall off the earth," I said. I had never done that before. Beyond us lay the great and forbidden Tibetan plateau, which the Chinese had officially sealed off. The gas was running low. I filled the tank with the gas we had brought. "It's time to turn back."

Chapter 54

We left Kathmandu after three months. I wanted to stay longer, but as a private citizen, I could do nothing about my tourist visa, which was limited to three months. There was a real need to continue my work here, but unlike Thailand, where the government extended my three-month visa for as long as I wanted at the request of the University, the rather unresponsive Nepalese government would make no such allowance despite the urgings of my colleagues.

"I am frustrated Rakesh," I said. "But they are difficult there. Completely inflexible. A bunch of government bureaucrats. Pathetic, really. Especially when you consider the need. But they wouldn't budge. I wish I could stay. I love it here. I could make Nepal my home."

"We wish you could as well," Rakesh said. "But we have no influence over them. They are in their own world – and control ours."

The conditions here were perfect for a vagabond like me. Ying loved it too. There was a good hospital with a devoted team, and endless pathology and opportunity to cut and cure. We had friends. It was a Hindu country with Tibetan Buddhism, both of great interest to me. There was a center of Theravada Buddhism, which resonated with me even more. The culture was enthralling. The Himalayan scenery inspiring. It was the perfect blending of all that I sought. On top of that, the food was great and everything was cheap. Even with my limited budget and no income I could have gone on for months.

The indifference on the part of the government served no one. It reminded me, in contrast, of the open-mindedness of the Thai government, which never failed to accommodate its universities in assisting visiting faculty, at least in my case, when there was a need or benefit for the country. There were reasons that some nations prospered and others did not.

There was a farewell dinner for Ying and I at Rakesh's home. There were also friends and colleagues from the Nepal Medical Council. "We hope you will return again," Rakesh said. "I would like that very much," I said. "We appreciate all you have done," Dr. Amatya said, "and for no compensation. We will always remember your kindness."

There were more gracious thanks and requests to return for a longer stay. The next day, Ying and I were on the road again.

We took an 8-hour bus trip from Kathmandu to Pokhara. It was a bumpy, long ride tracking along rivers at the bottom of ravines with impressive views of rushing streams, gorges, terraced fields, and the Himalayas. I was saddened to leave Kathmandu, a town I loved and had grown very comfortable in. But Asia beckoned and the journey continued. We arrived in Pokhara and spent a few days.

Pokhara was a laid back town with many inexpensive places to stay and eat. Although a popular destination for backpackers, there was none of the bustle and chaos of Kathmandu. It was famous for its magnificent scenery with the majestic Annapurna massif looming nearby and beautiful Phewa Lake. "Annapurna" referred to a number of mountains, but it was Annapurna I-IV plus Annapurna South that were best known. Annapurna I, at more than 8000 meters or 26,545 feet, was the highest of the Annapurna massif and tenth highest in the world. Then there was the famous "Machhapuchhare," the brilliant pyramidal shaped, snow-crested peak that dominated Pokhara, easily visible at all times. It was actually lower than the Annapurna Five at 22,943 feet but because of its proximity, appeared larger. It also stood apart from the other mountains and so was more visually stunning. Many of the postcards and pictures of Pokhara and Annapurna featured Machhapuchhare because of its distinct features and shape and its apparent size.

We stayed "lakeside," as they called it, which meant at an inn alongside placid Phewa Lake. We took hikes, boated on Phewa Lake, and enjoyed the wonder of Annapurna. The food was good, the ambience pleasant, and the scenery spectacular. "I miss Kathmandu, but this is wonderful," I said. "Very relaxing," Ying said, "like a real vacation. Much less frantic than Kathmandu."

We took a bus to the town of Bhairawa, some 180 km away on the Siddhartha highway, built by the Indian government in 1968. The scenery, as everywhere in Nepal, was magnificent. The road twisted and turned as it wound its way down from the Himalayan slopes toward the plains of northern India. We traveled up and down hills, clung to the sides of dells and valleys, crossed rivers, wandered over gorge floors, and finally arrived at the dusty, frenetic town of Bhairawa.

We found a cheap hotel and the next day took a bus ride some 20km west to the Buddhist pilgrimage site of Lumbini, the place of Buddha's birth. "I have dreamed of coming here," Ying said. I was excited too. "This will be the first of the four great Buddhist pilgrimage sites," I said.

"What are the other three?" my Buddhist wife asked me, the Jew.

"Bodhgaya, Sarnath, and Kushinagar, where he attained enlightenment, gave his first sermon, and died, respectively."

"Wow, you are such a good Buddhist," Ying said, laughing.

We got off the bus, followed the signs, and arrived at the site. I was surprised to find the place nearly deserted other than a few workers tending the grounds. There were no other tourists or pilgrims. "I can't believe we've got the birthplace of the Buddha to ourselves," I said.

After the bustle of Kathmandu, the laidback but still heavily touristed Pokhara, and even the busy little town of Bhairawa where we spent the night, this was a surprise. I assumed it would be a place of much activity with vendors, hotels, restaurants, tourists, and the like. But it was pastoral and serene and almost devoid of human presence.

"The Buddha would not mind this," Ying said.

We walked amidst the ruins. I had studied the history and lore of the site.

"The Buddha's mother," I recited, "'Queen Maya Devi,' was pregnant and traveling with her entourage to visit her parents in Devadaha from her palace at Kapilavastu nearby. She stopped to admire the beauty of the area and to bathe in the pond. She felt labor pains, left the pond, and grabbed hold of a branch of a pipal tree when the baby, the future Buddha, was born."

"In the year 623 BC," Ying added.

"You've been reading."

"I can't let you be the only expert on Buddhism."

We sat by the sacred pond surrounded by a tiered stone border where the Buddha's mother bathed just prior to his birth. So much history emerged from this small pool of water. There was the large pipal tree, grasped by the Buddha's mother whereupon she gave birth to her son, Siddhartha. We visited the Maya Devi temple, built in honor of the Buddha's mother. It was a neglected, disheveled structure, not flashy or compelling at all, which in a way was fitting.

"It is 25 paces from the pool. That was the distance Maya Devi walked from the pond when she gave birth," Ying said.

"Pretty good Ying."

We came upon the Ashokan Pillar, placed by India's greatest emperor, Ashoka, in honor of his pilgrimage to the Buddha's birthplace in 249 BC. Ashoka had placed many such pillars and other stone carved decrees throughout India (and Nepal) to indicate his presence and the extent of his empire. "He became a Buddhist after a great victory at the battle of Orissa. He saw much bloodshed," Ying said. "Then he spread Buddhism throughout India."

There were other mounds and the ruins of foundations for stupas and monasteries scattered through the grounds, some dating from the second century BC but little of their original glory remained. Simple stones gathered about the ground in some sequence or order, barely excavated, but other than its location here of no obvious significance or meaning. Yet centuries before, Buddhists had gathered here to practice and worship. They had built temples and monasteries and endeavored to live Buddhist lives and expound on the Buddha's teachings.

"And now only stone ruins are left to mark their time and labors," I said.

"What happened to this place? It must have been magnificent before." Ying said.

"Neglect, weather... and the Muslim invasions."

This phenomenon that I had observed in different variations in my travels, in particular Indonesia, was upon us again. I did not belabor it. I knew that Buddhism had not fared well in India, where it had originated, in large measure because of the spread of Islam. Islam would not abide such a faith with its images, temples and glorification of the life and teachings of the Buddha. Hence, it disappeared from the land of its birth, an historical tragedy. This, I imagined, more than anything, accounted for the stark, bare ruins we saw today strewn about, bricks and stones, scarcely arranged, unembellished and austere, that had once been the foundations of majestic edifices, looted, plundered, and razed to the ground.

But we were on another pilgrimage. A pilgrimage of healing. And wandering. We were in the midst of the journey. And the hunt. Nepal had been the third station in my voyage through the realm of third world medicine. But there would be new chapters as we wound our way through Asia, for my zeal for this way of life had not diminished. The odyssey would continue, as would the ordeal. Fresh triumphs and crushing defeats would come my way. We had come to Bhairawa for another reason besides visiting Lumbini. It was close to the border crossing at Sunauli with India.

Why India? Because it was there, close by, inexpensive, and accessible, and because I imagined it would be a critical element in the healing journey. It was poor, backward, and overpopulated, a nation that was almost synonymous with third world poverty. There would be neglect and advanced disease. I knew it would be a great challenge medically, which was my primary interest. It also possessed vast cultural and spiritual riches, unrivaled sites and sacred structures that Ying and I would revel in along the way. It was, in other words, exactly what I was looking for.

We were bound for India!

VI. India

Chapter 55

January 5, 1990

The Indian subcontinent was a vast and troubled land, permeated by powerful and sometimes devastating historical and religious forces. It was one of the world's great repositories of culture, spirituality, and learning, and yet it had also been referred to as a "wounded civilization." India had suffered many invasions, wars and periods of foreign domination; each though had added a vital new chemistry and layer to the strange and ever changing admixture of Indian culture. India was a state of mind, a magnificent and prismatic vision, kaleidoscopic in its permutations and angles. It was the birthplace of two great world religions, Buddhism and Hinduism. There were more than two hundred languages and dialects spoken in India, myriad styles of dress, cuisine, art, and music. It had its own form of medicine. There were resplendent temples, mosques, and palaces. India's cultural legacy was unsurpassed in the world, and it was as alive and vivid today as it had ever been in its 4,000-year history. It was also a bitch to travel around in.

Ying and I were at the train station in Varanasi waiting to board a train for New Delhi. We had arrived early but as departure time approached the crowd swelled. Coolies were running around loaded down with bags on top of their heads or balanced on their shoulders. Passengers carried suitcases, crates and sacks filled with all manner of earthly belongings. Other travelers had forewarned me that the trains of India were rife with pickpockets. The train from Varanasi to New Delhi was especially notorious because of the many tourists that traveled between the two cities. Varanasi was the holiest pilgrimage site for the Hindus because of the sacred Ganges River that passed through it. Indians from all over the country came here to bathe in its waters and after death to be cremated. Between the tourists and the Indians, the train was invariably packed.

The train appeared in the distance. Immediately, the hundreds of waiting passengers stood up, anxiously clasping their belongings or the hands of young children. A nervous excitement filled the air as the huge crowd began inching towards the edge of the platform. Bags were hoisted atop heads, suitcases placed on shoulders, babies carried, the elderly gently led forward. As the train came closer, the jockeying for position became even more intense. In India, there was no such thing as forming orderly lines and waiting your turn. This was a 17-hour journey, and no one wanted to stand. As the train rolled in a human tidal wave converged on the open doors. People burst forward smashing others with their suitcases. Mothers carrying children lunged head first like battering rams. Everyone thrashed and grappled like demons desperately focused on the urgent goal of passing through the narrow doors and finding a place to sit.

Ying and I had a simple plan. I would carry the luggage while Ying, who was as small and agile as any Indian, would try to find two seats. I placed my wallet in my front left pocket to avoid having it lifted. I watched Ying dash fearlessly into the crowd, twisting and finally squeezing through the narrow doors into the train. I followed behind and got as far as the top step, but with the luggage soon found myself completely immobilized, pressed tightly amidst a tangle of arms, legs, bodies and faces. In the midst of this great crush, I felt a strange sensation in the area of my left thigh. I paid no attention at first, but the feeling didn't go away. I looked down and noticed a small brown hand very deftly lifting my wallet out of the same front left pocket I had so cleverly placed it into. I was being robbed!

In one swift movement, a completely reflexive response, I allowed the pack resting on the top of my head to fall while I swung my right fist into the body of a small, skinny Indian wearing a white turban. I caught him flush in the chest. He was slammed back by the blow, but he hung on to the wallet and instantly disappeared into the crowd. My wallet, credit cards and travelers checks gone, and with my two packs there was no way I could pursue him. Ying was ahead. I yelled to her, "Ying, that little Indian guy in the white turban! He took my wallet!" She looked around, not sure whom I meant. "There. That little guy. Over there!" Ying spotted the thief as he passed her and grabbed his arm. He shook free and kept running. Ying followed in hot pursuit bumping and dodging around the crowded car, never losing sight of him. She chased the little bandit down until she caught up with him, jumped on his back, wrapped her legs around his waist, and, with jungle swiftness, plunged her teeth into his neck. "Ahhhhh. Stop. Stop," the brigand screamed. He twisted, writhed and whipped around like a trapped animal trying to shake Ying off his back. Ying clamped down harder. "Ahhhhh, noooo. Stop, please. Take the wallet!" Ying kept biting. The thief held the wallet up in the air. "Take it. Pleeeaase!" Ying let go of his neck, grabbed the wallet and leaped off his back. The thief disappeared into the crowd. Ying then found two seats and we were on our way to New Delhi.

Ying and I had arranged to work at the Goa Medical College in the small southern state of Goa. The Dean, who came to know me by way of a mutual friend, had invited us there. From the border of Nepal, it was a two thousand mile journey and in the process of getting there we planned to see something of this amazing country.

It was not long into our travels before we realized that India possessed a near endless succession of world centers of religious, spiritual and cultural significance. We began our Indian journey more than two weeks before, traveling first to Bodhgaya, the seat of world Buddhism and its holiest pilgrimage site. It was here where the Buddha sat beneath the legendary Bodhi tree more than 2500 years ago and vowed never to leave until, "I have attained the supreme and absolute wisdom." As an admirer of Buddhism, I was thrilled at the prospect of visiting the place where the Buddha had sat, gained enlightenment, and formed his philosophy; from here his doctrine had spread through much of Asia and beyond, and now into the Americas, molding human thought and belief and developing into one of the great world religions. It had persisted, like Judaism, through the continents and the vagaries of history, through the quirks and antagonisms of human caprice and aggression, to this instant.

We had boarded a rickety crowded bus that took us the twelve miles from the train station in Gaya to the small town of Bodhgaya. It was dark when we arrived so we hired a bicycle rickshaw to carry us the next kilometer or two to the Thai temple - one of many beautiful temples in Bodhgaya from around the world - where the monks welcomed us. "Fantastic," I said. "We're here! I've have been imagining this since Wat Satchatam." "It will be a fulfillment for both of us," Ying said. "Many Thai dream of coming here."

I felt Buddhism's tolerant and rational approach to the human predicament offered hope for the individual – and for mankind. I recognized what I considered flaws or inaccuracies in Buddhist thought. Life was not all suffering or even disappointment or disaffection, there was also joy, which Buddhism did not seem to acknowledge. I believed there was an independent self or soul, which Buddhism denied. Desire was not always bad; sometimes it was good, and a force for accomplishment, innovation and personal satisfaction. Notwithstanding this, I still held Buddhism up as a lamp of wisdom, particularly its emphasis on mindfulness or *sati*, as Jaroon called it. Siddhartha Gautama, the Buddha, was a world historical figure that had established a teaching that provided succor and insight for everyone regardless of faith. He ranked among the great men of history, with Aristotle, Isaiah and the Hebrew prophets, and Confucius, and other giants of his era and beyond. And now I was in his house, his sanctuary, in what had been a forest where he had dedicated himself to conquering suffering.

In the morning, Ying and I visited the many temples and monasteries built to honor the Buddha from every Buddhist nation in the world. Each sanctuary reflected the artistic and architectural style of the nation represented. There were shrines from Bhutan, China, Japan, Burma, Sri Lanka, Taiwan, Thailand, Tibet, and Vietnam, and we sampled each one like wine. It was an overwhelming display of creativity in the service of spirituality and revealed the intense heterogeneity of the Buddhist world.

The main focus of veneration was the Bodhi tree, an offshoot of the actual tree the Buddha sat under when he attained enlightenment. The original tree had died, but Emperor Ashoka's son, Mahinda, brought a sapling of it to Sri Lanka when he spread Buddhism there in the third century BC. A sprout from that tree, which still thrived in Sri Lanka, was later taken to Bodhgaya where it bloomed today. A red stone by the tree, called the *Vajrasan* or diamond throne, marked the place where the Buddha sat.

Behind the bodhi tree was the colossal and imposing Mahabodhi temple, built in the fifth century AD. This was a large grey sloping monument with a pyramidal summit, some 50 meters tall. A classical *Torana* or Buddhist style portal led through the temple courtyard into a hallway to a large gilded Buddha image with the right hand touching the ground, "holding earth as witness to his attained enlightenment." Intricate and delicately chiseled stone molding encircled the structure. The Lotus Pond, where the Buddha meditated and bathed lay outside the main enclosure. This reminded me of the pond at Lumbini that we had visited where Queen Maya Devi, the Buddha's mother, bathed just before giving birth to him. Circumambulating the Mahabodhi temple or praying and meditating under the Bodhi tree were thousands of pilgrims from around the Buddhist world. It was this wonderful sea of humanity representing Buddhism in all its pageantry and variety that was most memorable about Bodhgaya.

There was a blind, toothless Tibetan monk with Hollywood sunglasses, purple robes, dirty sneakers and all manner of beads and necklaces draped over his chest, selling small buttons of a smiling Dalai Lama for a rupee. A poised Sri Lankan monk, barefoot, in gleaming orange robes, walked in meditation with the airy lightness of a geisha. A congregation of Thai monks appeared with incandescent brilliance, a forest of luminous newly-shaved heads, stunning yellow robes, chanting from the Pali scriptures, while kneeling and bowing in unison like rows of flowing golden irises. Droves of long-haired Westerners sat solemnly in close-eyed contemplation. Crack Japanese monks, in white and purple robes, meditated in full lotus while intoning mantras with the martial crispness of samurai. There were Bhutanese women with weathered faces uttering sacred formulas, rubbing their bodhi beads fervently with one hand and with the other turning squeaking prayer wheels in clockwise rotation. Close to the Mahabodhi temple were the other temples with characteristic styles from each of the Buddhist nations of the world. The color and diversity of this peaceful religion that had grown and evolved in so many different ways was in full glory in Bodhgaya.

Bodhgaya, India

"This is the universe of Buddhism condensed into a single point like Jerusalem for Judaism, Rome for Catholicism, and Mecca for Islam," I said. I was at home in this Buddhist universe, much as I had been at Wat Satchatam and Kathmandu with its many Buddhist temples and monasteries.

There was an American lady staying at the Thai temple. She was middle aged, plump, and outgoing. She was eager to chat with us. In the course of our conversation she mentioned, out of thin air, that she was disturbed that women could only become nuns and not monks. "Why are women not granted full equality?" she wondered. I thought to myself, what a thing to bring up here in Bodhgaya. Buddhism was a very tolerant religion yet her question suggested the opposite; that it somehow oppressed women. I did not take kindly to it.

"Are there women priests in Catholicism?" I asked. "Would you visit the Vatican in Rome and ask the same question of its clergy? Or to imams in Mecca? Buddhism does not persecute women. It is an ancient religion with rules regarding its sangha. This is not a concern here, least of all among women."

Ying too was perturbed. "Thai women do not want to be monks," she said, shaking her head emphatically. "We do not think of such things. It is ridiculous. Women want to be nuns not monks!"

The lady was flummoxed. She must have assumed we would be sympathetic. Rather, I thought she was tone-deaf and political. "Women are making strides in east Asia," I said. "I worked with many female doctors in Thailand including one who was my boss. They are very accomplished and respected. If you want to fight for women's rights consider visiting Muslim countries. They need you there. But I don't think you will be well received."

Chapter 56

From Bodhgaya we continued to Varanasi, also known as Banaras, the abode of Shiva and India's holiest city. Located on the banks of the Ganges River, Hindus visited it at least once in their lives to bathe in and cleanse themselves of earthly sins. Hindus held that acts of charity, sacrifices, fasts, chants and meditation yielded far more good and benefit in Varanasi than anywhere else because of its spiritual ascendancy. It was one of seven holy cities for Hindus and its most important pilgrimage site.

The Ganges River originated from the Gangotri Glacier at Gaumukh (also a Hindu pilgrimage site) in Uttarakhand, India, an area bordering China in the Indian Himalayas. Hindus worshipped the river as the deity Ganga or Ganga Maiya (Mother Ganga). Like Pashupatinath Temple in Kathmandu, life and death comingled here. Bathing in its waters cleansed a lifetime of sins. Indians came here to die because they hoped doing so brought *moksha* or liberation from *samsara*, the cycle of death and rebirth. Families brought their dead to the *ghats* lining the river to be cremated and to receive the benefit of *moksha*. As Bodhgaya was for Buddhism, Varanasi was the epicenter of Hinduism, a mystical and potent focus of spirituality, devotion, and worship. It was also a chaotic city, more than 3000 years old, with winding, labyrinthine streets and alleys, suffocating traffic, vendors, food stalls, touts, and rickshaws, interspersed amidst sacred temples, shrines, *sadhus* (Hindu holy men) and ascetics. It was magic.

We stayed at the Imperial Hotel. The room was spacious with an extravagant canopy bed fit for royalty and a walkout balcony overlooking the vast city. It was lavish. Most memorable was the shower. It had a massive showerhead the size of a large cauliflower, vertically oriented and directly overhead, not angled. A metal cord was pulled releasing an incredible stream of steaming hot water, wrapping you in a cocoon of warmth, a wondrous cascade, the most richly satisfying shower I have ever had. The price for this decadence - one hundred rupees or about five bucks.

"I can't believe this place," I said. "It's the best deal we've ever had."

"We have nothing but good deals in India," Ying said. "India itself is a good deal, I think the best in Asia."

We walked around this bustling and tumultuous city with its wild traffic, streams of exotic humanity, flamboyant religiosity, pungent street food, animals of varying sorts intermingled with the teeming humanity, hot milk vendors, ear-cleaners, holy men, and all manner of general Indian madness.

"This is India," I said, "in its brash, chaotic, and dazzling essence."

We rented a boat and sailed out onto the Ganges at dawn and watched as thousands of Indians stood by the bathing ghats (the steps leading to the river) and immersed themselves in the hallowed waters. Further down from the bathing ghats, corpses decorated in wreathes and brilliant ritual cloaks were carried to the banks of the Ganges, placed atop funeral pyres and set ablaze. All along the shores of the river the fires burned, greeting the first rays of the rising sun with their light and smoke.

"What a sight," I said, mesmerized by this striking vision of devotion and reverence. "The Hindus perform this last service to their loved ones, that they may receive *moksha*. I admire this country and its ways."

After the flames had consumed the bodies, the ashes were gathered and strewn about the river. This final bodily remnant of the deceased were thusly merged with the sacred waters of Mother Ganga, which began in the frozen Himalayas, flowed down to Varanasi, the holy city, across northern India and Bangladesh nearly 2000 miles to the Bay of Bengal and to the oceans beyond. It was a haunting and glorious vision.

Sarnath, another of the four major Buddhist pilgrimage sites, was only 12 km from Varanasi. Ying and I took a bus there. It was here where the Buddha, having attained enlightenment under the Bodhi tree in Bodhgaya, gave his first sermon before the five ascetics he had practiced with earlier in his spiritual career, an event known as the "turning of the wheel of Dhamma." The Buddha taught of the Four Noble Truths (the truth of suffering and how to end it) and the Eight Fold Noble Path. The five ascetics became his disciples and formed the original *sangha* or Buddhist clergy.

We walked amidst the ruins and sacred structures. "India has an embarrassment of riches," I said. "There is so much culture and spirituality here. So many places of religious significance. Bodhgaya, Varanasi and now Sarnath. And we are only just beginning. However poor India may be economically, it is a cultural and spiritual world power."

The Dhamekha Stupa was the most prominent edifice in Sarnath and the spot where the Buddha gave his first sermon. It had a rounded, conical shape, some 128 feet tall. There were Buddhist pilgrims circumambulating it. Sarnath was not nearly as crowded or busy as Bodhgaya, almost deserted really although not quite as devoid of human presence as Lumbini, yet it was here where the voice of Buddhism, the dhamma, was first spoken and heard. The wheel referred to *samsara* or the endless cycle of death and rebirth that continued due to cravings and attachment, which the Buddha's dhamma tried to end.

"Much of Sarnath was destroyed during the Muslim invasions," I said. "They sacked the place and used the building materials for other structures including mosques. It had been, in its day, a wonder. What a pity to have lost it all."

I lamented this as I did other such examples of Muslim aggression in India and elsewhere. So much had been lost to time, never to be recovered.

"They build mosques over Hindu or Buddhist temples to show the power of Islam over other religions," Ying said.

"Like the Dome of the Rock in Jerusalem, sacred to Jews and Christians, or the Hagia Sophia, the most spectacular church in the world in its day, converted into a mosque after the Ottoman Muslims conquered Constantinople in 1453."

From Varanasi we traveled to New Delhi. There we visited among other things, the Mahatma Gandhi Memorial with the eternal flame. It was a moving tribute to a man who was properly considered the father of modern India having led the movement for independence from Great Britain. I had read several books on Gandhi and in general admired him as a model of non-violent civil disobedience *("satyagraha")* in the pursuit of reasonable social and political aims.

He did also make some preposterously stupid comments regarding Britain and the Nazis, advising the British to "lay down the arms you have as being useless for saving you or humanity. You will invite Herr Hitler... to take what [he] wants... you will allow yourselves... to be slaughtered, but you will refuse to owe allegiance to them."

To the Jews of Europe he was even more irrational and bizarre. In 1946, in response to the Holocaust, he said "...the Jews should have offered themselves to the butcher's knife... [and] thrown themselves into the sea from the cliffs." He felt that this "collective suicide" would have been "heroism." He apparently was not clever enough to recognize that the methods of civil resistance he employed against a Western democracy like Britain were ludicrous in the face of a totalitarian regime like Nazi Germany. These comments displayed a moral blindness and obtuseness that for me were unforgivable.

From New Delhi we journeyed to Agra to see the Taj Mahal. The Moghul emperor Shah Jahan built the Taj, in 1629, in memory of his wife, Mumtaz Mahal who died in childbirth after producing fourteen children. Said to be the most extravagant monument ever built for love, it loomed like a brilliant white vision, more dream than substance, as it hovered seamlessly above the reflecting lakes below it. At night it glowed by the light of the full moon, the white marble lustrous in the surrounding darkness, it's timeless grandeur and subtle beauty made even more hypnotic.

In this and other examples, I noted Islam's grand contributions to human civilization for these splendid palaces and structures were moving and impressive, awe-inspiring in their scale, contours, detail, and beauty.

"We have seen the greatness of Islam too," I said.

We continued on to Jaisalmer, a small fortress city in the middle of the Thar Desert in the Indian state of Rajasthan not far from the border of Pakistan. It had a rugged medieval feel and the homes, mansions, temples and palaces were hewed in blonde-yellow sandstone, creating a golden aura that against the backdrop of the receding beige sands of the desert was stunning. While in Jaisalmer, Ying and I spent two days and nights traveling through the desert on the back of a camel. We visited sand dunes, villages and ancient temple ruins. At night, the guide made a fire, cooked our food, and sang Rajasthani songs for us. We slept under the stars in the cool desert night, warmed by the fading embers and the smelly body of our camel, who insisted on lying beside us. Upon our return to Jaisalmer, exhausted and aching, we dusted the sand off our bodies and went out for a meal. We chose a restaurant with rooftop dining to enjoy the view of the desert and the city below. The waiter appeared with the menus.

One of the items listed in the beverage section was something known as "bhang lassi." A lassi was a common Indian drink, akin to a yogurt smoothie. "Bhang," on the other hand, was something I had only recently heard about since coming to Jaisalmer. This was a form of cannabis that was sold legally on the streets in government controlled "bhang" shops. When bought just as "bhang" it came as a tightly wrapped leafy green ball to be held in your mouth between the cheek and gum, chewed and sucked on for a while and then swallowed. Its effect was said to be between that of hashish and peyote and many in Jaisalmer appeared to partake. They had glazed, delirious looks on their faces and seemed to be having a great time. In restaurants it was usually blended with a lassi so you wouldn't have to put up with the taste. "You want to try a bhang lassi?" I asked Ying. "Yes," she said. I had a feeling she wanted one. "Do you want your own or do you want to share?"

"Let's share."

"Okay," We ordered our food and a large bhang lassi. I then sat back in my chair and browsed through the India Times.

Ten minutes later the food arrived, and with it a tall glass of bhang lassi. Normally, lassi was a white colored drink, but in this case it was green tinged from the bhang. I didn't think very much about it and sipped it slowly from time to time while reading the paper and eating. Ying had some also but I wound up drinking most of it. About half an hour later I realized that something strange was happening when I realized that I had been reading the same line in the newspaper over and over again for the last twenty minutes. Something about the rising costs of lentils in rural India. I slowly lifted my eyes off the page and glanced at Ying. She had that same weird smile that everybody else had in Jaisalmer. Her eyes were glazed, her pupils dilated and she was looking right at me and giggling. She seemed to be having a great time while I, on the other hand, was not feeling so great. I had this odd feeling that Ying knew exactly what I was thinking, and I started to get a little paranoid.

"Hi, Rick." Ying giggled.

"Uhh, hi Ying."

"How do you feel, Rick?" she smiled.

"Uhh, okay, I think."

"You have been staring at the newspaper a while, Rick."

"Uh huh."

"Are you sure you're okay, Rick?"

"Uhh, yeah I think."

"Do you feel funny, Rick?"

"Uhh, a little, how about you?"

"Yeah, me too," she continued to giggle.

I tried to giggle back although I didn't feel like it. This of course made Ying giggle more. I responded with some giggling just to show Ying I was enjoying myself, and before long we were both giggling hysterically. The only thing was that I wasn't having such a good time. I noticed that my mind and body had split off from one another. My body was shaking with laughter, but my mind was lost somewhere in a rush of chaotic perceptions and disconnected thoughts. Everything was filtered through a series of prisms, broken down by composite colors and angles like a psychedelic cubist painting. The world had fragmented into photons and wavelengths, and I could barely function.

"Are you ready to go," Ying asked, still giggling. She seemed to have much more control than I did. I was glad she had taken less bhang.

"Uhh, yeah."

"Sure?"

"Uhh, yeah."

"Let's go." She stood up and waited. I looked at her. Somewhere there was a thought that said, "get up" but it had gotten lost in a billow of clouds.

"Do you need some help," Ying laughed.

"Uhh, I think so..." Thank Buddha for Ying.

Ying and I somehow made it down the steps of the restaurant to the street below. She hung on to my arm and carefully guided me through the anarchy of Indian street life. Everything was a blur. At one point, as we were approaching our hotel, Ying asked me if I knew which way to go. From here we usually made a right turn to our hotel only two blocks away. I looked down one street, then another, and another, but could not figure out the way. I made one desperate attempt to answer her question. "That way." I pointed stuporously. "Which way?" Ying asked jokingly, knowing I had no idea. She laughed and dragged me to our hotel opposite the direction I had recommended. That was the first and last time I tangled with the great Indian god Bhang.

We then traveled to the Brahmin city of Pushkar, also in Rajasthan, a beautiful white village built around a holy lake on the edge of the desert. Pushkar Lake was said to have been formed by the tears shed by Shiva upon the death of his wife Sati. Surrounding this small desert city were miles of empty windswept sand dunes. We arrived in Pushkar as the sun was setting. A young man in a long white shirt and a red dot painted on his forehead introduced himself to us at the bus station.

"I am a Brahmin, of the priestly cast," he said. "I can perform ritual blessings for a fee and have a beautiful hotel for you to stay in."

We dumped our bags in a cart pulled by a large camel and rode into town with him. From the roof of our hotel, we could see the Hindu shrines and temples and homes of the city all covered in white stucco, reflecting in the hallowed lake's dark waters. As the sun fell the white city was aflame in the glow of the desert sunset.

The streets of Pushkar were typical India in all its plumage and eccentricity. There were saints and beggars, holy men and snake charmers, Brahmin priests and traveling minstrels. Musicians played traditional stringed instruments for barefoot dancers with bells on their ankles. Fierce desert people with thick mustaches and turbans rode in on their camels carrying rugs and blankets. There were juice vendors who blended delicious concoctions from exotic Indian fruits and vegetables; sugar cane pressers who ran long stalks of sugar cane through rollers extracting green frothy juice. Hot milk vendors sat like monks before vats of bubbling, creamy milk. Restaurants with amazing aromas prepared curries, masalas, kormas, biryanis and delicious breads baked in large mud ovens. There were barbers and scalp massagers, tailors, psychics, Ayurvedic dispensers, artists, tattooists, jewelers, rug dealers, craft and clothing vendors. You could get a shave and a scalp massage right on the street, have your palm read, your fortunes told, your dreams interpreted. There were festivals and ceremonies with the Hindu faithful chanting and making offerings. Camel drivers offered night rides in the desert, hailing us as "Maharaja and Maharini" (prince and princess), promising romantic desert sojourns by the light of the moon.

From Pushkar, we continued on our journey, traveling to Udaipur, a romantic city of palaces, castles and lakes and then to Ajanta and Ellora. These were the two sites of the world famous Buddhist, Jain and Hindu cave temples carved into solid rock, in some cases, almost two thousand years ago. We had also been to Jaipur, the "Pink City," and Jodhpur, the "Blue City," both in Rajasthan with historic and opulent palaces, temples, and forts. Afterwards we traveled to Poona, where we stopped by the ashram of Osho, more commonly known in the West as Rajneesh.

Rajneesh was an Indian guru with tens of thousands of followers in the West who became somewhat controversial in the US when he created an ashram community in Oregon. As it turned out Ying and I arrived at his ashram to find that Rajneesh had died only four days before. True to Osho's spirit, four days after his death there was a big bash at the ashram, with wild dancing and rock and roll music that could be heard for blocks in celebration of Osho's *Samadhi* (union with the Divine at or before death). His adherents, perhaps a little unconvincingly, explained that "...It was only his body that died but his spirit remains..."

Osho's ashram was a three ring spiritual circus, the Club Med of alternative consciousness, with just about every conceivable spiritual practice or therapy offered. There was shiatsu, acupressure, dance therapy, *kundalini* yoga, astral travel, dynamic vegetarianism, enemas that cured everything, and many more of the exotic and bizarre. And there were thousands there from around the world, particularly Europe and the US, most of them garbed in purple robes, sandals, and beaded chains with a picture of their beloved guru around their necks. It was a scene.

After Poona, we boarded a train to the state of Goa where I had arranged to visit and teach at the local hospital. A dapper Indian, an ENT doctor named Naveen Kumar, received us at the train station in Vasco. He shook my hand and ushered Ying and I into a taxi. The three of us sped off to Panaji, the capital of Goa, where the hospital was located. When we arrived Naveen handed me the bill for the taxi. It was an omen of things to come.

Chapter 57

The next morning, while Ying and I were asleep in our small room in the hospital dorm, I heard a knock on the door. I opened it and was greeted by a short, portly Indian man in a white coat.

"Good morning, Dr. Moss, I am Dr. Pradip with the ENT department. I am so happy you have arrived safely. We were all so worried about you. Please, I have brought you and your wife something for breakfast." He entered the room and handed us a small bag of Indian sweets. "Did Naveen meet you at the train station last night?" he asked.

"Yes, we took a taxi back together." I answered.

"Oh, wonderful, I am very pleased. I would have come myself but I could not get free." Dr. Pradip seemed very polite. "I will not keep you long, Dr. Moss, I only wanted to welcome you to Goa and wish you a good stay. Let us meet later for lunch in the cafeteria. Afterwards Dr. Joseph, the Dean, wants to see you."

We met later in the hospital cafeteria and were introduced to some of the members of the department. Naveen had come, and another rather sickly looking fellow who had just joined the staff by the name of Arjun. We sat around a few tables eating chickpeas and potatoes in curry sauce along with rather tart lassies and were soon joined by Pradip and the residents. Except for one individual, the residents were all women, beautifully dressed in traditional saris, some of them, as seemed to be the custom in India, quite hefty. Chubbiness seemed to be something of a status symbol in India, possibly denoting wealth, higher caste or both. It never seemed to fail that the people with the most expensive jewelry and clothing were also the heaviest. Pradip headed the ENT department and seemed genuinely pleased that I had come to Goa. "We were really looking forward to your visit Dr. Moss and thank you for traveling so far. We will try to learn everything we possibly can from you."

Afterwards, Pradip and I went to pay our respects to Dr. Joseph, the dean. Dr. Joseph had been the one who had arranged my visit. We had been in contact by mail. Pradip and I checked in with the secretary and were politely given seats on a long wooden bench in the reception area. After about twenty minutes the Dean was ready to meet us. We walked through two tall wooden doors and entered a cavernous room with high ceilings. A thin red carpet led to a large lonely desk in the distance, behind which sat, in full papal glory, the Dean. We walked cautiously into the silent room and sat in two chairs opposite him. Dr. Joseph was a middle-aged man who wore bifocals that rested at the tip of his nose. He was silently reading over some documents and did not lift his eyes to greet us. I noticed Pradip twitching nervously as we waited. Finally, the great man placed the papers on his desk and looked up.

"...Hello, this must be Dr. Moss," he said to Pradip in a business like tone.

"Y-y-yes, sir, r-r-right, sir, this is Dr. Moss, sir," Pradip stammered.

"Pleased to meet you, Dr. Moss, I am Dr. Joseph." He had a formal British manner about him. "So glad you could make it." He did not offer his hand.

"Thank you."

"We have arranged a place for you to stay at the dorm, I hope it will be alright for you and your wife."

"I'm sure it will be fine."

"Good. Please let me know if there is anything I can do for you. My Mrs. and I will, of course, have you over some night for dinner." So proper. But an invite to the papal residence just the same.

"Thank you, I'll look forward to it."

"How long do you think you will be staying with us?"

"About three months or possibly longer."

"Excellent. I'm sure Dr. Pradip and the residents will gain a great deal from you. Isn't that so Pradip?" Joseph shot a quick glance over at Pradip.

"Y-y-yes, sir, it is our great pleasure to have him, sir."

We chatted amiably for another twenty minutes. Dr. Joseph seemed delighted I had come all this way, referring to me, in the best British tradition, as a "fine chap." He mentioned that he had studied in Britain years ago and received a degree in comparative anatomy. He had long since given up his academic pursuits to become a fulltime administrator at the hospital where he had served as Dean for the last seven years.

"But you are still an outsider in Goa, no matter how long you have been here," Joseph said.

"Are you Hindu," I asked.

"No, actually I am a Christian, but that doesn't matter really. There is something about Goa and Goans. Unless you are from here, you are never truly accepted, no matter who you are." I noticed Joseph pause. "Uhh, Dr. Moss, one small thing."

"Yes," I answered.

"Sorry to bother you with this, really. I don't know if Dr. Pradip mentioned, but since you are from a western country, it is mandatory that you have an *Elisa* done."

"Elisa?"

"Yes, the Elisa, you know, for HIV."

I had been out of the states for too long. "You mean the blood test for AIDS," I asked.

"Yes."

"Oh, of course. Why?"

"Well surely you must have heard."

"No."

"True, you have only just arrived. Well, all you have to do is pick up a newspaper. There are stories every day. We have an AIDS epidemic in Goa. With all the westerners, you see, at the beaches. Alot of drugs. Bad business, really. But don't worry, it's just a formality. Apologies for the inconvenience."

"Right. Where do I get this done?"

"Dr. Pradip will arrange it for you."

So AIDS had moved to India's shores. It had become quite an issue in Thailand, as well, with the prostitution and drugs there. One of the advantages I had remembered thinking about when leaving the US in the first place was getting away from AIDS. Especially since I had been working in the two AIDS capitols of the world, New York City and San Francisco. Now the AIDS scourge had arrived on these distant and exotic lands too. Pradip and I stood to dismiss ourselves, "Good to meet you, Dr. Joseph," I said.

"Thank you for coming," he answered, "please keep in touch."

Ying and I found our way over to our new home. The accommodations Joseph had alluded to consisted of a single room with two hospital beds pushed together and a squeaky ceiling fan that operated at only one speed - gale force. There was a small balcony that I was urged to keep locked because of recent thefts in the area. We had to use a large communal bathroom at the end of the hall with the other house staff that generally stank. The toilets were Indian squat style, with a footpad on either side of a porcelain pit to place your feet on. There was a small faucet with a little bucket for cleaning your hands. As I had already learned, trees in India rarely became toilet paper. I was also to receive a stipend of 3000 rupees a month or about 167 dollars. Fairly modest for an American surgeon but I wasn't complaining. It was better than Nepal. Overall though, Ying and I were pleased. We had a place to stay, were getting some compensation and had an eager staff that on first glance appeared very interested in learning.

Chapter 58

"... It is the same issue Dr. Moss. We cannot get the blood," Dr. Pradip said. He smiled sympathetically, his broad white teeth gleaming. "Of course you know we all want to watch you operate, but it is not possible this week."

"What's the problem again?"

"The same as always, Doctor Moss. We cannot find the blood."

"Isn't there anything you can do?"

"You know how difficult it is."

"Have you spoken with the family?"

"We have tried everything, Dr. Moss. I hope next week it will be better."

The polite toothy smile and "sincere" apologies, followed by an abrupt departure - the pattern became familiar. Weeks had passed since coming to Goa and as yet I had not picked up a knife. There were cases that needed to be done but for a variety of reasons none of them found their way to the operating room. With each passing week, I grew increasingly frustrated. Most of the time the reason cited was lack of blood replacement, and in fact this was true. A very curious thing about Goa was that no one could be found to donate blood. On several occasions I had to send patients home to die of cancer because of lack of blood. Even family members of cancer patients refused to donate. Partly I wondered if the Hindu caste system had something to do with this - carving a society up by caste for thousands of years could present problems in getting people to volunteer their veins for one another. Perhaps also, it had to do with superstition or lack of education or fear of blood tainted by AIDS. And maybe it also had something to do with Pradip. Despite the difficulties in obtaining blood, other surgical departments were performing big cases. From the ENT department of Dr. Pradip, no blood and no major surgery. I began to wonder if lack of blood hadn't become the perfect alibi for Pradip, his way of keeping me from operating. I had endured his stall tactics for weeks now, the toothy smile, the polite apologies, the story about the blood, but it was obvious that things were not right.

The warm sunny relationship that Pradip and I seemed to enjoy that first day had gone decidedly downhill. I had quickly observed that as an ENT surgeon Pradip was not particularly adept. He could perform the most basic procedures but not much else. His motives for resisting me could be understood on the basis of personal insecurity, unfortunate but understandable. What was more confusing though was how someone with his level of expertise could rise to become chairman of a surgical department at a teaching center. The answer to this, I soon found, was simple - Pradip was an "untouchable."

There were four Hindu castes in traditional Indian society. These included the Brahmins (priests), Kshatriyas (rulers, warriors), Vaishyas (merchants, artisans, farmers), and Shudras (laborers). Historically, certain groups were excluded from the caste system altogether, considered completely outside and beneath its purview and referred to as "untouchables." For centuries, the "untouchables" had been a despised underclass in India, looked upon by their Hindu countrymen as unclean and impure. Anyone born into this lowest of classes was ostracized from birth as an "outcaste," given the most menial of occupations with little or no chance of bettering themselves. Gandhi had tried to elevate their status and referred to them as "Harijans" ("Children of God"). With India's independence in 1947, an effort to correct the social wrongs of the caste system began that included a quota system. This reserved a specified number of posts in the government and universities for the untouchables, an Indian version of affirmative action and every bit as divisive and controversial as its counterpart in the US. The term "untouchable" was illegal now and never used in India, at least not in public. They were referred to instead as the "scheduled caste." Whether he deserved it or not, as a member of the scheduled caste, Pradip had landed himself a damn good job.

Dr. Phillip Fonseca was the chief of the surgery department. He was a Christian, one of the Portuguese Old Guard who still hearkened back to the days (not long ago) when Goa was a colony of Portugal. Like many surgeons he could be cantankerous especially when it came to the topic of Pradip. He had learned through the grapevine of the problems I was having getting surgery scheduled and asked me to meet him in his office.

"Am I an Indian or a Portuguese, Richard, aye, I don't even know anymore," Phillip said. "Sometimes I wish we could cut our little state off from these heathens. We were much happier under the Portuguese." He puffed on his cigarette and furrowed his brow. "We are like a mongrel half breed in this state, half Christian and half Hindu, and see the problems we have as a result. Pradip is a headache but there is very little to be done. You see it is much bigger than us. This began millennia ago with their godless caste system and now they try to repair it in their clumsy way from a thousand miles away. And we and our patients must suffer the consequences." He frowned as he looked over at me. "There are ten thousand Pradips throughout the land, many who are as unqualified as he. I ask only that you not judge us by Pradip, Richard, please don't do that to us. That would be unfair. The other departments here are very strong, believe me. It is our *enlightened* leaders in New Delhi, may they rot in hell for an eternity, who have done this."

Pradip, as I had suspected, was in over his head. But once entrenched as the chairman of the department it was impossible to dislodge him. A former ENT doctor in the department here, "a very good one too" Phillip had informed me, "an old Portuguese by the name of Alfonso," had taken it to Pradip and was fired the next day. No one would stand in the way of India's march to social equality, regardless of problems and poor outcomes. My arrival on the scene had undoubtedly given Pradip indigestion. As an outsider, he could not confront me directly, and the Dean himself had sanctioned my visit. But Pradip was an actor. Through a facade of polite humble-pie, he could smile me into oblivion, keep me at arms length from the residents, and, more importantly, from the head and neck cancer patients whom he was unable to treat himself. He would not suffer the embarrassment of being outdone in front of his staff. But he would do it by attrition, hoping that I would slowly get the message and quietly disappear. All knew his strategy, but as Phillip indicated, there was nothing they could do. "Richard, do your cases with us. We would be happy to watch and learn. You will not be able to work with Pradip," Phillip said.

As the reality of the situation unfolded, I could not have felt more appalled. Ying and I had come a long way on the trains and buses of India at our own expense for the sole purpose of teaching local doctors and helping patients. Our accommodations and stipend, which we happily accepted, were modest to say the least. To then suffer this kind of treatment was intolerable – not just for us, but the residents and especially the patients.

One morning Ying and I were making rounds with Pradip and the residents. This was one of the few activities at Goa that I found professionally fulfilling, as we were unable to do surgery. It gave me a chance to interact with the residents and teach, an important part of my mission. We did this weekly, something I insisted on, a major concession by Pradip who had no interest as long as I was leading it. We moved from bed to bed, examining the patients and making recommendations. The young doctors and students seemed to enjoy it. They were eager and attentive. Pradip was distracted. He seemed to resent that I could hold forth in this fashion and retain the interest of the staff, even stirring them with the wonders of head and neck pathology and its treatment.

We came upon a patient with a large mass that completely engulfed his right parotid gland, a salivary gland located in the cheek just in front of the ear. He was a young man and in considerable pain. The bulging mass deformed his cheek. It was rock hard and fixed, which was to say, immobile, having invaded the surrounding soft tissue and perhaps bone, in this case the mandible. It may even have involved the base of the skull, which would have made resection impossible. It was an advanced tumor, likely incurable, a pity for so youthful an individual.

I palpated the nasty tumor, felt its rigidity, sensed, given its presentation, what it might be and opened up the floor for debate and questions. "So what do we do?" I asked, looking around at the small group of physicians. Hands shot up. "He will need surgery, Dr. Moss, but it is so big," one young doctor said.

"It would be good if we could get a CT scan," a student suggested.

"We do not have one here," a resident responded.

"Has he received antibiotics?" I asked.

"Yes, but to no effect, sir."

"It is a large tumor," Pradip piped in. "Too large to operate on here and we do not have blood. It is the same problem, Dr. Moss. Very unfortunate but nothing we can do." He seemed keen to move on.

"Not so fast, Pradip," I said smiling through my teeth. "Someone get me a syringe and an 18 gauge needle." Pradip rolled his eyes. "Has anyone needled this thing?" I asked.

The residents shook their heads.

"It is one of the glories of ENT," I said, "that most neck masses can be needled. Especially something as large as this. It is always among the first things to do in managing neck masses. Find out what you're dealing with."

"Our resources are limited Dr. Moss. We can barely do basic surgery let alone something major like this. Let's continue," Pradip said.

The politics here were in play. Pradip and I were not on the best of terms. That was unfortunate. Nonetheless, the team wanted to see the procedure so they could learn. But they also knew that I was here only temporarily. They were torn between observing me and protecting themselves from future retaliatory attacks. In the end, they wisely but reluctantly shuffled to the next bed so as not to annoy Pradip.

Unfortunately for Pradip the student arrived with the needle and syringe. "Here it is, sir," he said as he handed them to me. He cringed as Pradip glowered at him. The crowd returned once more to the patient. Ying looked at me in the same way she did when I was burring down on that man's skull in Kathmandu. She was nervous and hoped that I would not make a fool of myself.

A nurse handed me a gauze pad. I wiped the area with alcohol. I arranged the needle and syringe and told the patient not to move. I plunged the little dart into the center of the mass. I drew back on the syringe. Pure pus. I filled the syringe with the disgusting green fluid and reaspirated over and over until there was nothing left and not less than 75 milliliters of pus had been evacuated from the abscess. The large mass decompressed immediately. His distorted face looked normal again.

I handed the syringe over to the resident. "Run a culture on this. He can probably go home later today."

The patient stood up and shook my hand, thanking me excitedly in Hindi, obviously grateful and already feeling much better. The faculty, residents, students and nurses smiled. The man who was about to be sent home mistakenly with an "incurable" tumor could now return to his family cured of a large abscess that had been drained with a minor bedside procedure.

I patted the patient on the shoulder. Ying smiled. I smiled. Pradip scowled. We moved on to the next patient.

Chapter 59

More than a month had passed since I had come to Goa, and I had had enough. The frustration and inactivity of the last few weeks had slowly boiled over. It was time to resolve it. I found Pradip looking over some charts by the ENT clinic. "I want to speak with you," I said. He seemed surprised by the tone in my voice.

"Excuse me, Dr. Moss, I'm busy now, can we speak later."

"We need to speak *now*."

His face stiffened. "If you insist."

We walked into a conference room where some of the residents were reading.

"What is the problem, Dr. Moss," Pradip asked petulantly.

"The problem, Pradip, is you."

"And what is that supposed to mean?"

"It means I'm leaving."

"Oh?" he said, clumsily pretending to be disappointed.

"You got me and my wife to come two thousand miles to help you and the others, and you're not interested. You know very little about treating cancer patients, and you don't want to know. My only question is why didn't you say so before? Why drag us all the way down here?"

"That's ridiculous."

"What about the cancer patients you send home to keep me from operating?"

"It's the blood, Dr. Moss," he said.

"The general surgeons are operating daily."

"But there is still a problem."

"Yes, there is. The problem is you, Pradip."

"What do you want from me?"

"Nothing."

"I-I'm sorry if things did not work out."

"I don't want your apologies, Pradip."

"W-what is it then?"

"You are way out of your depth, and you wasted our time. You should know your limits and listen to those who can help you. But you have a miserable attitude and made that impossible."

I left him.

I had already decided to leave Goa. I had mixed feelings about it. I had come a long way, spent a month and accomplished virtually nothing, yet the idea of leaving ran against my grain. I wanted to take care of these patients and to teach the local physicians and residents. But it was impossible with Pradip standing in my way. It was also unbearable to send patient's home when they could have been treated.

"Richard, stop torturing yourself," Phillip said to me when we spoke later in his office. "It is just bad luck. You had no way of knowing this until you got here. No one could warn you or tell you of the pitfalls of Indian politics and how the foolish policies from New Delhi reach down and touch every nook and cranny of our lives, ruining everything."

"It seems so easy to remedy," I said, "the solution so obvious, and yet there is some invisible barrier preventing us from doing what is proper for the patients."

"It is bigger than us. We have no power over this. It serves some 'greater' goal. We must bow and scrape before our heathen masters and accept our ugly fates."

"If I explained to someone what is going on, maybe they would understand."

"There is no hope, Richard, except with us. We have cases. Work with us. We want to learn from you."

"General surgeons used to do head and neck. Some of the founding fathers of modern head and neck surgery were general surgeons."

"Now you are talking, Richard. And truly we would like to learn. It is no longer part of our training. Maybe we can start again with your help."

"Do you have any cases?"

"We have one waiting for you."

I saw the patient in the General Surgery clinic the next day. She was an elderly woman with a tongue cancer. It required a flap, which the surgery residents were eager to see. We scheduled the case the next day. I was amazed at how swiftly the surgeons arranged it. They had the blood typed and crossed, anesthesia notified, and a crack team of young general surgery residents along with Phillip on hand to assist me. We removed part of the mandible and half the tongue along with a neck dissection. We reconstructed with a flap and a K-wire for the jaw, an old technique but still good. It went well and Phillip and his staff very much appreciated it.

"Thank you, Dr. Moss," the residents said after the case.

"I want to thank you too," Phillip said, "it was excellent. For our patient and the residents."

I hung around a few days to check the patient with the residents. She looked good and the flap had good color. Everything was fine. That solitary case with Phillip was the one bright spot in a bitter month.

We had a farewell dinner with Dr. Joseph, the Dean, and his wife at his home. It was pleasant. He was very cordial. During the meal he had mentioned to his wife, referring to me, that "the poor chap is crestfallen, unable to do surgery," and he smiled sympathetically as if speaking of a youngster deprived of a toy. I realized the man had no understanding of my purpose in coming here or what was going on with Dr. Pradip. Perhaps he thought of my visit as a kind of cultural exchange? When I mentioned something about Pradip he quickly changed topics. Perhaps he knew but could do nothing given the political headwinds. Nothing further was said about it.

"You blew it, Rick," Ying said to me after dinner. "You failed. Pradip has no power. He was your ordeal, Rick, and you failed. You are a buffoon sometimes, blind to everything around you. Just another emotional fool letting your anger get the better of you. I am disappointed in you."

"But what about Pradip? I could do nothing with him."

"You should have gone around him. You had Phillip Fonseca, the chief of surgery, on your side. You had just done a successful case with him. He and his team were happy to work with you. You just had dinner with the Dean, more than an hour of uninterrupted time, and not once did you discuss the problem with him."

"But Phillip said there was nothing to be done."

"Phillip was your ally. You could have mobilized him along with other surgeons to go around Pradip. You could have continued working with Phillip and the other surgeons if nothing else. Or maybe you could have gone together to the Dean. Pradip was the guardian at the gate, but you were too emotional to see it. You had to outwit him. It should have been easy for you. Everything was in your favor. Goa should have been a great success like Nepal, a critical part of your mission of healing, not the disappointment it became, depressing you and making you feel as a failure.

"You have spent weeks studying and discussing Buddhism with Uttamo. You lived in a forest monastery practicing *sati* with Jaroon. But you have no *sati*. No mindfulness. And this was so easy, Rick. You should have seen this. If you cannot work around a common pack mule like Pradip than there is no hope for you, and you will fail other tests that come your way. Most important, you are a Jew. You are supposed to be clever. But you are not. You are just another dumb ox like Pradip."

She was right. Pradip was the guardian at the threshold. I had merely to tip toe around him to enter the realm of power, to be initiated and gain insight and knowledge. I had failed to see beyond him.

"Should I pack my bags and go home and give up on myself?" I asked aloud. "I am defeated now. But what we lack in guile and skill we make up with brute force. I am not done yet. There are missteps in every journey. I will find a way to continue my work as a surgeon in the third world."

The next day, Ying and I visited the Basilica of Bom Jesus in old Goa where St. Francis Xavier's incorrupt body lay in state in a silver casket within a glass case. He was born in 1506 in present day Spain and was a cofounder of the Society of Jesus with Saint Ignatius of Loyola. He took the vow of poverty and chastity and led a mission into Asia through the Old Portuguese Empire, mostly in India but then Japan, Borneo, Malacca, and the Maluku Islands. He died enroute to China in 1552. He was considered the greatest Christian evangelist since Saint Paul himself. Originally buried on a beach in an island off the coast of China, his body was eventually brought back to Goa in 1553.

I did not have a "Christian" purpose to visit his church and casket. It was more a sense of paying tribute to a fellow traveler. As a Jew, I was agnostic on the matter of Christian evangelization, if not a little cynical, preferring to leave the native populations alone with the great Eastern faiths. But I valued Christianity, notwithstanding some of its historical flaws. There was no question it was a force for good in the world, part of the Judeo-Christian foundation of Western civilization, a legacy of which I was a recipient and a defender. My purpose here was to show respect to the memory of a great man, one of the founding Jesuits, who had risked everything for his faith and mission. I thought I would find his stalwart vision salutary.

We circled the casket and walked through the church.

"I am on my own mission, not the same as St. Francis', but with some similarities," I said.

"Yes, you are. It is good what you do, Rick," Ying said.

"We can pick up from here."

"Yes, we can, Rick."

"Even a dumb ox can make things happen?"

"Yes," Ying said chuckling, "even a dumb ox – who happens to be a great surgeon."

"Those were good words yesterday, Ying. Memorable."

"I hope you understood."

"I did. It was good."

"Sometimes it is better to speak honestly."

"I understand. It was strong medicine, but necessary."

"Yes."

"St. Francis risked everything and died for his belief."

Ying nodded.

"He traveled through India and the Far East."

"It is a powerful story."

"I take some consolation."

"Good."

Chapter 60

Before long, Ying and I were on the road again. Naveen, who had become our good friend over the month, took us to the train depot in Vasco. Life sometimes enacts a certain poetic symmetry, I thought, remembering how Naveen had only recently met us here on our arrival to Goa. It had gone by quickly. We bid farewell, and Ying and I boarded the train.

I felt betrayed by my experience in Goa. In coming here, I had expended considerable time and energy and for pure motives. For this I had been repaid with a slap in the face. "You had some triumphs here too, Rick," Ying said. "There will be more."

With the train moving swiftly, I reconciled myself with this latest chapter and lost myself instead in the changing landscapes of the Indian countryside.

It was an eight-hour ride to Hampi, formerly the capitol of the Vijayanagara Kingdom, one of the largest Hindu empires in Indian history. Like so many places in India, Hampi was beautifully preserved despite the wars and ravages of time. In a mystic, almost surreal landscape, the deserted temples and dwellings stood silently in the hot sand along the Tungabhadra river with it's huge grey rocks, blue waters and herds of cattle trudging along it's banks.

"India itself will help you forget Goa," Ying said.

We continued on to Hyderabad, the capitol of the state of Andhra Pradesh, a city of two and a half million, and an important center of Islamic culture in the south. Then to Vijayawada to visit the father of an Indian doctor friend of mine from New York. Dr. Rau met us at our hotel and, after one look at the place, had us immediately pack our bags and move to a "better" hotel, while picking up the tab. Ying and I did not mind staying in cheap joints, we were used to it by now. Nor did we mind staying at fancier places as long as we weren't footing the bill. To our minds and wallets though, the first place was fine. To my friend's father, Dr. Rau, on the other hand, it was unthinkable. I realized how curious I must have seemed to Dr. Rau, an American surgeon traveling through India with his wife, staying in budget flophouses with barely a rupee to his name.

From Vijayawada, we took an overnight train to the temple town of Bhubaneswar, the capitol of the state of Orissa. Ying and I were anticipating this visit, excited to see the place that had had such impact on the history of Buddhism. The reign of Kalinga came to an end here in 261 B.C., in a bloody battle with the great emperor Ashoka. As I had already learned, the bloodshed and loss of life so affected Ashoka that he converted to Buddhism and spread that gentle religion throughout his vast empire. We had seen the Ashoka pillars at important Buddhist pilgrimage sites such as Lumbini and Sarnath.

We visited Puri near Bhubaneswar. It was a delightful beachside town with a famous "casteless" temple built to *Jagannath*, "Lord of the Universe" (considered a form of Vishnu). It was particularly popular in India because it was open to all regardless of caste. Along the beach, thirty-three kilometers to the north, was the famous temple of *Konorak*, a magnificent and vast structure carved and conceived as a chariot for the sun god, Surya. Around the base were twenty-four gigantic chiseled stone wheels, pulled by seven powerful horses. The entire edifice was covered with engravings, statuary, and sculpture in bas-relief, many in the erotic style that Konorak and Khajuraho were famous for.

We continued on the last leg of our Indian journey, an eight-hour overnight train to Calcutta, the former seat of "British India."

Founded some 300 years before by the British, Calcutta was notorious for it's squalor and poverty, many of it's ten million inhabitants reduced to begging on the streets or pulling rickshaws in their bare feet, the so called "human horses." Calcutta had been the unhappy recipient of thousands, even millions of refugees at various times in the recent past including the partition of India in 1947, the Pakistani civil war in 1971, and from the many devastating floods that have occurred in West Bengal over the years, all of which have only served to worsen it's already tenuous condition. Yet it was also a beautiful city with lovely residential neighborhoods, a booming film industry, and world-class museums. A hot bed of intellectual ferment, left wing politics, and the home of some of India's greatest poets, scholars and artists, Calcutta was a major economic and cultural center for the country. For Ying and I though it was the place to get visas to enter our next country. After two days of discussion, letters from the American consul, and a little baksheesh, the officials at the Bangladesh consulate on Circus Avenue did us the great service of allowing us to enter one of the poorest nations on earth, Bangladesh.

In the same way as Calcutta but even more so, Bangladesh summoned up visions of human suffering and poverty. I imagined the disease and neglect here would transcend anything I had yet experienced. Between the poverty and overpopulation and lack of resources, I knew it would be challenging – and exactly what I was looking for. I had no idea if I would be able to satisfy my wish to heal and teach here, but somehow I believed I could. I wanted to revive my mission and rekindle my passion to treat patients. After Goa I was running out of steam. My funds were low. Maybe I could make a last stand in Bangladesh. After nearly three years on the road, my goals were the same. Only I had vastly more experience and could offer so much more than before fresh out of residency. I had been given the name of a professor in Bangladesh. I had mailed him earlier. I never heard back, but then how could I since I was on the road. I trusted the fates and hoped for the opportunity to do what I most wanted: to restore patients suffering with oppressive disease.

We boarded a train the next day for the two-hour journey to the border of Bangladesh. Ying and I were to begin the most difficult phase of my medical work. Despite my experiences of the last several years, Bangladesh would test me in ways I could only imagine.

VII. Bangladesh

Chapter 61

April 13, 1990.

The train pulled out of the station in Calcutta. It was noisy and crowded with life. The women in saris. The beggars in rags. The coolies and the sadhus. There were no seats.

Ying and I placed our bags by an open door. I bent my aching knees and squatted on my bag. I felt the warm air hit my face as the train picked up speed. The squalor and congestion of Calcutta gave way to the green fields of jute and rice.

Ying and I hardly stood out in the crowd. I looked Indian but it was more than that. I had become Asian. I acted like one. Thought like one. Asia had entered me. Without knowing it. When I first arrived, I thought I was merely visiting when in truth I was returning home. Spiritually, psychically, and through my work as a surgeon, I belonged here.

It was a two-hour ride to the border. I was about to enter the world's poorest country with barely a dime in my pocket wondering what I was doing with my life. I had the name of one doctor in Dhaka whom I never met. The life of an itinerant surgeon was wonderful, but I was broke. If I didn't figure out a way to make money soon my journey would have to end. I had been traveling on a ridiculously tight budget. Cheap hotels. Street food. Second class train tickets. I loved what I was doing, but I questioned myself. If I had become a monk or sadhu, I would have been supported. But not as a surgeon. I could create a new order, the surgeon-mendicant-monk. I could carry a scalpel, begging bowl, and don orange robes.

Why did I keep going? Was my healing quest at an end? Would Bangladesh breathe new life into my little enterprise?

I took the measure of my journey thus far. It had been nearly 3 years. I had major stopovers in Chiang Mai, Songkla, Nepal, and India. Between

Songkla and Nepal, I enjoyed a prolonged expedition through Malaysia, Singapore, and Indonesia with brief glimpses of third world medicine, particularly in Yogyakarta. Each place was unique and provided extraordinary experiences. And now we were about to enter Bangladesh. Along the way I had met my wife. The circumstances were not ideal, which was putting it mildly, but we had grown together. She had a different perspective on things. I should have given more weight to her concerns. We had argued over money, and she was right. My vision of medicine was too pure. I was still unwilling to compromise. But the reality of my pauperhood was closing in around me. My dilemma was how to continue my work with no income. In the meantime, I would travel on buses, eat street food, and stay in budget flophouses. But it would not be enough. I was seeking a middle way, like the Buddhists. I had to find a way to do charity work *and* earn a living. I had to rework the mission and myself.

The train from Calcutta pulled in at the town of Bongaon, close to the border with Bangladesh. From here it was a seven-mile ride on the back of a wooden cart. We bargained the rickshaw walla down to twenty-five rupees for the two of us. Along the way locals desperate to change rupees for dollars swore up and down their rates were better than at the border. We continued on our bumpy path.

The scene at the border crossing was the typical madness: changing money, customs officials checking your bags, asking absurd questions, taking their time trying to squeeze a little baksheesh out of you. It reminded me of the shenanigans at the border crossing at Sunauli when we entered India from Nepal a few months back. Not too many westerners passed into Bangladesh this way so I was quite a curiosity. Most usually flew into Dhaka. I had two weeks on my visa but I figured I could change that once inside the country.

We finally passed into Bangladesh to a little border town by the name of Benapole. The bus to Dhaka had just left. We had to wait until 7 PM to catch the next one. The ride to Dhaka took ten hours including several river crossings on ferries in the middle of the night. It was a nightmare. The whole night they blasted Hindi music. At stops hawkers boarded the bus and screamed in your face peddling snacks and wares. The heat was oppressive, and the driver was a maniac. Blowing his horn psychotically, he picked up speed whenever he approached a curve or switched lanes with an oncoming vehicle approaching rapidly. He enjoyed coming as close to total annihilation as possible, escaping only at the final split second. Ying and I spent the entire night quaking in mortal fear. Arriving in Dhaka at five in the morning, having slept not a minute all night, we swore never to ride a Bangladeshi bus again.

We got into a three-wheeled Bangladeshi taxi and roamed the city looking for the cheapest hotel. At five in the morning the town was asleep. We checked in at a place called the "Asia Hotel." It was 180 taka or about six bucks - a big splurge. We put our bags on the floor and slept.

The nation known today as Bangladesh was formerly the Bengali region of India. This region, primarily Muslim, became the eastern wing of Pakistan during the bloody partition from India in 1947. Bangladesh itself was born in 1971 when civil war tore it from Pakistan. The Bengalis had supplied the major share of foreign exchange earnings for Pakistan through its jute exports but received little of the development or foreign aid programs and were excluded from political power. In 1970, the first elections ever to give the eastern wing an equal vote were held. The Bengali, Sheikh Mujibur Allaudin, came to power. The West Pakistanis, not about to be led by a Bengali, promptly jailed him. Civil war broke out. More than three million Bengalis, many of them innocent civilians, were killed. The war and wholesale slaughter did not stop until India stepped in. After the war in 1971 East Pakistan became Bangladesh. Since then the newly formed nation of Bangladesh had been plagued by natural disasters, corruption, poverty, and a high population rate. There were some 120 million people packed into a country the size of Wisconsin, most of them impoverished. One of the basket cases of the world, I could only guess what the patients here would be like.

I still had the name and phone number of the ENT doctor I had mailed more than a year ago, Professor Nurul Amin. Other than that there had been no contact between us. I called. He could hardly believe his ears when he picked up the phone.

"Moss. Yes, yes. You are here? When did you come? Where are you? I never thought..."

"I'm at the Asia hotel off Kakrail Road."

"What are you doing in such a place? Are you okay? How did you get here?"

"I took the bus."

"From where?"

"Benapole."

"At the border?"

"Yes."

"You're not serious?"

Professor Amin was the patriarch of Ear, Nose and Throat in Bangladesh. I met him at his office on the fifth floor at the Institute of Post Graduate Research and Medicine, or simply PG Hospital. One of his residents had picked us up in a car and brought us to his office. Prior to entering, the resident stopped and listened. He placed his ear against the door.

"He is praying. He bows toward Mecca. We must wait."

Several minutes passed. The resident listened again. I could make out the sound of people talking. We walked in.

Inside the room were a number of doctors sitting around a desk. Behind the desk sat a silver haired, husky man in glasses who stood up to greet me.

"Moss. Come in. I asked some colleagues to meet with you. Moss, you really surprised me. I received your letter, but you see things move slowly in our country. To arrange a license and accommodations takes time. I am Dr. Amin, sit down." Amin snapped his fingers and nodded towards several of the residents standing against the wall. Two chairs instantly appeared for Ying and I.

"Moss, you come at the wrong time. This is our holy month, Ramadan. We are all fasting. Or almost everyone." He nodded and smiled at one of the doctors sitting by the desk, a dark skinned individual. "Our country is 83% Muslim and about 17% Hindu with a small amount of Buddhist and Christian. But at this time of year our nation is divided into the eaters and the noneaters. Moss, you and your wife must be hungry." He pointed at the residents, speaking quickly in Bengali. Two of them left the room.

"We will get you some food. You see Moss, I don't think it will be very busy for you. Everyone is tired. No one will want to have surgery now."

Amin was a forceful bundle of energy. He sat up in his chair, leaned forward against his desk and bounced his leg up and down. He had a habit of pursing his upper lip between sentences to accentuate his point. When he spoke everyone listened with the respectful air of obedient children.

I was introduced to some of the other elder statesmen of ENT in the room. There was Abdullah Haroon, a pale thin man who was the chief at Mitford Hospital, part of Sir Salimullah Medical College in the old city. He was accompanied by a chubby, round faced man in glasses, named Narouz. There were two of Amin's associates at PG Hospital, Zaman and a dark skinned Hindu named Dowlut. Also seated was the chief resident, a small feisty individual named Mokhtar.

"I only hope that they will learn from you and become better than me," Amin said beaming at his two younger associates, "You see Moss, we are a very poor country with so much disease. The tumors grow so large and still the patients refuse to get treatment. It is inconceivable how they can wait so long."

"I have seen a lot of that in my travels," I said.

"Moss, I know you have seen many things in your journey. But whatever you have seen, as bad as it may have been, it will be worse in Bangladesh. This is not bragging, Moss. If anything, I wish it were not true. It will be ten times worse. It will astound you. I am not exaggerating."

"You have such a large population."

"Yes. And much neglect. The other day we had a little boy with a tumor of his jaw. We had to remove the entire bone. I could not believe such a case. And to repair it?" Amin again showed favor to his younger colleagues, nodding at them. "They bent some wire and twisted it to make a new jaw."

"Sounds like a good case."

"Yes, we have many good cases. But you see we cannot do that for everyone. In this country we must choose. We do not have the resources to help every patient. If I do a major operation for one person then I will not be able to do it for another. That is our reality. We must select carefully and pick the ones who have the best chance. In Bangladesh, we are often forced to play the role of God."

"It must be challenging."

"It is Moss, because everything costs money, and we have none. Sutures. Medicines. Intravenous fluid. Dressings. Who will pay for it? One hundred and twenty million people and only two or three hospitals in the entire country that can help them. Outside of Dhaka, in the smaller cities and towns, you are better off not going because the facilities are inadequate. Even here I am not so sure. How many times we must turn away patients. Or choose between sick patients. Or send patients home to die. We are so poor. Oooof. It is hot. Moss, please have some soda."

Two bottles of Coca Cola magically appeared. Amin continued without taking a breath.

"Have you ever worked in a country without nurses, Moss? This is the only country in the world without nurses. But we have alot of manpower." A smile and glance over at the residents standing in the back. "It is difficult to find nurses in a Muslim country."

Amin paused for an instant as if contemplating his thoughts. "You see Moss, we have one major problem in this country. The military. They are like a cancer in our system sucking up all our resources. Think of it Moss. One hundred thousand people - the soldiers and their families taking 90% of all the money spent on health in the country. While we are left to treat the rest, 120 million people, with nothing. It makes you sick just to think of it. Ah! Your food has arrived."

Two small paper boxes filled with white rice and chicken legs were opened and handed to Ying and me.

"Moss, please, you and your wife enjoy. You must be starved. Do not mind us. We all look forward to our meal after sunset." Amin watched carefully as the boxes were opened for us, making sure it was satisfactory. I felt self-conscious eating in front of them, but they didn't seem to mind. I liked Amin and the others. Without a clue as to who I was or what I could offer, they had received me as an honored son.

"It must be difficult to go the entire day without eating," I said as I devoured a chicken leg.

"We do not mind. It is our holy month so we must do it."

"The entire month without eating?"

"Yes, but it is not so bad now, Moss. You see the month of Ramadan follows the lunar calendar. When it falls in the summer months the days are especially long."

"And everyone must follow this?"

"Everyone should. But our prophet is merciful. If there are special circumstances then you may eat or drink - if you are sick or must travel."

"You cannot drink?"

"Nothing should touch your lips. Even your own saliva you should not swallow. There are some who spit our their saliva rather than swallow it."

"I shouldn't be eating in front of you."

"Never mind Moss. Have some soda. You must be thirsty."

"When do you eat?"

"From sunset to sunrise. We have a big breakfast at 3 AM."

"Is it difficult?"

"It is our duty."

"And what happens at the end of the month?"

"It is a celebration. We call it `Eid'. We have a feast. It is our Christmas."

I heard a knock. The door burst open and two soldiers walked in dressed in green army uniforms and boots. One of them advanced towards Amin and flashed a crisp salute. *"Suh,"* I heard him say, 'sir'. He then twisted and faced the other ENT power brokers of Bangladesh and offered them equally crisp salutes "Suh. Suh." They all nodded disinterestedly. Finally, the young soldier wheeled and saluted me. He then clapped his two hands to his sides and marched backward to stand against the wall. He stood apart from the residents who eyed him with smug curiosity. The second soldier then sort of glided in. He walked up first to pay homage to the great patriarch Amin who actually stood to shake his hand.

"Moss, please, this is Colonel Masadur Khan, the chief of ENT at CMH, the Combined Military Hospital," Amin said. The colonel turned and shook my hand. He wore thick black glasses. He was short, handsome, and in his mid forties.

"Dr. Moss, I am so happy to see you. You cannot imagine my delight when Professor Amin called me this morning to tell me you were here." Khan had a regal air about him. When he spoke there was total concentration. "I hope you will not mind if I tell you of one very troubling case," he said.

"Not at all," I responded.

"For three months I have suffered with one poor patient," he began, "a man I operated on with a large tongue cancer. After the surgery, everything fell apart. His neck. His tongue. Everything is open. He cannot eat. Everything runs out onto his skin. Even his saliva. And he has so much pain. I have caused this. I operated on him to help him, but how many times since the operation I have found myself wishing that I never touched him. I have tried to repair it but I cannot. I must bear the burden for having caused my patient so much suffering." Khan looked at me, a glimmer of despair surfacing on his smooth face. "I don't know what to do with him. I have prayed for some answer. Now you have appeared. God is great. He has heard my prayers." Khan smiled broadly at me. He seemed to glow. His nostrils dilated rhythmically in accordance with his breathing. His eyes remained steady. What wonderful presence! "Please tell me when you can come to my department. I will arrange for your transportation." Khan said.

"I will be happy to come anytime."

"Thank you." Khan was smiling easily now, relieved somehow of a great weight. He shook my hand warmly and sat down next to me.

All of us were now sitting around Amin. I had to admire the ability and swiftness of the great man. In a single day he had arranged for the chiefs of the major ENT departments in the capitol city of Bangladesh to appear at the same time in his office. No small accomplishment. It suggested a number of things. First, there was a need in this country for what I had to offer. Second, there was an unusual willingness to learn. A pleasing sort of humility. A far cry from my bitter memory of Goa. Third, there was a single individual who had the experience, respect, authority, and contacts to bring it all together. That man was Amin.

"Uuuhh Dr. Moss." It was Abdullah, the chief of Mitford, stirring slowly. "Uuuhh, I've got a couple of cases I'd like you to take a look at too." Colonel Khan had gotten things going. "The only problem is that my hospital is in the old city. I cannot drive you there. We have to take a rickshaw."

"I'm used to rickshaws. I've been in Asia almost three years."

"Wwweeelll." Abdullah was slow motion personified. Every gesture and word meandered leisurely. "Gooood." he gradually announced.

"Moss," Amin said, "We have plenty of things for you to look at here at PG also." Amin nodded at his two young associates, Zaman and Dowlut. These two were much closer to me in age and of course felt some threat. They looked up at me in a half interested way.

"You have some difficult cases here too?" I said.

"Yes, but we can do the big cases."

"You do the radical necks and larynxes?" I asked.

"Yes. We do them."

"And the flaps?"

"We do them."

"The pec majors?"

"No, we use the forehead flaps."

This was an old technique not used in the states for more than 10 years. Sensing their unease I did not probe further.

"Good," I responded.

"Moss," Amin interrupted, "we are very pleased that in your south Asia adventure you have decided to include our poor country. The only problem now is that I cannot let you stay at that hotel. You see you are my guest. If something were to happen to you it would be a great burden on me. I have spoken with another colleague who has arranged for you to stay in a better part of town. He will meet you at your hotel later today. His name is Allaudin."

Chapter 62

Dr. Mohammed Allaudin had a prosperous air about him. He was middle-aged, dressed casually, and had a boyish face. He met Ying and me at our hotel.

"Hello, Richard and Ying," he said, "welcome to Bangladesh."

He graciously paid our bill, and then escorted us to a waiting car where his driver was patiently waiting.

"Please," he said, opening the door for us. I was reminded that in every country, even one as poor as Bangladesh, there will always be a wealthy class. "Richard, I have arranged for you to stay temporarily at the Mennonite Christian Center near my home. It will serve for now until we can find more permanent accommodations."

"Thank you."

"In Bangladesh, we have thousands of non-government organizations, or NGO's. They are international relief aid organizations. Some are religious, some secular, but they are all drawn to our impoverished country."

"I have encountered some in my travels." I recalled 'Interplast' in Nepal.

"Yes, but there will be many more here. Our country is so poor and the government has no money."

I nodded.

Allaudin brought us to his home after we dropped off our luggage. We met his wife, a pretty dark-haired woman who was dressed in a colorful sari. She brought us tea and engaged us in lively conversation.

"What a journey you are on. How long has it been?" she asked.

"Nearly three years."

"What has brought you to our poor country?"

"A letter to Dr. Amin more than a year ago. It has taken us that long to get here."

"I am amazed at what you are doing. Traveling as you are with no assistance, no organization. It is so unusual. I know our doctors will be eager to learn from you. And our patients will benefit. There is great need here."

Allaudin soon joined us. What a curious sight Ying and I must have presented to our hosts. Two ragamuffins in the ultimate ragamuffin country. Still, appearances not withstanding, Allaudin seemed very keen on working with me.

"Richard, I run the ENT department at the main referral center for the entire country, Dhaka Medical College. I received my training in Great Britain years ago. We have many cases. I will be happy to take you there tomorrow."

"I am looking forward to it."

"I have also arranged for your Bangladeshi Medical license to be delivered tomorrow."

This was no small feat. Something like obtaining a license to practice medicine could take months, even years. "I am surprised that you can make that happen so quickly."

Allaudin winked. "I have some friends, Richard. But don't worry yourself about it. They wanted a 1000 taka, but I told them absolutely not. Under no circumstances. You came here to help us."

"I appreciate that very much."

"We see a fair amount of head and neck cancer," Allaudin continued. "I do what I can in my own small way," he added modestly.

I knew from experience that when someone understates himself in that way generally it means they are a big gun. Knowing that their work will speak volumes, they say little about themselves.

"Richard, you will see tomorrow how it is here in Bangladesh. I will pick you up in the morning. The Medical College is like a museum. A Museum of ENT pathology. You will be amazed."

The Dhaka Medical College was built almost a hundred years before during the British Raj. The hospital itself was a large grey building with turn of the century architecture surrounded by a tall black metal fence. We entered the building and took the elevator to the 13th floor, the ENT floor. The elevator was run by a small Bangladeshi and had no door inside the elevator itself. We watched the aging walls of the elevator shaft pass as we ascended. On the thirteenth floor we walked out and were led by Allaudin to the wards. When Allaudin passed I noticed everyone would stop in their tracks and stand at attention, raising their right hands to their hearts sharply as he passed them, a kind of Bangladeshi salute or gesture of respect reminiscent of the *wai* in Thailand only with martial crispness. Allaudin nodded almost imperceptibly or responded not at all. He walked briskly through several sets of double doors with Ying and I chasing after him, and the nurses, doctors and aids receiving him as a conquering lord.

We approached the wards themselves. Allaudin made a turn to the left towards his office. By this time there was a line-up of young doctors and residents trailing behind him with Ying and I taking up the rear. As we came to the door of his office, he turned suddenly and began shouting orders in Bengali. Allaudin's face had abruptly transformed to one of utter ferocity. His eyes narrowed to tiny slits while he pierced the air with his jabbing finger. The crowd instantly began scrambling, looks of terror writ over their faces.

The emperor had spoken. Just as suddenly his eyes softened and an angelic smile replaced the momentary hardness.

"Richard and Ying, let's go into my office. It is air conditioned there. They will bring us some coffee and donuts."

We sat in his office in front of his desk while he spoke to several of his lieutenants. I was astonished to see the abject fear Allaudin stirred in the young doctors. A far cry from the paternal albeit dominant manner of Amin. Allaudin controlled his army with steel and fire. I was equally mystified at his ability to transform himself into a pudgy teddy bear whenever he spoke with Ying and me.

"Richard, there are some interesting cases that have come in yesterday. I want to show them to you. We will make rounds after you are done with your breakfast."

We followed Allaudin out to the wards and were met with the entire team of residents and faculty. There were some brief nods of greeting but otherwise very little reaction to my presence. Under the watchful eyes of the emperor, the team of doctors silently entered the first communal patient ward.

The wards here were packed with patients and their families in austere, antiquated, poorly lit rooms. We moved quickly from bed to bed. The pure concentration of disfiguring disease was astounding. First, a young man, probably in his early 20's, with a tumor the size of a grapefruit bursting through the skin of his neck. How such a young man came down with this kind of disease at so early an age I did not know. I had seen this before, but the youth of the patients was different. So many, as I came to see, were in their twenties, decades younger than most head and neck cancer patients in other countries. And then there was the incredible profusion of such cases. Allaudin did not stop for questions. The march was on. The next patient was a man in his 30's with an equally large tumor, only actively bleeding. Huge swaths of gauze that hadn't been changed in days were wrapped tightly around the tumor. The dressing was removed for my benefit. When the final layer was pulled off, the blood poured.

"Hurry up," Allaudin shouted to the residents. "Get some gauze pads."

A new dressing was quickly pressed against the wound. The patient hardly seemed to care. He stared vacantly at the wall.

"Come see this, Richard," Allaudin said.

In the next bed, an older brother was caring for a little boy about five years old. At first, I didn't notice anything

"Turn the head," Allaudin said.

Growing out of his right cheek was a large tumor about the size of a melon, completely distorting his face and nose and pressing his right eye shut. It was so large that his head was permanently tilted to the right and his brother had to support it to keep the head upright.

"We will operate next week," Allaudin said, barely stopping as he moved to the next patient.

There was no discussion or questions. Allaudin had seen all this before. A mere sentence announcing his intentions was sufficient. He moved on.

A patient approached the advancing army of doctors. He wanted to show Allaudin something. I saw instantly what it was. A tumor had pushed his left eye almost completely out of the socket by a tumor. The eye was red, swollen and desiccated from exposure, green discharge streaming down from both corners. He was blind in that eye. "It is a lymphoma, difficult to treat as chemo is very expensive." We passed quickly.

I noticed that no questions were being asked. No attempt at teaching. It seemed a strange way to make teaching rounds. The residents were too terrified of Allaudin to even think of asking something. Still I wondered why there was no instruction. There was such an obvious need, an almost palpable hunger from the residents to be taught something. But maybe there was too much to overcome in Bangladesh to indulge such niceties as education and discourse? Too many patients with unspeakable pathology, too few doctors able to care for them, too few centers with adequate means? Was Allaudin correct in his approach as a matter of necessity? It may have been the only way to survive the deluge, the crush of the multitudes with late stage disease and insufficient resources to treat them.

"Come, Richard, I want to show you this."

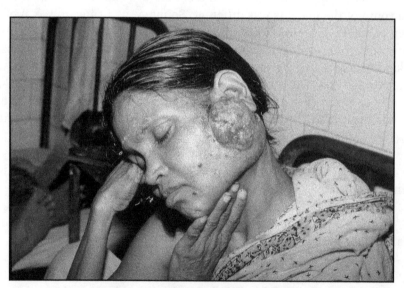

Large Cancer, Dhaka, Bangladesh

In another communal ward we came upon the bed of woman in her late 30's. She lied curled up like a fetus, barely stirring, oblivious to the clamor around her, consumed by her own private torment.

"Have her sit up," Allaudin said to the residents.

She grimaced, obviously in great discomfort and turned her head to the left allowing me to get a better look at her malady. It was grotesque. The entire left side of her face had been turned into ground beef by cancer. The tumor had digested all of the skin. She was unable to move her face or even close her eye as the tumor had already destroyed the facial nerve, the nerve responsible for facial movement. Allaudin glanced over at me, gave me a wink and smile as if to say, "I told you." I thought of his comment yesterday about the "Museum of ENT Pathology."

Almost all of the patients were severely malnourished. They were emaciated and sick in every sense of the word, quite apart from the specific problem of their cancer. The cancer seemed to be only one of many manifestations of their general debilitation, although certainly the most dramatic. But it was deeper than that. Every aspect of their physical system was diseased: their blood, viscera, muscle, and marrow. The basic fiber and sinew that bound them had been weakened, enfeebled by years of malnutrition and hunger. There was an illness here as well beyond the suffering of the patients, a disease of the culture or system or government that did not permit the nation to provide a better life for its citizens.

At one point, I found myself staring at a patient lying flat on his bed. His eyes were hollow and empty, his mouth open and dry, lips cracked. Almost, a corpse. He barely breathed. I also noticed that he seemed to be moving. I didn't quite get it. I took a closer look.

"Ying, take a look at this."

She glanced over.

"It seems like he's moving. Am I imagining this?"

I looked again. I realized that it was not the patient who was moving but something else.

"He's covered with lice," I said, shocked. "His face, neck, chest and body."

There were no nurses or family members present. He didn't care. He was going to die anyway. Underneath his bed were insects. On the walls were insects. Roaches, and ants. A couple of beds over, I noticed small bowls of rice and dhal. They too were infested with insects, maggots, and lice. I saw the patients picking up the bowls and eating the food. Insects, maggots, lice, and all. They were oblivious to the presence of the creatures in the food. There was no one around to clean. I noticed the residents and Allaudin were equally oblivious. It was life in the ENT museum. I looked at Ying. "It *is* worse here," I said, remembering Amin's words yesterday.

Finally, Allaudin arrived at the bedside of the patient he wanted me to see.

"Richard, what do you think?" he asked.

A man in his early 30's was sitting comfortably with his legs hanging over the side of his bed. Allaudin turned his head to the side exposing a large tumor of the jaw running right through from his mouth to the overlying skin. Solid, massive tumor. The man could barely open his mouth because of the bulk of the cancer and its invasion into the muscles of the jaw. Despite it all he seemed unperturbed, displaying Asian stoicism.

"I plan to operate tomorrow, Richard. It is an ameloblastoma of the mandible. We will have to take skin on this. I will need a flap."

I felt the man's face. The tumor was big. The whole jaw would have to go. And much of the skin. This was a big case. Allaudin seemed breezy about it.

"He'll definitely need a flap," I responded.

"You can show me the pec major?"

"Yes."

I would have preferred further evaluation of this patient. Maybe a CT scan. An angiogram. Check the carotids. Get an idea of what I was dealing with. No way. There was only one CT scan in the entire country and that was in the military hospital where Colonel Khan worked. This was Bangladesh.

"Don't worry Richard. You let me cut this little thing out and you can reconstruct it after. Okay?" Allaudin said with a twinkle in his eye.

"Sure," I responded hesitantly.

I was accustomed to doing big surgery with next to nothing. Still I had the distinct impression that I was going to receive a lesson from the emperor of Dhaka Medical College tomorrow.

"Come, Richard and Ying, it is late, and I am hot. You must be hungry."

Within minutes we were sitting in Allaudin's air-conditioned car being whisked along the crowded streets of Dhaka with his personal driver behind the wheel looking for a place to eat.

Chapter 63

Allaudin picked Ying and I up early next morning from the Mennonite Christian Center.

"Good morning," Allaudin said with a smile. He seemed very relaxed.

We drove down to the Medical College and parked. We took the old elevator up to the 13th floor, went straight to his office and changed into our scrubs. We walked to the operating room.

Inside the OR it was pandemonium. In addition to the routine madness before a major case, there was a large audience of onlookers, partly, I imagined, because I was operating.

"The word has spread, Richard," Allaudin said, confirming my suspicions. "They are here for you. We never have such a crowd." He poked me playfully in the ribs and winked. "You are already a star."

I was doing a procedure never done before in Bangladesh, the pectoralis major myocutaneous flap or, simply, the pec flap. This was a reconstructive technique that brought skin and muscle up from the chest to repair defects in the head and neck region after cancer surgery. In Bangladesh, they were still using an older technique, the forehead flap that had been long superseded, at least in the states, by the pec flap.

"You are making history today, Richard. We have never seen the pec flap. That is what they are here for. And me as well," Allaudin said.

It promised to be a good show. With the emperor performing the tumor resection, and me on the reconstruction, the place was jammed with a crowd of some 30 ENT physicians and professors from around Dhaka, including some I had met in Amin's office. This didn't make it easier for me. It was my first case in one of the poorest countries in the world, and I had no idea about the equipment or the skill level of my assistants. No matter how good a surgeon was, a weak or inexperienced operating team with inadequate equipment on a major case with a sick patient could be a challenge. Also I was with the emperor, and I didn't know what to expect. With a big throng on hand, you could be sure that news of any screw-ups by me would spread quickly and damage my reputation. This was the test run. If things went well, as in Nepal, patients and cases would quickly follow.

We accompanied Allaudin into the OR. Instantly, the large crowd stiffened and cleared a path. There was silence. Allaudin was angry. I didn't know if this was his typical OR personality, but he was in a rage. He shouted orders in Bengali, scattering the troops in every direction. The audience cowered against the wall, frightened and trembling, hoping to avoid the venom and fire pouring from Allaudin. In the center of the room lay the patient, blissfully sleeping with a tube coming out of his mouth. The anesthesiologist slowly pumped air in and out of his lungs.

"Hello, Dr. Moss, welcome," he said.

Two of Allaudin's assistants were painting the patient's face and chest with betadine and preparing the drapes.

As promised, there were no nurses. Residents were on hand to assist Allaudin and me with our sterile gowns. I noticed that almost all of the onlookers were in street clothes so sterility was not a high priority here. Probably there weren't enough sterile gowns to go around in this impoverished country.

Allaudin and I stood on either side of the patient's head. Altogether, we had looked at this patient for about 30 seconds before bringing him to the OR. There had been no CT scan or X-ray or any other type of study, no discussion with the patient or family. A quick look and feel and it was off to the OR. Yet this was the premier teaching institution in the country. Perhaps it was a question of numbers. There were too many patients with mind-numbing disease that had to be dealt with expeditiously. Even then it was not possible to keep pace with the waves of critically ill patients appearing daily.

"Knife," Allaudin said.

After this, everything was a blur. He sliced through the patient's lip and neck, raising the cheek up off the jaw, cutting around tumor, retracting the entire right side of the patient's face up towards the top of the head.

"Saw," Allaudin said.

He grabbed the instrument and split the patient's jaw in half using broad, savage strokes. He grunted and pulled and yanked on the tumor. Blood poured and spurted in every direction, but nothing fazed the great warrior. The rest of us scrambled to control the hemorrhaging, shouting for clamps and hemostats, throwing them into the wound, packing and mopping up the blood with suction and sponges. Allaudin was after bigger game. He was in the midst of the hunt. Stalking his prey, the malignant tumor ravaging the man's jaw and neck. He continued the horrific onslaught, never hesitating.

At one point, after a deep cut, a powerful scarlet plume of blood came spilling out of the corner of the man's neck. For one instant everyone froze thinking Allaudin had cut the carotid artery, the dominant vessel of the neck that carries blood to the brain.

"Suction! Clamp! Sponge!" I said as we desperately tried to stem the crimson tide. Still the blood poured. Allaudin then let out a mighty roar.

"HOLD IT. HOLD IT! I WILL GET IT! GET OUT OF THE WAY. I WILL

GET IT," he screamed at the top of his lungs. He grasped a long clamp with his right hand and plunged it into the center of this spurting geyser. "CLAMP. HURRY. GET ME ANOTHER CLAMP!"

He thrust the second clamp into the patient's neck like a spear. The bleeding stopped.

With even greater savagery he now cut and hacked and yanked at the tumor, flailing at it, fuming and snarling, furious that he should be challenged, even interrupted, in the midst of battle by something so trivial as bleeding. With one last great heave and cut, he yanked the massive tumor out of the patient's face like a giant turkey leg and tossed it into a metal bowl.

It was inelegant, bloody and could not be duplicated. He came close to transecting tumor, and we did we not check margins with frozen section. But when he was done a mere 25 minutes had elapsed. In almost anyone else's hands, including my own, it would have taken hours. I looked over at Ying. This was jungle surgery at its best.

"It is all yours now, Richard," Allaudin said to me.

I began the reconstruction of the face and jaw using the pec flap. It was routine, even anti-climactic. I had done it many times. Of course, this was the first of its kind in Bangladesh, a fact not lost on my audience or me. I felt dozens of pairs of eyes boring into me, watching every detail and technical nuance. I raised the flap from the chest, preserved its blood supply, tunneled the flap under the neck skin and into the defect and reconstructed the oral cavity and face. When the case was over, everyone in the room including Allaudin congratulated me.

"Richard, it was excellent. We have a technique now that we can use to reconstruct our patients. You have made history here, and I mean that," Allaudin said.

"Thank you, Professor."

"The news will spread. The whole ENT universe in Bangladesh was here today watching you."

The first case had been done before a large crowd and the word would go out. In this tormented nation, with unthinkably advanced disease and appalling human suffering, I knew I would be busy soon.

Chapter 64

Through his many connections, Amin had arranged for Ying and me to stay at a fancy hostel, known as the Highspeed guesthouse, the official inn for visitors of a major shipping firm in Bangladesh by the same name. Amin was a friend of the owner who agreed to let me stay because, as he said, I was "helping the poor people of Bangladesh."

The guesthouse was located in a district of Dhaka known as Banani. This was to the north of town and was located right next to another district known as Gulshan. These two quiet residential neighborhoods were the fancy parts of town, far from the noise, traffic, and beggars. They were also the unofficial diplomatic and expatriate zones. Almost every nation that maintained diplomatic relations with Bangladesh had their embassy in one of these two districts. Also, major firms, NGOs and wealthy Bangladeshi were based here. The homes were plush, the streets tree-lined and immaculate, and signs of the overwhelming poverty found everywhere else, blissfully absent. It could have been a wealthy suburb in southern California. There was a heavy security presence too. The main military base for the country was not far away. The only reminder that we were in Bangladesh was the occasional rickshaw driver, barefoot and in rags, sweating and struggling, while pedaling an overweight sahib down a quiet, manicured avenue. The airport was just to the north of Gulshan. I wondered what a skewed but agreeable view of Bangladesh a visitor would have if upon landing at the airport he was whisked off to Gulshan in an air-conditioned car only 15 minutes away to stay in a lovely home, complete business matters, and leave the same way, a couple of days later. It could go on forever that way and the visitor would never get an inkling of what was really going on here.

My new home was spacious with a large bathroom and bedroom and an elegant living room. I had a screened-in patio adjacent to my bedroom and a backyard. There was an official dining area with a long table and candles in the center and three houseboys who cooked, cleaned, and gardened. It was luxury. In just a few days - and one major operation - I had made it to the diplomat zone. I had arrived.

Dr. Abdullah Haroon lived close by. The next day the phone rang and I heard an already familiar voice.

"Uuhhrr, Rriichard," I heard him say in that leisurely drawl of his. "It's Abdullah. I was wondering if I could show you some patients tomorrow."

"Sure, Abdullah, what time?"

"Wwweell, about, uuhhrr ... let's try for niiine ... or so." The `nine' poured out of Abdullah's mouth like molasses.

"Sounds good, Abdullah, I'll be waiting."

The next morning, Abdullah rolled in at about ten. He lived about five minutes from my house, so Ying and I had been waiting outside figuring he would be pulling up any minute. He got out of his car and casually walked over to us. He had that same tired look on his face. He didn't say a word about keeping us waiting an hour, so I figured this was the norm for Abdullah. Everything slow and easy. That was okay with me.

We drove down to the center of town and parked. From here, Abdullah commissioned two rickshaws to take us the rest of the way. We were entering the old city now where the streets were narrow and travel by car difficult.

The old city was archetypal third world chaos. Crowded, narrow, lab-yrinthine streets, beggars in rags, people lying half dead on the pavement, hawkers, small storefronts, street vendors, animals of all sorts, fumes, dirt, smoke, noise, carts, oxen, pedestrians, bicycles, scooters, rickshaws, trucks, cars, coolies, and utter traffic paralysis. People screamed at each other, horns blared, human and animal excrement were everywhere. Police and soldiers armed with billy clubs and whistles smacked little dark skinned beggars or rickshaw wallahs who got in their way or slowed traffic. The roads were cluttered with potholes, litter, and pools of oil. Ying and I bounced around in the back of the rickshaw like two sacks of potatoes. It was hot and humid. Abdullah took this ride everyday, back and forth. No wonder he moved slowly in the morning.

I watched the back of my rickshaw driver as he strained every muscle pedaling through old Dhaka. His skin was black as night. He was small and rail thin. His clothing consisted of a dirty piece of cloth wrapped around his waist. He was barefoot and had no shirt. He sweated and struggled against the weight of the rickshaw and the blazing Bangladeshi sun. Other rickshaw drivers yelled at him, cut him off, bumped him for moving in front of them and he did the same thing back. Police beat him with their clubs and berated him or blew their whistles in his face. He sat waiting in the traffic, breathing in the fumes, listening to the Bengali curse words, the horns, the clamor all about him. The press of humanity, concentrated into an impoverished critical mass, fell upon him and everyone else who fought to survive in the old city.

We arrived at the hospital in our separate rickshaws at the same time. The ride lasted about 40 minutes. Abdullah peeled off 20 taka, less then a buck, and told them to split it. They both seemed happy to get it.

Mitford Hospital was part of the Sir Salimullah Medical College. It was a large yellow building surrounded by an imposing iron fence, built like Dhaka Medical College at the turn of the century. It rested on the north bank of the Buriganga River in the old city. We entered the hospital and walked up a ramp five flights to the ENT floor. There were no elevators. A number of young doctors and students were waiting for Abdullah when we arrived and greeted him respectfully. He looked over at Ying and me and said, "Richard and Ying, come here, I want to show you something."

We walked over to a large patio just beyond his office. I immediately felt a refreshing breeze. The hospital overlooked the Buriganga River, a long, serpentine river, filled with sea crafts of all sizes that emptied into the Bay of Bengal. You could smell the ocean in the air. For a moment, you forgot where you were. Abdullah pointed out some of the sights, including some famous mosques on the river's edge.

"Richard, this view makes that long, terrible trip worth it. If it wasn't for this, I would never do it." We walked back inside to Abdullah's office and met with the other doctors and residents. There were many faces, some quite young, waiting excitedly for the visit with the American doctor.

I sat down in front of Abdullah's desk and within seconds two cups of tea appeared for Ying and I. Some of the more senior doctors introduced themselves to me. Jaket was an unusually burly Bangladeshi with a big smile who welcomed me warmly. Narouz, the older doc whom I met the first day at Amin's office, was also on hand to greet me. He was second in command here under Abdullah and always seemed to have a sly sort of grin on his face. I wondered why. There were many others whom I did not formally meet, most of them students or residents. They all were remarkably shy and self-effacing in a way that reminded me of Thailand. Asians in general, with the possible exceptions of the Indians and Chinese, were far more humble and ingratiating then their western counterparts. Even the Japanese, who have no reason to take a second seat to anyone, were remarkably modest. Thus far, the Bangladeshi I had met had shown themselves to be a receptive open-minded people, unencumbered by false pride or ego. It made it easier and more pleasant for me.

Abdullah leaned back in his chair and relaxed. He sipped his tea and waited. With Abdullah, it seemed like there was all the time in the world. His manner was different too. He dealt with his subordinates in a more gentle, fatherly way then the other big chiefs I had met. Amin, too, had a paternal quality, but underneath that veneer was a determined fighter. He had struggled to earn his place at the top of the heap. Allaudin was in another league altogether. There was not the slightest pretense at civility with his lessers. It was war at the Medical College where the emperor reigned and took no prisoners. Abdullah, on the other hand, was benign and the atmosphere at

Mitford much more relaxed. I also learned that Abdullah was a diabetic. Perhaps that slowed him down as well.

Narouz was winking at me. I looked over at him. "You know Dr. Moss, I have spent time in Thailand myself. In the south. In Hat-Yai," he said. Again I noticed the sly grin. Of course. The old codger had made the rounds with the heathen bombshells in the clubs and brothels of Hat-Yai. No wonder he was always smiling.

"I worked in Malaysia. In Penang. Do you know Penang?" he asked.

"Yeah. I've been there twice." I said. Once was to get my Thai visa and the other to catch a boat to the island of Sumatra.

"We used to go to Hat-Yai on the weekends. It was so much fun." he smiled again at the memory. "And you know the Thai women. They are really quite lovely." I was surprised to hear him go on like this. This was, after all, Bangladesh, a Muslim country. But then some of the biggest playboys in the world were Muslims. I also didn't like it because my wife was, of course, Thai. Unfortunately, many around the world had the impression that all women in Thailand were prostitutes and that was not true. Roughly 1-2% of the female population of Thailand was engaged in some form of prostitution, which left you with 98-99% of the women who were not. Still, there was this perception, which often prompted me to emphasize that my wife was a nurse whom I met while working at one of the hospitals.

"They certainly are lovely, and they make wonderful wives." I responded.

"They say the Japanese make the best wives in the world. Maybe now we will change that to Japanese and Thai," Narouz said, smiling. Everyone, including Ying and Abdullah, laughed. The awkward moment passed.

"Richard," Abdullah interjected, "I have a patient I would like you to examine. He is a young man with a big family. A farmer with four children, a wife, and parents."

"Sure."

"He has a big throat cancer. His larynx is involved, and it has spread to both sides of his neck. He is only 28."

"Twenty-eight! Amazing. It usually afflicts patients in their fifties and sixties."

"It is routine here. Many of our patients are young. Perhaps it is the malnutrition. And they all wait so long. Anyway, Richard, this is Bangladesh. We will bring him in for you to examine."

The crowd of residents and doctors opened to allow a handsome, muscular man walk in and sit in front of me. I never would have guessed that he had cancer. On closer exam though I could make out a large tumor on the left side of his neck that had already grown into the skin. I felt it. It was hard. I looked down his throat with a light. Bad smell. There was a foul broth of saliva and exudate covering a large cancer invading his throat. I could barely make anything out because the normal structures had been so badly chewed up. There wasn't much guesswork here. Everything had to go.

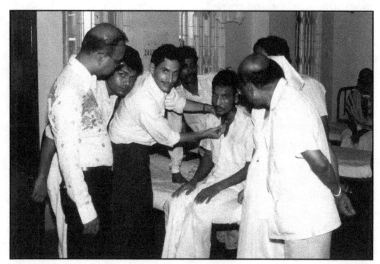

With Dr. Haroon and staff, Mitford Hospital, Bangladesh

"He'll need the entire throat and voice box removed, also bilateral necks. We'll have to reconstruct the throat and the skin of the neck. Is anyone doing gastric pull-ups here?" I asked.

"I believe they tried at the Medical College," Abdullah said, "but five out of seven died on the operating table."

"Well, we won't try the eighth. We'll use the pec flap again. I can use it for both the pharynx and the skin of the neck. When can we do it?"

"Tomorrow."

Chapter 65

The scene in the OR at Mitford was even crazier than at the Dhaka Medical College the other day. It was a smaller room and there were more people. The word had gotten out that I was doing another pec flap and everyone wanted to watch. There was also a television crew from the Ministry of Education to tape the event. Abdullah had arranged this to record the second pec major flap ever performed in the country for posterity and, I imagined, for educational purposes.

Before the case, I consulted with the anesthesiologists who seemed worried. They were not used to doing such major cases. They were also concerned about the general condition of the patient. They told me that my 28 year old, healthy-looking, muscular patient had a hemoglobin of eight.

"Eight!" I exclaimed.

"Yes."

"Why so anemic?"

"Everyone in Bangladesh is like this. It is from malnutrition. Iron deficiency anemia, or possibly worms."

"Everyone?"

"Just about. It is quite common."

A hemoglobin of eight was about half of the normal level. It was less than optimal to perform major surgery on someone with a blood count that low.

"What about blood replacement? Do we have anything to transfuse him?"

"We have four units. Usually we cannot get that much. Several of the residents had to donate their own blood to replace what was taken from the bank. Also, his brother and wife."

Four units of blood with major surgery and a hemoglobin of eight. It would have to do. I was glad to see that unlike Goa, family members and even the doctors in Bangladesh were willing to help by donating their own blood.

"What else?" I asked.

"You understand, Dr. Moss, that our equipment for such major surgery is very primitive. We do not have all the sophisticated monitoring devices you are used to."

"What do you have?"

"Well, I mean, we have basically nothing."

"Nothing?"

"I'm afraid so."

"What do you mean?"

"I mean, Dr. Moss, we have nothing."

"You've got to have something. You can't give anesthesia with nothing."

"Very primitive, I'm afraid, sir."

"Well, what do you have?"

"Two things," he said hesitantly.

"Well?"

"A stethoscope and a blood pressure cuff."

"That's it?"

"Yes."

"No EKG or anything?" I asked.

"No."

"How are you going to ventilate him?"

"By hand, sir."

"You're kidding me."

He wasn't. A nine or ten hour case, bagging the patient by hand. This meant ventilating or "breathing" for the patient with an air bag, pressing the bag by hand, delivering oxygen through the intubation tube to the lungs for each and every breath for some nine or ten hours. It would be a challenge. Usually, in the States and elsewhere including all of the Asian countries I had worked in, this was done by machine, something known as a ventilator.

We were about to embark on a major cancer operation on a very sick patient with hardly any blood and virtually no equipment. A similar case in the US would be bristling with expensive, state of the art, high tech equipment, armed to the hilt in preoperative preparation and intraoperative monitoring. The room would be alive with gadgets and devices, buzzers, alarms, printouts, digital screens, sounds, and warning lights. There would be gas analyzers, *Swan Ganz* catheters, central and arterial lines, pulse oxymetry, temperature probes, peripheral nerve stimulators, heating or cooling blankets, ventilators, and heart monitors. Every conceivable physiologic parameter would be continuously gauged throughout the procedure. There would be as much blood as needed for any contingency, and the patient would have been transfused and medically stabilized prior to the operation. The same case in Bangladesh? A stethoscope and a blood pressure cuff. Not even an EKG monitor! And the anesthesiologists would have to ventilate the patient by hand. Ten hours of non-stop bagging. I figured they would tire of me quickly.

"And we must use re-sterilized endotracheal tubes. They are old already. We are not allowed to discard anything. Maybe, you can help us, Dr. Moss. We have nothing. If you could speak to someone about our conditions." He seemed to be in a daze.

"I'll do what I can," I said.

Which, as far as I knew, was next to nothing. But then the royal Saudi family would have trouble making a dent in this place.

We walked back to the OR. There were so many people it seemed more like a convention than an operating room. Before entering the OR, Abdullah handed me a pair of white scrubs and a used bar of soap. I looked at the soap. "That's for washing your hands," he mentioned. "Thanks." We changed into our scrub suits in an abandoned room filled with junk next to the OR. I noticed Abdullah wore long underwear. The weather in Bangladesh was tropical. What was this about?

"We do not like to show our naked flesh to God," Abdullah said. "He is everywhere, you see. There are some of us who even bathe in our clothing for shame of appearing naked before him."

We walked over to the sink room just outside the OR. There was a rack with old blood stained sneakers. I tried to find a matching pair. Abdullah and I then washed our hands by two old kitchen sinks with the used bars of soap he had found. We entered the OR.

Inside, it was tumult once again, coupled with, I thought, gut burning nervous anxiety on the part of the young doctors. I realized that Abdullah and his fledgling crew were not old hands in the area of major head and neck surgery like Allaudin. We were about to start a long case on a sick patient with a big tumor, precious little equipment, and very green assistants. Abdullah, more from general temperament and, perhaps, his medical condition, did not seem like someone who could go the full 15 rounds.

There were more doctors here then for the first case with Allaudin. But, in addition, we had a TV crew to tape the second pec flap in the history of Bangladesh. There were technicians holding floodlights and cameras, testing the equipment and lighting. Instrument trays were opened. The assistants prepped the patient. As at the Medical College, almost everyone was dressed in street clothes.

The young residents preparing the instruments were in a panic. In Bangladesh, as Amin warned, there were no nurses, so the residents had to arrange everything. And these poor fellows had never seen this kind of surgery before. What they did have were women in traditional Muslim dress that served as "aids." They wore saris, covering their heads and bodies in beautiful colored fabrics. They were friendly but limited. There was no air conditioning in the room, so the residents carried in two big fans from Abdullah's office. I watched the anesthesiologist sitting peacefully amidst the confusion, gently ventilating the patient and checking the heart rate and blood pressure with his stethoscope and blood pressure cuff. It would be a long day for him.

It wasn't 10 minutes into the case before I realized it was going to be a long day for me also. Without a scrub nurse to organize the instruments, the lower part of the patient's abdomen, where I tended to place the instruments,

had quickly become a disorganized heap. The simplest of requests degener-
ated into major expeditions requiring seconds of valuable time just to find a
simple clamp. In addition, the bovie, the cauterizing instrument that controls
bleeding, as well as the suction, stopped working. I also noticed that two of
the young doctors assisting me in this major case seemed to hate the sight
of blood. One of them, a short, pudgy fellow with a pencil mustache was so
nervous he was sweating into the wound. He also shook with fear every time
I asked him to do something, especially, if it meant cutting human flesh.

"Cut," I said, while spreading my clamp underneath some tissue.

No discernible movement.

"Cut, please." I requested again.

I noticed a visible tremor in the young doctor's hand.

"Uhh, do you mind cutting, please?" I asked again.

By now the hand holding the knife was shaking. I noticed the sound of
rapid, shallow breathing. The pudgy doctor was hyperventilating. I studied
his face. His pupils were dilated. Beads of sweat had formed over his brow.
He was pale.

"Cut please."

He didn't look at me, nor did he make any meaningful gesture with the
knife. He reminded me of Jaruan in Thailand, only much worse.

I noticed a high-pitched humming sound.

"nnnnnnnnnnnnnnnn."

What was that strange sound?

"nnnnnnnnnnnnnnnn."

I couldn't tell if it was human or machine. I looked at the patient. No
leaks around the trache. I looked over at the anesthesiologist. Nothing there.

"nnnnnnnnnnnnnnnn."

Who was making that noise? I looked at the pudgy doctor. "nnnnnnnnn-
nnnnn." It was coming from him. I looked into his eyes. He didn't recognize
me. He was not aware of the sound he was making.

"Are you okay?" I asked.

No response. No recognition of the question either. His hand was now
jerking back and forth. Ten minutes into the case and my first assistant
was decompensating. I suggested that he step away from the table, leave
the room, and sit down somewhere. He handed the knife to his nervous
co-resident and left the OR, bloodstained gown and all.

The case progressed. The floodlights were on, the TV cameras were
taping the event, and the large audience seemed to be enjoying the show.
Abdullah, bless his diabetic soul, was having trouble keeping up. At one
point, in the middle of a crucial juncture he informed me that it was time for
his afternoon prayer. The Muslims prayed five times a day but in the middle
of surgery?

"Of course, Abdullah."

Later in the case the room blacked out. Utter darkness. The fans stopped, the floodlights went out, and everything was silent. It was steaming hot in the room.

"Uhh, what's going on?"

"Oh, it is nothing, Dr. Moss, only the generator. It happens all the time," said an unknown but comforting voice. "Especially during the monsoons."

"What happens now?"

"Oh, it will be all right. It's from all the rain, you see."

"Uh huh."

"Don't worry, they'll be working on it."

"How long does it usually take?"

"Oh, not too long."

"How long?"

"Possibly an hour. Sometimes as little as a half hour."

With a patient on the table?

At that moment, in a small hot dark crowded room in Bangladesh filled with sweating bodies in the middle of surgery, I heard a sound I had never heard before or since inside an operating room.

"Tssszzzz." The unmistakable sound of someone lighting a match. The entire room suddenly lit up by this single match in the hand of a young doctor.

"You see, Dr. Moss, we are prepared for every contingency." That same comforting voice.

I noticed some ruffling of bodies in the darkness. Voices. The sound of equipment being moved. Suddenly, there was a very dim yellow light focused on the open neck of the patient. Flashlights. Then, an even more bizarre sight. The individual holding the lit match was now lighting several candles. How romantic.

"You see, Dr. Moss, nothing to worry about."

I heard more sounds.

"Where are the batteries?" someone asked.

"Here they are," another voice said.

A bright white light illuminated the patient. It is a battery-operated hand held fluorescent light carried by one of the doctors. This apparently happened all the time!

"Will that do, Dr. Moss," the same voice inquired.

"It's fine. Don't you have back up generators here?"

"This is Bangladesh, sir."

"Right."

The residents held flashlights, candles, and a fluorescent light for 45 minutes before the regular lights returned.

Towards the end of the case my assistants were fading. It was probably over 100 degrees. One of my assistants asked if he could rest while another resident took his place. I said sure. As he backed away from the table his replacement stepped in. This individual was someone I had just seen remove his t-shirt, wring it out in the operating room, forming a small puddle of sweat on the floor, only to step up to the OR table unscrubbed, sweating, bare-chested, and barehanded to assist me in surgery. Sterile conditions took on a whole new meaning here.

The only other event of the day worthy of note was that at one point in the operation, probably from all the sweat, blood, and time, my pants fell down, only I didn't realize it. I stood at the side of the table surrounded by doctors from all over Dhaka as well as the lovely nursing aids waltzing around the room in their saris, operating for more then 45 minutes in my underwear. Everyone felt too shy to point out to the visiting American surgeon that his pants had fallen down. Finally, one courageous soul, informed me. I didn't know if the cameras caught it.

Ten hours after starting this adventure, we finished. It was grueling. I had never before felt my heart get pinched quite as it did for that first case at Mitford. Fortunately, my wife Ying, a fully trained nurse, stepped in at one point to assist, which helped a great deal. She also, by the way, had a good laugh when it was discovered that my pants had fallen down. The patient was taken off the table. Ten days later he had healed up, was eating, and ready to leave the hospital.

Chapter 66

Allaudin stopped by our house to visit. "Richard, I want to take you and Ying to see our National Museum. It is one of the largest in South Asia."

"Wonderful," I said, impressed at how generous he was given his hectic schedule.

We entered the museum and leisurely strolled through the many halls and chambers with elaborate collections of sculpture, terracottas, wood and metalwork, artifacts of natural history, and much else. There were stone sculptures of various Buddhist subjects including the Buddha himself in classical postures, and statues of "Tara," a much beloved Buddhist image, and other Mahayana deities. There were also Hindu artifacts.

"I am amazed by the Buddhist art," I said.

"It is part of our history," Allaudin said. "Bangladesh was a part of India before the partition in 1947."

The acceptance of that part of their history intrigued me. I also wasn't expecting displays of statues portraying individual subjects, whether it be of the Buddha or others. I assumed that in a Muslim country such images would be forbidden.

We passed through a section of the museum dedicated to contemporary art in particular the work of Zainul Abedin. "He is one of our own," Allaudin said with pride. "A Bengali. He died in 1976. He is considered the father of modern art in Bangladesh."

The pieces were stunning. Some of the paintings could have come from the Museum of Modern Art in New York. There was a fair amount of "Impressionist" art by Abedin and others, with indistinct figures, the purposeful imprecision, the play of light, all exquisitely rendered, yet by local Bangladeshi artists. The influence of Van Gogh, Gauguin, Monet, Renoir, and others was manifest.

"I could not be more impressed with a museum," I said. I did not mention that part of the reason was that it was in Bangladesh, a Muslim country. In truth, it was a great museum apart from that. But that it was in a Muslim country, to me, made it even more valuable and unexpected. Knowing the prohibition against "graven images" or "idols" in Islam, I did not anticipate a museum stocked with thousands of just such images. I was gratified that there seemed to be room in at least this Muslim country for the sharing of

317

artistic traditions from around the world even if ostensibly it may have con-
flicted with strict Islamic belief and practice.

"I thought you would like it. It is also a small token of my thanks for your
coming here and helping us."

We continued. Along the way we came upon a painting of the iconic
Biblical scene of Abraham about to sacrifice his son Isaac with knife raised
as the angel intervened. I was surprised to see this, coming straight out of
the Judeo-Christian fold as it did.

"It is of Ibrahim," Allaudin said, using the Islamic pronunciation of
Abraham.

"Yes, I know."

"This event is important in Islam. We have a holiday to celebrate it."

"Really?"

"Yes. Eid al-Adha. The Feast of the Sacrifice. It is one of our two holiest
days. The other is Eid al-Fitr, which is coming soon right after Ramadan,
our month of fasting."

"I knew about Eid al-Fitr. I did not know of Eid al-Adha."

"It is the more important. On this day, Muslims throughout the world
sacrifice animals to God."

I recalled Ying's reaction to animal sacrifices in Nepal. "It is the more
holy of the two?" I asked.

"Yes, because it honors Ibrahim's submission to God."

I nodded.

"That Ibrahim was willing to listen to God and sacrifice his son Ishmael."

What! I looked at him. *Was he kidding?* I held my tongue. I glanced at
Ying who did not appreciate the historical switch that had just occurred. *Was
that what Islam taught?*

Did Muslims not realize that there was an obscure, little book known as
the Bible written 1600 years before the birth of Mohammed that had already
told that story? That it was Isaac not Ishmael that had been bound and nearly
sacrificed by Abraham. That every Christian and Jew knew this story and
that you could not, 1600 years after the fact, change protagonists to suit the
preferences of your faith.

While I recognized that Islam believed that it had "superseded" the two
previous "Abrahamic" faiths, Judaism and Christianity, that out of respect
and general knowledge, one should accord those faiths deference for their
contribution to the religious narrative, especially in that it had been become
part of the Muslim heritage. Even Christianity, as anti-Semitic as it had been
throughout much of its history, preserved the Jewish Bible, albeit under
the rubric of the "Old Testament." It at least gave Judaism its due, however
begrudgingly.

By co-opting this 3000-year-old story, known by virtually every

Christian and Jew, and altering it in so transparent a way, Islam displayed an extraordinary arrogance. It was an obvious error that anyone familiar with the narrative would instantly recognize, yet Islam and its adherents did not seem to care. To conveniently insert one's champion over another to serve a narrow self-interest made me question if Islam could be taken seriously. I also wondered, based on this not insignificant anecdote, whether Islam could conduct itself civilly amongst the family of nations, religions, and cultures of the world. As I knew Muslims held that the Koran was the direct word of God, I questioned whether Islam *could* reform itself. It didn't seem that there was room in such a faith and belief system to modify itself. I saw it as a harbinger of ongoing strife between Islam and the rest of the world - and itself.

Allaudin had already continued through the halls of the great National Museum, oblivious to my thoughts, which was good. I did not, of course, bring any of this up to him. I understood that one could not judge Muslims by Islam, one had to look at individuals. My Muslim friends here in Bangladesh had treated me with the utmost respect. They were as gracious as could be. They opened doors that allowed me to continue my work. This was the most important thing and more than enough to satisfy me. Still, I thought it was the strangest thing. I also recognized that I was giving a very polite interpretation of the matter. There was reason for pessimism.

"It has been a wonderful visit," I said to Allaudin. "It is truly an amazing museum. Thank you for taking time out of your busy schedule to show it to us."

"I am so happy you liked it."

Chapter 67

I heard the sound of a car rolling into the carport at our guesthouse where Ying and I were finishing our breakfast. The door opened and two soldiers in full uniformed regalia entered. They wheeled, spun, snapped their boots together and belted out crisp salutes while I sat there with my mouth half open with toast and eggs.

"Suh, Major Akel reporting, suh."

It was the same young man I had seen at Amin's office a couple of weeks ago with Colonel Khan.

"Suh, very sorry suh to bother you at meal time suh." Akel said. I loved the way he said `sir'. "No problem, Akel, we're just finishing."

"Shall we wait outside, suh?"

"No, don't worry, just relax. Have a seat."

"Are you sure, suh?"

"Yeah. Don't worry. Take it easy. Sit down."

"Very kind of you, suh."

After finishing breakfast I noticed Akel giving some money to the houseboy.

I looked at him. "Don't worry, suh, I will be taking good care of you. The military does a fine job of it, suh. I will make sure everything is just right for you and your lady suh."

He was very British in manner a throwback, I imagined, to the former colonial era.

"I watched you at surgery, suh, at the Medical College, suh. A fine job, suh, very impressive, really. Everyone has heard, suh. Colonel Khan is really looking forward to your visit today, suh."

"I don't remember seeing you there, Akel."

"Oh, I was there, suh," he laughed lightly. " You didn't recognize me, suh, because I was in my civvies, suh."

"Oh."

"Suh."

"Akel?"

"Suh?"

"You don't have to call me, `sir', all the time."

"Suh?"

"You don't have to call me `sir' all the time. `Rick' is okay, or Doctor Moss." Still American, after all this time, I maintained an American discomfort with formality.

"Suh, excuse me, suh, I don't read you."

"I mean it's not necessary to call me `sir'."

"Oh, I see, suh. Oh, no bother, suh, really, suh, I prefer it. It is the military way, suh."

In every country I worked in there was always one individual who got the job of baby-sitting me. I remembered Rak and Kowit in Thailand, Dharma in Nepal, Naveen in Goa, and now Akel appeared poised to assume that role here in Bangladesh. These individuals were indispensible to me, running errands, translating, cutting through red tape, assisting with the hassles and inconveniences of life in a developing country. They invariably became my closest friends.

We got into the army jeep waiting outside in the carport. Ying and I sat in the back.

"We are really looking forward to your visit, suh. Colonel Khan is very excited. You see, suh, we have a very bad case, suh. Colonel Khan has suffered so much with this poor chap, suh, really, he has."

"I remember Colonel Khan telling me something about that in Dr. Amin's office."

"Right, suh, you have a very good memory, suh."

We were going to the Combined Military Hospital, or CMH, the main military hospital for the entire country. I remembered Amin's description of the military as a cancer consuming the resources of the country. I figured the facilities would be better than elsewhere since they received the lion's share of government expenditure for health care with relatively few patients (compared with the 120 million non-military population the rest of the health care system was obliged to treat). They were also likely to be healthier. This was not unusual. In most third world countries the military had most if not all of the power notwithstanding the occasional half-hearted attempts at democratic reform, a small bone thrown out for the benefit of western donor nations who needed this sort of window dressing to justify the billions of dollars spent in foreign aid.

We passed through a series of gates prior to actually entering the compound, each with a sentry carrying a machine gun who checked Akel's papers, stepped back, saluted, and allowed us to continue. We passed the main hospital at CMH, which Akel pointed out to me and parked just outside a long barrack. We walked inside, passing a small ENT clinic with several young doctors examining patients who all stood to salute me. We came to a door, which Akel opened slowly after knocking.

"Hello, Richard and Ying, good, good, so good to see you, please come in.

Sit down," Colonel Khan said exuberantly, getting up from his chair to greet us. He shook my hand warmly. He had that same glowing face I remembered when I first met him at Amin's office. "Richard, Ying, please, would you like to have some tea and cookies? Akel, please get our guests some tea."

"Suh, right away, suh." Akel hurried off.

"Richard, how are you and Ying enjoying our poor country?" Khan asked.

"Very much, Colonel. We have been very busy."

"Yes, I have heard. Akel has told me of your work. We are very pleased you have come to our country. How are your accommodations?"

"Very pleasant. The best I've had in three years."

"Good, good. You are comfortable, then?"

"Yes."

"Banani is a nice district. How do you like the food? Are you getting used to our diet. A lot of lentils, you know. It is the poor man's meat. In this country, for most people, that is the only protein they have. But they are preparing some chicken and meat dishes for you, also, right Richard?"

"Yes, we are very comfortable, Colonel."

Akel entered with a tray carrying four cups of tea and some cookies.

"Ah, good, the tea has arrived. Richard and Ying, please." Akel placed the tray on the table. Khan continued. "Richard, I want to tell you about that very terrible case of mine - the one I mentioned to you the first day - if you would mind to see him after your tea."

"Of course."

"He is a former soldier, a young man really, with a large cancer of the tongue. We operated six months ago and it has been a terrible agony for everyone, especially the patient, ever since. Everything has fallen apart. I have tried to reconstruct him many times but nothing works. We have been treating his wound, but he is miserable. My only consolation for all his suffering is that, at least, I have cured him of his cancer." Khan sighed. "Richard, if you will be so kind, please have a look at him on the wards. Akel will bring you to him."

Afterwards Ying and I joined Akel to look at Khan's patient. The wards consisted of large communal rooms, set up army style, that were clean and tidy. On first impression conditions here at CMH seemed a good deal better then the other hospitals I had worked at in Dhaka.

We came to the bed of Khan's patient. He was a short, light skinned individual, a former soldier, who appeared to be in his early thirties.

The man was bedridden and moribund. His neck was swathed in multiple layers of gauze, and a large dribble of saliva could be seen forming below the dressing and running down his neck. He had a nasogastric tube in his nose. Akel slowly removed the dressing.

I could see what he and Khan were talking about. In the upper right side of the patient's neck was a hole large enough to put your fist into that communicated directly with the back of the man's throat. Pools of saliva dripped onto his neck through the open wound. What was even more disconcerting was the sight of the man's tongue hanging down through the big hole in his neck. During the surgery the structures that supported the tongue had been removed causing the tongue to prolapse down and backward from his mouth and into his neck. It was bizarre.

"He has been this way for months, suh, since the surgery. I have been working on this poor chap everyday, suh, changing his dressing, cleaning his wounds. What do you think, suh?" Akel asked.

I was still examining the patient. "Do you have a flashlight and a tongue blade Akel?" I asked.

"Of course, suh. Will it be possible to reconstruct this, suh?"

"I think so. We'll have to use a flap. I just need to get a close look at the wound."

"Good, suh."

Akel handed me the flashlight. I took a long look at the wound, both from the outside and through the patient's mouth. I wondered when the last time Akel had examined the man closely. It was not good news. He had a massive recurrent tumor invading the tongue, tonsil, throat, and neck. It was rock hard tumor, rigid, and fixed. I felt the man's neck. The cancer had gotten into the bone, the base of the skull, everywhere.

"Uhh, Akel, when was the last time you looked at the patient?"

"Oh, everyday, suh."

"I don't think you were looking very carefully."

"What do you mean, suh?"

"I mean he's got tumor everywhere. I don't think I can help this man. I can't reconstruct this."

"Why, suh?"

"Take a look, Akel." It was hard to imagine how this could have been missed. Akel examined the patient's neck, feeling the same tumor I had just felt.

Akel somehow remained unconvinced.

"Why, suh?" The young doctor wasn't getting the picture.

"You can't reconstruct it when there's tumor! What are you going to do, cover the tumor with a flap? What good will that do? He has an incurable cancer."

The patient, who fortunately did not understand a word of English, remained blissfully ignorant of the conversation.

"But, suh, what about the poor chap, what will I tell him? I promised him you would be able to help him."

"Akel, I'm very sorry, but there's nothing I can do."

"Couldn't you try anyway? Suh, if you only knew how it has gone for this poor chap. Changing his dressings twice a day, not being able to eat and looking like that, suh. It has been terrible."

"I know Akel"

"But, suh, if you only knew how his spirits lifted when I told him about you. We told him you could help him, repair the hole, allow him to eat again, please, suh, reconsider! I've seen your flaps, suh. Couldn't you try anyway, suh?"

Poor Akel. It was touching to see how affected he was by the plight of his patient. He had gone out on a limb telling the patient I could help him before I had a chance to examine him myself. Now he would have to shatter the false hopes he had himself created.

"There's no way, Akel, I'm sorry."

"Suh, I beg of you, I cannot bear to tell him."

"Akel, you have to. We can't help him. We have to let him go. Make him comfortable. That's all you can do."

"Suh."

Akel bowed his head and closed his eyes, holding back tears.

I recalled my last patient in Chiang Mai, the young man who had become a monk and had incurable tongue cancer. We also had to deny him despite his youth and wish to live.

"I'm sorry, Akel."

That was it. Surgeons were not magicians or Gods, only mortals made of clay. Some patients could not be helped. Any good doctor agonized over his patients, especially when he may have contributed to their suffering. I knew Akel and Colonel Khan felt tremendous guilt. There were other patients at CMH that we helped. Akel, the Colonel, and I did many cases together. But not this one.

Chapter 68

Ying and I were having lunch one afternoon with Allaudin at his home. His wife was present, preparing the meal, and a friend of his, non-medical, sat next to Allaudin on the couch. It was Friday, the Muslim Sabbath day. Allaudin was barefoot and dressed casually in loose fitting garments, reflecting the peaceful, relaxed nature of the day. One leg was crossed almost in yogic fashion, and I thought to myself how tranquil and beatific he seemed here in contrast with the fierce warrior-surgeon I was accustomed to at the Medical College.

His wife appeared with a tray of sweets. "Richard and Ying, please enjoy," she said.

"Thank you," I said picking one of them, a pastry.

Ying had one, as did Allaudin and his guest.

"It will ruin my appetite, but I cannot resist," Allaudin said, smiling.

I saw Allaudin as a consummate fighter, a man who meant well notwithstanding his intense manner and who had dedicated himself to teaching - in his fashion. That he headed the ENT Department at one of the most prestigious medical centers in the country was a great and deserved honor for him, a commanding status in his field indicative of his accomplishment and expertise.

"Professor Allaudin, I must tell you, I am amazed at how swiftly and well you perform major head and neck cancer surgery," I had told him previously.

He smiled warmly. "Thank you, Richard. That means a lot coming from you."

"I know how important it is that you perform such cases quickly. The sheer volume of advanced disease necessitates it. I will always remember your description of the Medical College as the 'Museum of ENT pathology.'"

"I knew the cases would impress you, Richard, even with all you have seen in your travels and your training in the US. Truly, Bangladesh is unique in this way. I wish it were not so. I would prefer that we had more resources so patients could be seen sooner rather than at such late stages."

As a result of the pressure to move cases, he could be ruthless. He left no room for error. If something were amiss, someone would pay. When all went well he remained implacable and unforgiving. I did not judge him. I thought a less mercurial approach could have succeeded even in a place as overwhelming as the Medical College, but I understood him. Yet here in his home on the Muslim Sabbath I saw him in a different light. He was as serene and hospitable as could be, as he had always been toward Ying and me.

The television was on in the corner of the room. It was a news program that we viewed disinterestedly between snippets of conversation. At one point there was coverage of Israel. The first intifada was on. There were daily skirmishes between the Israelis and Palestinians. I felt a bubble of tension. I looked over at Ying. She too registered discomfort.

My colleagues had wondered about my religious background. Many of them thought I was Muslim and had inquired. As a Sephardic Jew (of Spanish origin), I was short and swarthy like the Bangladeshi. When I mentioned that I was Jewish it surprised them. They took it in stride. They smiled. Perhaps they admired me for it. Perhaps not. Perhaps they had negative impressions of Jews but did not say. They must have wondered why a Jew would volunteer to work in a Muslim country to help Muslim patients and doctors. But it affected nothing other than to perhaps make me more of a novelty. It was enough that I had materialized out of nowhere, a welcome but quixotic entry into their universe, to perform surgery on hopelessly ill patients, to teach and lecture, shuttle about the city from hospital to hospital for no compensation.

"Moss," Amin had said to me after our initial meeting," I had many Jewish professors in Britain. I learned so much from them. They were critical influences in my early career. That I was Muslim never came up. They treated me as anyone else. I will always remember that."

"Thank you Professor Amin, I appreciate your telling me that." I smiled at the great patriarch. I knew he must have heard through the grapevine that I was Jewish and had brought this up to reassure me that it was not an issue and to harbor no concerns. "I am very content here. I was apprehensive only about the insane bus driver that took us to Dhaka from the border that first night."

"Don't ever do that again, Moss. I forbid it."

"I promise you it will never be repeated."

We both laughed.

"I want you to be at ease here, Moss."

"I am, Dr. Amin, believe me I am."

At a dinner gathering of doctors, I was chatting with Abdullah. Another non-ENT physician appeared.

"This is Dr. Moss from the US," Abdullah said, introducing me.

I could tell he was studying my complexion and stature and wondering if I was perhaps a Bangladeshi Muslim trained in the US.

"Is he Muslim," I heard him whispering to Abdullah, somewhat hopefully.

Abdullah, who knew I was Jewish, answered with his slow drawl, "he's uhh... Christian," finally getting it out.

This was of no consequence. Most Americans were Christian, and so it was expected. Abdullah told a white lie, settling, perhaps wisely, on declaring me a Christian to avoid an incident – and to protect me. This reflected, however, an undercurrent of anti-Semitism from which I needed to be guarded. And there was other more blatant evidence.

I remembered reading an editorial in the main English daily of Bangladesh, the *Observer*, for which I had written a few columns upon the request of Abdullah shortly after my arrival. I showed it to Ying, shaking my head unhappily.

"If you want to see the ugly face of anti-Semitism, here it is."

Ying read it and shook her head as well.

"There is an exodus of Jews leaving the Soviet Union," I said. "Many of them are flocking to Israel. Look at their description of it."

"I saw."

"They liken the migration of Soviet Jews escaping the communist regime for Israel as a 'plague of locusts' settling in the Holy Land." This and other language like it against Jews and Israel in the press was not uncommon in Bangladesh. "It is every bit as derogatory and anti-Semitic as the language of Nazi Germany. It reminds me, I'm afraid, that anti-Semitism is entrenched in the Muslim world including here in the relatively moderate nation of Bangladesh far from the Middle East."

But from my colleagues and others I met, never. Not in general nor directed at me personally. It was quite the opposite.

Back in Allaudin's living room, the news program depicted Israeli soldiers firing tear gas at some of the Palestinian rock throwers. A battle ensued. At that moment, before anything offensive could be said by the unsuspecting guest who did not realize I was Jewish, Allaudin leaned over, cupped his hand and whispered into his guest's ear. Of course I did not hear it. It happened so swiftly as to be almost imperceptible. I observed only that the man looked at me, pushed his lower lip out in a manner to suggest surprise and nodded either mystified or impressed or both. I knew Allaudin had told him that I was Jewish, a way of cautioning him to avoid saying something unpleasant. The news coverage of Israel quickly passed and the moment of discomfiture ended. The atmosphere became light and convivial again.

"Richard and Ying, please, let's eat," Allaudin said as the food was brought to the table.

It was in this and many other ways that my Muslim friends and colleagues in Bangladesh shielded me. I appreciated them greatly.

Soon after our arrival in Bangladesh I was swamped. The needs of the many patients with terrible, often fatal disease coupled with the abiding interest of the local ENT surgeons to do cases together had me running all over Dhaka. One day, I might be operating at PG hospital. The next, seeing patients or operating at CMH. The day after, running to the Medical College or possibly to Mitford hospital in the old city with Abdullah - all the while keeping tabs on the many post-operative patients scattered throughout the city. I did not have my own personal car or motorcycle to get around with and had to rely on others. This generally worked out, but it was not always convenient. Overall, I preferred being chauffeured around mainly because I didn't trust myself in the Dhaka traffic. It was positively lethal. Between the bicycle rickshaws, numbering in the tens of thousands, the pedestrian traffic, the beggars, animals, three wheeled taxis, carts, roadside stalls, trucks, cars, kamikaze bus drivers, not to mention the potholes, fumes and the blazing sun, it was in my own best interests to let someone else drive.

But the word was getting around and not just among the local ENT doctors. Before long, I received calls from the Bangladeshi elite as well as from the expatriate/diplomatic community who had discovered that an American surgeon was in town. In general, for the expatriates and diplomats, as well as the wealthy Bangladeshi who could afford such extravagance, any significant medical problem usually meant a trip to Bangkok for treatment. Now, at least for ear nose and throat problems, such a trip was no longer necessary. And more and more of these kinds of calls were coming in. It was always interesting to see the differences in the complaints or concerns between the haves and have-nots of the world. It was like moving from one planet to another. In the morning, I may see someone from the British High Commission having a horrendous time with itchy ears and later on in the day, say, at Mitford Hospital, a 22 year old Bangladeshi kid with a tumor the size of a melon bursting out of the side of his neck, or perhaps, a little girl, less then two years of age with both lips completely eaten away by infection. I didn't mind treating the itchy ears, but there was no question where my heart and sympathies lied, and where I would rather be spending my time and energy. It required a major shifting of gears for me to bounce between the first and third world in the stretch of a 45 minute drive from the pleasant suburban diplomat ghetto of Gulshan to the steamy urban madness of the old city around Mitford.

Dealing with `first world' people was also a completely different trip. It necessitated lots of explanation and heaping tablespoons of empathy and solicitude over problems that, in the scheme of things, were relatively trivial. With the indigent population, it was a different picture. Very little explanation was needed, and they trusted you implicitly. They also showed tremendous respect and gratitude even when you could do nothing for them. It made me wonder if I could ever return to that most pampered of nations, the United States.

I did manage to meet some rather interesting and well-placed patients.

Once, while visiting Khan at CMH, we received a phone call from the office of the President of Bangladesh, Hussain Muhammad Ershad. Khan stiffened as he listened. A half hour later, the executive secretary to the President, General Hafiz, drove up with his wife, an obese woman who complained miserably of a tickle in the back of her throat. I spent 45 minutes trying to get a look down her throat with a mirror, but it was impossible. She gagged and sputtered and I could not visualize her larynx. I soon gave up to everyone's relief especially the wife. After a crisp thank you, the general, who walked around with a leather whipping stick held snugly in his right armpit, left with his wife in something of a huff.

Another time, while resting in my guesthouse in Banani, I received a phone call from a man who would become a good friend of mine, the Deputy Ambassador of the American embassy to Bangladesh in Dhaka, Ray Peppers. He had a problem with chronic nosebleeds that occurred at the most inopportune times, such as when he recently hosted a dinner for the Ambassador from France. In the middle of a "toast" he was giving to the French Ambassador, with wine glasses raised, his nose spurted and bright red blood poured onto his white shirt, tuxedo, white table cloth, dinnerware and food in front of the assembled diplomats. He was so desperate to do something about this that he agreed to brave the traffic of the old city to meet me at Mitford Hospital the next day. We traveled together in his chauffeur driven, air conditioned limousine through the narrow, bumpy, crowded streets of the old city. As luck would have it, in the midst of examining the Deputy Ambassador from the United States, in one of the poorest countries in the world, he again had a nosebleed. In that sorry old hospital, so short of supplies, I spent the next hour trying to control a major nasal hemorrhage with basically my bare hands. By luck, or the will of God, it stopped. I placed a couple of cotton balls in both nostrils and begged him not to blow his nose. Somehow, we still parted as friends.

From the perspective of my work as a surgeon, my experience in Bangladesh was perhaps the pinnacle of my young career. I was dealing with the sickest patients I had ever encountered, patients with disfiguring, advanced cancers of mind boggling dimension with little or no hope of salvage. Many of these patients had families who depended on them and the intensity of their need was heart wrenching. For a surgeon, trained to cut and to cure, there could be few opportunities more satisfying than this. Rescuing the poor and the infirm from the ravages of hopeless disease under the most daunting of conditions often using substandard equipment had been precisely my quest. Bangladesh tested my fortitude and ingenuity. I was fulfilling my own unspoken code of honor. I had expanded into a larger version of myself, shed my former layers and emerged altered and new, reborn in the fires of Bangladesh. Here I had found my calling. It was to treat the destitute, the stricken, and the neglected people of the developing world with all the power my training, experience, and will would allow.

The fact that this had all manifested in its most powerful and urgent form in a Muslim country was an irony not lost on me. It was here in Bangladesh, where a Jew working with Muslim colleagues on Muslim patients in a Muslim nation could bring the loose threads, ambitions, and desires of his life together to find his greatest challenge and fulfillment. I had noted earlier in my travels my concerns with Islam and its treatment of other religions in Thailand, Indonesia, Nepal, and India. Yet, I was at ease in this Muslim land with Muslim friends. They had received me and welcomed me as one of their own. I felt comfortable here. Bangladesh had been made my home. In the Middle East and elsewhere there was strife. But for this lone Jew in a nation of 120 million Muslims, there was peace and acceptance.

Chapter 69

The American Embassy in Dhaka stood out like a medieval fortress in the heart of another upscale district known as Baridhara. It was ringed by tall brown walls made of solid rock, topped by multiple layers of barbed wire and pointed black wrought iron fences. It was massive and imposing, occupied acres and acres of land, and could be seen for miles in any direction. In the center of the complex, hanging limply in the hot sun, high above the buildings and fences, was the American flag, proudly serving notice that this was American territory.

"I am always happy to see that flag," I said to Ying.

The American Embassy was different from other embassies in Dhaka, a separate realm that many people felt represented the seat of power in this sputtering, indigent and beleaguered nation. And the embassy was built to convey that impression. Like all American embassies throughout the world, this embassy was a powerful symbol of the United States, a projection of American power and prestige, a clear message meant to portray America's singular role and position in the world. The contrast between this symbol of the world's richest and most powerful nation situated within one of the world's poorest must have been intimidating.

Ying and I rode up to the embassy in a cycle rickshaw where the barefoot wallah let us off. We paid him a few takas, and he pedaled off in search of other customers. We entered the broad massive gate into the embassy and encountered the first layer of security consisting of several uniformed Bangladeshi who frisked us, took our bags and checked us with metal detectors. After passing their inspection, they cordially smiled and let us through the door. We were now actually in the embassy.

"This is officially US soil," I said to Ying. "Welcome to America."

She chuckled.

We continued up a narrow corridor until we came to the second line of defense, a thick metal door that buzzed as we approached it. Inside, was a large room with a smaller glass enclosed cubicle off to the side where I could discern an American face with a microphone. There were several heavily armed marines in the room with him.

"How can I help you?" the metallic voice inquired over the speaker.

"I have an appointment with Jim Howard." I responded.

331

"What time was that for?"

"2:30."

"One minute, please. Have a seat."

We sat down on a bench and waited. A few minutes later, an attractive American woman in a dress appeared at the door and introduced herself to us. She brought us to a desk and had us sign our names on a list, our time of arrival, and our purpose for visiting. She then handed us each a badge, identifying us as visitors, and escorted us out of the room. We passed through a series of carpeted, air-conditioned corridors, with beautiful framed pictures of pastoral scenes hanging on the walls and finally into a spacious room, buzzing with clerical activity. She led us to a large couch, smiled, and disappeared.

In stepping through the door it was as if we had been miraculously transported back to the states. There was wall-to-wall carpeting, stylish wallpaper, inset lighting, coffeemakers, air conditioning, and beautiful framed pictures. The secretaries, some Bangladeshi, some American, were all neatly dressed, clean and well groomed, pecking away on their computer keyboards, studying the monitors like religious artifacts, or else picking up their push-button telephones, speaking with unruffled American secretary voices, taking messages on note pads, transcribing, shuffling papers, dictating memos, sending faxes, making copies, discussing organizational matters, and in all ways carrying on like any major corporate or government office in America. There were several smaller chambers that led into the one larger office where Ying and I were waiting. I could hear the voices of people in conference discussing with great urgency the issues of the day. From one room, a single, dominant masculine voice expounded on the difficulties of convincing illiterate Muslim villagers in remote areas of the country to use condoms, which I could readily understand. In another hall, several feminine voices could be heard assessing family planning in this country with unstoppable population growth. After being out of the states for almost three years, this artificial re-entry into Americana was something of an awakening. I realized how many light years now separated me from the culture I had grown up in. I had to shift gears psychologically from a cycle rickshaw to a corporate boardroom in a matter of minutes. I felt better in the rickshaw.

"After three years, I had forgotten what its like to be in America. It's another world. I'm more comfortable on the streets of Bangladesh," I whispered to Ying.

The United States Agency for International Aid or USAID was the foreign aid branch of the US government. Much of the money spent in developing countries from the US was funneled through their offices. America sent Bangladesh about seven hundred million dollars a year, the most in the world until Japan outspent us recently with eight hundred million of their own. I had arranged to meet with one of the head honchos, a man by the name of Jim Howard, to see if, either through USAID itself, or through some of their connections with NGOs, I could arrange funding for my work.

"Mr. Howard will be able to see you," a male Bangladeshi secretary said. I was amazed at how Americanized the Bangladeshi man seemed. Except for his physical appearance, you could hardly tell him from an American.

"Thank you," I said.

We were escorted through a door leading into a cramped office where we encountered an individual with rolled up sleeves, a loosened tie, and open collar. He sat at a cluttered desk, a cup of coffee in his hand, feet up, and hurriedly skimmed papers as we came in. He stood to greet us, briefly shook my hand, and sat down. He had a slightly frazzled look and gave every indication that he considered himself important and that his time was very valuable.

"Yes, I remember our conversation on the phone the other day. Ray Peppers mentioned you also," he added.

"Right."

"And you're doing cancer surgery and teaching at some of the hospitals here?"

"Yes."

"You must see some unusual things?"

"Yes, very advanced cases."

"And you're on your own, no organization, NGO, nothing?"

"Right. I've been doing this for almost three years now."

"Very commendable. Uhh, how can I help you?" There was a sudden change in temperature.

"You remember our conversation about possible sponsorship for my work? You suggested you might be able to help." I said.

"Oh, right. Hmmm. Yeah. Well, let's see. Uhh, I, I'm not sure."

We had spoken earlier in the week about this very same question. He had indicated at the time, in fairly grand fashion, that USAID purse strings and generosity knew no bounds and for so noble a cause as mine surely something could be arranged.

"I've got an idea, just a second." He reached for his phone and called in his secretary, who entered the room promptly. "Do we have that book listing all the NGOs in Bangladesh?" Howard asked the secretary.

"I believe so, sir."

"Can you find it for the doctor?"

"Right away, sir." He left the room to find the book. I noticed a look of relief on Howard's face. The secretary returned with a thick tome listing every NGO in Bangladesh, a number totaling more then four thousand. The secretary handed it to Howard.

"Great, this is it," he said, while skimming the book. "This is the one." He handed the book to me.

I leafed quickly through it and realized that the assistance Howard was offering was a list of other organizations for me to go around and beg to.

"Uhh, thanks, Jim, but somehow I had the impression after our phone call that USAID might be able to help directly."

"We are helping. That's why I'm showing you the book."

"That's not what we discussed."

"I'm not sure I understand. You're welcome to look at the book as long as you like. You can sit outside and review it."

I reflected on this odd convergence. Here was a guy sitting at a desk in an air conditioned office, pulling upwards of six or seven thousand dollars a month, maybe a hundred grand a year, for the purpose of dispensing foreign aid to the poor of Bangladesh, dismissing from his office a man who had been doing jungle surgery on some of the sickest people in the country and not making a dime. I was in the trenches going to battle with my bare hands, and he was sitting in this plush office with his digital telephone and secretaries while sipping fresh coffee with cream and sugar. Looking around this place, it made you wonder. How much money was wasted? What percentage of "foreign aid" actually got to where it was supposed to go and how much went into salaries, the building, the slick, business offices, the cars, chauffeurs, maids, cooks, air travel, paid holidays, vacations, pensions, healthcare benefits, and other perks. On the face of it, it sounded so humanitarian. Living in Bangladesh, working with USAID, helping the needy. The fact was they were very comfortable and well compensated. Here I was, on the other hand, a one-man operation with no overhead, no salary, no organizational support, going right into the heart of a major health problem affecting tens of thousands of people and getting shown the door.

"Well thanks Jim," I said, taking the book.

"Just one American helping another, doctor," he replied.

Chapter 70

Abdullah picked Ying and me up at our guesthouse in the morning. We drove down to the Dhanmondi district, one of the most affluent areas in Dhaka, to meet with Amin and Khan. An appointment had been made with the supervisor of the World Health Organization, or WHO, in Dhaka, to see about the possibility of some funding to keep me going in Bangladesh. This meeting had been arranged by an influential general from the Combined Military Hospital who had attended a lecture I had given about the problem of head and neck cancer in Bangladesh. The slides of the advanced cases, the extensive surgery, the overwhelming nature of the problem, had impressed the general who then pushed a few buttons resulting in this meeting.

Abdullah parked his car just outside the WHO headquarters where Amin and Khan were already waiting. It was gratifying to see these three senior ENT surgeons take time out from their busy schedules to support me like this. We walked up to the second floor and were led into yet another air-conditioned office to be introduced to a short Indian fellow, Devdas Gupta, the local head of the WHO. Gupta reclined in his easy chair behind his desk and stood to greet us.

"Hello, hello, so good to see you. Please sit down, make yourselves comfortable." Gupta said. He came around from his desk and sat down with us. A secretary appeared with cups of tea.

The main headquarters for the WHO in south Asia was in New Delhi where Gupta was actually from. Gupta looked like he was doing all right here in his pleasant office with doctors and generals calling on him requesting assistance. I felt as if I was reliving my US Embassy experience from just a few days before. Like the USAID grandees, the upper level bureaucrats in the WHO and other big time foreign aid organizations made out very well in this poor country. They generally pulled in close to a hundred thousand a year, paid little or no taxes, and enjoyed all the perks. I didn't know what Gupta would have been making working for the Indian government back in New Delhi, but I'd guess it would have paled in comparison. The UN pay scales were modeled after the US government. After dealing with large NGOs since coming to Bangladesh, I had become cynical. They enjoyed a certain image of sanctity, an aura of selfless mission that, at least for the career bureaucrats, didn't fit the facts. The reality was that they had great jobs with tremendous benefits. They were history's best-paid saints. Among the many international organizations of the world, the UN, its various appendage agencies and departments, its officials, bean counters, and career apparatchiks, were the most bloated and corrupt.

Most of the money coming in to Bangladesh by way of the WHO and other major players in the foreign aid game was earmarked for two areas: family planning, for the outrageous population growth, and flood control. Both problems were wrecking the country and were not unrelated. There were upwards of a hundred and twenty million people crowded into this tiny nation with no sign of slowing down despite the billions spent every year on population control. And the floods were an almost annual nightmare of death and destruction despite huge sums of money spent. Bangladesh's notorious floods were a result of the nation's peculiar geography. The country was draped over the Ganges and Brahmaputra river deltas, both river systems originating in the Himalayan Mountains to the north. Monsoonal flooding, generally a positive thing in the Delta before the population exploded to occupy every seasonally dewatered area, even those most subject to extreme flooding, was now a catastrophe because permanent population centers had formed in regions that would have been only seasonally inhabited several generations ago. In addition, Bangladesh was below sea level and bordered the Bay of Bengal with its frequent cyclones and hurricanes. The resultant flooding, among the world's worst, also led to increased fecal-oral contamination and near epidemic diarrhea, especially among children. With such major league problems as these, I wondered if the WHO would have anything left over for something as narrow and focused as head and neck cancer.

"You see, Gupta, we need this transfer of technology," Amin began, sipping his tea.

"I see." Gupta sat back in his chair, pressing his two hands together in front of his face, weighing Amin's words with studied gravity. He seemed to enjoy his status as WHO mandarin.

"I know you are beginning the anti-tobacco campaign in the coming weeks, Gupta. But please, let us be honest, it is a waste of time." Amin pressed, armed with inside information.

"Hmmmmm." Gupta's eyes widened almost imperceptibly. Amin had scored a direct hit only seconds into the match.

"What good is a television or newspaper campaign when 90% of the people getting cancer cannot read and 100% of them will never in their lives come close to owning a TV?" Amin smiled. The old master was in control.

"Hmmmmm." Gupta twitched slightly.

"We are not asking for much, Gupta, only a little something to help our good friend from America who is doing so much to help our poor country." Amin was turning up the heat.

"Yeessss, I see."

"This is important, Gupta."

"Well, you realize, of course, I do not have the power to allot funding for new projects. That must arise first in Delhi." Gupta now countering.

"But this new anti-tobacco campaign is under your jurisdiction. You have additional funding now for that." Amin was on him like a cat.

"Wellll."

"Gupta, please, if you don't mind my saying, between you and me, it is a waste of time. We have thousands of cancer cases a year that need treatment. They come in from all over the country, from very remote areas. They will never even know of this anti-tobacco campaign."

"Wellll. We may be able to work something out. We have a certain `discretionary fund' for this sort of thing." Gupta was licking his lips. He enjoyed handing out little morsels for the peasants.

"Good, good. And how much are we talking about, Gupta?"

"Wellll."

"Dr. Moss is a foreign expert and should be paid like one. He will need at least five thousand dollars a month. "

"Five thousand a month!"

"Gupta, you know as well as I what you are making. Why should Dr. Moss get less?

"That cannot be arranged. By our rules, even though he is from another country because he is currently here he must be considered a local expert. He cannot be paid as a foreign expert."

"Very well, then, what are we talking about?"

"I have ten thousand dollars I can divert from the anti-tobacco campaign."

"Fine." Amin said. I was ecstatic.

"Only one thing, it must be approved."

I knew it.

"Approved?" Amin thundered.

"Yes, approved."

"But you just said it was `discretionary.'"

"Everything must be approved. "

Chapter 71

Colonel Khan and I drove up to an old government building from the turn of the century. He parked the car and we entered this dusty castle, passing two soldiers carrying machine guns who saluted as we passed. We ascended two flights of stairs and came to an office. We walked inside and Khan spoke to the male secretary sitting behind a desk.

"Colonel Khan and Dr. Moss to see the honorable Health Minister."

We were led through a maze of corridors and finally to a large wooden door. The secretary motioned for us to enter. Khan, ever polite, knocked instead. From what seemed like a long distance, we heard a voice thunder, "Come in."

We meekly entered into a cavernous hall, carpeted and air conditioned, and walked towards a large desk at the opposite end of the room. There was a tremendous chair, more like a throne, with the back turned toward us behind the desk. Just as we approached the desk the large swivel chair turned and a big bear of a man with a huge barrel chest and a large face greeted us.

"Come in, come in, sit down," he bellowed in a deep, cavernous voice that echoed from way down in his solar plexus. "I've been expecting you."

"Good morning sir," Khan saluted sharply.

"Sit down."

The same general that had arranged our meeting with Gupta at the WHO had also arranged a meeting with the honorable Minister of Health of Bangladesh, Azizur Rahman. A member of the executive cabinet, he was appointed by the great man himself, the supreme leader of the country for the last six years, President Ershad. Somehow, we had gotten in to see the number one health official in the country, a man not particularly well liked by Bangladeshi physicians, but someone known to have his fingers in many different pies and particularly some of the better funded NGOs including the Rockefeller Foundation. We sat down nervously before him. He rocked back on his throne looking outward beyond us as if surveying his kingdom.

"You know, I used to be a surgeon, a pediatric surgeon." he said, looking at no one in particular.

"I know, suh, we have all heard, suh." Khan too, said `sir' in the same curious way that Akel did.

"I used to do so many surgeries, everyday, dozens of operations. I never rested. " He seemed to be speaking to himself as if in a trance.

"Yes, suh, we have always known of your great abilities, suh." Khan responded.

"For hours and hours, never stopping."

"Yes, suh, we have always admired you."

"And now look at me."

"Suh, suh.

"You know," he began again, this time speaking to me, "I trained in your country."

"Oh?" I croaked.

"Yes, in Minnesota. Duluth. The University of Minnesota. Back in 1960. Oh, it's cold there. Can you see me coming from Bangladesh and living in Minnesota for four years? Cold. So cold."

"Yes, I can imagine."

"I enjoyed those years, living in your country."

"Yes."

"So innocent, the Midwest."

"Yes."

"So rich, so powerful. America. So removed from the great problems of the world.

"Yes."

"How I miss those simple days in college."

"Yes."

"The optimism and hope of America."

"Yes."

"You know who I used to love back then?"

"No."

"Bob Dylan. Oh, he was my favorite. Even now I still love to listen to Dylan. He was a hometown boy. I have all his tapes."

"You're kidding. I grew up listening to Dylan," I said.

"Nobody better. I loved his voice."

"Which albums did you like?"

"His early stuff. But it didn't matter. I loved them all." The Health Minister of Bangladesh, a Muslim, loved Bob Dylan, a Jew. We had something in common, an auspicious development. "My favorite," he continued, "was *Blonde on Blonde*. But I also loved *Highway 61 Revisited*."

We discussed the motorcycle accident that led to Dylan's going electric back in 1965, his days on the road singing folk songs with Joan Baez, his influence on John Lennon, and other important Dylan topics.

Several minutes into our Dylan reverie the phone rang. The Health Minister picked it up. In an instant, I witnessed an extraordinary transformation. This proud walrus of a man with an immense booming voice began to shake like a leaf. His spine stiffened, his face tensed, and his lower lip twitched.

"Suh, suh, suh, suh, suh," he lowered his head to the table obsequiously, cowering like a frightened child. "Suh, suh, suh, suh." Sweat formed over his brow; his deep voice became thin and quavering. "Suh, suh, suh, suh," he continued over and over, 'sir', in that Bangladeshi style. His hand trembled as he grasped the phone. Who was he speaking to? This giant of a man was scared out of his wits. I looked over at Khan and noticed he too was crapping in his pants. Who was on the phone? I realized it must have been none other then the President himself, Hussain Muhammad Ershad. Who else could strike such fear in these two powerful men? Just as suddenly, amidst a flurry of `suhs,' the Health Minister hung up the phone. Night became day. The swagger, the pride, the grandeur all returned. The Health Minister looked at me as if nothing had happened.

"So, how can I help you?" he asked, now all business.

"Suh," Khan began, "Dr. Moss has a lecture, a slide lecture of his work in Bangladesh, suh."

"Oh."

"We would like to hold a seminar in your honor, suh, under the auspices of the Cancer Institute and Research Hospital, suh.

"Hmmmmm, I see."

"We would be delighted, suh, if you would grace this seminar with your presence, suh," Khan said, buttering him up.

"Hmmmmm, yeeessss, I see."

"It will be on cancer surgery, suh. As a surgeon, suh, we thought you would find it interesting, suh."

"Yeeessss, hmmmmmm, it could be interesting. But you know I am very busy. I don't know when I'll be free."

"Of course, suh, only at your convenience."

"And where do you want to hold it?"

"At Birdem Hospital, suh."

"And who will attend?"

"We plan to invite over 200 of our most prominent physicians, suh. There will be residents and students and faculty from all the teaching hospitals, suh."

"Good, good." He was warming up to it. "And the press?"

"Absolutely, suh. We will notify the newspapers."

"Fine. We can do it. When?"

"At your convenience, suh."

"Good. Well, then, please speak to my secretary and arrange it."

"Fine, suh, I will do that, suh." Khan hesitated before standing to leave.

The Health Minister had taken the bait by agreeing to attend the lecture. Should Khan take a chance by airing the real purpose of his visit? He paused. The Health Minister eyed him suspiciously. "Well?" he asked.

"Uhh, excuse me, suh."

"What is it?" A tinge of annoyance.

"One small thing, suh."

"Yes?"

"Suh, excuse me for asking, suh."

"Go on."

"We are trying to help Dr. Moss, suh"

"Yeeessss?"

"Excuse me, suh, for being so bold, suh."

"Go on, go on."

"Well, suh, if it is possible to arrange funding through your many contacts with various NGOs, suh."

"Funding?"

"Suh."

"Funding is very difficult"

"I know, suh."

"You cannot just make money appear, you know."

"I understand, suh."

"I'm a busy man, Colonel, draw up a proposal and let me see it. I have work to do!"

"Excellent, suh, thank you, suh."

Chapter 72

The date for the seminar on Surgical Management of Head and Neck Malignancies and Reconstructive Surgery had been set for June 23, 1990, at the auditorium of Birdem Hospital in the heart of Dhaka just opposite PG Hospital. Professor Ali, a soft-spoken oncologist whom I had met once in Amin's office, arranged it under the auspices of "The Cancer Institute and Research Hospital." Notices had gone out to all the teaching hospitals, to numerous physicians and surgeons, and to the press. "The Honorable Minister of Health and Family Planning, Dr. Azizur Rahman, FRCS (Fellow of the Royal College of Surgeons), has kindly consented to grace the occasion by his presence. Speaker on the subject is Dr. Richard Moss, an eminent Head and Neck surgeon from the USA," read the notice. I was flying high here in Bangladesh. In only 3 months I had gone from beggar roaring into Dhaka on the overnight kamikaze express bus to "eminent surgeon."

In the meantime, Khan and I were hard at work on the proposal. It was several pages long and documented the overwhelming problem of Head and Neck cancer in Bangladesh. There were roughly 200,000 new cases of total body cancer each year in the country. Out of these, almost 50% occurred in the head and neck, making it the leading cancer in the nation. One hundred thousand new cases of head and neck cancer per year and only two or three centers capable of treating them in the entire country. And those facilities were located only in Dhaka. Outside of Dhaka there was often little that could be done. The neglect and delay in diagnosis and treatment resulted in horribly advanced, often incurable disease. It was a slow, miserable death for thousands of helpless Bangladeshi.

In The US, the incidence was 3-4%, compared with almost 50% in Bangladesh. The reason was the near universal use of betel nut. This was a nut known to contain carcinogens that the Bangladeshi (and Indians) loved to chew not unlike tobacco for Americans. On almost every street corner in every city, town, and village in Bangladesh little stands could be found selling betel nut, usually wrapped in a leaf with lime, spices, and syrups that the locals indulged in regularly. It created a disgusting red broth that coated the membrane of the oral cavity, stained the teeth, and made unappealing blood-red blotches on the streets and walls where the Bangladeshi spat it out. These vendors selling betel nut were little cancer factories dispersed throughout the cities and countryside. Smoking, malnutrition, poor oral hygiene, and general neglect played a role too. We recommended prevention, education and treatment, a three-pronged attack to counter the terrible disease at every point. Get the word out about betel nut and smoking, not an easy task in a largely illiterate nation with little or no avenues for mass communication. Educate the primary care doctors about the early signs and symptoms of head and neck cancer with emphasis on timely detection and treatment. And finally train as many specialists as possible in the surgery and management of the disease. This was where I came in. I hoped to participate in all areas but particularly the last.

The senior ENT surgeons in the country would review, support, and sign the proposal. I had lost touch with Allaudin, and Abdullah had gone to Mecca on the Haj, the pilgrimage every Muslim makes to their holiest city. As with everything else, Amin's support was paramount. Both he and Khan had reviewed it and appeared supportive. Khan would bring it to the seminar where he and Amin would sign it and submit it to the Health Minister after my presentation. The lecture would hopefully persuade the Health Minister by impressing upon him the magnitude of the problem, something he may not have realized given the many other pressing medical urgencies that prevailed in Bangladesh like malnutrition, infectious and diarrheal disease, and natural disasters. We wanted to demonstrate that extensive surgery and good outcomes could be accomplished here in Bangladesh. Sensitized to the problem of head and neck cancer in Bangladesh, this "national tragedy on a grand scale" as I would describe it, Rahman would seize the proposal and, in lavish fashion, in front of a large audience and the press, proclaim this as one of Bangladesh's most pressing health problems. We hoped he would agree to mobilize the health bureaucracy, the nation's hospitals and health-care workers, and the vast armies of NGOs, most particularly the Rockefeller Foundation, to provide the necessary funding for this noble mission, including a small allowance for me.

The monsoon's had started in Bangladesh several weeks before. We watched from inside our guesthouse the morning of the seminar as the rains pounded the streets. Akel, as usual, had come to pick Ying and me up.

"So good to see you, suh. How are you and the lady feeling, suh?"

"Fine, Akel, thanks."

"How is the lecture, suh, I am really looking forward to it."

"Okay, I think."

"Oh, wonderful, suh. The Health Minister, I'm certain, will really appreciate it, suh."

We drove to Birdem Hospital where I would deliver the lecture. With the downpour and the darkened sky, I had an unwelcome premonition. I doubted the plan. The hospital was swarming with the indigent of Bangladesh, the teeming crowds of penniless, sick people standing or sitting on the floors. The lecture would be in a large hall on the second floor. We arrived early to prepare. I arranged the projector, lights, microphone, and pointer; I reviewed the slides and rehearsed my opening lines. Everything was ready.

Slowly, the room filled. Doctors and residents poured in, some of whom I recognized. Many looked at me with odd expressions on their faces. I wondered what they were thinking? Questions like, why is he doing this? Others smiled and waved. It must have seemed odd, this American surgeon putting on this spectacle in Bangladesh.

Khan arrived along with Dr. Ali. The two would introduce me before the lecture. The entire hall was now crammed with all the seats in the auditorium taken and many standing on the sides and in the back. In the rear of the hall I noticed a commotion. A large entourage marched into the hall with cameras flashing, reporters asking questions, taking notes, aides clearing a path, a real scene. In the middle of this ruckus, I identified the unmistakable figure of the Health Minister. He wore a grey safari suit, his big, burly chest puffed out, his deep voice bellowing, a force of nature. He came barreling down the central aisle confidently, gesturing forcefully, with Amin at his right side. Several aides ran before him and dusted off the front row seats reserved for him and other dignitaries. I noticed Amin taking the seat to his right, talking to him with great intensity, handing him documents and folders. I realized these were papers concerning his hearing project, something he had been working on for years. I wondered if this was the ideal time to be discussing hearing conservation when we were trying to pique the Health Minister's interest in head and neck cancer.

In the back I noticed another VIP guest arrive. The ambassador from Thailand, Chiaya Windosongse, and his close friend, General Abed, retired from the Bangladeshi army. The ambassador had no background in medicine, but he had a very curious and open mind. Ying and I had met him earlier at a Thai party we had gone to. He was very gracious, the consummate diplomat, and we had become good friends. When I told him of my lecture he instantly expressed an interest in coming. I never imagined he would drive so far in the rain, but aside from being inquisitive he was very supportive of me. I watched them sneak in as the lights dimmed and occupy the two seats adjacent to the Health Minister. When Rahman saw the Thai ambassador, his regal posture dropped a notch or two. It was one thing to thunder and rant at aides and hirelings but quite another in the presence of an ambassador. He seemed surprised to see the Thai ambassador, but instantly recognizing him, welcomed him warmly in the best diplomatic tradition. Chaiya, as smooth and polished a man as I have ever met, responded in kind. The show was about to begin.

Dr. Ali remarked on the Cancer Institute, of which he was the director.

He was a mild mannered individual who spoke softly and self-effacingly. Within minutes of his discussion, the Health Minister shifted impatiently in his seat, making grunting sounds of displeasure. Rahman was not here to listen to Ali reflect on the hopes and aspirations of the Cancer Institute. He was here for red meat – blood sucking, industrial-age, cancer, Bangladesh style. He was in no mood to suffer the meek or long winded. A vortex of negative energy radiated about him. Ali sputtered and cringed. He eked out another sentence or two, ending his comments promptly before dismissing himself.

Next was Colonel Khan. He felt the desert winds that had just melted Ali off the stage and seemed shaky. Fortunately, he had prepared some notes of introduction about me. He reviewed my background in the states. He said I was well published, which was not quite true. I had at that time about ten articles in the ENT literature, hardly a drop in the ocean of articles, reviews, supplements, journals, and books churned out yearly in the Otolaryngology universe. He then described the last three years of my life, traveling and working in poor countries in Asia. He mentioned the four countries I had spent time in, Thailand, Nepal, India, and now Bangladesh. He then used a very touching metaphor. He spoke about different kinds of religious pilgrims, Muslim, Hindu or Christian, who go to their sacred places for religious purposes. He likened me to a religious pilgrim although modifying it, referring to me instead as a "pilgrim of knowledge." It was a very poetic description of the last three years of my life, and I would always remember it.

I stepped up to the podium, adjusted the microphone and spoke off the cuff about the terrible problem of head and neck cancer in Bangladesh. Although facing a large crowd with dignitaries, professors and colleagues, I experienced no anxiety. I called for the slides.

I reviewed the incidence of head and neck cancer in Bangladesh, some of the reasons for its preponderance here, and what could be done. I discussed and demonstrated specific cases I had encountered and performed surgery on. I chose the most difficult cases, both to dramatize the aggressive nature of the disease and to demonstrate the extensive surgery we performed. I showed examples involving men, women and children to point out that all ages and sexes were affected. Case after case, each more grotesque and disfiguring then the last, passed before the audience. The message was persuasive. Head and neck cancer was a major health challenge to the country.

I completed my lecture, asked for the lights, and opened the floor to questions. There were many. I listened and responded and could have continued for an hour. After a time, I received a signal from Amin to stop. I thought it was premature but followed his lead. Perhaps it was the Health Minister's schedule. Amin, the senior ENT doctor of the country, then came to the podium to address the audience. What I heard was disconcerting. He spoke at length about his hearing project and said nary a word about the topic I had just spent an hour reviewing. He mentioned something about cochlear implants and referred to head and neck surgery as impractical in a country as poor as Bangladesh. He suggested that the limited resources of the nation should be used for hearing loss.

Amin then introduced the "esteemed and honorable Health Minister, Azizur Rahman." This was the big moment. The Health Minister would now offer his own sentiments on what he had seen and heard. He stood in lordly fashion, gazing benevolently at the Thai ambassador and the vast audience. He ambled serenely and majestically with broad, measured steps to the podium. He adjusted his large frame. He shifted his weight back on his heels and inhaled deeply, then allowed the air to flow slowly out through his nostrils. His mood changed. His eyes narrowed to angry slits, and he stared menacingly at the crowd, which seemed to collectively flinch. He rolled his eyes back to the top of his head, and inhaled deeply through his nose a second time. His abdomen puffed and he rotated his head in a strange way, as if trying to contain his energy. He seemed to be building up to his very first syllable, wanting every ounce of power focused on that precise moment. The audience froze in tense anticipation, awaiting the great man's response. With chest expanded, nostrils dilated, and eyes burning, he let out an animal roar.

"Aaaarrrrgggghhhh," he roared as if consumed by loathing and disgust. He stared around the room, like an angry lion. "You know," he said, looking contemptuously at the throng, almost mocking them. "You know that I used to be a surgeon, too, aaaarrrrgggghhhh." He snarled and thumped his chest. "I KNOW ABOUT SURGERY TOO," he repeated.

This great fact of his life, having been a surgeon, meant everything to Rahman who wanted it known by one and all. He was no paper-pushing lackey to the President. The great Rahman, the Minister of Health, the primo health official in the land, had been a powerful surgeon-warrior too. He had grasped the polished, sacred scalpel in his massive hand, had carved and sculpted human flesh, had redeemed frail, sickly bodies from disease, had waged noble war in the arena of blood and sinew and ravaged tissue, had battled in the only endeavor worthy of his greatness – that of surgeon. His position as Health Minister, his authority, his manhood, his being, all drew strength from this essential piece of his past.

"I hear all the time that we... " He backed away from the podium in disgust. Glaring at the cowering audience, he twisted his face as if readying to spit. "...That we cannot do anything in this country. That we are too poor to do anything in this country." He inhaled, tensed his body, and expanded his abdomen. He tightened his face, and his right cheek twitched. He raised his right arm high above his head and slammed it down on the podium, roaring, "WHO SAYS WE CANNOT DO SURGERY HERE? WHO SAYS WE CANNOT DO BIG SURGERY IN THIS COUNTRY? LET THE MAN WHO SAYS WE

CANNOT DO SURGERY IN BANGLADESH, COME SAY IT TO MY FACE HERE AND NOW." Sweat and saliva flew from his tormented face. Banging the podium again and daring the throng, he thundered again, "SAY IT TO ME NOW! COME UP TO THIS STAGE AND TELL ME NOW, BECAUSE I AM TIRED OF ALL OF YOUR COMPLAINTS!" The audience was frozen in fear. He growled and snarled and shook the podium, almost lifting it. "I HAVE BEEN SAYING FOR YEARS THAT WE IN BANGLADESH CAN DO WHATEVER WE WANT TO DO!"

It was political theater at its best. No cabinet official in the US would put on a performance like this. But in Bangladesh, where life was lived in the raw, it was jungle politics. You could bang and bluster and weep and snarl. There was nothing else to offer the pauperized minions of this needy country. Ershad was known to break down in tears before large audiences and win them over. The Health Minister was making political hay over my lecture. Health care in Bangladesh was in dire straits, but by showing the difficult surgical cases I had performed here, Rahman saw a perfect opportunity to make the opposite claim. Health care was alive and well in Bangladesh after all – thanks to his leadership.

"LOOK AT WHAT THIS YOUNG SURGEON HAS DONE IN OUR COUNTRY. HE HAS NO FEAR. HE IS A MAN OF ADVENTURE! A MAN OF COURAGE! YOU SAW HIS SLIDES. HE HAS DONE ALL THIS IN BANGLADESH! WHO NOW SAYS WE CANNOT DO THIS IN BANGLADESH? THEY ARE WRONG. WE CAN DO IT AND THIS YOUNG MAN PROVES IT!"

With this final oration, Rahman reached over to shake my hand and then bounded down from the stage and into the crowd. People rushed to him, cameras flashed, questions poured in from the press. I followed behind and scores of well-wishers and colleagues engulfed me. The Thai ambassador and General Abed and many others congratulated me. We were rushed into a large room off from the lecture hall for a buffet lunch prepared for the occasion. A photographer assembled the Health Minister, the Thai ambassador and me for a picture. Rahman, in the middle, smiled broadly and squeezed us together like teddy bears. He was laughing, snarling, thrilled with the event. It had gone well, and he wasn't expecting this. In front of a large audience of prominent physicians he had thrown down the gauntlet and declared himself and his tenure as Health Minister vindicated. He was ecstatic. If there was ever a time to give him the proposal, it was now. So far, it seemed, everything was going according to plan.

I looked for Amin and Khan. I noticed them by one of the tables, standing toe to toe in what seemed to be a heated exchange. What was going on? Chaiya and I walked over to them. At so successful an occasion, with the Health Minister so pleased, I could not imagine why the two main sponsors of the event would be arguing in front of everyone like this. As we approached them I saw the fighting intensify. With the ambassador from Thailand and I standing in front of them, the bickering continued. I could hear Khan asking Amin why he refused to sign the proposal, why he didn't want to give it to Rahman now while he was here and in such a good mood. Tomorrow would be too late. Other needs and problems would occupy his attention. He was a busy man, and there were so many other urgent issues in the country. Now was the time! I watched Khan's face and saw his concern. He felt uncomfortable arguing with Amin, his senior, but pressed him. He had worked hard to get to this point and for some reason, at the very last minute, Amin was backing out. Amin claimed he needed more time to study it and refused to sign the proposal now. He would not be cowed either. Khan acquiesced to Amin and agreed to give him more time to "review it." I knew then the plan was sunk.

Chaiya pulled me away from the two doctors, saying, "Richard, don't waste your time. You have worked so hard and see what they do." Chaiya did not know of the proposal, but somehow sensed that I had been betrayed at the last minute. I suspected he was also appalled to see such behavior in front of him, an ambassador. "Go back to Thailand, Richard, if you want to help someone. We need you also, and we will treat you well." The party was over in Bangladesh. At the most inopportune moment, Amin had scuttled the deal.

Chapter 73

Over the next couple of days, I had become both despondent and enraged about the events at the seminar. It seemed that personal ambition had interfered with what I thought was our primary objective. I met with the doctors again, at Amin's office, including Khan, Amin, Ali, and others, and realized the game was up. Even Khan, recognizing that Amin was no longer behind the project, was lukewarm. At one point in the meeting, seeing that the rug had been pulled out from under me, I stood and announced heatedly that, "I have done my last case in this country!" Amin was conciliatory, but it was now clear that the proposal would never be signed by him or given to the Health Minister.

I tried to figure it out. Amin had expressed his support for me. He seemed to like me, I thought, and I looked to him as a father figure, as most people under him did. Several explanations came to mind. First, Amin had been developing a major hearing conservation project that he had invested considerable amounts of time, money, and personal influence on. It was coming together and several NGOs were supporting him. All of a sudden, this young upstart from the states appears out of the blue, cutting out cancers all over Dhaka and creating a stir, perhaps diminishing his status. Articles were published, letters written, lectures given, and out of this, a major funding proposal signed by the senior ENT doctors of the country, to be handed to the Health Minister at a well publicized seminar with over 200 doctors in attendance. It was a bit too much, even for the most generous of souls. No doubt he felt his own well-thought out plans threatened. He could have quashed the seminar early on but once the invitations and notices had gone out it was too late. Instead he turned it to his own advantage with the Health Minister in attendance.

I was now confronted with a reality I found intensely disagreeable - returning to the states for more gainful employment. Why did the thought offend me? The hassles, the paperwork, the third party payers, the government breathing down your neck, the lawyers, the demanding, litigious public. And more importantly, was I needed in America? Did I make a difference in a nation with hospitals and doctors and CT scans on every block? `Need' was relative, but after 3 years in Asia, and particularly after winding it up in one of the poorest countries in the world, America seemed well taken care of.

Any American who wanted to learn about true hardship should visit Dhaka or Calcutta or a remote mountain village in Nepal or Thailand. Americans had no idea how well off they were and to what lengths foreigners would go to enter our country. But for me, going from stark deprivation to overwhelming abundance, was, in a curious way, a step down. I was interested in being where the need was greatest and the suffering most intense. But, I also had to make a living.

"It seems we are coming to the end of our journey," I told Ying sadly.

Chapter 74

I was sitting with Khan in his office when I told him Ying and I would have to leave soon. Given the recent developments, he was not surprised. He had worked hard on my behalf and had gone out on a limb with his ENT colleagues. We were both disappointed, but that was now an old story. I told him I would not be performing any additional surgery. This, I knew, would raise an eyebrow. Khan turned to me and asked, "What about the ten year old boy?"

This was a case I had been worrying about for sometime. I had my doubts about doing this case before the fiasco with the Health Minister, and with things as they were now, I figured it would be better if I slipped quietly out of Bangladesh.

The boy was a frail lad whose father had been a former soldier in the Bangladeshi army. I had first seen the boy on one of my first visits to Khan's office. The father, a poor man who didn't speak a word of English, had carried the boy into the office in his arms and placed him into the chair for me to examine. He was so weak he could barely lift his head. He was emaciated and in pain. I watched as he groaned, wept, and grimaced. The father too was in agony over the fate of his son. He looked at me with anguished, mournful eyes.

I assessed the boy and quickly found that he had a massive tumor bulging out the right side of his face. It extended from the base of his skull to below his jaw and had already eaten into the overlying skin. It had pressed on his ear and pushed it back, almost squeezing the ear canal shut. The tumor was so large and firm it had stretched the skin of his face like a balloon. Biopsies showed osteogenic sarcoma, an uncommon bone tumor arising from his jaw.

I felt the tumor and knew this would be a very difficult case, maybe even impossible, especially in a malnourished ten-year-old child. The tumor was fixed to his skull. I couldn't budge it. I couldn't tell where it began or ended.

Akel appeared with his CT scan. Since this was the military hospital, luxuries like CT scans were available. I was glad they had gotten one on him. What I found confirmed my clinical impression. The tumor had arisen from the mandible and had eroded the entire right side of the jaw. Even more worrisome, as I examined the CT scan section by section, the tumor had grinded through the base of the skull and into the middle cranial fossa. The tumor was intracranial. There was no way I was going to operate on this kid. Any attempt with so advanced a tumor could leave you with a dead patient.

I explained my findings to Akel who translated for the father. I watched him nod in understanding to Akel. On occasion, he would steal a sad look over at me. After several minutes, he seemed to accept our pronouncements. He picked up his dying son and carried him out of Khan's office. It was painful to do this, but I had no choice. In Bangladesh, it was a sad but common occurrence.

The following week while sitting in Khan's office, Akel came in to have a word with me. "Suh, excuse me, suh, it's about the little boy. You remember, suh, the little ten-year-old boy you saw last week? It's his father, suh, he wishes to speak with you, suh."

"What about, Akel?" I asked.

"He is so unhappy, suh, he wishes to speak with you. He wants you to help his son, suh."

"You explained everything last week already."

"I know, suh, excuse me, suh, but if you could please have a chat with the poor fellow. He's a good chap, really, suh, a veteran, suh. If you don't mind, suh, to give him a moment."

"Okay, Akel."

Akel ushered him in. He stood before me and spoke in Bengali. He kept his sorrowful eyes on me and spoke as if I understood everything he was saying. Akel translated.

"What he is saying, suh, is that he wants you to do something for his son even if he may die. He cannot bear to watch his son suffering like this, suh. He begs you, suh, excuse me for this, suh, he begs you to do something. He understands the risks, suh, but if you do nothing, suh, his son will die anyway."

The man continued speaking right through Akel's words as if the intent of his words could be driven into me by the power of his emotion.

"He and his wife can no longer watch their son in such torment, suh. Even if he dies from the surgery, it will be better then living in such pain. He begs you, suh, to please do something." I felt as if he wanted me to put him out of his misery rather than prolong the agony, a form of mercy-killing or suicide by surgery.

What was I going to do? How could I get that damn tumor out without killing the boy? I didn't want his death on my hands. If the tumor killed him that was nature. If I killed him it was malpractice. I didn't mind taking on tough cases, but only if there was a chance for cure. Above all, a surgeon had to remember to "do no harm."

"But, suh, you can do it. We have seen the other cases you have done, suh. Do it for this poor man, suh, maybe it will be alright, suh."

"But the tumor is in his brain, Akel. I'm not a neurosurgeon. I can't get it out!"

The man spoke again. I noticed tears forming and running down his brown cheeks.

"Suh, once again, he begs you to do something to relieve his son's suffering."

I was not happy about this. Not because I felt Akel and the father were imposing on me, but because I wanted to do something but was afraid to. Could I do this case or not? Was it too advanced or not? Would I wind up with a dead patient? I had to answer this question since coming to Bangladesh regularly, but this was worse because the tumor had invaded intracranially. Everybody, even surgeon-warriors, had to know their limits. I was frightened of the case because I couldn't be sure of doing it safely. But watching the small Bengali father weeping affected me. I knew I had said no before when confronted by such situations. I had lectured Akel on this very matter not so long ago although that case was entirely different. But notwithstanding the challenges of this case, part of me felt that I could pull it off.

That was before. Things had changed now. The proposal was kaput, I was broke and leaving the country.

Khan looked at me. "What about the little boy, Richard? They were expecting you."

I know, I know. They were expecting me to perform a miracle. I had lost my appetite for miracles.

"It is up to you, Richard, but I will have to tell the father."

Ying looked at me. She knew I was weakening. But not yet. I was still bitter about the proposal. That was not the kid's fault or Khan's. But I had decided that I had done enough surgery in Bangladesh.

"Well, Richard?"

"To be honest, Colonel, Ying and I decided that we won't be doing anymore surgery."

"That is up to you. But the family. They were hoping."

"I know."

"It is up to you, Richard, I understand."

"Right."

"I will have to let them know."

"Right."

"However you decide, Richard, I will respect your decision."

"Rrriigght." I knew there were risks, none of which I had to accept. But I felt I could do the case - and I wanted to. For myself, the boy, and his father, I had decided. "Okay, let's do the surgery."

"Wonderful, Richard, I will let them know."

The case was on. My last case in Bangladesh and probably my most dangerous. I would have to postpone my departure from the country for at least three weeks if not longer, just to follow the patient through his recovery and take care of any complications.

The day before the surgery an earthquake shook Iran, killing more then twenty five thousand people, with many more feared dead. All of the Muslim nations of the world, including Bangladesh, responded with offers of humanitarian aid for their Muslim brethren. The Bangladesh contingency was under the leadership of Dr. Shah Zaman, the nation's most prominent neurosurgeon, from Dhaka Medical College, and the man who was supposed to help me with the surgery. I watched on the television as the jet flying Dr. Zaman and the other members of the medical team left for Iran, leaving me in the lurch.

The next morning I looked on as the anesthesiologist put the little boy to sleep. This was a man-size tumor on a sickly kid with a hemoglobin of eight, about half of what it should be. I would be watching every single capillary on this case. One of the things you fear most in any major surgery, but especially in someone with so little reserve, was bleeding. I planned to keep this case bone-dry. I had my usual assortment of assistants, most notably, Ying and Akel. As of now, though, I had no neurosurgeon to help me remove the part of the tumor that had invaded the brain. I have had to extemporize on many occasions since coming to Asia, but this was the first time I had to do neurosurgery.

The case required removing the skin on the right side of the face, the mandible and the base of the skull where the tumor had entered the intracranial cavity. I was hoping that the actual substance of the brain had been spared by the tumor and that we would be able to peel the tumor off the brain's outer lining, a structure known as the dura. If we could stay out of the brain itself, we might be all right. The second part of this adventure required reconstructing him, including repair of the big hole he would have on the side of his face.

The case began. I watched every blood vessel. A saw was used to cut the jaw in half, which allowed me to gently nudge my hand under the tumor and move it slightly. I cut through additional muscle tissue and the cheek bone, separated the tumor from the ear canal, placed my hand around the entire mass and pulled it away from the skull and out of the patient's face, a growth about the size of a mango. What was left, though, was the part of the tumor that had invaded the base of the skull.

I noticed another person enter the operating room. He introduced himself as Dr. Ahmed, a neurosurgeon and colleague of Dr. Zahman. Apparently Dr. Zahman had arranged for a replacement to assist in the case after all! He just showed up without notifying me. I didn't know, but I was delighted.

We finished the surgery by peeling the tumor off the dura and removing the involved bone. We never had to disturb the brain. I reconstructed the right side of the child's face with a large flap from his shoulder. The next morning when I came in to see the boy I found him sitting up in his bed and smiling for the first time. His father was standing alongside him holding his hand. In his eyes I could see relief and gratitude. He thanked me over and over in Bengali.

Chapter 75

Akel delivered Ying and me to the main railroad station in Dhaka. It was August 2, 1990. Akel mentioned that Saddam Hussein had invaded Kuwait. "He is a crazy man, suh, really crazy. Nasty business, suh," he said. Other then that it was an ordinary day except that I was ending my Asian odyssey as itinerant-surgeon. Akel embraced me, politely bid farewell to the "Lady Ying," and thanked me for all I had done. Akel had been a great and loyal friend, and it was sad to say goodbye.

Ying and I boarded the train and stowed our bags beneath our seats. I had decided to see the country that had meant so much to me and had given me so much - even as I had endeavored to give myself over to it. I wanted to witness its beauty as I had witnessed its misery. We would travel north through its heartland. As the train moved from the station through the city and to its outskirts, we observed the squalor and concrete of Dhaka dissolve before the broad, lush fields of jute and rice. From the depths of the grim poverty of Dhaka, an opulent palace of iridescent pastures and lavish grasslands appeared in its place. We had seen little of Bangladesh since arriving in Dhaka. Now we beheld it in its beauty and grandeur.

There were thatched-hut villages with no electricity or running water and bullocks pulling loaded carts. Cows yoked together dragged small Bengali boys perched on wooden-ploughs while churning the wet earth. The train shuttled over small bridges suspended above rivers and ravines. Black bulls cooled themselves in brown waters, only their bony horns, moist snouts, and blinking eyes visible above the surface. We saw women dressed in the flowing robes of their traditional saris. Young children waved and shouted as we passed. And everywhere around us was the splendid labyrinth of jade-green and butter-yellow meadows of rice and jute and the silken web of estuaries that laced their way through the fertile soil of this, the Ganges and Brahmaputra river delta over which Bangladesh was draped.

"It is another reality," I said to Ying. "You must leave Dhaka to know Bangladesh."

Half way into the journey we approached the mighty Jamuna River, one of the three great rivers along with the Ganges and the Meghna that both blessed and cursed this country with their powerful currents enroute to the Bay of Bengal. We left the train to board a ferry for the two-hour river crossing to a waiting train on the other side. In the ferry there were red-shirted coolies with brown turbans offering to carry baggage. Hordes of beggars, many with congenital malformations, flocked to us seeking some scrap of food or small change. We went up to the deck to escape the throng. The view was hypnotic. The Jamuna River was vast and wide and the lime fields emerging from its embankments were one of the most memorable visions I have had of Asia. After reaching the other side we resumed the train journey and arrived in the town of Pharbatipur, a grubby little depot, at ten P.M. We stayed in a shanty named the "Deluxe Hotel," all we could find at that late hour.

The next morning we boarded the train. Two hours later we reached the border town of Chiliharti. We stopped at the immigration check post. The border official, a small, balding Bengali, dusted off a book with the inscriptions of the previous foreign travelers who had braved the passage through Chiliharti into India. The pages were yellowed and faded. The last insert, from Poland of all places, dated back about a year. I scratched the required numbers, dates, and figures, while the official hovered over me. He shook my hand. There were tears in his eyes.

Outside the immigration station, several cycle-rickshaw wallahs prowled about anxious for a fare. The distance from Chiliharti to the Indian border was about eight kilometers. We hopped on one for this last leg of our journey out of Bangladesh.

We passed through Chiliharti, a small, dusty, desolate town roasting like a peanut in the stifling sun. We crossed over a number of streams and lakes on rickety bamboo bridges. We traveled through pristine villages with nursing mothers in saris and children frolicking about their primitive thatched-hut dwellings. Men with knotted, sinewy muscles and black sunbaked skin toiled in the fields of rice and jute. There was not the slightest hint of modernization. It seemed an Eden of simplicity and beauty. Here you did not encounter the crush of poverty. The people lived humbly but seemed to have enough.

The road ended and we continued on foot for another three kilometers through brush and tall grass past the final Bangladeshi check post. After a kilometer we came to a river. Beyond the river I sighted a small shack with several soldiers in uniforms grasping rifles. This was the Indian checkpoint and the river marked the border between Bangladesh and India. It was fairly deep. Ying was not a swimmer. I placed her on my shoulders and waded across. The water reached mid-chest. Ying squirmed. I deposited her on the other side. I returned for the luggage, balanced the bags on my head and crossed the river once more leaving Bangladesh to enter India. The Indian soldiers greeted me with yelps and laughter. We posed together for photos. They let me hold one of their rifles. We continued a few kilometers to the Indian border town of Haldibari and feasted on delicious Indian food.

From there we traveled to Darjeeling, Sikkim, and into Bhutan where we managed to sneak in for a couple of days without a visa. We took the train down to Calcutta and spent a week in a cheap hotel waiting for the next open flight to Bangkok. Once there I arranged for Ying to obtain her green card and with my last cash reserves bought two tickets to New York. Before leaving, we took a train down to Sungai Kolok to visit my good friend Uttamo. We spent a few days together in his Buddhist sanctuary, the same as before. I needed to hear his thoughts of my journey, and of my sense of failure. I told him of all that had happened since we were last together. I emphasized Bangladesh as that was most recent, and because it had the greatest impact on me.

"You did not realize Buddhist practice," Uttamo said to me almost caustically, as if displeased with his student. "Bangladesh was perfect for you, yet you allowed your disappointment with the failed proposal to affect your judgment."

Ying nodded even as she remained silent.

"You accomplished a great deal in your travels. You helped many patients. It opened your eyes and changed you in profound ways. Yet, in the end, your anger got the better of you. Instead of being mindful, you were petulant and bitter. The real world is where *dhamma* is most critical, Rick, not in the monastery or forest temple."

I never heard Uttamo speak so directly.

"Your concept of medicine was one-dimensional. You could have explored practice opportunities with one or more of your colleagues, Abdullah, Amin, Allaudin, or Khan, as Ying suggested. Or started a clinic or surgery center, even a hospital in Bangladesh, with you, the American cancer surgeon as their star. The opportunities for someone with your skills were endless. As undeveloped as the market is, Bangladesh would have been a gold mine. I might have invested myself," he said, winking.

"My Jewish Buddhist financial advisor. How did I miss this?"

"You forgot *dhamma*," Uttamo said.

"I should have called you. Really, I should have."

"You missed this because your transformation was not complete. You entered the arena but failed to adapt yourself. Your vision was unclear. You still have work to do, Rick. But so do we all."

I would start my life over in America. I would have to find a job, earn a living, and become a householder. I dreaded it. How conventional it seemed. How monotonous and routine. It was a profound let down after three years of wonder, peril, and abandon. How I recoiled at the prospect of such an existence. How I would long to return to my life as surgeon and wanderer. As seeker. As healer. As a man of courage and adventure as Rahman had called me. As a pilgrim of knowledge as Khan had described me. In truth, I would never be content until I was back where I belonged. In the third world among the destitute and the sick.

I had learned a great deal about the world, Asia, and the limits of medicine and surgery. I had witnessed unimaginable disease at advanced stages and tragic human suffering. I had seen the depths of poverty. Volunteers like myself were only a thimble in an ocean of wretchedness. It was beyond the scope of foreign aid, NGOs, and volunteers to make even a dent in the misery. The answers existed on a far deeper plane, on the level of culture, morality, religion, history, economics, science, and political philosophy. I did not delude myself that my work and the work of even tens of thousands of others could alter substantially the paradigm.

I would rely on the good graces of my family to support me while getting back on my feet. I had lost touch with America in my three years away, and I was returning with no money. I knew the re-entry into American life would be difficult. I remembered the Chinese fortune cookie, from the "Number 1" Chinese restaurant on Canal Street in lower Manhattan that had launched my crusade. It said nothing about this. Yet that was its wisdom.

I was a different person from the green, young surgeon that began this voyage. I had confronted my fears. I had made my mistakes. I had moved on. I knew what I wanted when I set out. I wanted to heal, to embark on a quest of healing. Yet I did not anticipate my confrontation with my limitations and myself. I managed the destitution around me but not my constrained vision within. I did not allow the suffering and wonder of the world to transform me as it could have. I performed surgery on others to heal and restore them but did not accept an internal surgery that would have elevated me. There were painful truths that I failed to grasp. Yet it was still worth it. I had my triumphs, and I had my failures. My own realization would continue. It was a good journey. A pilgrimage. An odyssey. And it was not over.

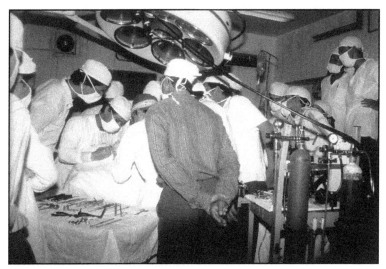

Dr. Moss (dark hat) operating at Dhaka Medical College

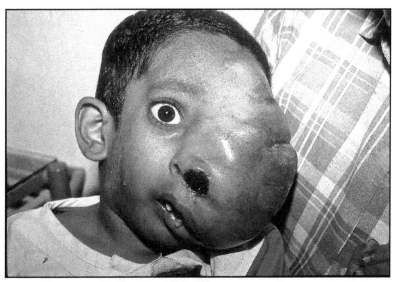

Large Head and Neck Cancer, Child, Bangladesh

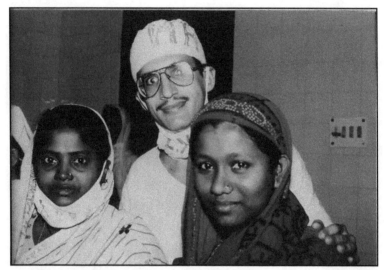

Dr. Moss with 'nurses' in saris in operating room, Bangladesh

With Dharma and Patient, Nepal

With Three ENT Patriarchs, Professors Khan, Amin, Haroon, Bangladesh

Head and Neck Clinic Team, Chiang Mai, Thailand

Bali, Indonesia

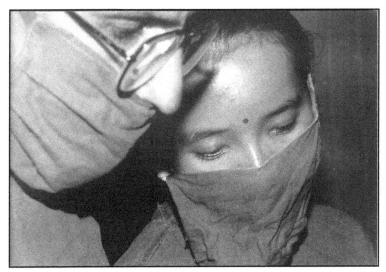

Ying assisting me in surgery, Nepal

Dr. Acharee Sorasuchart, Professor and Head of
ENT, Chiang Mai University, Thailand

With Combined Military Hospital Medical Faculty and Professors Amin, Khan, and Haroon, Bangladesh

Bio

Dr. Moss and Ying settled in Jasper, an enclave in southern Indiana, to begin a private practice after returning to the United States. He loves the area in part because it reminds him so much of Asia. The rolling hills and sprawling green fields of corn and soy are reminiscent of Thailand, and the small town of 12,000 with its family oriented "Hoosier" values remind Dr. Moss of the qualities he loves best about Asia. Dr. Moss gives frequent lectures and slide shows about his work in Asia and has helped colleagues from abroad arrange visits to teaching centers in the United States as well as to visit him in his practice. He gives multimedia presentations at local schools. Dr. Moss has continued to lecture and perform surgery overseas on a limited basis. He has been to Central and South America, Europe, Africa, and Asia. He and Ying have four children, all of them active in sports, music, and their studies, who have traveled with them on exciting journeys abroad. Dr. Moss has written another book, *Matilda's Triumph: A Memoir* about his mother and growing up in the Bronx. He writes regular columns for Indiana newspapers. At varying times he owned and operated a bagel shop, *Bronx Bagel*, and an Italian restaurant, *Simply Pasta*. He taught Yoga and had a Yoga TV show, *Yoga For Health*, on a local channel. He speaks publically and had a radio talk show for a time. He ran for state representative for Indiana's 63rd district and Congress for Indiana's 8th district. He has two websites, *exodusmd.com* and *richardmossmd.com* on which he regularly posts. He is on Facebook, Twitter, and Instagram. It is his intention to return to his overseas volunteer medical work again.

CPSIA information can be obtained
at www.ICGtesting.com
Printed in the USA
BVHW03*1129081018
529575BV00008B/229/P